Fodor's 96
Miami & the Keys

"When it comes to information on regional history, what to see and do, and shopping, these guides are exhaustive."

—*USAir Magazine*

"Usable, sophisticated restaurant coverage, with an emphasis on good value."

—Andy Birsh, *Gourmet Magazine* columnist

"Valuable because of their comprehensiveness."

—*Minneapolis Star-Tribune*

"Fodor's always delivers high quality...thoughtfully presented...thorough."

—*Houston Post*

"An excellent choice for those who want everything under one cover."

—*Washington Post*

D1602742

Reprinted from *Fodor's Florida '96*

Fodor's Travel Publications, Inc.
New York • Toronto • London • Sydney • Auckland

Fodor's Miami & the Keys

Editor: Andrea E. Lehman

Area Editor: Herb Hiller

Editorial Contributors: Robert Andrews, Robert Blake, Janet Foley, George and Rosalie Leposkey, Rebecca Miller, Mary Ellen Schultz, M. T. Schwartzman (Gold Guide editor), Dinah Spritzer

Creative Director: Fabrizio La Rocca

Cartographer: David Lindroth

Cover Photograph: Morton Beebe

Text Design: Between the Covers

Copyright

Special Sales

Fodor's Travel Publications are available at special discounts for bulk purchases for sales promotions or premiums. Special editions, including personalized covers, excerpts of existing guides, and corporate imprints can be created in large quantities for special needs. For more information, contact your local bookseller or write to Special Markets, Fodor's Travel Publications, 201 East 50th Street, New York, NY 10022. Inquiries from Canada should be directed to your local Canadian bookseller or sent to Random House of Canada, Ltd., Marketing Department, 1265 Aerowood Drive, Mississauga, Ontario L4W 1B9. Inquiries from the United Kingdom should be sent to Fodor's Travel Publications, 20 Vauxhall Bridge Road, London SW1V 2SA, England.

MANUFACTURED IN THE UNITED STATES OF AMERICA

10 9 8 7 6 5 4 3 2 1

CONTENTS

ON THE ROAD WITH FODOR'S

A GOOD TRAVEL GUIDE is like a wonderful traveling companion. It's charming, it's brimming with sound recommendations and solid ideas, it pulls no punches in describing lodging and dining establishments, and it's consistently full of fascinating facts that make you view what you've traveled to see in a rich new light. In the creation of *Miami & the Keys '96,* we at Fodor's have gone to great lengths to provide you with the very best of all possible traveling companions—and to make your trip the best of all possible vacations.

About Our Writer

Editor of *The Ecotourism Society Newsletter* and a Lowell Thomas Travel Journalism Award winner, **Herb Hiller** wrote the chapters on south Florida and is the conscience of this book. To keep his finger on the pulse of environmental, development, and cultural issues, he leaves the seclusion of his offshore island ("by boat or gator back") to travel from burgeoning metropolis to remote wilderness, with reverence for the joys of each. Much of his time is spent on wheels—bicycle wheels, that is; Herb is an avid cyclist and works to promote Florida cycling.

Editor **Andrea Lehman** has been vacationing in Florida since she took her first airplane ride there. She long ago traded sand pail for sunscreen and continues to be amazed at the state's transformations as well as its constants: warm weather and great beaches. Working from her home office in New Jersey, she's ready to take her two little girls down to discover Florida all over again, sand pails in hand.

What's New

A New Design

If this is not the first Fodor's guide you've purchased, you'll immediately notice our new look. More readable and easier to use than ever? We think so—and we hope you do, too.

Let Us Do Your Booking

Our writers have scoured Miami and the Keys to come up with an extensive and well-balanced list of the best B&Bs, inns, resorts, and hotels, both small and large, new and old. But you don't have to beat the bushes to come up with a reservation. Now we've teamed up with an established hotel-booking service to make it easy for you to secure a room at the property of your choice. It's fast, it's free, and confirmation is guaranteed. If your first choice is booked, the operators can line up your second right away. Just call 800/FODORS-1 or 800/363-6771 (0800/89-1030 when in Great Britain; 0014/800-12-8271 when in Australia; 1800/55-9101 when in Ireland).

Travel Updates

In addition, just before your trip, you may want to order a Fodor's Worldview Travel Update. From local publications all over Florida, the lively, cosmopolitan editors at Worldview gather information on concerts, plays, opera, dance performances, gallery and museum shows, sports competitions, and other special events that coincide with your visit. See the order blank in the back of this book, call 800/799-9609, or fax 800/799-9619.

How to Use This Book

Organization

Up front is the **Gold Guide,** comprising two sections on gold paper that are chock-full of information about traveling within your destination and traveling in general. Both are in alphabetical order by topic. **Important Contacts A to Z** gives addresses and telephone numbers of organizations and companies that offer destination-related services and detailed information or publications. Here's where you'll find information about how to get to Florida from wherever you are. **Smart Travel Tips A to Z,** the Gold Guide's second section, gives specific tips on how to get the most out of your travels, as well as information on how to accomplish what you need to in Florida.

Chapters in *Miami & the Keys '96* are arranged by region of the state. Each chapter covers exploring, shopping, sports, dining, lodging, and arts and nightlife and ends with a section called Essentials, which tells you how to get there and get around and gives you important local addresses and telephone numbers.

Stars

Stars in the margin are used to denote highly recommended sights, attractions, hotels, and restaurants.

Restaurant and Hotel Criteria and Price Categories

Restaurants and lodging places are chosen with a view to giving you the cream of the crop in each location and in each price range. Price categories are as follows:

For restaurants:

CATEGORY	COST*
$$$$	over $50
$$$	$35–$50
$$	$20–$35
$	under $20

per person for a three-course meal, excluding drinks, service, and 6% sales tax (some counties also have a local sales tax)

For hotels:

CATEGORY	COST*
$$$$	over $150
$$$	$90–$150
$$	$60–$90
$	under $60

All prices are for a standard double room, excluding 6% sales tax (some counties also have a local sales tax) and 1%–4% tourist tax.

Hotel Facilities

Note that in general you incur charges when you use many hotel facilities. We wanted to let you know what facilities a hotel has to offer, but we don't always specify whether or not there's a charge, so when planning a vacation that entails a stay of several days, it's wise to ask what's included in the rate.

Restaurant Reservation Policies

The nicer the restaurant, the more likely that reservations will be advised or even accepted. This is especially true in high season. In all but burger shacks, delis, and diners, it's always a good idea to call ahead—if not to make a reservation then to find out if and when there's likely to be a wait. We note only those places that require reservations.

Dress Code in Restaurants

Dress in Florida restaurants is quite casual. In nicer establishments, neat attire is the norm, but at the most-casual beachfront places, sometimes tank tops and swimsuits are even acceptable. In general, we note dress code only when men are required to wear a jacket or a jacket and tie.

Credit Cards

The following abbreviations are used: **AE,** American Express; **D,** Discover; **DC,** Diners Club; **MC,** MasterCard; and **V,** Visa.

Please Write to Us

Everyone who has contributed to *Miami & the Keys '96* has worked hard to make the text accurate. All prices and opening times are based on information supplied to us at press time, and the publisher cannot accept responsibility for any errors that may have occurred. The passage of time will bring changes, so it's always a good idea to call ahead and confirm information when it matters—particularly if you're making a detour to visit specific sights or attractions. When making reservations at a hotel or inn, be sure to mention if you have a disability or are traveling with children, if you prefer a private bath or a certain type of bed, or if you have specific dietary needs or any other concerns.

Were the restaurants we recommended as described? Did our hotel picks exceed your expectations? Did you find a museum we recommended a waste of time? We would love your feedback, positive and negative. If you have complaints, we'll look into them and revise our entries when the facts warrant it. If you've happened upon a special place that we haven't included, we'll pass the information along to the writers so they can check it out. So please send us a letter or postcard (we're at 201 East 50th Street, New York, NY 10022). We'll look forward to hearing from you. And in the meantime, have a wonderful trip!

Karen Cure

Karen Cure
Editorial Director

The Florida Peninsula

GEORGIA

Osceola
National
Forest

Amelia
Island

St. Marys R.

N

Jacksonville

ATLANTIC
OCEAN

Swannee River

Santa Fe R.

St. Johns River

St. Augustine

Gainesville

Ocala
National
Forest

Ocala

Daytona Beach

Cedar Keys

Titusville

John F. Kennedy
Space Center

Walt Disney
World

Orlando

Merritt Island

Cape Canaveral

Cocoa Beach

Tarpon Springs

Clearwater

Tampa

Winter
Haven

Florida's Turnpike

Melbourne

Sebastian Inlet
Recreation Area

St. Petersburg

Tampa
Bay

Bradenton

Manatee R.

Vero Beach

Fort Pierce

Sarasota

Peace R.

Kissimmee R.

Hutchinson
Island

Venice

Lake
Okeechobee

Caloosahatchee R.

West Palm
Beach

Singer
Island

Cape
Coral

Fort Myers

Loxahatchee
National
Wildlife
Refuge

Palm
Beach

Captiva Island

Boca Raton

Sanibel Island

Naples

Big Cypress
National
Preserve

Fort Lauderdale

Miami
Beach

Gulf of Mexico

Miami

Everglades
National
Park

Biscayne
Bay

Cape Sable

Florida Bay

0   100 miles

0   150 km

Key
West

Florida Keys

IMPORTANT CONTACTS A TO Z

An Alphabetical Listing of Publications, Organizations, and Companies That Will Help You Before, During, and After Your Trip

No single travel resource can give you every detail about every topic that might interest or concern you at the various stages of your journey—when you're planning your trip, while you're on the road, and after you get back home. The following organizations, books, and brochures will supplement the information in Fodor's *Miami & the Keys '96*. For related information, including both basic tips on visiting Florida and background information on many of the topics below, study Smart Travel Tips A to Z, the section that follows Important Contacts A to Z.

A

AIR TRAVEL

The major gateways to Florida include Miami International Airport and Palm Beach International, which offers a striking collection of art in public places. If you're destined for the north side of Dade (metro Miami), consider flying into Fort Lauderdale–Hollywood International; it's much easier to use than Miami International. Flying time is just over three hours from New York, about three hours from Chicago, and not quite five hours from Los Angeles.

CARRIERS

Most major U.S. airlines schedule regular flights into Florida, and some, such as Delta and USAir, serve Florida airports extensively. Delta (and its commuter affiliate, Comair) and USAir have regular service into West Palm Beach, Fort Lauderdale, Miami, and Key West.

Other major airlines that serve the Florida airports include American, American Trans Air, Continental, Northwest, TWA, and United. Many foreign airlines also fly into some of the major airports in Florida; the smaller, out-of-the-way airports are usually accessible through the commuter flights of major domestic carriers.

Packages that combine airfare and vacation activities at special rates are often available through the airlines.

For inexpensive, no-frills flights, contact Florida-based **Carnival Air Lines** (☎ 800/824–7386), which serves Fort Lauderdale and Miami; **Kiwi International** (☎ 800/538–5494), based in Newark and New York, serving West Palm Beach; **Midwest Express** (☎ 800/452–2022), based in Milwaukee, which serves 45 U.S. cities in the Midwest and on both coasts, including Fort Lau-

derdale; **Private Jet** (☎ 404/231–7571, 800/546–7571, or 800/949–9400), based in Atlanta, serving Miami; and **ValuJet** (☎ 404/994–8258 or 800/825–8538), also based in Atlanta and serving West Palm Beach.

COMPLAINTS

To register complaints about charter and scheduled airlines, contact the U.S. Department of Transportation's **Office of Consumer Affairs** (400 7th St. NW, Washington, DC 20590, ☎ 202/366–2220 or 800/322–7873).

CONSOLIDATORS

Established consolidators selling to the public include **Euram Tours** (1522 K St. NW, Suite 430, Washington, DC 20005, ☎ 800/848–6789) and **TFI Tours International** (34 W. 32nd St., New York, NY 10001, ☎ 212/736–1140 or 800/745–8000).

PUBLICATIONS

For general information about charter carriers, ask for the Office of Consumer Affairs' brochure **"Plane Talk: Public Charter Flights."** The Department of Transportation also publishes a 58-page booklet, **"Fly Rights"** ($1.75; Consumer Information Center, Dept. 133B, Pueblo, CO 81009).

For other tips and hints, consult the Consumers Union's monthly **"Consumer Reports Travel Letter"** ($39 a year; Box 53629, Boulder, CO 80322, ☎ 800/234–1970) and the newsletter **"Travel Smart"** ($37 a year; 40 Beechdale Rd., Dobbs Ferry, NY 10522, ☎ 800/327–3633); *The Official Frequent Flyer Guidebook,* by Randy Petersen ($14.99 plus $3 shipping; 4715-C Town Center Dr., Colorado Springs, CO 80916, ☎ 719/597–8899 or 800/487–8893); *Airfare Secrets Exposed,* by Sharon Tyler and Matthew Wonder (Universal Information Publishing; $16.95 plus $3.75 shipping from Sandcastle Publishing, Box 3070-A, South Pasadena, CA 91031, ☎ 213/255–3616 or 800/655–0053); and *202 Tips Even the Best Business Travelers May Not Know,* by Christopher McGinnis ($10 plus $3 shipping; Irwin Professional Publishing, 1333 Burr Ridge Parkway, Burr Ridge, IL 60521, ☎ 708/789–4000 or 800/634–3966).

B

BETTER BUSINESS BUREAU

In Miami, contact the **Better Business Bureau** (16291 N.W. 57th Ave., Miami 33014-6709, ☎ 900/225–5222, 90¢ per minute). For other local contacts, consult the **Council of Better Business Bureaus** (4200 Wilson Blvd., Arlington, VA 22203, ☎ 703/276–0100).

BUS TRAVEL

Greyhound Lines (☎ 800/232–2222) passes through practically every major city in Florida, including West Palm Beach, Fort Lauderdale, Miami, and Key West. For information about bus schedules and fares, contact your local Greyhound Information Center.

C

CAR RENTAL

All major car-rental companies are represented in Florida, including **Alamo** (☎ 800/327–9633), **Avis** (☎ 800/831–2847), **Budget** (☎ 800/527–0700), **Dollar** (known as Eurodollar outside North America, ☎ 800/800–4000 in the U.S. and Canada, 0181/952–6565 in the U.K.), **Hertz** (☎ 800/654–3131), **National** (☎ 800/227–7368), and **Thrifty** (☎ 800/367–2277). **Value** (☎ 800/468–2583) offers some of the state's lowest rates. Rates in Miami range from $25 to $40 a day and $130–$165 a week with unlimited mileage.

Besides the national rental companies, several local firms offer good deals in major Florida cities. In Fort Lauderdale, local companies include **Aapex Rent A Car** (☎ 305/782–3400) and **Florida Auto Rental** (☎ 305/764–1008 or 800/327–3791). In Miami, **Pass** (☎ 305/444–3923) and **InterAmerican Car Rental** (☎ 305/871–3030) sometimes beat the competition. Down

in Key West, try **Tropical Rent-a-Car** (☎ 305/294–8136).

CHILDREN AND TRAVEL

FLYING

Look into *Flying with Baby* ($5.95 plus $1 shipping; Third Street Press, Box 261250, Littleton, CO 80126, ☎ 303/595–5959), cowritten by a flight attendant. **"Kids and Teens in Flight,"** free from the U.S. Department of Transportation's Office of Consumer Affairs, offers tips for children flying alone. Every two years the February issue of *Family Travel Times* (*see* Know-How, *below*) details children's services on three dozen airlines.

LODGING

Florida may have the highest concentration of hotels with organized children's programs in the United States; sometimes they are complimentary, and sometimes there's a charge. Not all accept children who are still in diapers, and hotels sometimes offer programs when their central reservations services say they don't. The following list gives representative examples of what's available, though programs may not be available all week or all year. Most hotels allow children under a certain age to stay in their parents' room at no extra charge, while others charge them as extra adults; be sure to ask about the cut-off age.

MIAMI AREA> For Just Us Kids, ages 5–13, contact the **Sonesta Beach Hotel Key Biscayne** (350 Ocean Dr., Key Biscayne 33149, ☎ 800/766–3782).

FORT LAUDERDALE> Look into the Beachside Buddies program for ages 5–12 at **Marriott's Harbor Beach Resort** (3030 Holiday Dr., Fort Lauderdale 33316, ☎ 305/525–4000 or 800/228–9290).

PALM BEACH AND THE TREASURE COAST> **Club Med** (40 W. 57th St., New York, NY 10019, ☎ 800/258–2633) operates the Sandpiper resort village in Port St. Lucie; there's a Baby Club (4–24 months) and Mini Club (2–11 years). **Indian River Plantation** (555 N.E. Ocean Blvd., Hutchinson Island, Stuart 34996, ☎ 407/225–3700 or 800/444–3389) offers the Pineapple Bunch Children's Camp year-round for children 3–12 as well as a teen program with snorkeling, parties, movie nights, a game room, and instruction in golf and tennis.

THE KEYS> Florida's only environmentally oriented children's program, conducted by marine-science counselors, is Camp Cheeca for ages 6–12 offered at **Cheeca Lodge** (MM 82, Upper Matecumbe Key, Box 527, Islamorada 33036, ☎ 800/327–2888). However the program is offered only during summers and holiday weekends, including the entire Christmas–New Year's period. **Sheraton Key**

Largo (MM 97, BS, Key Largo 33037, ☎ 305/852–5553 or 800/325–3535) offers its Keys Kids Club, for ages 5–12, throughout its high season but otherwise only on weekends.

KNOW-HOW

Family Travel Times, published 10 times a year by Travel With Your Children ($55 a year; TWYCH, 45 W. 18th St., New York, NY 10011, ☎ 212/206–0688), covers destinations, types of vacations, and modes of travel.

The *Family Travel Guides* catalogue ($1 postage; ☎ 510/527–5849) lists about 200 books and articles on family travel. Also check *Take Your Baby and Go! A Guide for Traveling with Babies, Toddlers and Young Children,* by Sheri Andrews, Judy Bordeaux, and Vivian Vasquez ($5.95 plus $1.50 shipping; Bear Creek Publications, 2507 Minor Ave., Seattle, WA 98102, ☎ 206/322–7604 or 800/326–6566).

TOUR OPERATORS

Contact **Rascals in Paradise** (650 5th St., Suite 505, San Francisco, CA 94107, ☎ 415/978–9800 or 800/872–7225).

CUSTOMS

CANADIANS

Contact **Revenue Canada** (2265 St. Laurent Blvd. S, Ottawa, Ontario K1G 4K3, ☎ 613/993–0534) for a copy of the free brochure "I Declare/Je Déclare" and

for details on duties that exceed the standard duty-free limit.

U.K. CITIZENS

HM Customs and Excise (Dorset House, Stamford St., London SE1 9NG, ☎ 0171/202–4227) can answer questions about U.K. customs regulations and publishes "A Guide for Travellers," detailing standard procedures and import rules.

D

FOR TRAVELERS
WITH DISABILITIES

COMPLAINTS

To register complaints under the provisions of the Americans with Disabilities Act, contact the U.S. Department of Justice's **Public Access Section** (Box 66738, Washington, DC 20035, ☎ 202/514–0301, TTY 202/514–0383, FAX 202/307–1198).

ORGANIZATIONS

FOR TRAVELERS WITH HEARING IMPAIRMENTS> Contact the **American Academy of Otolaryngology** (1 Prince St., Alexandria, VA 22314, ☎ 703/836–4444, TTY 703/519–1585, FAX 703/683–5100).

FOR TRAVELERS WITH MOBILITY PROBLEMS> Contact the **Information Center for Individuals with Disabilities** (Fort Point Pl., 27–43 Wormwood St., Boston, MA 02210, ☎ 617/727–5540, 800/462–5015 in MA, TTY 617/345–9743); **Mobility International USA** (Box 10767, Eugene, OR 97440, ☎ and TTY 503/343–1284, FAX 503/343–6812), the U.S. branch of an international organization headquartered in Belgium (*see below*) that has affiliates in 30 countries; **Moss-Rehab Hospital Travel Information Service** (1200 W. Tabor Rd., Philadelphia, PA 19141, ☎ 215/456–9603, TTY 215/456–9602); the **Society for the Advancement of Travel for the Handicapped** (347 5th Ave., Suite 610, New York, NY 10016, ☎ 212/447–7284, FAX 212/725–8253); the **Travel Industry and Disabled Exchange** (TIDE, 5435 Donna Ave., Tarzana, CA 91356, ☎ 818/344–3640, FAX 818/344–0078); and **Travelin' Talk** (Box 3534, Clarksville, TN 37043, ☎ 615/552–6670, FAX 615/552–1182).

FOR TRAVELERS WITH VISION IMPAIRMENTS➤ Contact the **American Council of the Blind** (1155 15th St. NW, Suite 720, Washington, DC 20005, ☎ 202/467–5081, FAX 202/467–5085) or the **American Foundation for the Blind** (15 W. 16th St., New York, NY 10011, ☎ 212/620–2000, TTY 212/620–2158).

IN THE U.K.
Contact the **Royal Association for Disability and Rehabilitation** (RADAR, 12 City Forum, 250 City Rd., London EC1V 8AF, ☎ 0171/250–3222) or **Mobility International** (Rue de Manchester 25, B1070 Brussels, Belgium, ☎ 00–322–410–6297), an international clearinghouse of travel information for people with disabilities.

PUBLICATIONS
Several free publications are available from the U.S. Information Center (Box 100, Pueblo, CO 81009, ☎ 719/948–3334): **"New Horizons for the Air Traveler with a Disability"** (address to Dept. 355A), describing legally mandated changes; the pocket-size **"Fly Smart"** (Dept. 575B), good on flight safety; and the Airport Operators Council's worldwide **"Access Travel: Airports"** (Dept. 575A).

Fodor's **Great American Vacations for Travelers with Disabilities** ($18; available in bookstores, or call 800/533–6478) details accessible attractions, restaurants, and hotels in U.S. destinations. The 500-page **Travelin' Talk Directory** ($35; Box 3534, Clarksville, TN 37043, ☎ 615/552–6670) lists people and organizations who help travelers with disabilities. For specialist travel agents worldwide, consult the **Directory of Travel Agencies for the Disabled** ($19.95 plus $2 shipping; Twin Peaks Press, Box 129, Vancouver, WA 98666, ☎ 206/694–2462 or 800/637–2256). The Sierra Club publishes **Easy Access to National Parks** ($16 plus $3 shipping; 730 Polk St., San Francisco, CA 94109, ☎ 415/776–2211 or 800/935–1056).

You can request a free copy of **"Florida: Planning Companion For Travelers with Disabilities"** from the Florida Governor's Alliance (345 S. Magnolia Dr., Suite D-11, Tallahassee 32301, ☎ 904/487–2222, FAX 904/922–9619, TTY 904/487–2223), which lists by region agencies and organizations that offer resources and referrals.

TRAVEL AGENCIES AND TOUR OPERATORS
The Americans with Disabilities Act requires that travel firms serve the needs of all travelers. However, some agencies and operators specialize in making group and individual arrangements for travelers with disabilities, among them **Access Adventures** (206 Chestnut Ridge Rd., Rochester, NY 14624, ☎ 716/889–9096), run by a former physical-rehab counselor, and **Tailored Tours** (Box 797687, Dallas, TX 75379, ☎ 214/612–1168 or 800/628–8542).

FOR TRAVELERS WITH HEARING IMPAIRMENTS➤ One agency is **International Express** (7319-B Baltimore Ave., College Park, MD 20740, ☎ and TTY 301/699–8836, FAX 301/699–8836), which arranges group and independent trips.

FOR TRAVELERS WITH MOBILITY IMPAIRMENTS➤ The following operators specialize in working with travelers with mobility impairments: **Hinsdale Travel Service** (201 E. Ogden Ave., Suite 100, Hinsdale, IL 60521, ☎ 708/325–1335 or 800/303–5521), a travel agency that will give you access to the services of wheelchair traveler Janice Perkins; **Wheel-**

chair **Journeys** (16979 Redmond Way, Redmond, WA 98052, ☎ 206/885–2210), which can handle arrangements worldwide.

FOR TRAVELERS WITH DEVELOPMENTAL DISABILITIES➤ Contact the nonprofit **New Directions** (5276 Hollister Ave., Suite 207, Santa Barbara, CA 93111, ☎ 805/967–2841).

DISCOUNTS

Options include **Entertainment Travel Editions** (fee $28–$53, depending on destination; Box 1068, Trumbull, CT 06611, ☎ 800/445–4137), **Great American Traveler** ($49.95 annually; Box 27965, Salt Lake City, UT 84127, ☎ 800/548–2812), **Moment's Notice Discount Travel Club** ($25 annually, single or family; 163 Amsterdam Ave., Suite 137, New York, NY 10023, ☎ 212/486–0500), **Privilege Card** ($74.95 annually; 3391 Peachtree Rd. NE, Suite 110, Atlanta, GA 30326, ☎ 404/262–0222 or 800/236-9732), **Travelers Advantage** ($49 annually, single or family; CUC Travel Service, 49 Music Sq. W, Nashville, TN 37203, ☎ 800/548–1116 or 800/648–4037), and **Worldwide Discount Travel Club** ($50 annually for family, $40 single; 1674 Meridian Ave., Miami Beach, FL 33139, ☎ 305/534–2082).

DRIVING

For current information on tolls and other services, try the **Florida's Turnpike** public informa-

tion number (☎ 800/749–7453).

G
GAY AND
LESBIAN TRAVEL

ORGANIZATION

The **International Gay Travel Association** (Box 4974, Key West, FL 33041, ☎ 800/448–8550), a consortium of 800 businesses, can supply names of travel agents and tour operators.

PUBLICATIONS

The premier international travel magazine for gays and lesbians is **Our World** ($35 for 10 issues; 1104 N. Nova Rd., Suite 251, Daytona Beach, FL 32117, ☎ 904/441–5367). The 16-page monthly **"Out & About"** ($49 for 10 issues; ☎ 212/645–6922 or 800/929–2268) covers gay-friendly resorts, hotels, cruise lines, and airlines.

TOUR OPERATORS

Cruises and resort vacations are handled by **Toto Tours** (1326 W. Albion, Suite 3W, Chicago, IL 60626, ☎ 312/274–8686 or 800/565–1241), which has group tours worldwide.

TRAVEL AGENCIES

The largest agencies serving gay travelers are **Advance Travel** (10700 Northwest Fwy., Suite 160, Houston, TX 77092, ☎ 713/682–2002 or 800/695–0880), **Islanders/ Kennedy Travel** (183 W. 10th St., New York, NY 10014, ☎ 212/242–3222 or 800/988–1181), **Now Voyager**

(4406 18th St., San Francisco, CA 94114, ☎ 415/626–1169 or 800/255–6951), and **Yellowbrick Road** (1500 W. Balmoral Ave., Chicago, IL 60640, ☎ 312/561–1800 or 800/642–2488). **Skylink Women's Travel** (746 Ashland Ave., Santa Monica, CA 90405, ☎ 310/452–0506 or 800/225-5759) works with lesbians.

I
INSURANCE

Travel insurance covering baggage, health, and trip cancellation or interruptions is available from **Access America** (Box 90315, Richmond, VA 23286, ☎ 804/285–3300 or 800/284–8300), **Carefree Travel Insurance** (Box 9366, 100 Garden City Plaza, Garden City, NY 11530, ☎ 516/294–0220 or 800/323–3149), **Near** (Box 1339, Calumet City, IL 60409, ☎ 708/868–6700 or 800/654–6700), **Tele-Trip** (Mutual of Omaha Plaza, Box 31716, Omaha, NE 68131, ☎ 800/228–9792), **Travel Insured International** (Box 280568, East Hartford, CT 06128-0568, ☎ 203/528–7663 or 800/243–3174), **Travel Guard International** (1145 Clark St., Stevens Point, WI 54481, ☎ 715/345–0505 or 800/826–1300), and **Wallach & Company** (107 W. Federal St., Box 480, Middleburg, VA 22117, ☎ 703/687–3166 or 800/237–6615).

IN THE U.K.

The **Association of British Insurers** (51

Gresham St., London EC2V 7HQ, ☎ 0171/600–3333; 30 Gordon St., Glasgow G1 3PU, ☎ 0141/226–3905; Scottish Provident Bldg., Donegall Sq. W, Belfast BT1 6JE, ☎ 01232/249176; and other locations) gives advice by phone and publishes the free "Holiday Insurance," which sets out typical policy provisions and costs.

L

LODGING

APARTMENT AND VILLA RENTAL

Among the companies to contact are **Hometours International** (Box 11503, Knoxville, TN 37939, ☎ 615/588–8722 or 800/367–4668), **Rent-a-Home International** (7200 34th Ave. NW, Seattle, WA 98117, ☎ 206/789–9377 or 800/488–7368), **Vacation Home Rentals Worldwide** (235 Kensington Ave., Norwood, NJ 07648, ☎ 201/767–9393 or 800/633–3284), and **Villas and Apartments Abroad** (420 Madison Ave., Suite 1105, New York, NY 10017, ☎ 212/759–1025 or 800/433–3020). Members of the travel club **Hideaways International** ($99 annually; 767 Islington St., Portsmouth, NH 03801, ☎ 603/430–4433 or 800/843–4433) receive two annual guides plus quarterly newsletters, and arrange rentals among themselves.

CAMPING AND RV FACILITIES

Contact the national parks and forests you plan to visit directly for information on camping facilities (*see* National Parks, *below*). For information on camping facilities in state parks, contact the Florida Department of Environmental Protection (*see* State Parks, *below*).

The free annual "Florida Camping Directory," published each December, lists 220 commercial campgrounds in Florida with 66,000 sites. It's available at Florida welcome centers, from the Florida Division of Tourism, and from the **Florida Association of RV Parks & Campgrounds** (1340 Vickers Dr., Tallahassee 32303-3041, ☎ 904/562–7151, FAX 904/562–7179).

CONDOS

See *The Condo Lux Vacationer's Guide to Condominium Rentals in the Southeast*, by Jill Little ($9.95; Vintage Books/Random House, New York).

HOME EXCHANGE

Principal clearinghouses include **Intervac International** ($65 annually; Box 590504, San Francisco, CA 94159, ☎ 415/435–3497), which has three annual directories, and **Loan-a-Home** ($35–$45 annually; 2 Park La., Apt. 6E, Mount Vernon, NY 10552-3443, ☎ 914/664–7640), which specializes in long-term exchanges.

HOTELS

The **Florida Hotel & Motel Association** (200 W. College Ave., Box 1529, Tallahassee 32301-1529, ☎ 904/224–2888) publishes an "Annual Travel Directory," which you can obtain from the association if you send a No. 10 SASE and $2 for handling ($4 outside the United States), or without charge from the **Florida Division of Tourism** (Department of Commerce, 126 Van Buren St., Tallahassee 32399, ☎ 904/487–1462).

INNS AND B&BS

Inn Route, Inc. (Box 6187, Palm Harbor 34684, ☎ and FAX 813/786–9792 or 800/524–1880), a statewide association of small, architecturally distinctive historic inns, will send you a free brochure. *Florida's Country Inns,* put out by Buchan Publications (Box 7218, St. Petersburg 33734, ☎ 813/526–9121), describes 100 favorites of author Robert Tolf.

Bed-and-breakfast referral and reservation agencies in Florida include **Bed & Breakfast Co., Tropical Florida** (Box 262, Miami 33243, ☎ and FAX 305/661–3270), **Bed & Breakfast Scenic Florida** (Box 3385, Tallahassee 32315-3385, ☎ 904/386–8196), **RSVP Florida & St. Augustine** (Box 3603, St. Augustine 32085, ☎ 904/471–0600), and **Suncoast Accommodations of Florida** (8690 Gulf Blvd., St. Pete Beach 33706, ☎ 813/360–1753).

VACATION OWNERSHIP RESORTS

Most are affiliated with one of two major exchange organizations—

Interval International (6262 Sunset Dr., Penthouse One, South Miami 33143, ☎ 305/666–1861 or 800/828–8200, FAX 305/665–2546) or **Resort Condominiums International** (3502 Woodview Trace, Indianapolis, IN 46268-3131, ☎ 317/876–8899 or 800/338–7777, FAX 317/871–9335).

To rent at vacation ownership resorts where unsold intervals remain and/or owners have placed their intervals in a rental program, contact the exchange organizations **Worldex** (☎ 800/235–4000, FAX 305/667–5372) or **Resort Condominiums International** (☎ 800/338–7777), the individual resort, or a local real-estate broker in the area where you want to rent.

M

MARINE CHARTS

A packet of charts to the Keys (and elsewhere in Florida) helpful to boaters, divers, and fisherfolk is available for $7.95 ($3.60 each individual chart) from **Teall's, Inc.** (111 Saguaro La., Marathon 33050, ☎ 305/743–3942, FAX 305/743–3942). A directory of available charts is free.

MONEY MATTERS

ATMS

For specific **Cirrus** locations in the United States and Canada, call 800/424–7787. For U.S. **Plus** locations, call 800/843–7587 and enter the area code and first three digits of the number you're calling from (or

of the calling area where you want an ATM).

WIRING FUNDS

Funds can be wired via **American Express MoneyGram**[SM] (☎ 800/926–9400 from the U.S. and Canada for locations and information) or **Western Union** (☎ 800/325–6000 for agent locations or to send using MasterCard or Visa, 800/321–2923 in Canada).

P

PARKS AND PRESERVES

NATIONAL PARKS

Consult the **"Guide and Map of National Parks of the U.S."** (GPO No. 024005008527; $1.25 from the U.S. Government Printing Office, Washington, DC 20402) for park addresses and facilities. For further details, contact each site directly.

STATE PARKS

The **Florida Department of Environmental Protection** (Marjory Stoneman Douglas Bldg., MS 535, 3900 Commonwealth Blvd., Tallahassee 32399-3000, ☎ 904/488–2850, FAX 904/488–3947) is responsible for hundreds of historic buildings, landmarks, nature preserves, and an expanding state-park system. When you request a free copy of the *Florida State Park Guide,* mention which parts of the state you plan to visit. For information on camping facilities at the state parks, ask for the free "Florida State Parks, Fees and Facilities"

and "Florida State Parks Camping Reservation Procedures" brochures. Delivery takes 10–14 days.

Responding to cutbacks in its budget, the DEP has established a citizen support organization called **Friends of Florida State Parks.** Membership information is available from ☎ 904/488–8243.

PRIVATE PRESERVES

Contact the **National Audubon Society** (Sanctuary Director, Miles Wildlife Sanctuary, R.R. 1, Box 294, W. Cornwall Rd., Sharon, CT 06069, ☎ 203/364–0048), or, for information about **Nature Conservancy** preserves, contact its Florida chapter (2699 Lee Rd., Suite 500, Winter Park 32789, ☎ 407/628–5887). Visitors are welcome at the Winter Park office and at offices in Tequesta (250 Tequesta Dr., Suite 301, 33469, ☎ 407/575–2297), Key West (201 Front St., Suite 222, 33040, ☎ 305/296–3880), Lake Wales (225 E. Stuart Ave., 33853, ☎ 813/678–1551), Tallahassee (625 N. Adams St., 32301, ☎ 904/222–0199), and West Palm Beach (Comeau Bldg., 319 Clematis St., Suite 611, 33401, ☎ 407/833–4226). All offices are open weekdays 9–5.

PASSPORTS AND VISAS

U.K. CITIZENS

For fees, documentation requirements, and to get an emergency passport, call the **London passport**

IMPORTANT CONTACTS / THE GOLD GUIDE

office (☎ 0171/271–3000). For visa information, call the **U.S. Embassy Visa Information Line** (☎ 0891/200–290; calls cost 48p per minute or 36p per minute cheap rate) or write the **U.S. Embassy Visa Branch** (5 Upper Grosvenor St., London W1A 2JB). If you live in Northern Ireland, write the **U.S. Consulate General** (4 Queen St., Belfast BTI 6EQ).

PHOTO HELP

The **Kodak Information Center** (☎ 800/242–2424) answers consumer questions about film and photography.

R

RAIL TRAVEL

Amtrak (☎ 800/872–7245) provides north–south service on two routes to the major cities of Jacksonville, Orlando, Tampa, West Palm Beach, Fort Lauderdale, and Miami and east–west service through Jacksonville, Tallahassee, and Pensacola, with many stops in between on all routes.

S

SENIOR CITIZENS

EDUCATIONAL TRAVEL

The nonprofit **Elderhostel** (75 Federal St., 3rd Floor, Boston, MA 02110, ☎ 617/426–7788), for people 60 and older, has offered inexpensive study programs since 1975. The nearly 2,000 courses cover everything from marine science to Greek myths and cowboy poetry. Fees for programs in the

United States and Canada, which usually last one week, run about $300, not including transportation.

ORGANIZATIONS

Contact the **American Association of Retired Persons** (AARP; membership $8 per person or couple annually; 601 E St. NW, Washington, DC 20049, ☎ 202/434–2277). Its Purchase Privilege Program gets members discounts on lodging, car rentals, and sightseeing, and the AARP Motoring Plan furnishes domestic trip-routing information and emergency road-service aid for an annual fee of $39.95 per person or couple ($59.95 for a premium version).

For other discounts on lodgings, car rentals, and other travel products, along with magazines and newsletters, contact the **National Council of Senior Citizens** (membership $12 annually; 1331 F St. NW, Washington, DC 20004, ☎ 202/347–8800) and **Mature Outlook** (subscription $9.95 annually; 6001 N. Clark St., Chicago, IL 60660, ☎ 312/465–6466 or 800/336–6330).

PUBLICATIONS

The 50+ Traveler's Guidebook: Where to Go, Where to Stay, What to Do, by Anita Williams and Merrimac Dillon ($12.95; St. Martin's Press, 175 5th Ave., New York, NY 10010, ☎ 212/674–5151 or 800/288–2131), offers many useful tips. *"The Mature Traveler"* ($29.95; Box 50400, Reno, NV 89513,

☎ 702/786–7419), a monthly newsletter, covers travel deals.

SPORTS

The **Governor's Council on Physical Fitness and Sports** (1330 N.W. 6th St., Suite D, Gainesville 32601, ☎ 904/955–2120, FAX 904/373–8879) puts on the annual Senior Games each December.

SPORTS

The **Governor's Council on Physical Fitness and Sports** (*see* Senior Citizens, *above*) puts on the Sunshine State Games each July in a different part of the state, and promotes the business of sports. The **Florida Sports Foundation** (107 W. Gaines St., Suite 466, Tallahassee 32399-2000, ☎ 904/488–8347) publishes guides on Florida boating, diving, fishing, golf, and baseball spring training.

Florida is steadily making it easier for visitors to get in touch with its natural attractions. New publications for guiding visitors include *Florida Wildlife Viewing Guide,* by Susan Cerulean and Ann Morrow ($7.95 plus $2.95 shipping; Falcon Press, Box 1718, Helena, MT 59624, ☎ 800/582–2665). The guide lists 96 wildlife-watching sites identified by Florida Department of Transportation signs. The Florida Division of Tourism (*see* Visitor Information, *below*) publishes **"Florida Trails: A Guide to Florida's Natural Habitats,"** a review of bicycling, canoeing, horseback riding, and walking trails, with additional information on camping, snorkeling and diving, and Florida ecosystems and a good set of sources for finding out still more. You can request a free trails-oriented **"Recreational Guide"** from the Southwest Florida Water Management District (☎ 800/423–1476) or the free **"Recreation Guide to District Lands,"** with detailed descriptions of 32 marine, wetland, and upland recreational areas from the St. Johns River Water Management District (Box 1429, Palatka 32178-1429).

Information on canoeing, kayaking, bicycling, and hiking trails statewide is available from the **Florida Department of Environmental Protection** (Office of Greenways, Mail Station 585, 3900 Commonwealth Blvd., Tallahassee 32399-3000, ☎ 904/487–4784).

BICYCLING

Contact **Florida's Department of Environmental Protection** (*see above*) for information on bicycle tours and trails.

Florida's Department of Transportation (DOT) publishes free bicycle trail guides, which you can request from the state bicycle-pedestrian coordinator (605 Suwannee St., Mail Station 82, Tallahassee 32399-0450, ☎ 904/487–1200); you can also request a free touring information packet. Also contact the DOT for names of bike

coordinators around the state. In Greater Miami, contact **Dade County's bicycle-pedestrian coordinator** (Office of County Manager, Metro-Dade Government Center, 111 N.W. 1st St., Suite 910, Miami 33128, ☎ 305/375–4507).

CANOEING

A free guide issued by the Florida Department of Environmental Protection (*see above*), *Florida Recreational Trails System Canoe Trails* describes nearly 950 miles of designated canoe trails of a total canoe/kayak trail network now up to 1,550 miles. The DEP guide lists support services along 36 Florida creeks, rivers, and springs. Two additional guides are *Canoe Liveries and Outfitters Directory,* which lists organizations that offer livery and rental services for canoe trails in the system, and *Canoe Information Resources Guide,* which lists canoe clubs and organizations and gives a bibliography of maps, books, films, etc., about canoeing.

Two Florida canoe-outfitter organizations publish free lists of canoe outfitters who organize canoe trips, rent canoes and canoeing equipment, and help shuttle canoeists' boats and cars. The **Florida Association of Canoe Liveries and Outfitters** (Box 1764, Arcadia 33821) publishes a free list of 22 canoe outfitters who organize trips on 47 creeks, rivers, and bays. The nonprofit **Florida Canoeing and**

Kayaking Association (Box 20892, West Palm Beach 33416, ☎ 407/575–4530) publishes a quarterly newsletter, sponsors events, and can provide up-to-date information on many trail conditions. **"Canoe Outpost System"** is a brochure listing five independent outfitters serving eight Florida rivers (2816 N.W. Rte. 661, Arcadia 33821, ☎ 813/494–1215).

FISHING

For a free copy of the annual *Florida Fishing Handbook,* write to the **Florida Game and Fresh Water Fish Commission** (620 S. Meridian St., Tallahassee 32399-1600, ☎ 904/488–1960). You can also request fishing guides for five Florida regions as well as educational bulletins on catch-and-release fishing and on largemouth and striped bass.

Write the **Florida Sea Grant Extension Program** (Bldg. 803, University of Florida, Gainesville 32611, ☎ 904/392–5870) for a free list of publications on saltwater fishing, pier fishing, Florida varieties of fish, and much more.

HORSEBACK RIDING

Contact the **Sunshine State Horse Council** (temporary ☎ 800/792–3833) or **Horse & Pony** (6229 Virginia La., Seffner 33584, ☎ 813/621–2510).

HUNTING

Each year in June, the **Florida Game and Fresh Water Fish Commission** (620 S. Meridian St.,

THE GOLD GUIDE / IMPORTANT CONTACTS

Tallahassee 32399-1600, ☎ 904/488–4676) announces the dates and hours of the fall hunting seasons for public and private wildlife-management areas. Contact the commission for a free copy of the annual *Florida Hunting Handbook*.

JOGGING, RUNNING, AND WALKING

Local running clubs all over the state sponsor weekly public events for joggers, runners, and walkers. For a list of local clubs and events, call or send a SASE to **USA Track & Field–Florida** (Attn. Event Marketing & Management Int'l., 1322 N. Mills Ave., Orlando 32803, ☎ 407/895–6323, FAX 407/897–3243), the Florida affiliate for the governing body of the sport and a complete source of information. For information about events in south Florida, contact the 1,600-member **Miami Runners Club** (7920 S.W. 40th St., Miami 33155, ☎ 305/227–1500, FAX 305/220–2450).

PARI-MUTUEL SPORTS

You can request a schedule, updated every six months, from the **Department of Business & Professional Regulations, Division of Pari-Mutuel Wagering** (8405 N.W. 53rd St., Suite C-250, Miami 33166, ☎ 305/470–5675, FAX 305/470–5686).

TENNIS

For a schedule of tournaments and other tennis events in Florida, you can order the yearbook of the **United States Tennis Association Florida Section** (1280 S.W. 36th Ave., Suite 305, Pompano Beach 33069, ☎ 305/968–3434, FAX 305/968–3986). It's $11 by credit card including postage and handling.

STUDENTS

GROUPS

A major tour operator is **Contiki Holidays** (300 Plaza Alicante, Suite 900, Garden Grove, CA 92640, ☎ 714/740–0808 or 800/466–0610).

HOSTELING

Contact **Hostelling International–American Youth Hostels** (733 15th St. NW, Suite 840, Washington, DC 20005, ☎ 202/783–6161) in the United States, **Hostelling International–Canada** (205 Catherine St., Suite 400, Ottawa, Ontario K2P 1C3, ☎ 613/237–7884) in Canada, and the **Youth Hostel Association of England and Wales** (Trevelyan House, 8 St. Stephen's Hill, St. Albans, Hertfordshire AL1 2DY, ☎ 01727/855215 and 01727/845047) in the United Kingdom. Membership ($25 in the U.S., C$26.75 in Canada, and £9 in the U.K.) gets you access to 5,000 hostels worldwide that charge $7–$20 nightly per person.

I.D. CARDS

To get discounts on transportation and admissions, get the **International Student Identity Card** (ISIC) if you're a bona fide student or the **Go 25 Card** if you're under 26. In the United States, the ISIC and Go 25 cards cost $18 each and include basic travel accident and illness coverage, plus a toll-free travel hot line. Apply through the Council on International Educational Exchange (*see* Organizations, *below*). Cards are available for $15 each in Canada from Travel Cuts (187 College St., Toronto, Ontario M5T 1P7, ☎ 416/979–2406 or 800/667–2887) and in the United Kingdom for £5 each at student unions and student travel companies.

ORGANIZATIONS

A major contact is the **Council on International Educational Exchange** (CIEE, 205 E. 42nd St., 16th Floor, New York, NY 10017, ☎ 212/661–1450), with locations in Boston (729 Boylston St., Boston, MA 02116, ☎ 617/266–1926), Miami (9100 S. Dadeland Blvd., Miami, FL 33156, ☎ 305/670–9261), Los Angeles (10904 Lindbrook Dr., Los Angeles, CA 90024, ☎ 310/208–3551), 43 college towns nationwide, and the United Kingdom (28A Poland St., London W1V 3DB, ☎ 0171/437–7767). Twice a year, it publishes *Student Travels* magazine. The CIEE's Council Travel Service offers domestic air passes for bargain travel within the United States and is the exclusive U.S. agent for several student-discount cards.

Campus Connections (325 Chestnut St., Suite 1101, Philadelphia, PA 19106, ☎ 215/625–8585 or 800/428–3235) specializes in discounted accommodations and airfares for students. The **Educational Travel Centre** (438 N. Frances St., Madison, WI 53703, ☎ 608/256–5551) offers rail passes and low-cost airline tickets, mostly for flights departing from Chicago.

In Canada, also contact **Travel Cuts** (*see above*).

T
TOUR OPERATORS

Among the companies selling tours and packages to Florida, the following have a proven reputation, are nationally known, and have plenty of options to choose from.

GROUP TOURS

For escorted tours to Florida, contact **Maupintour** (Box 807, Lawrence, KS 66044, ☎ 913/843–1211 or 800/255–4266) and **Tauck Tours** (11 Wilton Rd., Westport, CT 06880, ☎ 203/226–6911 or 800/468–2825). Another operator, falling between deluxe and first class, is **Globus** (5301 S. Federal Circle, Littleton, CO 80123, ☎ 303/797–2800 or 800/221–0090). In the first-class and tourist range, try **Collette Tours** (162 Middle St., Pawtucket, RI 02860, ☎ 401/728–3805 or 800/832–4656) and **Domenico Tours** (750 Broadway, Bayonne, NJ 07002, ☎ 201/823–8687 or

800/554–8687). For budget and tourist-class programs, try **Cosmos** (*see* Globus, *above*).

PACKAGES

Independent vacation packages are available from major tour operators and airlines. Contact **American Airlines Fly AAway Vacations** (☎ 800/321–2121), **Continental Airlines' Grand Destinations** (☎ 800/634–5555), **Delta Dream Vacations** (☎ 800/872–7786), **Globetrotters** (139 Main St., Cambridge, MA 02142, ☎ 617/621–9911 or 800/999–9696), **Kingdom Tours** (300 Market St., Kingston, PA 18704, ☎ 717/283–4241 or 800/872–8857), **United Vacations** (☎ 800/328–6877), and **USAir Vacations** (☎ 800/455–0123). **Funjet Vacations,** based in Milwaukee, Wisconsin, and **Gogo Tours,** based in Ramsey, New Jersey, sell Florida packages only through travel agents.

Regional operators specialize in putting together Florida packages for travelers in their local area. Arrangements may include charter or scheduled air travel. Contact **Apple Vacations** (25 Northwest Point Blvd., Elk Grove Village, IL 60007, ☎ 708/640–1150 or 800/365–2775) and **Travel Impressions** (465 Smith St., Farmingdale, NY 11735, ☎ 516/845–7000 or 800/224–0022).

FROM THE U.K.

Tour operators offering packages to Florida include **British Airways**

Holidays (Astral Towers, Betts Way, London Rd., Crawley, West Sussex RH10 2XA, ☎ 01293/518–022), **Jetsave Travel Ltd.** (Sussex House, London Rd., East Grinstead, West Sussex RH19 1LD, ☎ 01342/312–033), **Key to America** (1–3 Station Rd., Ashford Middlesex TW15 2UW, ☎ 01784/248–777), and **Virgin Holidays Ltd.** (The Galleria, Station Rd., Crawley, West Sussex RH10 1WW, ☎ 01293/562–944).

Some travel agencies that offer cheap rates to Florida include **Trailfinders** (42–50 Earl's Court Rd., London W8 6FT, ☎ 0171/937–5400, **Travel Cuts** (295a Regent St., London W1R 7YA, ☎ 0171/637–3161), and **Flightfile** (49 Tottenham Court Rd., London W1P 9RE, ☎ 0171/700–2722).

THEME TRIPS

ADVENTURE➣ **Wilderness Inquiry** (1313 5th St. SE, Box 84, Minneapolis, MN 55414, ☎ 612/379–3858 or 800/728–0719) runs canoeing trips through the Florida Everglades.

FISHING➣ **Cutting Loose Expeditions** (Box 447, Winter Park, FL 32790, ☎ 407/629–4700) can arrange a charter yacht or resort fishing vacation.

GOLF➣ **Golfpac** (Box 162366, Altamonte Springs, FL 32716-2366, ☎ 800/327–0878) and **Great Florida Golf** (Box 590, Palm Beach, FL 33480, ☎ 407/820–9336 or

800/544–8687) sell golf packages at resorts throughout the state.

HEALTH> **Spa-Finders** (91 5th Ave., New York, NY 10003, ☎ 800/255–7727) represents several spas in Florida.

LEARNING VACATIONS> The **Smithsonian Institution's Study Tours and Seminars** (1100 Jefferson Dr. SW, Room 3045, Washington, DC 20560, ☎ 202/357–4700) and the **National Wildlife Federation** (1400 S. 16th St. NW, Washington, DC 20036, ☎ 703/790–4363 or 800/245–5484) operate natural-history programs. **Earthwatch** (680 Mount Auburn St., Box 403SI, Watertown, MA 02272, ☎ 617/926–8000 or 800/776–0188) recruits volunteers to serve in its EarthCorps as short-term assistants to scientists on research expeditions.

SAILING> **Annapolis Sailing School** (Box 3334 STI, Annapolis, MD 21403, ☎ 800/638–9191) has vacation packages to the Florida Keys that include sailing instruction.

YACHT CHARTERS> For crewed or uncrewed yachts, try **Sail Away** (15605 S.W. 92nd Ave., Miami 33157, ☎ 305/253–7245 or 800/724–5292).

ORGANIZATIONS

The **National Tour Association** (546 E. Main St., Lexington, KY 40508, ☎ 606/226–4444 or 800/682–8886) and **United States Tour Operators Association** (USTOA, 211 E. 51st St., Suite 12B, New York, NY 10022, ☎ 212/750–7371) can provide lists of member operators and information on booking tours.

PUBLICATIONS

Consult the brochure **"Worldwide Tour & Vacation Package Finder"** from the National Tour Association (*see above*) and the Better Business Bureau's **"Tips on Travel Packages"** (publication No. 24-195, $2; 4200 Wilson Blvd., Arlington, VA 22203).

TRAVEL AGENCIES

For names of reputable agencies in your area, contact the **American Society of Travel Agents** (1101 King St., Suite 200, Alexandria, VA 22314, ☎ 703/739–2782).

V
VISITOR
INFORMATION

Contact the **Florida Division of Tourism** (126 Van Buren St., Tallahassee 32399, ☎ 904/487–1462, FAX 904/487–0132) for information on tourist attractions and answers to questions about traveling in the state. Canadian travelers can get assistance from

Travel, U.S.A. (☎ 900/451–4050, US$2 per minute).

The Florida Division of Tourism operates welcome centers on I–10, I–75, I–95, and U.S. 231 (near Graceville) and in the lobby of the New Capitol in Tallahassee (Department of Commerce, 126 Van Buren St., Tallahassee 32399, ☎ 904/487–1462). For more information, contact the regional tourist bureaus and chambers of commerce in the areas you wish to visit (*see* individual chapters for listings).

In the United Kingdom, also contact the **United States Travel and Tourism Administration** (Box 1EN, London W1A 1EN, ☎ 0171/495–4466). For a free USA pack, write the USTTA (Box 170, Ashford, Kent TN24 0ZX). Enclose stamps worth £1.50.

W
WEATHER

For current conditions and forecasts, plus the local time and helpful travel tips, call the **Weather Channel Connection** (☎ 900/932–8437, 95¢ per minute) from a Touch-Tone phone.

SMART TRAVEL TIPS A TO Z

Basic Information on Traveling in Florida and Savvy Tips to Make Your Trip a Breeze

The more you travel, the more you know about how to make trips run like clockwork. To help make your travels hassle-free, Fodor's editors have rounded up dozens of tips from our contributors and travel experts all over the world, as well as basic information on visiting Florida. For names of organizations to contact and publications that can give you more information, *see* Important Contacts A to Z, *above.*

A
AIR TRAVEL

If time is an issue, **always look for nonstop flights,** which require no change of plane and make no stops. If possible, **avoid connecting flights,** which stop at least once and can involve a change of plane, although the flight number remains the same; if the first leg is late, the second waits.

CUTTING COSTS

The Sunday travel section of most newspapers is a good source of deals.

MAJOR AIRLINES➤ The least-expensive airfares from the major airlines are priced for round-trip travel and are subject to restrictions. You must usually **book in advance and buy the ticket within 24 hours** to get cheaper fares, and you may have to **stay**

over a Saturday night. The lowest fare is subject to availability, and only a small percentage of the plane's total seats are sold at that price. It's good to **call a number of airlines—and when you are quoted a good price, book it on the spot**—the same fare on the same flight may not be available the next day. Airlines generally allow you to change your return date for a $25 to $50 fee, but most low-fare tickets are nonrefundable. However, if you don't use it, you can apply the cost toward the purchase price of a new ticket, again for a small charge.

CONSOLIDATORS➤ Consolidators, who buy tickets at reduced rates from scheduled airlines, sell them at prices below the lowest available from the airlines directly—usually without advance restrictions. Sometimes you can even get your money back if you need to return the ticket. Carefully read the fine print detailing penalties for changes and cancellations. If you doubt the reliability of a consolidator, **confirm your reservation with the airline.**

ALOFT

AIRLINE FOOD➤ If you hate airline food, **ask for special meals when booking.** These can be

vegetarian, low cholesterol, or kosher, for example; commonly prepared to order in smaller quantities than standard catered fare, they can be tastier.

SMOKING➤ Smoking is banned on all flights within the United States of less than six hours' duration and on all Canadian flights; the ban also applies to domestic segments of international flights aboard U.S. and foreign carriers. Delta has banned smoking system-wide.

C
CAMERAS, CAMCORDERS, AND COMPUTERS
LAPTOPS

Before you depart, **check your portable computer's battery,** because you may be asked at security to turn on the computer to prove that it is what it appears to be. At the airport, you may prefer to **request a manual inspection,** although security X-rays do not harm hard-disk or floppy-disk storage.

PHOTOGRAPHY

If your camera is new or if you haven't used it for a while, **shoot and develop a few rolls of film** before you leave. Always **store film in a cool, dry place**—never in the car's glove com-

SMART TRAVEL TIPS / THE GOLD GUIDE

partment or on the shelf under the rear window.

Every pass through an X-ray machine increases film's chance of clouding. To protect it, carry it in a clear plastic bag and **ask for hand inspection at security.** Such requests are virtually always honored at U.S. airports. Don't depend on a lead-lined bag to protect film in checked luggage—the airline may increase the radiation to see what's inside.

VIDEO

Before your trip, **test your camcorder, invest in a skylight filter to protect the lens, and charge the batteries.** (Airport security personnel may ask you to turn on the camcorder to prove that it's what it appears to be).

Videotape is not damaged by X-rays, but it may be harmed by the magnetic field of a walk-through metal detector, so **ask that videotapes be hand-checked.**

CHILDREN AND TRAVEL

BABY-SITTING

To find a local sitter, **check with your hotel desk for recommendations.**

DRIVING

If you are renting a car, **arrange for a car seat when you reserve.** Sometimes they're free.

FLYING

On domestic flights, children under two not occupying a seat travel free, and older children currently travel on the "lowest applicable" adult fare.

BAGGAGE➤ In general, the adult baggage allowance applies for children paying half or more of the adult fare.

SAFETY SEATS➤ According to the FAA, it's a good idea to **use safety seats aloft.** Airline policy varies. U.S. carriers allow FAA-approved models, but airlines usually require that you buy a ticket, even if your child would otherwise ride free, because the seats must be strapped into regular passenger seats. If you choose not to buy a seat for your child, many airlines will allow you to use a vacant seat (if there is one) free of charge and will often rearrange seating to accommodate you. When reserving seat assignments, **ask to have an empty seat in the middle of your traveling party.** Often it will remain vacant, and you can use it for your child, so bring your safety seat just in case. If the flight is full, you can check the safety seat at the gate.

FACILITIES➤ When making your reservation, **ask for children's meals or a freestanding bassinet** if you need them; the latter are available only to those with seats at the bulkhead, where there's enough legroom. If you don't need the bassinet, **think twice before requesting bulkhead seats**—the only storage for in-flight necessities is in the inconveniently distant overhead bins.

KNOW-HOW

Periodicals for parents that are filled with listings of events, resources, and advice are available free at such places as libraries, supermarkets, and museums.

LODGING

Most hotels allow children under a certain age to stay in their parents' room at no extra charge, while others charge them as extra adults; be sure to **ask about the cut-off age.**

CRUISES

To get the best deal on a cruise, **consult a cruise-only travel agency.**

CUSTOMS AND DUTIES

BACK HOME

IN CANADA➤ Once per calendar year, when you've been out of Canada for at least seven days, you may bring in C$300 worth of goods duty-free. If you've been away less than seven days but more than 48 hours, the duty-free exemption drops to C$100 but can be claimed any number of times (as can a C$20 duty-free exemption for absences of 24 hours or more). You cannot combine the yearly and 48-hour exemptions, use the C$300 exemption only partially (to save the balance for a later trip), or pool exemptions with family members. Goods claimed under the C$300 exemption may follow you by mail; those claimed under the lesser exemptions must accompany you.

Alcohol and tobacco products may be included in the yearly and 48-hour exemptions but not in the 24-hour exemption. If you meet the age requirements of the province through which you reenter Canada, you may bring in, duty-free, 1.14 liters (40 imperial ounces) of wine or liquor *or* 24 12-ounce cans or bottles of beer or ale. If you are 16 or older, you may bring in, duty-free, 200 cigarettes, 50 cigars or cigarillos, and 400 tobacco sticks or 400 grams of manufactured tobacco. Alcohol and tobacco must accompany you on your return.

An unlimited number of gifts valued up to C$60 each may be mailed to Canada duty-free. These do not count as part of your exemption. Label the package "Unsolicited Gift— Value under $60." Alcohol and tobacco are excluded.

IN THE U.K.➤ From countries outside the EU, including the United States, you may import duty-free 200 cigarettes, 100 cigarillos, 50 cigars or 250 grams of tobacco; 1 liter of spirits or 2 liters of fortified or sparkling wine; 2 liters of still table wine; 60 milliliters of perfume; 250 milliliters of toilet water; plus £136 worth of other goods, including gifts and souvenirs.

D

DINING

One cautionary word: Raw oysters have been identified as a problem for people with chronic illness of the liver, stomach, or blood, or who have immune disorders. Since 1993, all Florida restaurants serving raw oysters are required to post a notice in plain view of all patrons warning of the risks associated with consuming them.

FOR TRAVELERS WITH DISABILITIES

When discussing accessibility with an operator or reservationist, **ask hard questions.** Are there any stairs, inside *or* out? Are there grab bars next to the toilet *and* in the shower/tub? How wide is the doorway to the room? To the bathroom? For the most extensive facilities, meeting the latest legal specifications, **opt for newer properties,** which more often have been designed with access in mind. Older properties or ships must usually be retrofitted and may offer more limited facilities as a result. Be sure to **discuss your needs before booking.**

DISCOUNT CLUBS

Travel clubs offer members unsold space on airplanes, cruise ships, and package tours at as much as 50% below regular prices. Membership may include a regular bulletin or access to a toll-free hot line giving details of available trips departing from three or four days to several months in the future. Most also offer 50% discounts off hotel rack rates. Before booking with a club, **make sure the hotel or other sup-** **plier isn't offering a better deal.**

DRIVING

Three major interstates lead to Florida from various parts of the country. I–95 begins in Maine, runs south through New England and the Mid-Atlantic states, and enters Florida just north of Jacksonville. It continues south past Daytona Beach, the Space Coast, Vero Beach, Palm Beach, and Fort Lauderdale, eventually ending in Miami.

I–75 begins at the Canadian border in Michigan and runs south through Ohio, Kentucky, Tennessee, and Georgia before entering Florida. The interstate moves through the center of the state before veering west into Tampa. It follows the west coast south to Naples, then crosses the state, and ends in Fort Lauderdale.

California and all the most southern states are connected to Florida by I–10. This interstate originates in Los Angeles and moves east through Arizona, New Mexico, Texas, Louisiana, Mississippi, and Alabama before entering Florida at Pensacola on the west coast. I–10 continues straight across the northern part of the state until it terminates in Jacksonville.

Travelers heading from the Midwest or other points west for the lower east coast of Florida will want to use Florida's Turnpike from

Wildwood, which crosses the state for 304 miles and terminates in Florida City. Coin service plazas have replaced the use of toll cards through the urban southern sections of the turnpike.

SPEED LIMITS

In Florida the speed limits are 55 mph on the state highways, 30 mph within city limits and residential areas, and 55–65 mph on the interstates and on Florida's Turnpike. These limits may vary, so be sure to watch road signs for any changes.

H

HEALTH
CONCERNS

DIVERS' ALERT

Scuba divers take note: **Do not fly within 24 hours of scuba diving.**

I

INSURANCE

BAGGAGE

Airline liability for your baggage is limited to $1,250 per person on domestic flights. On international flights, the airlines' liability is $9.07 per pound or $20 per kilogram for checked baggage (roughly $640 per 70-pound bag) and $400 per passenger for unchecked baggage. However, this excludes valuable items such as jewelry and cameras that are listed in your ticket's fine print. You can buy additional insurance from the airline at check-in, but first **see if your home-** **owner's policy covers lost luggage.**

FLIGHT

You should **think twice before buying flight insurance.** Often purchased as a last-minute impulse at the airport, it pays a lump sum when a plane crashes, either to a beneficiary if the insured dies or some-times to a surviving passenger who loses eyesight or a limb. Supplementing the airline's coverage de-scribed in the limits-of-liability paragraphs on your ticket, it's expen-sive and basically unnecessary. Charging an airline ticket to a major credit card often automatically entitles you to coverage and may also embrace travel by bus, train, and ship.

HEALTH

FOR U.K. TRAVELERS➤ According to the Asso-ciation of British Insur-ers, a trade association representing 450 insur-ance companies, it's wise to **buy extra medical coverage when you visit the United States.** You can buy an annual travel-insurance policy valid for most vacations during the year in which it's pur-chased. If you go this route, make sure it covers you if you have a preexisting medical condition or are preg-nant.

TRIP

Without insurance, you will lose all or most of your money if you must cancel your trip due to illness or any other reason. Especially if your airline ticket, cruise, or package tour is nonrefundable and cannot be changed, it's essential that you **buy trip-cancellation-and-interruption insurance.** When considering how much coverage you need, look for a policy that will cover the cost of your trip plus the nondiscounted price of a one-way airline ticket should you need to return home early. Read the fine print carefully, especially sections defining "family mem-ber" and "preexisting medical conditions." Also **consider default or bankruptcy insurance,** which protects you against a supplier's failure to deliver. How-ever, such policies often do not cover default by a travel agency, tour operator, airline, or cruise line if you bought your tour and the coverage directly from the firm in question.

L

LODGING

APARTMENT AND VILLA RENTALS

If you want a home base that's roomy enough for a family and comes with cooking facilities, **consider a furnished rental.** It's generally cost-wise, too, although not always—some rentals are luxury properties (economical only when your party is large). Home-exchange directories do list rentals—often second homes owned by prospective house swappers—and some services search for a house or apartment for you (even a castle if that's your fancy) and handle the paperwork.

Some send an illustrated catalogue and others send photographs of specific properties, sometimes at a charge; up-front registration fees may apply.

HOME EXCHANGE

If you would like to find a house, an apartment, or other vacation property to exchange for your own while on vacation, **become a member of a home-exchange organization,** which will send you its annual directories listing available exchanges and will include your own listing in at least one of them. Arrangements for the actual exchange are made by the two parties to it, not by the organization.

HOTELS AND MOTELS

Florida, with some 40 million visitors in 1995, has every conceivable type of lodging, everything from tree houses to penthouses, from mansions for hire to hostels. Recession in the early 1990s discouraged investors from adding to Florida's hotel-room supply, but even with occupancy rates inching up above 70%, there are always rooms for the night, except maybe during Christmas and other holiday weekends. Even the most glittery resort towns have affordable lodgings, typically motel rooms that may cost as little as $30–$40 a night—not in the best part of town, mind you, but not in the worst, either, perhaps along busy highways where you'll need the roar of the air-condi-

tioning to drown out the traffic. Since beachfront properties tend to be more expensive, **look for properties a little off the beach for the best bargain;** still, many beachfront properties are surprisingly affordable, too, as in places like Olde Naples in the far southwest and Amelia Island in the far northeast.

Travelers who favor vintage hotels can find them everywhere. The classics include the Breakers and the Boca Raton Resort & Club, both in Boca Raton; the Biltmore in Coral Gables; and the Casa Marina in Key West. Florida also has more than 200 historic inns, from the Miami River Inn in downtown Miami to the Governors Inn in Tallahassee and the New World Landing Inn in Pensacola.

Often the best bet for traveling with children is to **book space that comes with a kitchen and more than one bedroom.** Such properties are especially plentiful around Orlando, where hoteliers expect steady family trade. Children are welcome generally everywhere in Florida. Pets are another matter, so **inquire ahead of time if you're bringing an animal with you.**

In the busy seasons—over Christmas, from late January through Easter, and during holiday weekends in summer—**always reserve ahead for the top properties.** St. Augustine stays busy all summer because of its historic flavor. Key

West is jam-packed for Fantasy Fest at Halloween. If you're not booking through a travel agent, **call the visitors bureau or the chamber of commerce in the area where you're going** to check whether any special event is scheduled for when you plan to arrive. If demand isn't especially high for the time you have in mind, you can often **save by showing up at a lodging in mid- to late afternoon**—desk clerks are typically willing to negotiate with travelers in order to fill those rooms late in the day. In addition, **check with chambers of commerce for discount coupons for selected properties.**

INNS AND B&BS

Small inns and guest houses are becoming increasingly numerous and popular in Florida. Many offer the convenience of bed-and-breakfast accommodations in a homelike setting; many, in fact, are in private homes, and the owners treat you almost like a member of the family.

VACATION OWNERSHIP RESORTS

Vacation ownership resorts sell hotel rooms, condominium apartments, or villas in weekly, monthly, or quarterly increments. The weekly arrangement is most popular; it's often referred to as "interval ownership" or "time sharing." Of more than 3,000 vacation ownership resorts around the world, some 500 are in Florida. As an owner, you can **join your resort's exchange organization and swap your interval** for another someplace else in any year when you want a change of scene. Even if you don't own an interval, you can **rent at many vacation ownership resorts** where unsold intervals remain and/or owners have placed their intervals in a rental program.

M
MONEY AND EXPENSES

ATMS

Chances are that you can **use your bank card at ATMs** to withdraw money from an account and get cash advances on a credit-card account if your card has been programmed with a personal identification number, or PIN. Before leaving home, **check on frequency limits** for withdrawals and cash advances.

On cash advances you are charged interest from the day you receive the money from ATMs as well as from tellers. Transaction fees for ATM withdrawals outside your home turf may be higher than for withdrawals at home.

TRAVELER'S CHECKS

Whether or not to buy traveler's checks depends on where you are headed; **take cash to rural areas and small towns, traveler's checks to cities.** The most widely recognized are American Express, Citicorp, Thomas Cook, and Visa, which

are sold by major commercial banks for 1% to 3% of the checks' face value—it pays to **shop around.** Both American Express and Thomas Cook issue checks that can be countersigned and used by you or your traveling companion. Record the numbers of the checks, cross them off as you spend them, and keep this information separate from your checks.

WIRING MONEY

You don't have to be a cardholder to send or receive funds through MoneyGram^{SM} from American Express. Just go to a MoneyGram agent, located in retail and convenience stores and in American Express Travel Offices. Pay up to $1,000 with cash or a credit card, anything over that in cash. The money can be picked up within 10 minutes in cash or check at the nearest MoneyGram agent. The cost, which includes a free long-distance phone call, runs from 3% to 10%, depending on the amount sent, the destination, and how you pay.

You can also send money using Western Union. Money sent from the United States or Canada will be available for pickup at agent locations in 100 countries within 15 minutes. Once the money is in the system, it can be picked up at any one of 25,000 locations. Fees range from 4% to 10%, depending on the amount you send.

P
PACKAGES AND TOURS

A package or tour to Florida can make your vacation less expensive and more convenient. Firms that sell tours and packages purchase airline seats, hotel rooms, and rental cars in bulk and pass some of the savings on to you. In addition, the best operators have local representatives to help you out at your destination.

A GOOD DEAL?

The more your package or tour includes, the better you can predict the ultimate cost of your vacation. Make sure you know exactly what is included, and **beware of hidden costs.** Are taxes, tips, and service charges included? Transfers and baggage handling? Entertainment and excursions? These can add up.

Most packages and tours are rated deluxe, first-class superior, first-class, tourist, or budget. The key difference is usually accommodations. If the package or tour you are considering is priced lower than in your wildest dreams, **be skeptical.** Also, **make sure your travel agent knows the hotels** and other services. Ask about location, room size, beds, and whether it has a pool, room service, or programs for children, if you care about these. Has your agent been there or sent others you can contact?

THE GOLD GUIDE / SMART TRAVEL TIPS

BUYER BEWARE

Each year consumers are stranded or lose their money when operators go out of business—even very large ones with excellent reputations. If you can't afford a loss, take the time to **check out the operator**—find out how long the company has been in business, and ask several agents about its reputation. Next, **don't book unless the firm has a consumer-protection program.** Members of the United States Tour Operators Association and the National Tour Association are required to set aside funds exclusively to cover your payments and travel arrangements in case of default. Nonmember operators may instead carry insurance; look for the details in the operator's brochure— and the name of an underwriter with a solid reputation. Note: When it comes to tour operators, **don't trust escrow accounts.** Although there are laws governing those of charter-flight operators, no governmental body prevents tour operators from raiding the till.

Next, **contact your local Better Business Bureau and the attorney general's office** in both your own state and the operator's; have any complaints been filed? Last, **pay with a major credit card.** Then you can cancel payment, provided that you can document your complaint. Always **consider trip-cancellation insurance** (*see* Insurance, *above*).

BIG VS. SMALL➤ An operator that handles several hundred thousand travelers annually can use its purchasing power to give you a good price. Its high volume may also indicate financial stability. But some small companies provide more personalized service; because they tend to specialize, they may also be experts on an area.

USING AN AGENT

Travel agents are an excellent resource. In fact, large operators accept bookings only through travel agents. But it's good to **collect brochures from several agencies,** because some agents' suggestions may be skewed by promotional relationships with tour and package firms that reward them for volume sales. If you have a special interest, **find an agent with expertise in that area;** the American Society of Travel Agents can give you leads in the United States. (Don't rely solely on your agent, though; agents may be unaware of small niche operators, and some special-interest travel companies only sell direct.)

SINGLE TRAVELERS

Prices are usually quoted per person, based on two sharing a room. If traveling solo, you may be required to pay the full double-occupancy rate. Some operators eliminate this surcharge if you agree to be matched up with a roommate of the same sex, even if one is not found by departure time.

The northern part of the state is much cooler in winter than the southern part. Winters are mild in the Orlando area, with daytime temperatures in the 70s and low 80s. But the temperature can dip to the 50s, even in the Keys, so **take a sweater or jacket,** just in case. Farther north, in the Panhandle area, winters are cool and there's often frost at night.

The Miami area and the Tampa–St. Petersburg area are warm year-round and often extremely humid during the summer months. Be prepared for sudden summer storms, but keep in mind that plastic raincoats are uncomfortable in the high humidity.

Dress is casual throughout the state, with sundresses, jeans, or walking shorts appropriate during the day; **bring a pair of comfortable walking shoes or sneakers** for the major theme parks. A few of the better restaurants request that men wear jackets and ties, but most do not. Be prepared for air-conditioning working in overdrive.

You can generally swim year-round in peninsular Florida from about New Smyrna Beach south on the Atlantic coast and from Tarpon Springs south on the Gulf Coast. Be sure to **take a sun hat and a good sunscreen** because the sun can be fierce, even in winter.

THE GOLD GUIDE / SMART TRAVEL TIPS

Bring an extra pair of eyeglasses or contact lenses in your carry-on luggage, and if you have a health problem, **pack enough medication** to last the trip. In case your bags go astray, **don't put prescription drugs or valuables in luggage to be checked.**

LUGGAGE

REGULATIONS➤ Free airline baggage allowances depend on the airline, the route, and the class of your ticket; ask in advance. In general, on domestic flights you are entitled to check two bags—neither exceeding 62 inches, or 158 centimeters (length + width + height), nor weighing more than 70 pounds (32 kilograms). A third piece may be brought aboard; its total dimensions are generally limited to less than 45 inches (114 centimeters), so it will fit easily under the seat in front of you or in the overhead compartment. In the United States, the Federal Aviation Administration gives airlines broad latitude to limit carry-on allowances and tailor them to different aircraft and operational conditions. Charges for excess, oversize, or overweight pieces vary.

SAFEGUARDING YOUR LUGGAGE➤ Before leaving home, **itemize your bags' contents** and their worth, and label them with your name, address, and phone number. (If you use your home address, cover it so that potential thieves can't see it.) Inside your bag, **pack a**

copy of your itinerary. At check-in, **make sure that your bag is correctly tagged** with the airport's three-letter destination code. If your bags arrive damaged or not at all, file a written report with the airline before leaving the airport.

PASSPORTS AND VISAS

British citizens need a valid passport. If you are staying fewer than 90 days and traveling on a vacation, with a return or onward ticket, you will probably not need a visa. However, you will need to fill out the Visa Waiver Form, 1-94W, supplied by the airline.

While traveling, **keep one photocopy of the data page** separate from your wallet and leave another copy with someone at home. If you lose your passport, promptly call the nearest embassy or consulate, and the local police; having the data page can speed replacement.

R
RENTING A CAR

Florida is a car renter's bazaar, with more discount companies offering more bargains—and more fine print—than any other state in the nation. For the best deal, **look for the best combination rate for car and airfare.**

CUTTING COSTS

To get the most savings, **book through a travel agent and shop around.** When pricing cars, **ask where the rental lot is located.** Some off-

airport locations offer lower rates—even though their lots are only minutes away from the terminal via complimentary shuttle. You may also want to **price local car-rental companies,** whose rates may be lower still, although service and maintenance standards may not be up to those of a national firm. Also **ask your travel agent about a company's customer-service record.** How has it responded to late plane arrivals and vehicle mishaps? Are there often lines at the rental counter, and, if you're traveling during a holiday period, does a confirmed reservation guarantee you a car?

INSURANCE

When you drive a rented car, you are generally responsible for any damage or personal injury that you cause as well as damage to the vehicle. Before you rent, **see what coverage you already have** by means of your personal auto-insurance policy and credit cards. For about $14 a day, rental companies sell insurance, known as a collision damage waiver (CDW), that eliminates your liability for damage to the car; it's always optional and should never be automatically added to your bill.

SURCHARGES

Before picking up the car in one city and leaving it in another, **ask about drop-off charges or one-way service fees,** which can be substantial. Note, too, that some rental agencies charge extra if you return the car before the time specified on your contract. To avoid a hefty refueling fee, **fill the tank just before you turn in the car.**

FOR U.K. CITIZENS

In the United States you must be 21 to rent a car; rates may be higher for those under 25. Extra costs cover child seats, compulsory for children under five (about $3 per day), and additional drivers (about $1.50 per day). To pick up your reserved car you will need the reservation voucher, a passport, a U.K. driver's license, and a travel policy covering each driver.

S

SENIOR-CITIZEN DISCOUNTS

To qualify for age-related discounts, **mention your senior-citizen status up front** when booking hotel reservations, not when checking out, and before you're seated in restaurants, not when paying your bill. Note that discounts may be limited to certain menus, days, or hours. When renting a car, **ask about promotional car-rental discounts**—they

can net lower costs than your senior-citizen discount.

SHOPPING

Malls in Florida are full of nationally franchised shops, major department-store chains, and one-of-a-kind shops catering to a mass audience. For the best souvenirs, **look for small shops in out-of-the-way places.**

T

TELEPHONES

LONG-DISTANCE

The long-distance services of AT&T, MCI, and Sprint make calling home relatively convenient and let you avoid hotel surcharges; typically, you dial an 800 number in the United States and a local number abroad.

W

WHEN TO GO

Florida is a state for all seasons, although most visitors prefer October–April, particularly in southern Florida.

Winter remains the height of the tourist season, when southern Florida is crowded with "snowbirds" fleeing the cold weather in the

North. Hotels, bars, discos, restaurants, shops, and attractions are all crowded. Hollywood and Broadway celebrities appear in sophisticated supper clubs, and other performing artists hold the stage at ballets, operas, concerts, and theaters.

For the college crowd, spring vacation is still the time to congregate in Florida, especially in Panama City Beach and the Daytona Beach area; Fort Lauderdale, where city officials have refashioned the beachfront more as a family resort, no longer indulges young revelers, so it's much less popular with college students than it once was.

Summer in Florida, as smart budget-minded visitors have discovered, is often hot and very humid, but ocean breezes make the season bearable along the coast. Besides, many hotels lower their prices considerably during summer.

CLIMATE

What follows are average daily maximum and minimum temperatures for major cities in Florida.

Climate in Florida

KEY WEST (THE KEYS)

Jan.	76F	24C	May	85F	29C	Sept.	90F	32C
	65	18		74	23		77	25
Feb.	76F	24C	June	88F	31C	Oct.	83F	28C
	67	19		77	25		76	24
Mar.	79F	26C	July	90F	32C	Nov.	79F	26C
	68	20		79	26		70	21
Apr.	81F	27C	Aug.	90F	32C	Dec.	76F	24C
	72	22		79	26		67	19

MIAMI

Jan.	74F	23C	May	83F	28C	Sept.	86F	30C
	63	17		72	22		76	24
Feb.	76F	24C	June	85F	29C	Oct.	83F	28C
	63	17		76	24		72	22
Mar.	77F	25C	July	88F	31C	Nov.	79F	26C
	65	18		76	24		67	19
Apr.	79F	26C	Aug.	88F	31C	Dec.	76F	26C
	68	20		77	25		63	17

1 Destination: Miami & the Keys

WHAT'S WHERE

The Everglades

Created in 1947, this national park in the southernmost extremity of the peninsula preserves a portion of the slow-moving "river of grass"—a 50-mile-wide stream that flows through marshy grassland en route to Florida Bay. Biscayne National Park, nearby, is the largest national park in the continental United States with living coral reefs.

The Florida Keys

This slender necklace of landfalls off the southern tip of Florida is strung together by a 110-mile-long highway. The Keys have two faces: one a wilderness of flowering jungles and shimmering seas amid mangrove-fringed islands dangling toward the tropics, the other a traffic jam with a view of billboards, shopping centers, and trailer courts. You don't come here for the beaches, but for the deep-sea fishing and the snorkeling and diving.

Fort Lauderdale

Once known for its wild spring breaks, this southern Florida city on the east coast is newly chic. Just as the beach has renewed itself, so has downtown—with residential construction and an emerging cultural arts district.

Miami and Miami Beach

In the '80s, *Miami Vice* brought notoriety to this southernmost of big Florida cities; South Beach put it on the map again in the '90s with its revamping of the Deco District. Through all this, the city went from an enclave of retired northeasterners to the ultimate joyride with a Latin beat—over half the city's population is Latin. Don't miss Coconut Grove, the south Florida mainland's oldest settlement. It's chic and casual, full of bistros, cafés, and galleries.

Palm Beach and the Treasure Coast

For 100 years, high society has made headlines along south Florida's Atlantic shore from Palm Beach south to Boca Raton—part of the Gold Coast. The coast north of Palm Beach County, called the Treasure Coast, is also worth exploring. Comprising Martin, St. Lucie, and Indian River counties, it's dotted with nature preserves, fishing villages, and towns with active cultural scenes.

PLEASURES & PASTIMES

Beaches

Florida rates 12 of the top 20 U.S. beaches, while no point in the state is more than 60 miles from salt water. The long, lean peninsula is bordered by a 526-mile Atlantic coast from Fernandina Beach to Key West and a 792-mile coast along the Gulf of Mexico and Florida Bay from Pensacola to Key West. If you were to stretch Florida's convoluted coast in a straight line, it would extend for about 1,800 miles. What's more, if you add in the perimeter of every island surrounded by salt water, Florida has about 8,500 miles of tidal shoreline—more than any other state except Alaska. Florida's coastline comprises about 1,016 miles of sand beaches.

From Daytona Beach south, Hurricane Gordon caused considerable erosion of beaches late in 1994, and the usual cycle of seasonal tides and winds has so far been slow to rebuild these beaches. Major beach-rehabilitation projects have been completed in Fort Lauderdale, Miami Beach, and Key Biscayne. By 1996, the experimental renourishing of beaches in metro Miami's Surfside will be complete.

In the Florida Keys, coral reefs and prevailing currents prevent sand from building up to form beaches. The few Keys beaches are small, narrow, and generally have little or no sandy bottom. A happy exception is the beach at Bahia Honda State Park.

Although the state owns all beaches below the mean high-tide line, even in front of hotels and private resorts, gaining access to them can be a problem along much of Florida's coastline. You must pay to enter and/or park at most state, county, and local beachfront parks. Where hotels dominate the beach frontage, public parking may be limited or nonexistent.

If you are unaccustomed to strong subtropical sun, you run a risk of sunburn and heat prostration, even in winter. Natives go to the beach early in the day or in the late afternoon. If they must be out in direct sun at midday, they limit their sun exposure and strenuous exercise, drink plenty of liquids, and wear hats. Wherever you plan to swim, ask if the water has a dangerous undertow.

Biking

Florida has many, many cyclists on the road traveling many, many miles. The key to cycling's popularity is the terrain—flat in the south. Most cities of any size have bike-rental shops, which are good sources of information on local bike paths.

Florida's Department of Environmental Protection has developed three overnight bicycle tours of different areas of the state. The tours vary in length between 100 and 450 miles (for two–six days of cycling) and use state parks for rest stops and overnight camping.

Canoeing

The Everglades has areas suitable for flat-water wilderness canoeing that are comparable to spots in the Boundary Waters region of Minnesota. Contact individual national forests, parks, monuments, reserves, and seashores for information on their canoe trails. Local chambers of commerce have information on canoe trails in county parks. The best time to canoe in Florida is winter, the dry season, when you're less likely to get caught in a torrential downpour or be eaten alive by mosquitoes.

Dining

Florida's cuisine changes as you move across the state, based on who settled the area and who now operates the restaurants. You can expect seafood to be a staple on nearly every menu, however, with greater variety on the coasts. Florida has launched some big-league culinary stars. Restaurateurs like Fort Lauderdale's Mark Militello are nationally acclaimed, while others who got their start here, such as Douglas Rodriguez, formerly of Yuca in Coral Gables, have gone on to glory in Manhattan.

South Florida's diverse assortment of Latin American restaurants offers the distinctive national fare of Argentina, Brazil, Colombia, Cuba, El Salvador, Mexico, Nicaragua, and Puerto Rico, and it's also easy to find island specialties born of the Bahamas, Haiti, and Jamaica. A new fusion of tropical, Continental, and nouvelle cuisine—some call it Floribbean—has gained widespread popularity. It draws on exotic fruits, spices, and fresh seafoods. The influence of earlier Hispanic settlements remains in Key West.

All over Florida, Asian cuisine no longer means just Chinese. Indian, Japanese, Pakistani, Thai, and Vietnamese specialties are now available. Continental cuisine (French, German, Italian, Spanish, and Swiss) is also well represented all over Florida.

Every Florida restaurant claims to make the best Key lime pie. Pastry chefs and restaurant managers take the matter very seriously—they discuss the problems of getting good lime juice and maintaining top quality every day. Traditional Key lime pie is yellow, not green, with an old-fashioned graham cracker crust and meringue top. The filling should be tart and chilled but not frozen. Some restaurants serve their Key lime pie with a pastry crust; most substitute whipped cream for the more temperamental meringue. Each pie will be a little different. Try several, and make your own decision.

Fishing

Opportunities for saltwater fishing abound from the Keys all the way up the Atlantic Coast to Georgia and up the Gulf Coast to Alabama. Many seaside communities have fishing piers that charge admission to anglers (and usually a lower rate to watchers). These piers generally have a bait-and-tackle shop. It's easy to find a boat-charter service that will take you out into deep water. The Keys are dotted with charter services, and Key West has a big sportfishing fleet. Depending on your taste, budget, and needs, you can charter anything from an old wooden craft to a luxurious, waterborne palace with state-of-the-art amenities.

In addition to the state's many natural freshwater rivers, South Florida also has an extensive system of flood-control canals. In

1989 scientists found high mercury levels in largemouth bass and warmouth caught in parts of the Everglades in Palm Beach, Broward, and Dade counties, and warned against eating fish from those areas. Those warnings remain in effect, and warnings have been extended to parts of northern Florida.

In Atlantic and Gulf waters, fishing seasons and other regulations vary by location and by the number and size of fish of various species that you may catch and retain. Licenses are required for both saltwater and freshwater fishing. The fees for a saltwater fishing license are $30 for nonresidents and $12 for residents. A nonresident seven-day saltwater license is $14. Nonresidents can purchase freshwater fishing licenses good for seven days ($15) or for one year ($30); residents pay $12 for an annual license. Combined annual freshwater fishing and hunting licenses are also available at $22 for residents. Typically, you'll pay a $1.50 surcharge at most any marina, bait-and-tackle shop, Kmart, WalMart, or other license vendor.

Golf

Except in the heart of the Everglades, you'll never be far from one of Florida's nearly 1,100 golf courses. Palm Beach County, the state's leading golf locale, has 150 courses, and the PGA, LPGA, and National Golf Foundation all have headquarters in the state. Many of the best golf courses in Florida allow visitors to play without being members or hotel guests.

Especially in winter, you should reserve tee times in advance. Ask about golf reservations when you make your lodging reservations.

Jogging, Running, and Walking

All over Florida, you'll find joggers, runners, and walkers on bike paths and city streets—primarily in the early morning and after working hours in the evening. Some Florida hotels have set up their own running trails; others provide guests with information on measured trails in the vicinity. The first time you run in Florida, be prepared to go a shorter distance than normal because of higher heat and humidity.

Two major Florida festivals include important running races. Each year in December the **Orange Bowl 10K,** one of the state's best-known running events, brings world-class runners to Miami. In April, as part of the Florida Keys annual Conch Republic Days, runners congregate near Marathon on one of the world's most spectacular courses for the **Seven Mile Bridge Run.** Other major events include the **Office Depot Corporate Challenge,** which attracts 15,000 runners to Miami the first week of May, and the **Heart Run,** which takes place February 4 each year in Fort Lauderdale.

National and State Parks

Although Florida is the fourth-most-populous state in the nation, more than 10 million acres of public and private recreation facilities are set aside in national forests, parks, monuments, reserves, and seashores; state forests and parks; county parks; and nature preserves owned and managed by private conservation groups. All told, Florida now has some 3,500 miles of trails, encompassing 1,550 miles of canoe and kayak trails, about 670 miles for bicycling and other uses, 900 miles exclusively for hiking, about 350 exclusively for equestrian use, plus some 30 miles of purely interpretive trails, chiefly in state parks. An active greenways development plan, which seeks to protect wildlife habitat as much as foster recreation, identified 150 greenways in use or under development in 1995.

On holidays and weekends, crowds flock to Florida's most popular parks. Come early or risk being turned away. In winter, northern migratory birds descend on the state. Many resident species breed in the warm summer months, but others (such as the wood stork) time their breeding cycle to the winter dry season. In summer, mosquitoes are voracious and daily afternoon thundershowers add to the state's humidity, but it's during the early part of this season that sea turtles come ashore to lay their eggs and you're most likely to see frigate birds and other tropical species.

NATIONAL PARKS➤ The federal government maintains no centralized information service for its natural and historic sites in Florida.

Everglades National Park was established in 1947, and **Biscayne National Park** in 1980. Another natural site in Florida under federal management includes **Big Cypress National Preserve** in the Everglades.

National wildlife refuges in Florida include the **Great White Heron National Wildlife Refuge, Crocodile Lakes National Wildlife Refuge,** and **National Key Deer Refuge** in the Keys and **Loxahatchee National Wildlife Refuge** near Palm Beach. The federal government also operates the **Key Largo National Marine Sanctuary, Looe Key National Marine Sanctuary,** and the **Florida Keys National Marine Sanctuary,** largest in the national system.

STATE PARKS➤ The Florida Department of Environmental Protection manages hundreds of historic buildings, landmarks, and nature preserves as well as beaches, recreation areas, and parks as part of an expanding state park system.

Pari-Mutuel Sports

Florida has a big variety of venues for sports you can lawfully bet on. These include greyhound race tracks, tracks for harness and Thoroughbred racing, and jai-alai frontons.

Scuba Diving and Snorkeling

South Florida and the Keys attract most of the divers and snorkelers, but the more than 300 statewide dive shops schedule drift-, reef-, and wreck-diving trips for scuba divers all along Florida's Atlantic and Gulf coasts. The low-tech pleasures of snorkeling can be enjoyed throughout the Keys and elsewhere where shallow reefs hug the shore.

Shopping

ANTIQUES➤ Antiques lovers should explore Southwest 28th Lane and Unity Boulevard in Miami (near the Coconut Grove Metrorail station).

CITRUS FRUIT➤ Fresh citrus is available most of the year, except in summer. Two kinds of citrus grow in Florida: the sweeter and more costly Indian River fruit from a thin ribbon of groves along the east coast, and the less-costly fruit from the interior, south and west of Lake Okeechobee.

Citrus is sold in ¼, ½, ¾, and full bushels. Many shippers offer special gift packages with several varieties of fruit, jellies, and other food items. Some prices include U.S. postage; others may not. Shipping may exceed the cost of the fruit. If you have a choice of citrus packaged in boxes or bags, take the boxes. They are easier to label and harder to squash.

NATIVE AMERICAN CRAFTS➤ Native American crafts are abundant, particularly in the southern part of the state, where you'll find billowing dresses and shirts, hand-sewn in striking colors and designs. At the Miccosukee Indian Village, 25 miles west of Miami on the Tamiami Trail (U.S. 41), as well as at the Seminole and Miccosukee reservations in the Everglades, you can also find handcrafted dolls and beaded belts.

SEASHELLS➤ Shell shops, selling mostly kitschy items, abound throughout Florida. The coral and other shells sold in shops in the Florida Keys have been imported for sale because of restrictions on harvesting these materials.

Tennis

Many Florida hotels have a resident tennis pro and offer special tennis packages with lessons. Many local park and recreation departments throughout Florida operate modern tennis centers like those at country clubs, and most such centers welcome nonresidents, for a fee.

FODOR'S CHOICE

No two people will agree on what makes a perfect vacation, but it's fun and helpful to know what others think. We hope you'll have a chance to experience some of Fodor's Choices yourself. For detailed information about each entry, refer to the appropriate chapter in this guidebook.

Views to Remember

★ **Everglades National Park from the tower on Shark Valley Loop.** This 50-foot observation tower yields a splendid panorama of the wide "river of grass" as it sweeps southward toward the Gulf of Mexico.

★ **Ocean Drive in the Art Deco District, Miami Beach.** Feast your eyes on brilliantly restored vintage Art Deco hotels at every turn. Since their restoration, this palm-lined beachfront is hopping 24 hours a day.

★ **Sunset scene at Mallory Square, Key West.** Here, sunset draws street performers, vendors, and thousands of onlookers to Mallory Dock and the eponymous square nearby.

Hotels

★ **The Breakers, Palm Beach.** This palatial Italian renaissance hotel, sprawling over 140 acres of splendor, is the standard of Florida resort excellence. $$$$

★ **Casa Grande, Miami Beach.** It's the only hotel on Ocean Drive that captures the street's fashionable imperative yet with fine classical taste. It's also one of the rare establishments in the area with spacious baths. $$$$

Restaurants

★ **Cafe des Artistes, Key West.** Chef Andrew Berman's brilliant tropical version of French cuisine is served in a series of intimate dining rooms filled with tropical art and an upstairs, outdoor patio. $$$

★ **Louie's Back Yard, Key West.** The Key West paintings and the ocean views seen from under the mahoe tree outside alone would have made it an institution; Susan Ferry's loosely Spanish-Caribbean cuisine shares pride of place. $$$

★ **Mark's Place, North Miami Beach.** The deco-style dining room is as much a feast for the eyes as owner-chef Mark Militello's absolutely fresh, regional Florida gourmet fare is a feast for the palate. $$$

FESTIVALS AND SEASONAL EVENTS

MID-DEC.➤ **Winterfest Boat Parade** is on the Intracoastal Waterway, Fort Lauderdale (☎ 305/767–0686).

LATE DEC.➤ **Coconut Grove King Mango Strut** is a parody of the Orange Bowl Parade (☎ 305/858–6253).

EARLY JAN.➤ **Polo Season** opens at the Palm Beach Polo and Country Club (☎ 407/793–1440).

MID-JAN.➤ **Art Deco Weekend** spotlights Miami Beach's historic district with an Art Deco street fair, a 1930s-style Moon Over Miami Ball, and live entertainment (☎ 305/672–2014).

MID-JAN.➤ **Taste of the Grove Food and Music Festival** is a popular fundraiser put on in Coconut Grove's Peacock Park by area restaurants (☎ 305/444–7270).

LATE JAN.➤ **Miami Rivers Blues Festival** takes place on the south bank of the river next to Tobacco Road (☎ 305/374–1198).

FEB.–MAR.➤ **Winter Equestrian Festival** includes more than 1,000 horses and three grand-prix equestrian events at the Palm Beach Polo and Country Club in West Palm Beach (☎ 407/798–7000).

MID-FEB.➤ **Miami Film Festival** is 10 days of international, domestic, and local films sponsored by the Film Society of America (☎ 305/377–3456).

MID-FEB.➤ **Coconut Grove Art Festival** is the state's largest (☎ 305/447–0401).

EARLY MAR.➤ **Carnaval Miami** is a carnival celebration staged by the Little Havana Tourist Authority (☎ 305/644–8888).

LATE APR.➤ **River Cities Festival** is a three-day event in Miami Springs and Hialeah that focuses attention on the Miami River and the need to keep it clean (☎ 305/887–1515).

LATE APR.–EARLY MAY➤ **Conch Republic Celebration** in Key West honors the founding fathers of the Conch Republic, "the small island nation of Key West" (☎ 305/296–0123).

FIRST WEEKEND IN MAY➤ **Sunfest** includes a wide variety of cultural and sporting events in West Palm Beach (☎ 407/659–5980 or 800/833–5733).

FIRST WEEKEND IN JUNE➤ **Miami-Bahamas Goombay Festival,** in Miami's Coconut Grove, celebrates the city's Bahamian heritage (☎ 305/443–7928 or 305/372–9966).

MID-JULY➤ **Hemingway Days Festival,** in Key West, includes plays, short-story competitions, and a Hemingway look-alike contest (☎ 305/294–4440).

LATE OCT.➤ **Fantasy Fest** in Key West is an unrestrained Halloween costume party, parade, and town fair (☎ 305/296–1817).

EARLY NOV.–LATE FEB.➤ **Orange Bowl** and **Junior Orange Bowl Festival,** best known for the King Orange Jamboree Parade and the Federal Express/Orange Bowl Football Classic, also include more than 20 youth-oriented events in the Miami area (☎ 305/371–3351).

MID-NOV.➤ **12th Annual Miami Book Fair International,** the largest book fair in the United States, is held on the Miami-Dade Community College Wolfson Campus (☎ 305/237–3258).

2 Miami and Miami Beach

In the '80s, Miami Vice *brought notoriety to this southernmost of big Florida cities; South Beach put it on the map again in the '90s with its revamping of the Deco District. Through all this, the city went from an enclave of retired northeasterners to the ultimate joyride with a Latin beat—over half the city's population is Latin. Don't miss Coconut Grove, the south Florida mainland's oldest settlement. It's chic and casual, full of bistros, cafés, and galleries.*

WHAT MAKES MIAMI different from the rest of
the United States is quickly apparent when you
fly in. With the vast Everglades at the west-
By Herb Hiller ern edge and the Atlantic to the east, Miami clings to a ribbon of drained
land near the southeastern tip of the country. Still vulnerable to
mosquitoes, periodic flooding, and potential devastation by hurricanes, Miami a hundred years after its founding is still the wrong
place for a city, but it's the right place for a crossroads. And that's exactly what Miami is.

Long before Spain's gold-laden treasure ships passed offshore in the Gulf
Stream, the Calusa Indians who lived here had begun to trade with mainland neighbors to the north and island brethren to the south. Repeat-
ing this pattern, more than 150 U.S. and multinational companies now
locate their Latin American headquarters in Greater Miami. The city
has unparalleled airline connections to the Western Hemisphere, its cruise
port ranks number one in the world, and it leads the nation in the number of Edge Act banks. Miami hosts 20 foreign trade offices, 29 bina-
tional chambers of commerce, and 49 foreign consulates. No city of the
Western Hemisphere is so universally *simpatico*.

First-time visitors are always struck by the billboards in Spanish. Ini-
tially these seem an affectation, an attempt to promote Miami's exotic
international image. Only after you hear Spanish spoken by hotel help
all around you or after the elevator you're in announces the floor
stops as *primer piso* and *segundo piso* do you realize that the city
Newsweek called "America's Casablanca" is really the capital of Latin
America. Metro Miami is more than half Latin. Cubans make up most
of this Spanish-speaking population, but significant communities come
from Colombia, El Salvador, Nicaragua, Panama, Puerto Rico, and
Venezuela. The Spanish place-names George Merrick affixed to the streets
in Coral Gables 75 years ago—Alhambra, Alcazar, Salzedo—may have
been romantic pretense, but today's renamed Avenida Gen. Maximo
Gomez and Carlos Arboleya Way are earnest celebrations of a contemporary city's heroes. Frank Sinatra and Barbra Streisand have given
way in the hearts of Miamians to Julio Iglesias and Gloria Estefan.

In addition to the dominant Spanish-speaking population, Miami is
home to some 200,000 Haitians along with Brazilians, Chinese, Ger-
mans, Greeks, Iranians, Israelis, Italians, Jamaicans, Lebanese,
Malaysians, Russians, and Swedes—all speaking a veritable Babel of
tongues. Most either know or are trying to learn English; you can help
them by speaking slowly and distinctly.

Established Miami has warmed up to its newcomers. That's a big step
forward. Only a few years ago metropolitan government enacted an
ordinance forbidding essential public information from appearing in
Spanish. In 1993 that restrictive affront was rescinded, and resisters
have adjusted or moved north. Yesterday's immigrants have become
today's citizens, and the nation's most international city now offers a
style expressed in its many languages, its world-beat music, and its wealth
of restaurants enjoyed by Miamians and visitors alike.

Miami has changed fast. Only yesterday old Miami Beach was a rundown geriatric center. Today it's South Beach, the deco darling of the
world. Summer especially brings young people; two of every three are
male, and three of every four are single. Lincoln Road, once the 5th
Avenue of the South and only recently an embarrassing derelict row,

has been stunningly brought back to life. On weekends it rivals the pedestrian malls of Cambridge, Lyons, or Munich for crowds and sheer hoi polloi festivity. Next slated for revival is North Beach, as all of Miami Beach becomes a magic kingdom in the real world, proving it's possible and relatively inexpensive to build community by preserving distinctive architecture rather than by "imagineering" pseudo worlds. (Miamians—especially Miami's immigrant newcomers—do still adore Disney, however).

More changes are in store in this city that seems fueled on caffeine. (Stop by the window serving station of any Cuban café for a *tinto,* the city's high-test fuel.) Not surprisingly, much of the change is taking place to the south, in areas hard hit by Hurricane Andrew in 1992. In the Redland district, the Redland Conservancy is introducing bicycle trails and bed-and-breakfasts as a way of preserving the south county's agricultural heritage. Coral-rock walls and avocado groves may prove as distinctive in their own way as art deco hotels. A network of 200 miles of trails should link Biscayne and Everglades national parks by the end of the decade. For those interested in a quicker pace, Homestead has become a state-of-the-art hub for America's love affair with car racing (*see* Chapter 3, The Everglades).

As a big city, Miami also earns its bad rap. It has the highest percentage of citizens living in poverty. Its traffic is the fourth most congested in the United States. It ranks first in violent and property crimes and does the worst job of any city in putting and keeping criminals behind bars. Yet the widely publicized crimes against tourists in 1993 led to stepped-up visitor-safety programs that by 1995 had turned visitor safety around. Police patrols have been upgraded in primary visitor areas. New red, sunburst-logo, highway direction signs have been installed at ¼-mile intervals on major roads. Indicia that made rental cars conspicuous to would-be criminals have been removed, and multilingual pamphlets with tips on how to avoid crime are widely distributed. Despite all the problems and hyped headlines, Miami is still incredibly appealing. It has the climate, the beaches, and the international sophistication that few places can match.

A slew of international celebrities has moved here: Madonna, Sylvester Stallone, Cher, Gianni Versace. Four major-league sports franchises call Miami home, as do the Doral-Ryder Open Tournament, the Lipton Championships, the Miami City Ballet, and Florida Grand Opera. On the verge of its centennial year and barely two years after Hurricane Andrew roared through, Miami played host to both the Summit of the Americas and the Super Bowl. Visitors find in Miami a multicultural metropolis that works and plays with vigor and that welcomes the world to celebrate its diversity.

EXPLORING

Disney captured Miami's family trade, *Miami Vice* smacked the city upside the head with notoriety, South Beach made it a global resort for the turn of the 21st century, and through all this, the city went from an enclave of retired northeasterners to the ultimate joyride with a Latin beat. Hardly any part of the city isn't caught up in change. Where once people came to lie on the beach, even that's dangerous nowadays, though people do it anyway. (Good sunblock helps.) Meanwhile sightseeing— which used to be pretty much limited to picking fruit off citrus trees and watching alligator wrestling—has become a fun way to glimpse the city at work and at play.

Downtown has become the live hub of the mainland city, now more accessible thanks to the Metromover extension (*see* Getting Around by Train *in* Miami Essentials, *below*). Other major attractions include Coconut Grove, Little Havana, and South Beach/the Art Deco District, but since these districts are spread out beyond the reach of public transportation, you'll have to drive.

Finding your way around Greater Miami is easy if you know how the numbering system works. Miami is laid out on a grid with four quadrants—northeast, northwest, southeast, and southwest—which meet at Miami Avenue and Flagler Street. Miami Avenue separates east from west, and Flagler Street separates north from south. Avenues and courts run north–south; streets, terraces, and ways run east–west. Roads run diagonally, northwest–southeast.

Many named streets also bear numbers. For example, Unity Boulevard is Northwest and Southwest 27th Avenue, and LeJeune Road is Northwest and Southwest 42nd Avenue. However, named streets that depart markedly from the grid, such as Biscayne Boulevard and Brickell Avenue, have no corresponding numerical designations. Dade County and most other municipalities follow the Miami numbering system.

In Miami Beach, avenues run north–south; streets, east–west. Numbers rise along the beach from south to north and from the Atlantic Ocean in the east to Biscayne Bay in the west.

In Coral Gables, all streets bear names. Coral Gables uses the Miami numbering system for north–south addresses, but begins counting east–west addresses westward from Douglas Road (Southwest 37th Avenue).

Hialeah has its own grid. Palm Avenue separates east from west; Hialeah Drive separates north from south. Avenues run north–south and streets east–west. Numbered streets and avenues are designated west, east, southeast, southwest, northeast, or northwest.

Tour 1: Miami Beach

Numbers in the margin correspond to points of interest on the Tour 1: Miami Beach map.

Most visitors to the Greater Miami area don't realize that Miami and Miami Beach are separate cities. Miami, on the mainland, is southern Florida's commercial hub. Miami Beach, on 17 islands offshore in Biscayne Bay, is sometimes considered America's Riviera, luring refugees from winter to its warm sunshine, sandy beaches, and graceful palms.

In 1912 what would become Miami Beach was little more than a sand spit in the bay. Then Carl Graham Fisher, a millionaire promoter who built the Indianapolis Speedway, began to pour much of his fortune into developing the island city.

Ever since, Miami Beach has experienced successive waves of boom and bust—thriving in the early 1920s and the years just after World War II, but enduring the devastating 1926 and 1992 hurricanes, the Great Depression, and travel restrictions during World War II. During the 1960s, jets full of onetime Beach winter vacationers began winging to the more reliably warm Caribbean, and the flow of summer family vacationers was dammed midstate in 1971 by Walt Disney World.

Today Miami Beach—chiefly known for the South Beach area—revels in renewed world glory as a lure for models and millionaires, an affordable multilingual resort where anything goes from fancy dress to gender-free dress to undress. The comeback of the Beach was marked in 1993 by a record $232 million in building permits, almost double the previous high of $135 million only five years before. The hub of South Beach is the mile-square Art Deco District. About 650 significant buildings in the district are listed on the National Register of Historic Places. That is not to say that the City of Miami Beach yet respects the resource. The section immediately below the official Art Deco District, which also includes several outstanding properties, is slated for massive overbuilding in the near future after years of neglect. Bulky skyscrapers seem destined for lower Ocean Drive.

From the mainland, cross the **MacArthur Causeway** (U.S. 41), which spans Biscayne Bay, to reach Miami Beach. (To reach the causeway from downtown Miami, turn east off Biscayne Boulevard north of Northeast 11th Street. From I–95, turn east onto I–395. The eastbound Dolphin Expressway, Route 836, becomes I–395 east of the I–95 interchange.) As you approach the MacArthur Causeway bridge across the Intracoastal Waterway, you'll see the *Miami Herald* building, which occupies the Biscayne Bayfront on your left.

❶ Cross the bridge to **Watson Island,** created by dredging in 1931. To your right is the seaplane base of **Chalk's International Airlines** (*see* Guided Tours *in* Miami Essentials, *below*), the oldest scheduled international air carrier, founded in 1919. Today it operates seaplanes to Key West, Bimini, and Nassau.

❷ ❸ East of Watson Island the causeway leaves Miami and enters Miami
❹ Beach. On the left you'll pass the bridge to **Palm** and **Hibiscus islands** and then the bridge to **Star Island.** Celebrities who have lived on these islands include Al Capone (93 Palm Ave., Palm Island), author Damon Runyon (271 Hibiscus Island), and actor Don Johnson (8 Star Island).

East of Star Island the causeway mounts a high bridge. Look left to see
❺ an island with an obelisk, the **Flagler Memorial Monument.** The memorial honors Henry M. Flagler, who built the Florida East Coast Railroad, which opened all of east coast Florida to tourism and commerce, reaching Miami in 1896 and Key West in 1912. Flagler's hotels set a new standard for opulent vacationing and ushered in a long train of imperial developers, the list crowned in our own time by Walt Disney.

Just beyond the bridge, turn right onto Alton Road past the **Miami Beach Marina** (300 Alton Rd., ☎ 305/673–6000), where dive boats depart for artificial reefs offshore in the Atlantic Ocean. Continue to the foot of Alton Road, turn left on Biscayne Street, and then right at Wash-
❻ ington Avenue to enter **South Pointe Park** (1 Washington Ave.). From the 50-yard Sunshine Pier, which adjoins the mile-long jetty at the mouth of Government Cut, you can fish while watching huge ships pass. No bait or tackle is available in the park. Other facilities include two observation towers and volleyball courts.

TIME OUT   **South Pointe Seafood House** (1 Washington Ave., ☎ 305/673–1708) provides the catbird seat for enjoying this brew pub's beer while watching the mammoth cruise ships sail out Government Cut from the Port of Miami Friday through Monday.

Exit the park onto Biscayne Street, turn right, go to the end, and turn left onto Ocean Drive. Right away you'll start to see a line of pastel-hue Art Deco hotels on your left, and then at 5th Street, palm-fringed
★ **Lummus Park** and the beach on your right. This is the **Art Deco District,** a 10-block stretch along Ocean Drive that has become the most talked-about beachfront in America. Less than 15 years ago, the vin-

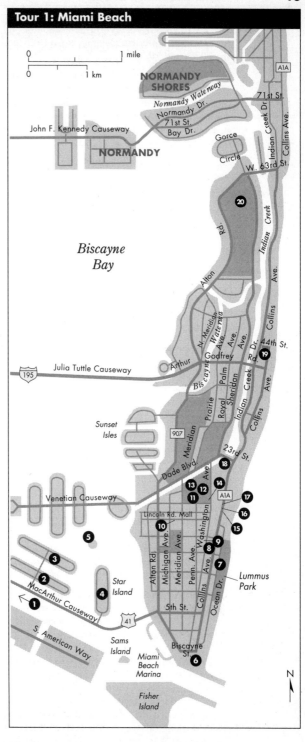

Tour 1: Miami Beach

tage hotels were badly run down, catering to infirm retired people. But a group of visionaries saw this collection of buildings as an architectural treasure, a peerless grouping of Art Deco modern architecture from the 1920s and 1930s.

In the early 1980s, investors started fixing up the interiors of these hotels and repainting their exteriors with vibrant colors. International bistro operators then moved in, sensing the potential for a new café society. The media took note, and celebrities came, among them singer Gloria Estefan, designer Gianni Versace, and record executive Chris Blackwell, who bought pieces of the action.

Now the place hums 24 hours a day, as fashion photographers pose beautiful models for shoots that make backdrops of the throngs of visitors. Pop singer and actress Madonna photographed scenes in her controversial 1992 book *Sex* up and down the beach.

As you progress up Ocean Drive, notice that the forms and decorative detail of buildings are drawn from nature (including birds, butterflies, and flowers); from ancient Aztec, Mayan, Babylonian, Chaldean, Egyptian, and Hebrew designs; and from the streamlined, aerodynamic shapes of modern transportation and industrial machinery. To

❼ get oriented, start at the **Art Deco District Welcome Center.** It is located on the beach side in the Oceanfront Auditorium (a 1950s building, not Deco). *1001 Ocean Dr., ☎ 305/531–3484. ☛ Free. ☉ Daily 11–6 (to later Thurs.–Mon. in season).*

You may want to get out of your car to stroll around the district, but from mid-morning on, parking is scarce along Ocean Drive. You'll do better on Collins or Washington avenues, the next two streets paralleling Ocean Drive to the west. Be warned: Tickets are handed out freely when meters expire, and towing charges are high. Additional parking garages are likely to materialize in 1996.

Turn left on 15th Street and left again at the next corner to cruise down **Collins Avenue.** Follow Collins south to 5th Street, and turn right. Turn right again at the next corner to go back north on **Washington Avenue,** a mix of chic restaurants, avant-garde shops, delicatessens, and produce markets.

❽ Continue north on Washington Avenue to the new **Wolfsonian Foundation Gallery,** displaying the 50,000-item collection of modern design and so-called propaganda arts amassed by Miami native Mitchell Wolfson, Jr., a world traveler and connoisseur. The gallery and its adjoining study center open fully in 1995. *1001 Washington Ave., ☎ 305/531–1001. ☛ $1 adults, 50¢ senior citizens and children. ☉ Weekdays 1–5.*

TIME OUT   Turn right on 12th Street to **Muff'n Man** (234 12th St., ☎ 305/538–6833). Multiberry, apple, and cinnamon-raisin muffins and brownies and cookies are baked here daily. The interior is filled with Deco District photos, silk pillows, and interesting art.

❾ Back on Washington Avenue, walk past 14th Street to **Espanola Way,** a narrow street of Mediterranean-revival buildings constructed in 1925 and frequented through the years by artists and writers. In the 1930s, Cuban bandleader Desi Arnaz performed in the Village Tavern, now part of the **Clay Hotel & AYH International Youth Hostel** (1438 Washington Ave., ☎ 305/534–2988). For one block of Espanola Way, west of Washington Avenue to Drexel Avenue, the way for cars has been narrowed to a single lane, and Miami Beach's trademark pink sidewalks have been widened to accommodate new sidewalk cafés. As recently as 1990, this street was troubled by derelicts; now it has miraculously popped up clean, safe, and redeemed, chockablock with imaginative clothing, jewelry, and art shops.

★ ⑩ Continue two blocks beyond Drexel to Meridian Avenue, and turn right. Three blocks north of Espanola Way is **Lincoln Road Mall.** Here you can expect throngs of new visitors who up until 1990 wouldn't have been caught dead on the mall, which had turned into a sideshow of freaks and panhandlers. During its heyday in the 1950s, Lincoln Road was known as the 5th Avenue of the South, but, like all of the Beach, by the '60s it had been bypassed. It was closed to traffic and turned into a pedestrian mall between Washington Avenue and Alton Road, but that couldn't halt the decline. When rents bottomed out, however, artists and arts groups moved in and rehabilitated their buildings. Cafés and restaurants followed, and then retailers. Today the mall is thriving, and even the Miami Beach City Commission, notoriously slow to recognize revival, is at least proving helpful here. A new, playful re-design, due for completion in 1996, includes a grove of 20 towering date palms with misters likely to spritz passersby, five linear pools di-vided by strips of jungle, and a simulated aquarium behind a curtain-like waterfall. The mall has become twinned with Ocean Drive as part of "must-see" South Beach, especially on Saturday night, when art gal-leries schedule openings together. Don't miss it.

Park in the municipal lot a half block north of the mall, between Washington and Meridian avenues; then either walk along the mall or catch one of the trams that shuttle shoppers. At 541–545 Lincoln Road you'll see a classical four-story Deco gem with its friezes repainted in wavy greens—this is where the **New World Symphony** (*see* The Arts and Nightlife, *below*), a national advanced-training orchestra led by Michael Tilson Thomas, rehearses and performs. As you walk west, toward Biscayne Bay, the street is lined with chic food markets like **Lyon Freres** (600 Lincoln Rd., ☎ 305/534–0600), with exotic businesses like the **Mideastern Dance Exchange** (622 Lincoln Rd., ☎ 305/538–1608), with artistic cafés like the **Beehive Diner** (630–A Lincoln Rd., ☎ 305/538–7484), and with brilliant boutiques like **Diamonds & Chicken Soup** (828 Lincoln Rd., ☎ 305/532–7687). Go farther west, and you'll find the **South Florida Art Center** (924 Lincoln Rd., ☎ 305/674–8278), one of the first arts groups to help resurrect the area. The building houses visual artists' studios and showrooms; they are open to the public, with no admission charge, weekdays 9–5. Farther on, a black-and-white Deco movie house with a Mediterranean barrel-tile roof has become the **Colony Theater** (*see* The Arts and Nightlife, *below*).

⑪ ⑫ The first main street north of Lincoln Road Mall is 17th Street, named **Hank Meyer Boulevard** for the publicist who persuaded the late come-dian Jackie Gleason to broadcast his TV show from Miami Beach in the 1950s. East on 17th Street, beside the entrance to **Miami Beach City Hall** (1700 Convention Center Dr., ☎ 305/673–7030), stands *Red Sea Road,* a huge red sculpture by Barbara Neijna. Also to your left east across Con-vention Center Drive is the **Miami Beach Convention Center** (1901 Con-vention Center Dr., ☎ 305/673–7311), a stucco 1960s-vintage building that gained its peach-tone, art deco look in a 1990 renovation and ex-pansion. It's the Miami area's largest convention space, with 1.1 mil-lion square feet.

⑬ Behind the Convention Center north along Convention Center Drive at the northwest end of the parking lot near Meridian Avenue, is the **Holocaust Memorial** (1933–1945 Meridian Ave., ☎ 305/538–1663 or 305/538–1673), a monumental sculpture and a graphic record in memory of the 6 million Jewish victims of the Holocaust. Admission is free, but a small donation is requested for literature on the memorial. A garden conservatory (2000 Convention Center Dr., ☎ 305/673–7256) next door is worth a visit, but has limited public hours.

Just south of the convention center, at 17th Street and Washington Avenue, you'll see another large sculpture, *Mermaid,* by Roy Lichtenstein, in front of the **Jackie Gleason Theater of the Performing Arts** (1700 Washington Ave., ☎ 305/673–7300), where Gleason's TV show originated. Now the 3,000-seat theater (*see* The Arts and Nightlife, *below*) hosts touring Broadway shows and classical-music concerts. Near the sculpture, performers who have appeared in the theater since 1984 have left their footprints and signatures in concrete. This **Walk of the Stars** includes the late George Abbott, Julie Andrews, Leslie Caron, Carol Channing, and Edward Villella.

Go one block east to Collins Avenue and turn right (south) toward three of the largest Art Deco hotels, all built in the 1940s. Their streamlined tower forms reflect the 20th century's transportation revolution. The round dome atop the 11-story **Hotel National** (1677 Collins Ave., ☎ 305/532–2311) resembles a balloon. The tower at the 12-story **Delano Hotel** (1685 Collins Ave., ☎ 305/538–7881) has fins suggesting the wings of an airplane or a Buck Rogers spaceship. (The hotel was acquired in 1994 by New York hotelier Ian Schrager, who has invested more than $20 million into the property and plans to turn it into a five-star urban resort in time for the 1995–96 winter season.) The 11-story **Ritz Plaza** (1701 Collins Ave., ☎ 305/534–3500) rises to a cylindrical tower resembling a periscope.

Go north on Collins Avenue. At 21st Street turn left beside the Miami Beach Public Library in Collins Park, go two blocks to Park Avenue, and turn right. You're approaching the **Bass Museum of Art,** which houses a diverse collection of European art, including *The Holy Family,* a painting by Peter Paul Rubens; *The Tournament,* one of several 16th-century Flemish tapestries; and works by Albrecht Dürer and Henri de Toulouse-Lautrec. A current expansion project will double the museum's size to 40,000 square feet in time for the 1997–98 winter season. Park in back and walk around to the entrance, past massive tropical baobab trees. *2121 Park Ave., ☎ 305/673–7530.* ☛ *$5 adults, $4 students with ID and senior citizens, $3 ages 13–17, $2 children 6–12; donations Tues.; some exhibitions may be more expensive.* ⊙ *Tues.–Sat. 10–5, except 2nd and 4th Weds. of each month 1–9; Sun. 1–5.*

Return on 21st or 22nd Street to Collins Avenue, and turn left. As you drive north, a triumphal archway looms ahead, framing a majestic white building set in lush vegetation beside a waterfall and tropical lagoon. This vista is an illusion—a 13,000-square-foot outdoor mural on an exterior wall of the **Fontainebleau Hilton Resort and Towers** (*see* Lodging, *below*). Artist Richard Haas designed the mural to illustrate how the hotel and its rock-grotto swimming pool would look behind the wall. Locals call the 1,206-room hotel Big Blue. It's the giant of Miami Beach.

Turn left on 65th Street, left again at the next corner onto Indian Creek Drive, and right at 63rd Street, which leads into **Alton Road,** a winding, landscaped boulevard of gracious homes styled along art deco lines. You'll pass **La Gorce Country Club** (5685 Alton Rd., ☎ 305/866–4421), which developer Carl Fisher built and named for his friend Oliver La Gorce, then president of the National Geographic Society.

To return to the mainland on the MacArthur Causeway, stay on Alton Road south to 5th Street, then turn right.

Tour 2: Downtown Miami

*Numbers in the margin correspond to points of interest on the Tour
2: Downtown Miami map.*

From a distance you see downtown Miami's future—a 21st-century skyline already stroking the clouds with sleek fingers of steel and glass. By
day this icon of commerce and technology sparkles in the strong subtropical sun; at night it basks in the man-made glow of floodlights.

Here staid, suited lawyers and bankers share the sidewalks with Latino
merchants wearing open-neck, intricately embroidered shirts called
guayaberas. Fruit merchants sell their wares from pushcarts. European
youths with backpacks stroll the streets. Foreign businesspeople hag-
gle over prices in import-export shops. You hear Arabic, Chinese, Creole, French, German, Hebrew, Hindi, Japanese, Portuguese, Spanish,
Swedish, Yiddish, and even a little English now and then.

The metropolis has become one of the great international cities of the
Americas, yet Miami's downtown is sorely neglected. Although office
workers crowd the area by day, the city, but for Bayside and the Miami
Arena, is deserted at night, and patrons of the Arena rarely stay downtown when the basketball and hockey games or other events are over.
Those who live close to downtown stay at its fringes, as on Claughton
Island at the mouth of the Miami River, where a half dozen residential towers have risen to house thousands in the last decade. Visitors,
too, spend as little time here as possible, since most tourist attractions
are in other neighborhoods. Miami's oldest downtown buildings date
from the 1920s and 1930s—not very old compared to the historic districts of St. Augustine and Pensacola. What's best in the heart of downtown Miami today is its Latinization and the sheer energy of Latin
shoppers. The following walking tour doesn't include many must-see
sights, but it can help you get to know this hub city.

Thanks to the Metromover (*see* Getting Around by Train *in* Miami Essentials, *below*), which has inner and outer loops through downtown
plus north and south extensions, this is an excellent tour to take by
rail. Attractions are conveniently located within about two blocks of
the nearest station, so the tour approximately follows the outer loop.
Parking downtown is no more inconvenient or expensive than in any
city, but the best idea is to leave your car at an outlying Metrorail station and take the train downtown.

Get off the Metrorail train at **Government Center Station,** where the
21-mile elevated Metrorail commuter system connects with Metromover.

❶ As you leave the station, notice the **Dade County Courthouse** (73 W.
Flagler St.). It's the building to the east with a pyramid at its peak, where
turkey vultures roost in winter. Built in 1928, it was once the tallest
building south of Washington, D.C.

❷ You'll enter **Metro-Dade Center** (111 N.W. 1st St.), the county government's sleek 30-story office building. Designed by architect Hugh
Stubbins, it opened in 1985.

★ **❸** Across Northwest 1st Street stands the **Metro-Dade Cultural Center** (101
W. Flagler St.), one of the focal points of Miami's downtown. The city's
main art museum, historical museum, and library are gathered here in
a 3.3-acre complex. Opened in 1983, it is a Mediterranean expression
of architect Philip Johnson's postmodern style. An elevated plaza provides a serene haven from the city's pulsations and an open-air setting
for festivals and outdoor performances.

The **Center for the Fine Arts,** an art museum in the tradition of the European *kunsthalle* (exhibition gallery), has no permanent collection (though a push toward forming one has come with the arrival, in 1995, of a new director). Throughout the year CFA organizes and borrows temporary exhibitions on diverse themes. ☎ *305/375–3000.* ☛ *$5 adults, $2 children 6–12; donations Tues.* ☉ *Tues.–Wed. and Fri.–Sat. 10–5, Thurs. 10–9, Sun. noon–5.*

The **Historical Museum of Southern Florida** is a regional museum that interprets the human experience in southern Florida from prehistory to the present. Artifacts on permanent display include Tequesta and Seminole Indian ceramics, clothing, and tools; a 1920 streetcar; and an original edition of Audubon's *Birds of America.* ☎ *305/375–1492.* ☛ *$4 adults, $2 children 6–12; donations Mon.* ☉ *Mon.–Wed. and Fri.–Sat. 10–5, Thurs. 10–9, Sun. noon–5.*

The **Main Public Library** has nearly 4 million holdings and a computerized card catalog. Inside the entrance, look up at the rotunda mural, in which artist Edward Ruscha interpreted a quotation from Shakespeare: "Words without thought never to heaven go." You'll find art exhibits in the auditorium and second-floor lobby. ☎ *305/375–2665.* ☉ *Mon.–Wed. and Fri.–Sat. 9–6, Thurs. 9–9, Sun. 1–5; closed Sun. May–mid-Oct.*

④ Take the Metromover to the next stop, **Ft. Dallas Park Station,** and walk one block south to reach the **Miami Avenue Bridge,** one of 11 bridges on the Miami River that open to let ships pass. From the bridge approach, watch freighters, tugboats, research vessels, and luxury yachts ply this busy 5-mile waterway.

TIME OUT   Stroll across the bridge to **Tobacco Road** (625 S. Miami Ave., ☎ 305/374–1198) for a drink, snack, or meal. Built in 1912, this friendly neighborhood pub was a speakeasy during Prohibition.

⑤ The next Metromover stop, **Knight Center Station,** nestles inside **NationsBank Tower** (100 S.E. 1st St.), a wedge-shape 47-story skyscraper designed by I. M. Pei and Partners. The building is brilliantly illumi-
⑥ nated at night. Inside the tower follow signs to the **James L. Knight International Center** (400 S.E. 2nd Ave., ☎ 305/372–0929), a convention and concert hall in a bulbous concrete building appended to the Hyatt Regency Miami.

At Knight Center Station, you can transfer to the inner loop and ride
⑦ one stop to the **Miami Avenue Station,** a block south of **Flagler Street,** downtown Miami's commercial spine. Like most such thoroughfares, Flagler Street has lost business in recent years to suburban malls—but, unlike most, it found a new lease on life. Today the ½ mile of Flagler Street from Biscayne Boulevard to the Dade County Courthouse is the most important retail import-export center in the United States. Its stores and arcades supply much of the world with bargain automotive parts, audio and video equipment, medical equipment and supplies, photographic equipment, clothing, and jewelry.

TIME OUT   Walk about 2½ blocks north of Flagler Street to the **Jamaican Restaurant** (245 N. Miami Ave., ☎ 305/375–0156), an open-air Jamaican eatery as authentic as any in Kingston. The jukebox pours reggae onto Miami Avenue while waitresses pour Jamaican beer, Red Stripe, which goes well with the oxtail stew or curried goat.

Tour 2: Downtown Miami

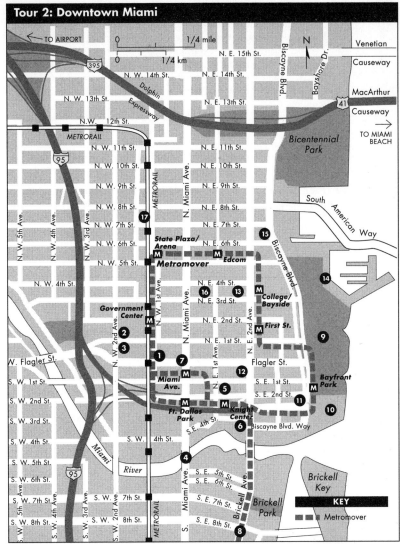

TO AIRPORT

0   1/4 mile

0   1/4 km

N. E. 15th St.

Venetian

Causeway

N. W. 14th St.   N. E. 14th St.

Biscayne Blvd.

Bayshore Dr.

MacArthur

N. W. 13th St.

Dolphin Expressway

N. E. 13th St.

41

Causeway

→

N. W. 12th St.

TO MIAMI
BEACH

METRORAIL

95

N. W. 11th St.   N. E. 11th St.

Bicentennial
Park

N. W. 10th St.   N. E. 10th St.

N. W. 9th St.   N. E. 9th St.

METRORAIL

N. Miami Ave.

N. W. 8th St.   N. E. 8th St.

South

N. W. 7th St.   N. E. 7th St.

American

Way

State Plaza/
Arena

N. E. 6th St.

15

N. W. 5th Ave.

N. W. 4th Ave.

N. W. 3rd Ave.

M   M   Edcom

Metromover

N. W. 4th St.

N. E. 4th St.

16

13

College/
Bayside

14

N. W. 1st Ave.

N. Miami Ave.

N. E. 3rd St.

M

Government
Center

2

N. E. 2nd St.

N. E. 2nd Ave.

First St.

N. W. 2nd Ave.

3

N. E. 1st St.

9

W. Flagler St.

1

7

Flagler St.

S. W. 1st St.

Miami
Ave.

M

12

Bayfront
Park

S. W. 2nd St.

N. 1st Ave.

S. E. 1st St.

S. W. 3rd St.

5

S. E. 2nd St.

M

11

S. W. 4th St.

Ft. Dallas
Park

M

Knight
Center

10

S. W. 5th St.

6

Biscayne Blvd. Way

S. W. 4th St.

Brickell
Key

Miami

S. W. 6th St.

4

River

S. E. 5th St.

S. E. 6th St.

Brickell
Park

95

S. W. 7th St.

Miami Ave.

S. E. 7th St.

S. W. 5th Ave.

S. W. 4th Ave.

S. W. 3rd Ave.

S. W. 2nd Ave.

Brickell Ave.

Brickell

KEY

S. W. 8th St.

METRORAIL

S. E. 8th St.

8

Metromover

Bayside
Marketplace, **14**

Brickell Avenue, **8**

Claude and Mildred
Pepper Bayfront
Park, **9**

Dade County
Courthouse, **1**

Flagler Street, **7**

Freedom Tower, **15**

Gusman Centerfor
the Performing
Arts, **12**

Hotel
Inter-Continental
Miami, **10**

James L. Knight
International
Center, **6**

Metro-Dade Center, **2**

Metro-Dade Cultural
Center, **3**

Miami Arena, **17**

Miami Ave. Bridge, **4**

Miami-Dade
Community
College, **13**

NationsBank
Tower, **5**

Southeast Financial
Center, **11**

U.S. Courthouse, **16**

Also from the Knight Center Station, you can ride the new Metromover spur that links downtown with the Brickell District, just across the Miami River along **Brickell Avenue,** a southward extension of Southeast 2nd Avenue. Heading south on Brickell Avenue through a canyon of tall buildings, you pass the largest concentration of international banking offices in the United States. From the end of the Metromover line, you can look south to where several architecturally interesting condominiums rise between Brickell Avenue and Biscayne Bay. Israeli artist Yacov Agam painted the rainbow-hue exterior of **Villa Regina** (1581 Brickell Ave.). Arquitectonica, a nationally prominent architectural firm based in Miami, designed three of these buildings: the **Palace** (1541 Brickell Ave.), the **Imperial** (1627 Brickell Ave.), and the **Atlantis** (2025 Brickell Ave.).

The next stop on the outer loop is **Bayfront Park Station,** opposite **Claude and Mildred Pepper Bayfront Park,** which extends east from busy, palm-lined Biscayne Boulevard to the edge of the bay. Japanese sculptor Isamu Noguchi redesigned the park just before his death in 1989; it now includes a memorial to the *Challenger* astronauts, an amphitheater, and a fountain (most often turned off as a budget-tightening measure) honoring the late Florida congressman Claude Pepper and his wife.

Just south of Bayfront Park, the lobby of the **Hotel Inter-Continental Miami** (*see* Lodging, *below*) contains *The Spindle,* a huge sculpture by Henry Moore. West of Bayfront Park Station stands the tallest building in Florida, the 55-story **Southeast Financial Center** (200 S. Biscayne Blvd.); towering royal palms stand in the 1-acre Palm Court plaza beneath its steel-and-glass frame.

As you continue north on the Metromover, take in the fine view of Bayfront Park's greenery, the bay beyond, the Port of Miami in the bay, and Miami Beach across the water. The next Metromover stop, **First Street Station,** places you a block north of Flagler Street and the landmark **Gusman Center for the Performing Arts** (*see* The Arts and Nightlife, *below*), an ornate former movie palace restored as a concert hall. Resembling a Moorish courtyard with twinkling stars in the sky, it hosts performances by the Miami City Ballet and the New World Symphony.

The **College/Bayside Station** Metromover stop serves the downtown campus of **Miami-Dade Community College.** In Building 1, you can browse through two fine galleries: the **Centre Gallery** on the third floor, with various exhibitions, and the **Frances Wolfson Art Gallery** on the fifth floor, which houses traveling exhibits of contemporary art. *300 N.E. 2nd Ave.,* ☎ *305/237–3278.* ☛ *Free.* ☉ *Weekdays 10–6 (both galleries).*

★ ⑭ College/Bayside Station is also the most convenient stop for **Bayside Marketplace,** a waterside entertainment-and-shopping center built by the Rouse Company between Bayfront Park and the entrance to the Port of Miami. After completing an $11 million renovation in 1992 and adding the Hard Rock Cafe to its list of attractions, Bayside at last is attracting crowds of locals and visitors, including cruise passengers who come over from the port for a few hours' shopping before their ships head for the Caribbean. Bayside's 235,000 square feet of retail space houses 150 specialty shops, pushcarts in the center's Pier 5 area, outdoor cafés, and an international food court. Street performers entertain throughout the day and evening, and free concerts take place every day of the year, typically calypso, jazz, Latin rhythms, reggae, and rock. *401 Biscayne Blvd.,* ☎ *305/577–3344.* ☉ *Mon.–Thurs.*

10–10, Fri.–Sat. 10–11, Sun. 11–8; extended hrs for restaurants and outdoor cafés; concerts (roughly): Mon.–Thurs. 7–11 PM, Fri.–Sat. 2–6 and 9 PM–1 AM, Sun. 1:30–5:30 and 7–11.

Look just north of Bayside to see the twin-span bridge that leads to the Port of Miami. More than 1.5 million cruise passengers a year go through this port; its 12 terminals are home base for 20 cruise liners. The first series of passenger "pods" were built in 1964 in concrete shapes sculpted in the form of wind scoops. Though the pods are now enclosed and climate controlled, in midweek when there are few ships docked here you can still see the graceful wavelike pod shapes inside.

⑮ As Metromover rounds the curve after College/Bayside Station, look northeast to see **Freedom Tower** (600 Biscayne Blvd.), where the Cuban Refugee Center processed more than 500,000 Cubans who entered the United States to flee Fidel Castro's regime in the 1960s. Built in 1925 for the *Miami Daily News,* this imposing Spanish-baroque structure was inspired by the Giralda, an 800-year-old bell tower in Seville, Spain. After years in derelict condition, Freedom Tower was renovated in 1988 and opened for office use in 1990, although, oddly, it has remained untenanted. To see it up close, walk north from **Edcom Station** to Northeast 6th Street then two blocks east to Biscayne Boulevard. (It's also at this point in the loop that the spur curves north to the Omni District.)

⑯ A two-block walk south from Edcom Station will bring you to the **U.S. Courthouse,** a handsome building of coquina coral stone, erected in 1931 as Miami's main post office. In what was the second-floor central courtroom is *Law Guides Florida Progress,* a huge Depression-era mural by Denman Fink. Surrounding the central figure of a robed judge are several images that define the Florida of the 1930s: fish vendors, palm trees, beaches, and a Pan Am airplane winging off to Latin America. No cameras or tape recorders are allowed in the building. *300 N.E. 1st Ave. Building open weekdays 8:30–5; security guards open courtroom on request.*

⑰ As you round the northwest corner of the loop, at **State Plaza/Arena Station,** look two blocks north to see the **Miami Arena** (701 Arena Blvd., ☎ 305/530–4444), built in 1988 as a home for the Miami Heat, Miami's National Basketball Association team, and currently also home of the Florida Panthers of the National Hockey League. Round, squat, windowless, and pink, the arena hosts other sports and entertainment events when the teams aren't playing.

Tour 3: Little Havana

Numbers in the margin correspond to points of interest on the Tours 3–7: Miami, Coral Gables, and Key Biscayne map.

★ Some 35 years ago the tidal wave of Cubans fleeing the Castro regime flooded an older neighborhood just west of downtown Miami with refugees. This area became known as **Little Havana.** Today, with a million Cubans and other Latins—more than half the metropolitan population—widely dispersed throughout Greater Miami, Little Havana and neighboring East Little Havana remain magnets for Hispanics and Anglos alike. They come to experience the flavor of traditional Cuban culture. That culture, of course, functions in Spanish. Many Little Havana residents and shopkeepers speak little or no English.

❶ From downtown go west on Flagler Street across the Miami River. Drive west on West Flagler Street to Teddy Roosevelt Avenue (Southwest 17th Avenue), and pause at **Plaza de la Cubanidad,** on the southwest corner. Redbrick sidewalks surround a fountain and monument with a quotation from José Martí, a leader in Cuba's struggle for independence from Spain: LAS PALMAS SON NOVIAS QUE ESPERAN (The palm trees are girlfriends who will wait), counseling hope and fortitude to the Cubans.

② Turn left at Douglas Road (Southwest 37th Avenue), drive south to **Calle Ocho** (the Spanish name for Southwest 8th Street), and turn left again. You are now on the main commercial thoroughfare of Little Havana.

TIME OUT   For a total sensory experience, have a snack or meal at **Versailles** (3555 S.W. 8th St., ☎ 305/445–7614), a popular Cuban restaurant. Etched-glass mirrors lining its walls amplify bright lights, and there's the roar of rapid-fire Spanish. Most of the servers don't speak English; you order by pointing to a number on the menu (choice of English or Spanish menus). Specialties include *palomilla* (beefsteak), *ropa vieja* (literally, "old clothes," a shredded-beef dish in tomato sauce), and *arroz con pollo* (chicken and yellow rice).

Drive east on Calle Ocho. After you cross Unity Boulevard (Southwest 27th Avenue), Calle Ocho becomes a one-way street eastbound through the heart of Little Havana, where every block deserves exploration. If your time is limited, try the three-block stretch from Southwest 14th Avenue to Southwest 11th Avenue. Parking is more plentiful west of Ronald Reagan Avenue (Southwest 12th Avenue).

③ At Avenida Luis Muñoz Marín (Southwest 15th Avenue) is **Dominoes Park** (technically Maximo Gomez Park), where especially elderly Cuban males pass the day with their black-and-white play tiles and their anti-Castro politics. Lately added here is a mural of the hemispheric Summit of the Americas held in Miami late in 1994; included are paintings of every leader who took part in the event. The park is open daily 9–6.

At Calle Ocho and Memorial Boulevard (Southwest 13th Avenue)
④ stands the **Brigade 2506 Memorial,** commemorating the victims of the unsuccessful 1961 Bay of Pigs invasion of Cuba by an exile force. An eternal flame burns atop a simple stone monument with the inscription: CUBA—A LOS MARTIRES DE LA BRIGADA DE ASALTO ABRIL 17 DE 1961. The monument also bears a shield with the Brigade 2506 emblem, a Cuban flag superimposed on a cross. Walk a block south on Memorial Boulevard to see other monuments relevant to Cuban history, including a statue of José Martí.

⑤ Drive five blocks south on Ronald Reagan Avenue to the **Cuban Museum of Arts and Culture.** Created by Cuban exiles to preserve and interpret the cultural heritage of their homeland, the museum has expanded its focus to embrace the entire Hispanic arts community and work produced by young local artists in general. The museum includes among its collection the art of exiles and of artists who continue to work on the island. Other exhibits are drawn from the museum's small permanent collection. *1300 S.W. 12th Ave., ☎ 305/858–8006. Donations welcome. ☺ Tues.–Fri. 11–3, Sat. noon–5.*

To return to downtown Miami take Ronald Reagan Avenue back north to Southwest 8th Street, turn right, drive east to Miami Avenue or Brickell Avenue, turn left, and continue north across the Miami River. To pick up the Coral Gables tour, which follows, drive south to the end of Ronald Reagan Avenue, where it intersects with Coral Way; turn right onto Coral Way and head west.

Tour 4: Coral Gables and South Miami

Coral Gables, a planned community of broad boulevards and Spanish Mediterranean architecture, justifiably calls itself "The City Beautiful." Developer George E. Merrick began selling Coral Gables lots in 1921 and incorporated the city in 1925. He named most of the streets for Spanish explorers, cities, and provinces. Street names are at ground level beside each intersection on whitewashed concrete cornerstones.

The 1926 hurricane and the Great Depression prevented Merrick from fulfilling many aspects of his plan. The city languished until after World War II, but then grew rapidly. Today Coral Gables has a population of about 41,000. In its bustling downtown more than 140 multinational companies maintain headquarters or regional offices. The University of Miami campus, in the south part of Coral Gables, brings a youthful vibrance to its corner of the area.

From downtown Miami drive south on Southeast 2nd Avenue across the Miami River, where the street becomes Brickell Avenue. One-half mile south of the river turn right onto Coral Way, which at this point is Southwest 13th Street. Within ½ mile, Coral Way doglegs left under I–95 and becomes Southwest 3rd Avenue. It continues another mile to a complex intersection, Five Points, and doglegs right to become Southwest 22nd Street.

Along the Southwest 3rd Avenue and Southwest 22nd Street segments of Coral Way, banyan trees planted in the median strip in 1929 arch over the roadway. The banyans end at the Miami–Coral Gables boundary, where **Miracle Mile** begins. Actually only ½ mile long, this five-block retailing stretch of Coral Way, from Douglas Road (37th Avenue) to LeJeune Road (42nd Avenue), is the heart of downtown Coral Gables.

6 The **Colonnade Building** (133–169 Miracle Mile) once housed the sales office for Coral Gables's original developer, George Merrick. Its rotunda bears an ornamental frieze and a Spanish-tile roof 75 feet above street level. The Colonnade Building has been restored and connected to the 13-story Colonnade Hotel and an office building that echoes the rotunda's roofline.

Immediately west of LeJeune Road, bear softly to the left onto Biltmore Way. The ornate Spanish Renaissance structure facing Miracle **7** Mile is **Coral Gables City Hall,** opened in 1928. It has a three-tier tower topped with a clock and a 500-pound bell. A mural by Denman Fink inside the dome ceiling depicts the four seasons and can be seen from the second floor. *405 Biltmore Way,* ☎ *305/446–6800.* ⊙ *Weekdays 8–5.*

TIME OUT   Break for a most affordable quick lunch at the **Cafe Cappuccino** (550 Biltmore Way, ☎ 305/441–2959) in the Shops at 550, the toniest little shopping mall in the city. Between 8 and 2:30, you can enjoy gorgeous muffins or an entrée or two among the marble, Persian rugs, and haute couture.

Continue west on Biltmore Way to the corner, turn right on Segovia, left **8** onto Coral Way, and right on Toledo Street to park behind **Coral Gables Merrick House and Gardens,** George Merrick's boyhood home. The city acquired the dwelling in 1976 and restored it to its 1920s appearance. It contains Merrick family furnishings and artifacts. *907 Coral Way,* ☎ *305/460–5361.* ☛ *House: $2 adults, $1 children; grounds: free.* ⊙ *House: Sun., Wed. 1–4; grounds: daily 8–sunset.*

Tours 3–7: Miami, Coral Gables and Key Biscane

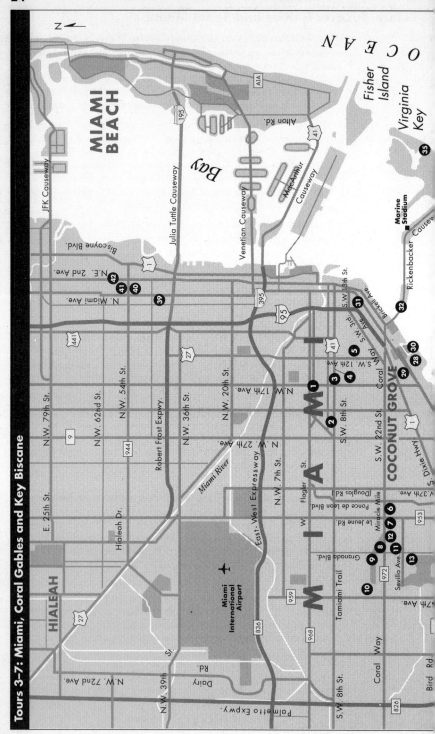

N

HIALEAH

MIAMI BEACH

Bay

O C E A N

Fisher Island

Virginia Key

Marine Stadium

Rickenbacker Causeway

COCONUT GROVE

M I A M I

Miami International Airport

JFK Causeway

Julia Tuttle Causeway

Venetion Causeway

MacArthur Causeway

A1A

Alton Rd.

195

41

1

395

95

441

27

41

9

944

959

836

968

826

953

972

Biscayne Blvd.

N. Miami Ave.

N.E. 2nd Ave.

N.W. 17th Ave.

N.W. 20th St.

N.W. 27th Ave.

N.W. 36th St.

N.W. 54th St.

N.W. 62nd St.

N.W. 79th St.

N.W. 7th Ave.

N.W. 39th St.

N.W. 72nd Ave.

E. 25th St.

Hialeah Dr.

Robert Frost Expwy.

Miami River

East-West Expressway

Palmetto Expwy.

Dairy Rd.

Flagler St.

W. Flagler St.

Tamiami Trail

Coral Way

S.W. 8th St.

Bird Rd.

Ponce de Leon Blvd.

(Douglas Rd.)

Le Jeune Rd.

Miracle Mile

Granada Blvd.

Sevilla Ave.

Coral Way

S.W. 22nd St.

S.W. 8th St.

S.W. 12th Ave.

S.W. 3rd Ave.

Brickell Ave.

S.W. 13th St.

S. Dixie Hwy.

S.W. 37th Ave.

7th Ave.

1

2

3

4

5

6

7

8

9

10

11

12

13

28

29

30

31

32

35

39

40

41

42

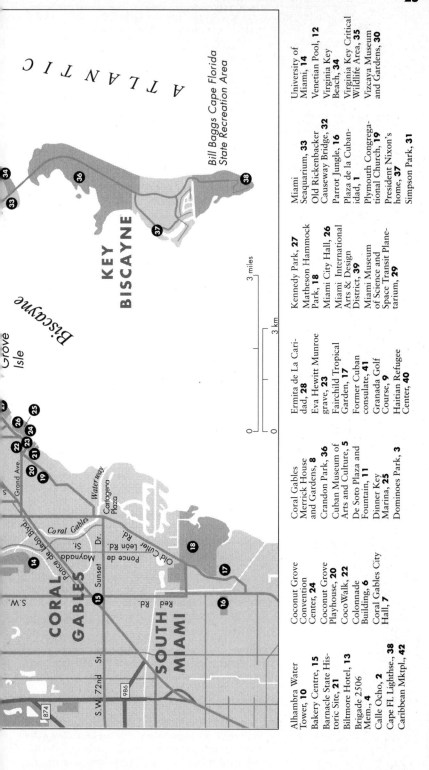

25

ATLANTIC

Bill Baggs Cape Florida State Recreation Area

KEY BISCAYNE

Biscayne

Grove Isle

3 miles

3 km

CORAL GABLES

SOUTH MIAMI

Alhambra Water Tower, **10**
Bakery Centre, **15**
Barnacle State Historic Site, **21**
Biltmore Hotel, **13**
Brigade 2506 Mem., **4**
Calle Ocho, **2**
Cape FL Lighthse., **38**
Caribbean Mktpl., **42**

Coconut Grove Convention Center, **24**
Coconut Grove Playhouse, **20**
CocoWalk, **22**
Colonnade Building, **6**
Coral Gables City Hall, **7**

Coral Gables Merrick House and Gardens, **8**
Crandon Park, **36**
Cuban Museum of Arts and Culture, **5**
De Soto Plaza and Fountain, **11**
Dinner Key Marina, **25**
Dominoes Park, **3**

Ermita de La Caridad, **28**
Eva Hewitt Munroe grave, **23**
Fairchild Tropical Garden, **17**
Former Cuban consulate, **41**
Granada Golf Course, **9**
Haitian Refugee Center, **40**

Kennedy Park, **27**
Matheson Hammock Park, **18**
Miami City Hall, **26**
Miami International Arts & Design District, **39**
Miami Museum of Science and Space Transit Planetarium, **29**

Miami Seaquarium, **33**
Old Rickenbacker Causeway Bridge, **32**
Parrot Jungle, **16**
Plaza de la Cubanidad, **1**
Plymouth Congregational Church, **19**
President Nixon's home, **37**
Simpson Park, **31**

University of Miami, **14**
Venetian Pool, **12**
Virginia Key Beach, **34**
Virginia Key Critical Wildlife Area, **35**
Vizcaya Museum and Gardens, **30**

As you leave the parking lot, turn left on Toledo Street and continue
to South Greenway Drive. You'll see the **Granada Golf Course** (2001
Granada Blvd., ☎ 305/460–5367), a gorgeous green open space and
one of two public courses in the midst of the largest historic district
of Coral Gables.

Turn left on South Greenway Drive, follow it to Alhambra Circle, and
turn right. One block ahead on your left, at the intersection of Alhambra Circle, Greenway Court, and Ferdinand Street, is the restored **Alhambra Water Tower.** This city landmark dates from 1924, when it stored
water and was clad in its decorative moresque, lighthouselike exterior.
After more than 50 years of disuse and neglect, the tower was completely
restored in 1993 with a copper-ribbed dome and multicolor frescoes.

Now drive south on Alhambra Circle four short blocks to Coral Way.
Turn left, and after six blocks turn right onto Granada Boulevard. You
are now approaching **De Soto Plaza and Fountain,** a classical column
on a pedestal with water flowing from the mouths of four sculpted faces.
The closed eyes of the face looking west symbolize the day's end. Denman Fink designed the fountain in the early 1920s.

Follow the traffic circle almost completely around the fountain to north-
east-bound De Soto Boulevard. On your right in the next block is **Venetian Pool,** a unique municipal swimming pool transformed from a rock
quarry. *2701 De Soto Blvd.,* ☎ *305/460–5356.* ☛ *Nonresident: $4 adults,
$3.50 ages 13–17, $1.60 children under 13; free parking across De Soto
Blvd.* ☉ *Weekends 10–4:30 and June–Aug., weekdays 11–7:30; Sept.–Oct.
and Apr.–May, Tues.–Fri. 11:30–5:30; Nov.–Mar., Tues.–Fri. 10–4:30.*

Return to the De Soto Fountain, and follow De Soto Boulevard southwest to emerge in front of the **Biltmore Hotel** (1200 Anastasia Ave., ☎
305/445–1926). Like the Freedom Tower in downtown Miami, the Biltmore's 26-story tower is a replica of the Giralda Tower in Seville, Spain.
After extensive renovations, the hotel reopened in 1992, looking better than ever. The Biltmore Golf Course, known for its scenic layout,
has been restored to its original Donald Ross design.

Just to the west, in a separate building, is the **Biltmore Country Club.**
Originally part of the hotel, the club then spent some years independent of it and was restored by the city in the late 1970s. In 1989 the
richly ornamented Beaux Arts–style structure with a superb colonnade
and courtyard was reincorporated into the hotel. On its ground floor
are facilities for golfers. In the former club lounge, meeting rooms include one lofty space paneled with veneer from 60 species of trees.

From the hotel, turn right on Anastasia Avenue, go east to Granada
Boulevard, and turn right. Continue south on Granada Boulevard
over a bridge across the **Coral Gables Waterway,** which empties into
Biscayne Bay. In the hotel's heyday, Venetian gondolas plied the waterway, bringing guests to a bayside beach.

At Ponce de León Boulevard turn right. On your left is Metrorail's Stone-
hengelike concrete structure, and on your right is the 260-acre main
campus of the **University of Miami.** With almost 14,000 full-time,
part-time, and noncredit students, UM is the largest private research
university in the Southeast.

Turn right at the first stoplight (Stanford Drive) to enter the campus, and
park in the lot on your right designated for visitors to UM's **Lowe Art
Museum.** The Lowe's permanent collection of 8,000 works includes Renaissance and Baroque art, American paintings, Latin American art, and
Navajo and Pueblo Indian textiles and baskets. The museum also hosts

traveling exhibitions. *1301 Stanford Dr., ☎ 305/284–3535 for recording or 305/284–3536 for museum office.* ☛ *$4 adults, $3 senior citizens, $2 students over 6.* ⊙ *Tues.–Sat. 10–5, Sun. noon–5.*

Exit the UM campus on Stanford Drive, pass under Metrorail, and cross Dixie Highway. Just beyond the Burger King on your right, bear right onto Maynada Street. Turn right at the next stoplight onto **Sunset Drive.** Fine old homes and mature trees line this city-designated "historic and scenic road." Sunset Drive leads to and through **South Miami,** a pioneer farming community that grew into a suburb but retains its small-town charm.

On the northwest corner of Sunset Drive and Red Road (57th Avenue), note the pink building with a mural in which an alligator seems ready to devour a horrified man. This trompe l'oeil fantasy, *South Florida Cascade,* by illusionary artist Richard Haas, highlights the main entrance to the **Bakery Centre** (5701 Sunset Dr., ☎ 305/662–4155). This oversize shopping mall, constructed on the former site of the Holsum Bakery, has failed to attract the hoped-for hordes of shoppers.

On the third level of the Bakery Centre, the **Miami Youth Museum** features arts exhibits, hands-on displays, and activities to enhance children's creativity and inspire interest in artistic careers. Late in 1996, the museum will move to quarters in neighboring Kendall that more than double the current size. *5701 Sunset Dr., ☎ 305/661–3046.* ☛ *$3 adults and children over 1, $2 senior citizens.* ⊙ *Mon., Fri. 10–5; Tues.–Thurs. 1–5; weekends 11–5. Closed holidays.*

Drive south on Red Road, and turn right just before Killian Drive (Southwest 112th Street) into the 13-acre grounds of **Parrot Jungle,** where more than 1,100 exotic birds are on display. Many of the parrots, macaws, and cockatoos fly free, and they'll come to you for seeds, which you can purchase from old-fashioned gum-ball machines. Attend a trained-bird show, watch baby birds in training, and pose for photos with colorful macaws perched on your arms. The "jungle" is a natural hammock surrounding a sinkhole. Stroll among orchids and other flowering plants nestled among ferns, bald cypress, and massive live oaks. Other highlights include a primate show, small-wildlife shows, a children's playground, and a petting zoo. Also see the cactus garden and Flamingo Lake, with a breeding population of 75 Caribbean flamingos. Opened in 1936, Parrot Jungle is one of Greater Miami's oldest and most popular commercial tourist attractions. *11000 S.W. 57th Ave., ☎ 305/666–7834.* ☛ *$10.95 adults, $7.95 children 3–12.* ⊙ *Daily 9:30–6 (last admission at 5); café open daily 8–6.*

From Parrot Jungle follow Red Road ⅓ mile south, and turn left at Old Cutler Road, which curves north along the uplands of southern Florida's coastal ridge. Visit the 83-acre **Fairchild Tropical Garden,** the largest tropical botanical garden in the continental United States. Although the gardens lost most of their tropical foliage in the 1992 hurricane, the cycads survived and the gardens are flourishing again. Even so, visitors can get an idea of how tropical plants regenerate themselves after severe storms by visiting a portion of the gardens left untouched since Hurricane Andrew. In other developments, the rare-plant house is open again, concerts are a frequent new feature, and the entry and parking lot have been relandscaped. *10901 Old Cutler Rd., ☎ 305/667–1651.* ☛ *$7 adults, children under 13 free with parents.* ⊙ *Daily 9:30–4:30; a free tram runs hourly; Rain Forest Cafe open weekends 11–3. Closed Dec. 25.*

North of the garden, Old Cutler Road traverses Dade County's old-
⑱ est and most scenic park, **Matheson Hammock Park.** The Civilian
Conservation Corps developed the 100-acre tract of upland and mangrove swamp in the 1930s on land donated by a local pioneer, Commodore J. W. Matheson. The park's most popular feature is a bathing
beach, where the tide flushes a saltwater "atoll" pool through four gates.
A 90-slip marina is open, with an additional 162 slips to follow by 1997.
*9610 Old Cutler Rd., ☎ 305/667–3035. Parking fee for beach and ma-
rina: $3 per car, $5 per car with trailer, $6 per RV; limited free upland
parking. ☉ Daily 6–sunset. Pool lifeguards on duty winter (Eastern
Standard Time), daily 8:30–5; summer (Daylight Saving Time), daily
7:30–7.*

Continue north on Old Cutler Road to Cartagena Plaza, cross the bridge
over the waterway onto LeJeune Road, turn right on U.S. 1, and return to downtown Miami.

Tour 5: Coconut Grove

Coconut Grove is southern Florida's oldest settlement, inhabited as early
as 1834 and established by 1873, two decades before Miami. Its early
settlers included Bahamian blacks, "Conchs" from Key West, and New
England intellectuals. They built a community that attracted artists, writers, and scientists to establish winter homes. By the end of World War
I more people listed in *Who's Who* gave addresses in Coconut Grove
than anyplace else.

To this day Coconut Grove reflects its pioneers' eclectic origins. Posh
estates mingle with rustic cottages, modest frame homes, and starkly
modern dwellings—often on the same block. To keep Coconut Grove
a village in a jungle, residents lavish affection on exotic plantings while
battling to protect remaining native vegetation.

The historic center of the Village of Coconut Grove went through a
hippie period in the 1960s, laid-back funkiness in the 1970s, and a teeny-
bopper invasion in the early 1980s. Today the tone is upscale and urban,
with a mix of galleries, boutiques, restaurants, bars, and sidewalk
cafés. On weekends the Grove is jam-packed.

From downtown Miami follow U.S. 1 south to Southwest 27th Avenue (Grapeland Boulevard), turn left, and drive south to South
Bayshore Drive. Turn right, and follow this road until it jogs right and
becomes McFarlane Road. At the next intersection turn left onto Main
Highway, which passes through the heart of the Village of Coconut
Grove. Before you explore this trendy area, however, go on to Devon
⑲ Road, and turn right in front of **Plymouth Congregational Church.**
Opened in 1917, this handsome coral-rock structure resembles a Mexican mission church. The front door, of hand-carved walnut and oak
with original wrought-iron fittings, came from an early 17th-century
monastery in the Pyrenees. Also on the 11-acre grounds are natural
sunken gardens; the first schoolhouse in Dade County (one room), which
was moved to this property; and the site of the original Coconut Grove
waterworks and electric works. *3400 Devon Rd., ☎ 305/444–6521.
Call office 1 day in advance to see inside of church weekdays 9–4:30;
Sun. service 10 AM.*

★ Return to Main Highway, and head northeast toward the historic **Village of Coconut Grove,** a trendy commercial district with redbrick
sidewalks and more than 300 restaurants, stores, and art galleries. Parking can be a problem in the village—especially on weekend evenings,
when police direct traffic and prohibit turns at some intersections to

prevent gridlock. Be prepared to walk several blocks from the periphery into the heart of the Grove.

㉒ As you enter the village center, note the apricot-hue Spanish rococo **Coconut Grove Playhouse** (*see* The Arts and Nightlife, *below*) to your left. Built in 1926 as a movie theater, it became a legitimate theater in 1956, and is now owned by the state of Florida.

㉑ Benches and a shelter opposite the playhouse mark the entrance to the **Barnacle State Historic Site,** a pioneer residence built by Commodore Ralph Munroe in 1891. Its broad, sloping roof and deeply recessed verandas channel sea breezes into the house. A central stairwell and rooftop vent allow hot air to escape. Many furnishings are original. *3485 Main Hwy.,* ☎ *305/448–9445.* ☛ *$2. Reservations required for groups of 8 or more; others meet ranger on porch.* ☉ *Thurs.–Mon. 9–4; tours at 10, 11:30, 1, 2:30 (but best to double-check).*

TIME OUT Turn left at the next street, Commodore Plaza, and pause. Cafés at both corners overflow the brick sidewalks. Try the **Green Streets Cafe** (3110 Commodore Plaza, ☎ 305/567–0662) on the south side. It features, among other fare, breakfast until 3 as well as pastas, pizzas, salads, and sandwiches with a full bar.

㉒ At the north end of Commodore Plaza is Grand Avenue, a major shopping street. **CocoWalk** (3015 Grand Ave., ☎ 305/444–0777), a multilevel open mall of Mediterranean-style brick courtyards and terraces overflowing with people, opened early in 1991 and has revitalized Coconut Grove's nightlife. The mix of shops, restaurants, and theaters has renewed the Grove by creating a new circuit for promenading between these attractions and the historic heart of the Grove along Commodore Plaza. Across Virginia Street, **Mayfair Shops at the Grove** (*see* Malls *in* Shopping, *below*) gained new life in 1994, after several seasons of heavy vacancies, by the opening of the new club Planet Hollywood (3390 Mary St., ☎ 305/445–7277). The area now teems with Manhattan-like crowds, especially on weekend evenings.

Leaving the village center, follow McFarlane Road east from its intersection with Grand Avenue and Main Highway. **Peacock Park,** site of the first hotel in southeast Florida, is on your right. In an iron enclosure to the side of the Coconut Grove Library (a branch of the main **㉓** library system) is the **Eva Hewitt Munroe grave.** Ralph Munroe's first wife was reburied here at the site Munroe donated for the library.

If you turn north at the end of McFarlane Road onto South Bayshore **㉔** Drive, you'll pass the 150,000-square-foot **Coconut Grove Convention Center** (2700 S. Bayshore Dr., ☎ 305/579–3310), where antiques, **㉕** boat, and home shows are held, and **Dinner Key Marina** (3400 Pan American Dr., ☎ 305/579–6980), where seabirds soar and sailboats ride at anchor. Named for a small island on which early settlers held picnics, it's Greater Miami's largest marina, with 581 moorings at nine piers.

㉖ At the northeast corner of the same lot is **Miami City Hall,** built in 1934 as the terminal for the Pan American Airways seaplane base at Dinner Key. The building retains its nautical-style Art Deco trim. *3500 Pan American Dr.,* ☎ *305/250–5357.* ☉ *Weekdays 8–5.*

㉗ Continue north on South Bayshore Drive past Kirk Street to **Kennedy Park,** where you can park your car and walk toward the water. From a footbridge over the mouth of a small tidal creek, you'll enjoy an unobstructed view across Biscayne Bay to Key Biscayne. Film crews often use the park to make commercials and Italian westerns.

Drive north on South Bayshore Drive. At the entrance to Mercy Hospital, South Bayshore Drive becomes South Miami Avenue. At the next stoplight, turn right on a private road that passes St. Kieran's Church

(28) to **Ermita de La Caridad** (Our Lady of Charity Shrine), a conical building 90 feet high and 80 feet wide; it overlooks the bay so worshipers face toward Cuba. A mural above the shrine's altar depicts Cuba's history. *3609 S. Miami Ave.,* ☎ *305/854–2404.* ⊙ *Daily 9–9.*

(29) Another ³⁄₁₀ mile up South Miami Avenue, turn left to the **Miami Museum of Science and Space Transit Planetarium.** This is a participatory museum, chock-full of sound, gravity, and electricity displays for children and adults alike to manipulate and marvel at. A wildlife center houses native Florida snakes, turtles, tortoises, birds of prey, and large wading birds—175 live animals in all. Outstanding traveling exhibits appear throughout the year. *3280 S. Miami Ave.,* ☎ *305/854–4247 or 305/854–2222 for 24-hr Cosmic Hotline for planetarium show times and prices.* ☛ *$6 adults, $4 senior citizens and children 3–12; planetarium show: $5 adults, $2.50 senior citizens and children; laser-light rock-and-roll concert shows: $6 adults, $3 senior citizens and children.* ⊙ *Daily 10–6.*

★ **(30)** Across South Miami Avenue is the entrance to **Vizcaya Museum and Gardens,** an estate with an Italian Renaissance–style villa built in 1912–16 as the winter residence of Chicago industrialist James Deering. The house and gardens overlook Biscayne Bay on a 30-acre tract that includes a native hammock and more than 10 acres of formal gardens and fountains. The house contains 70 rooms, with 34 rooms of paintings, sculpture, antique furniture, and other decorative arts, open to the public. These objects date from the 15th through the 19th centuries and represent the Renaissance, Baroque, Rococo, and Neoclassical styles. *3251 S. Miami Ave.,* ☎ *305/250–9133.* ☛ *$8 adults, $4 children 6–12. Guided 45-min tours available, group tours by appointment.* ⊙ *House and ticket booth: daily 9:30–4:30; garden: daily 9:30–5:30. Closed Dec. 25.*

Continue north on South Miami Avenue to 17th Road, and turn left

(31) to **Simpson Park.** Enjoy a fragment of the dense tropical jungle—large gumbo-limbo trees, marlberry, banyans, and black calabash—that once covered the entire 5 miles from downtown Miami to Coconut Grove. You'll get a rare glimpse of how things were before the highrises towered. Avoid the park during summer, when mosquitoes whine as incessantly today as they did 100 years ago. You may follow South Miami Avenue the rest of the way downtown or go back two stoplights and turn left to the entrance to the Rickenbacker Causeway and Key Biscayne. *55 S.W. 17th Rd., Miami,* ☎ *305/856–6801.* ⊙ *Sunrise–sunset, though park gate is unlocked by neighbors so opening sometimes delayed weekends and holidays.*

Tour 6: Virginia Key and Key Biscayne

Government Cut and the Port of Miami separate the dense urban fabric of Miami from two of the city's playground islands, Virginia Key and Key Biscayne—the latter no longer the laid-back village where Richard Nixon set up his presidential vacation compound. Parks occupy much of both keys, providing congenial upland with facilities for basking on the beach, golf, tennis, softball, and picnicking, plus uninviting but ecologically valuable stretches of dense mangrove swamp. Unfortunately, these islands were hit hard in 1992 by Hurricane Andrew, and, although all the hotels have reopened, the tourist attractions—many of which are outdoors and near the water—are still recovering their foliage.

To reach Virginia Key and Key Biscayne, take the **Rickenbacker Causeway** (toll: $1 per car) across Biscayne Bay from the mainland at Brickell Avenue and Southwest 26th Road, about 2 miles south of downtown Miami. The causeway links several islands in the bay.

The high-level **William M. Powell Bridge** rises 75 feet above the water to eliminate the need for a draw span. The panoramic view from the top encompasses the bay, keys, port, and downtown skyscrapers, with Miami Beach and the Atlantic Ocean in the distance.

㉜ Just south of the Powell Bridge, a stub of the **Old Rickenbacker Causeway Bridge,** built in 1947, is now a fishing pier. Park at its entrance, about a mile from the tollgate, and walk past anglers tending their lines to the gap where the center draw span across the Intracoastal Waterway was removed. Here you can watch boat traffic pass through the channel, pelicans and other seabirds soar and dive, and dolphins cavort in the bay.

Next along the causeway, on **Virginia Key,** stands the 6,536-seat **Miami Marine Stadium** (3601 Rickenbacker Causeway, ☎ 305/361–3316), formerly site of summer pop concerts, occasional shows by name entertainers, and a spectacular Fourth of July fireworks display. The stadium has been closed partly due to under-use, partly for needed repairs, and there's no date scheduled for reopening.

★ **㉝** Down the causeway from Marine Stadium is the **Miami Seaquarium,** a popular attraction with six daily shows featuring sea lions, dolphins, and Lolita, a killer whale who cavorts in a huge tank. Exhibits include a shark pool, a 235,000-gallon tropical-reef aquarium, and manatees. *4400 Rickenbacker Causeway, ☎ 305/361–5705.* ☛ *$17.95 adults, $14.95 senior citizens, $12.95 children 3–12. ☉ Daily 9:30–6 (last admission at 4:30).*

㉞ Opposite the causeway from the Seaquarium, a road leads north to **Virginia Key Beach,** a City of Miami park with a 2-mile stretch of oceanfront, shelters, barbecue grills, ball fields, nature trails, and a fishing area. Ask for directions at the entrance gate. Parking is $2 per car. Likely to be added later this decade are an RV park with various ball fields and an improved beach with windsurfing facilities.

㉟ Plans are in progress to safeguard the 400-acre portion of this mangrove-edged island that has been dedicated as the **Virginia Key Critical Wildlife Area.** Birds to be seen here include reddish egrets, black-bellied plovers, black skimmers, and roseate spoonbills—but only May through July. The area is left undisturbed the other nine months, to be more amenable to migratory shorebirds. The entrance is at Virginia Key Beach.

㊱ From Virginia Key the causeway crosses Bear Cut to the north end of **Key Biscayne,** where it becomes Crandon Boulevard. The boulevard bisects 1,211-acre **Crandon Park,** which has a popular 3½-mile Atlantic Ocean beach with a nature center. Turnouts on your left lead to four parking lots and adjacent picnic areas. *4000 Crandon Blvd., ☎ 305/361–5421. Parking: $3 per vehicle. ☉ Daily 8–sunset.*

TIME OUT Enjoy that rarity among Miami-area restaurants, a freestanding waterfront dining room, at **Sundays on the Bay** (5420 Crandon Blvd., ☎

305/361–6777). A 60-item brunch is served Sunday 10:30–3:30, and lunch and dinner are served daily.

On your right are entrances to the **Links at Key Biscayne** and the **Tennis Center at Crandon Park,** where in 1994 a $16.5 million, 7,500-seat tennis stadium was opened for use at the annual spring Lipton Championships (*see* Spectator Sports, *below*).

From the traffic circle at the south end of Crandon Park, Crandon Boulevard continues for 2 miles through the developed portion of Key Biscayne. You'll come back that way, but first detour to the site of **㊲ President Nixon's home** (485 W. Matheson Dr.). Turn right at the first stoplight onto Harbor Drive, go about a mile, and turn right at Matheson Drive. A later owner enlarged and totally changed the house.

Continue south on Harbor Drive to Mashta Drive; turn left and return to Crandon Boulevard. Turn right to reach the entrance to **Bill Baggs Cape Florida State Recreation Area,** named for a crusading newspaper editor whose efforts prompted the state to create this 406-acre park. After Hurricane Andrew turned 98% of the exotic Australian pine forest (600,000 trees) to kindling, park rangers engaged in a year of cleanup and two years of replanting. Gone are the high pines and other exotic plants. Except for a few coconut palms, they have been replaced with native species, including saw palmetto, cabbage palm, gumbo-limbo, pigeon plum, crabwood, and shoreline mangroves. The park is now reopened and largely transformed. Visitors find new boardwalks, 18 picnic shelters, and a bicycle and pedestrian path along the leeward shore as well as a nature trail, 1¼ miles of beach, and a seawall along Biscayne Bay where anglers catch bonefish, grouper, jack, snapper, and snook. Also in the park is the oldest structure in south ㊳ Florida, the brick **Cape Florida Lighthouse,** erected in 1845 to replace an earlier one destroyed in an 1836 Seminole attack, in which the keeper's helper was killed. Sometime during 1996, you should once again be able to climb the 95 feet to the top, and a replica of the keeper's house should open, too. *1200 S. Crandon Blvd.,* ☎ *305/361–5811.* ☛ *Park: $3.25 per vehicle with up to 8 people.* ☉ *Park: daily 8–sunset.*

When you leave Cape Florida, follow Crandon Boulevard back to Crandon Park through Key Biscayne's commercial center, a mixture of posh shops and more prosaic stores catering to the needs of the neighborhood. On your way back to the mainland, pause as you approach the Powell Bridge to admire the downtown Miami skyline. At night the brightly lighted NationsBank Tower looks from this angle like a clipper ship running under full sail before the breeze.

Tour 7: Little Haiti

Of some 200,000 Haitians who have settled in south Florida, almost half live in Little Haiti, an area on Miami's northeast side covering about 200 city blocks. More than 400 small Haitian businesses operate in Little Haiti. Yet the future of the district is uncertain: Immigration from Haiti has virtually ceased, while the majority already in Miami question their economic future in the ghetto. As their fortunes improve, many move out. Still, the neighborhood is one of the city's most distinctive. If you walk or drive along its side streets, you might see Haitian women carrying their burdens atop their heads, as they do on their home island.

For many Haitians, English is a third language. French is Haiti's official language, but much day-to-day conversation takes place in Creole, a French-based patois.

From downtown Miami, follow Biscayne Boulevard north to Northeast 38th Street; turn left, and drive about ⁹⁄₁₀ mile west as the street curves and becomes 39th Street. At North Miami Avenue, turn right, and at 40th Street, turn right again onto the main street of the **Miami International Arts & Design District.** Here, close by Little Haiti, some 225 wholesale stores, showrooms, and galleries feature interior furnishings and decorative arts. Since 1993 the district has been undergoing a revival, and there are several new art studios and showrooms.

Immediately north is the gentrified neighborhood of Buena Vista, which merges with Little Haiti. The area contains some of Miami's oldest dwellings, dating from the dawn of the 20th century through the 1920s land-boom era. Drive the side streets to see elegant Mediterranean-style homes and bungalows with distinctive coral-rock trim.

Return to North Miami Avenue and drive north. A half block east on 54th Street is the tiny storefront office of the **Haitian Refugee Center** (119 N.E. 54th St., ☎ 305/757–8538), a focal point of activity in the Haitian community. The building's facade is decorated by the painting of an uncomprehending Haitian standing in front of the Statue of Liberty, which denies him entry to America. Continue north on North Miami Avenue past the **former Cuban consulate** (5811 N. Miami Ave.), a pretentious Caribbean-Colonial mansion that is now the clinic of Haitian physician Lucien Albert.

North of 85th Street, cross the Little River Canal into **El Portal,** a tiny suburban village of modest homes, where more than a quarter of the property is now Haitian-owned. Turn right on Northeast 87th Street and right again on Northeast 2nd Avenue. You are now southbound on Little Haiti's tree-lined main commercial street. Along Northeast 2nd Avenue between 79th and 45th streets, rows of storefronts in faded pastels reflect a first effort by area merchants to dress up their neighborhood and attract outsiders.

Barely more successful, and showing the strains of uncertainty in this immigrant community, is the **Caribbean Marketplace** (5927 N.E. 2nd Ave., no phone), which the Haitian Task Force (an economic-development organization) opened in 1990. The building beautifully evokes the Iron Market in Port-au-Prince. Its handful of merchants surrounding a medical clinic sell handmade baskets, Caribbean art and craft items, books, records, videos, and ice cream.

To return to downtown Miami follow Northeast 2nd Avenue south to Northeast 35th Street, turn left, drive east one block to Biscayne Boulevard, and turn right to go south.

Tour 8: South Dade

Numbers in the margin correspond to points of interest on the Tour 8: South Dade map.

This tour directs you to major attractions in the suburbs southwest of Dade County's urban core. Although the population was largely dislocated by Hurricane Andrew in the fall of 1992, little damage is evident today. All attractions have reopened.

From downtown Miami follow the Dolphin Expressway (Route 836) west to the Palmetto Expressway (Route 826) southbound. Bear left south of Bird Road (Southwest 40th Street) onto the Don Shula Expressway (Route 874). Exit westbound onto Killian Drive (Southwest 104th Street), and drive west to Lindgren Road (Southwest 137th Avenue). Turn left, and drive south to Southwest 128th Street, the entrance
❶ to the Tamiami Airport and **Weeks Air Museum.** Rebuilt since its destruction by the hurricane, the museum now displays some 30–35 planes, including a B–17 Flying Fortress bomber and a P–51 Mustang from World War II. Most of the fragile WWI planes were destroyed by the storm. *14710 S.W. 128th St.,* ☎ *305/233–5197.* ☛ *$5 adults, $4 senior citizens, $3 children under 13.* ☉ *Daily 10–5; closed Thanksgiving, Dec. 25.*

Continue south on Lindgren Road to Coral Reef Drive (Southwest
❷ 152nd Street). Turn left, and drive east to **Metrozoo,** a cageless 290-acre zoo where animals roam free on islands surrounded by moats. Devastated by the hurricane, the zoo has reopened but without its monorail or "Wings of Asia," a 1½-acre aviary where hundreds of exotic birds from Southeast Asia fly through a rain forest beneath a protective net. Although that is not scheduled to reopen before the end of 1996 at the earliest, most of the animals, including elephants, koalas, and flamingos, are back, after having been shipped to other zoos after the storm. "Paws," a petting zoo for children, features three shows daily. *12400 Coral Reef Dr. (S.W. 152nd St.),* ☎ *305/251–0401 or 305/251–0400 for recorded information.* ☛ *During rebuilding: $5.33 adults, $2.66 children; 45-min tram tour: $2.* ☉ *Daily 9:30–5:30 (last admission at 4).*

❸ Next to the zoo, the **Gold Coast Railroad Museum** displays a 1949 *Silver Crescent* dome car and the *Ferdinand Magellan,* the only Pullman car ever constructed specifically for U.S. presidents, used by Roosevelt, Truman, Eisenhower, and Reagan. The museum was damaged in the hurricane, but most trains were expected back at the site before the end of 1995, when the replacement of the great shed over the trains should be nearing completion. *12450 Coral Reef Dr. (S.W. 152nd St.),* ☎ *305/253–0063.* ☛ *$4 adults (train rides included).* ☉ *Weekends 11–4 until repairs completed.*

Drive south on the Homestead Extension of Florida's Turnpike, exit at Hainlin Mill Drive (Southwest 216th Street), and turn right. Cross South Dixie Highway (U.S. 1), drive 3 miles west, and turn right into
❹ **Monkey Jungle,** home to more than 400 monkeys representing 35 species—including orangutans from Borneo and Sumatra, golden lion tamarins from Brazil, and brown lemurs from Madagascar. Its rainforest trail, damaged in the hurricane, is expected to reopen fully in 1996. Performing-monkey shows begin at 10 and run continuously at 30-minute intervals. The walkways of this 30-acre attraction are caged; the monkeys roam free. *14805 Hainlin Mill Dr. (S.W. 216th St.),* ☎ *305/235–1611.* ☛ *$10.50 adults, $9.50 senior citizens, $5.35 children 4–12.* ☉ *Daily 9:30–5 (last admission at 4).*

Continue west on Hainlin Mill Drive, past Krome Avenue (Southwest 177th Avenue), to Redland Road (Southwest 187th Avenue), and turn left to Coconut Palm Drive (Southwest 248th Street). You are at the
❺ **Redland Fruit & Spice Park,** a Dade County treasure since 1944, when it was opened as a 20-acre showcase of tropical fruits and vegetables. It has since expanded to 30 acres, and there's the prospect of a 3-acre lake by 1996. Two of the park's three historic buildings were ruined by the hurricane, as well as about half of its trees and plants, but relandscaping has begun and the park has reopened. Plants are now

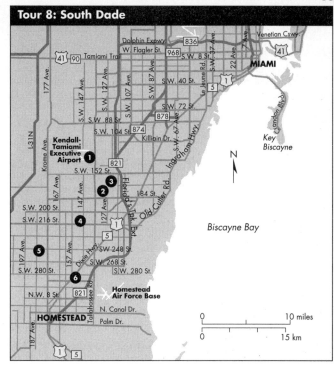

Tour 8: South Dade

grouped by country of origin and include more than 500 varieties of exotic fruits, herbs, spices, nuts, and poisonous plants from around the world. A sampling reveals 50 varieties of bananas, 40 varieties of grapes, and 100 varieties of citrus. A gourmet-and-fruit shop offers many varieties of tropical-fruit products, jellies, seeds, aromatic teas, and reference books. *24801 Redland Rd. (S.W. 187th Ave.),* ☎ *305/247–5727.* ☛ *$1 adults, 50¢ children; guided tour: $1.50 adults, $1 children.* ⊗ *Daily 10–5; tours weekends at 1, 3.*

Drive east on Coconut Palm Drive (Southwest 248th Street) to Newton Road (Southwest 157th Avenue). Continue south on Newton Road to South Dixie Highway (U.S. 1), and turn left. Almost immediately **6** you'll find **Coral Castle of Florida,** on your right. It was built by Edward Leedskalnin, a Latvian immigrant, between 1920 and 1940. The 3-acre castle has a 9-ton gate a child can open (though it was still not functioning in 1995), an accurate working sundial, and a telescope of coral rock aimed at the North Star. *28655 S. Dixie Hwy.,* ☎ *305/248–6344.* ☛ *$7.75 adults, $6.50 senior citizens, $4.50 children 7–12.* ⊗ *Daily 9–6.*

To return to downtown Miami after leaving Coral Castle, take South Dixie Highway to Biscayne Drive (Southwest 288th Street) and go east to the turnpike. Follow the turnpike back to the Don Shula Expressway (Route 874), which leads to the Palmetto Expressway (Route 826), which leads to the Dolphin Expressway (Route 836).

What to See and Do with Children

Greater Miami is a family-oriented vacation destination. Most of the major hotels can provide access to baby-sitters for young children. Free publications worth looking into include "A Kid's Guide to Greater Miami," which lists festivals and special events, and "Arts in Education Directory" (☎ 305/375–4634 for both), as well as "South Florida Parenting" (4200 Aurora St., Coral Gables, ☎ 305/448–6003), a monthly that covers Dade, Broward, and Palm Beach counties with a calendar of events, restaurant reviews by kids, and recommendations of places to visit, among other information. It's available at more than 2,200 locations, including libraries and children's retail stores, in addition to the address above.

The following sights are of particular interest to children:

American Police Hall of Fame and Museum exhibits more than 10,000 law enforcement–related items, including weapons, a jail cell, and an electric chair, as well as a 400-ton marble memorial listing the names of more than 3,000 police officers killed in the line of duty since 1960. *3801 Biscayne Blvd., Miami,* ☎ *305/573–0070.* ☛ *$6 adults, $4 senior citizens, $3 children under 12.* ☉ *Daily 10–5:30.*

The **Ancient Spanish Monastery** is the oldest building in the Western Hemisphere. It was built in 1141 in Segovia, Spain. Newspaper magnate William Randolph Hearst had it removed in pieces and stored it in California for 25 years. In 1954 Miami developers rebuilt it at its present site. *16711 W. Dixie Hwy., North Miami Beach,* ☎ *305/ 945–1461.* ☛ *$4 adults, $2.50 senior citizens, $1 children 7–12.* ☉ *Mon.–Sat. 10–4, Sun. noon–4.*

Coconut Grove Farmers Market (*see* Outdoor Markets *in* Shopping, *below*).

Coral Castle of Florida (*see* Tour 8, *above*).

Fairchild Tropical Garden (*see* Tour 4, *above*).

Gold Coast Railroad Museum (*see* Tour 8, *above*).

Historical Museum of Southern Florida (*see* Tour 2, *above*).

Lummus Park (east of Ocean Dr., between 5th and 15th Sts., Miami Beach) attracts beachgoing families with its children's play area.

Metromover rides (*see* Tour 2, *above*).

Metrozoo (*see* Tour 8, *above*).

Miami Museum of Science and Space Transit Planetarium (*see* Tour 5, *above*).

Miami Seaquarium (*see* Tour 6, *above*).

Miami Youth Museum (*see* Tour 4, *above*).

Monkey Jungle (*see* Tour 8, *above*).

Parrot Jungle (*see* Tour 4, *above*).

Venetian Pool (*see* Tour 4, *above*).

Vizcaya Museum and Gardens (*see* Tour 5, *above*).

Weeks Air Museum (*see* Tour 8, *above*).

SHOPPING

Except in the heart of the Everglades, visitors to the Greater Miami area are never more than 15 minutes from a major shopping area. Downtown Miami long ago ceased to be the community's central shopping hub, as most residents moved to the suburbs. Today Dade County has more than a dozen major malls, an international free-trade zone, and hundreds of miles of commercial streets lined with storefronts and small neighborhood shopping centers. Many of these local shopping areas have an ethnic flavor, catering primarily to one of Greater Miami's immigrant cultures.

In the Latin neighborhoods, for example, children's stores sell *vestidos de fiesta* (party dresses) made of organza and lace. Men's stores sell the *guayabera,* a pleated, embroidered shirt that replaces the tie and jacket in much of the tropics. Traditional bridal shops display formal dresses that Latin families buy or rent for a daughter's *quince,* a lavish 15th-birthday celebration.

No standard store hours exist in Greater Miami, though most malls observe the typical seven-day hours of malls everywhere. Call ahead. When you shop, expect to pay Florida's 6% sales tax unless you have the store ship your goods out of Florida.

Shopping Districts

There are 500 garment manufacturers in Miami and Hialeah, and many sell their clothing locally in the **Miami Fashion District** (5th Ave. east of I–95, between 25th and 29th Sts., Miami), making Greater Miami the fashion marketplace for the southeastern United States, the Caribbean, and Latin America. Most of the more than 30 factory outlets and discount fashion stores are open Monday–Saturday 9–5. The **Miami Free Zone** (MFZ) (2305 N.W. 107th Ave., Miami) is an international wholesale trade center open to the public, a vast operation occupying 850,000 square feet on three floors. You can buy goods duty-free for export or pay duty on goods released for domestic use. More than 140 companies sell products from more than 100 countries, including aviation equipment, chemicals, clothing, computers, cosmetics, electronics, liquor, and perfumes. The 51-acre MFZ is 15 minutes west of Miami International Airport off the Dolphin Expressway (Route 836) and about 40 minutes from the Port of Miami. It's open weekdays 9–5. The **Miami International Arts & Design District** (*see* Tour 7 *in* Exploring, *above*), also known as 40th Street, is full of showrooms and galleries specializing in interior furnishings and decorative arts. **Miracle Mile** (Coral Way between 37th and 42nd Aves., Coral Gables) consists of some 160 shops along a wide, tree-lined boulevard. Shops range from posh boutiques to bargain basements, from beauty salons to chain restaurants. As you go west, the quality increases. In the old section known as Allapattah, the **Wholesale District** (20th St., between N.W. 17th and 27th Aves.) comprises hundreds of merchants lining either side of the street. Merchandise includes apparel, shoes and handbags, luggage and accessories, jewelry, perfumes, and electronic and pharmaceutical products, and many small, affordable restaurants are tucked in as well. The district is about 10 minutes east of Miami International Airport off the East–West Expressway (Route 112).

Malls

Aventura Mall (19501 Biscayne Blvd., Aventura), in a northern suburb that became Dade's 28th municipality in 1995, has more than 200 shops anchored by Macy's, Lord & Taylor, JCPenney, and Sears. **Bal Harbour Shops** (9700 Collins Ave., Bal Harbour) is a swank collection of boutiques, featuring Chanel, Gucci, Cartier, Nina Ricci, Fendi, Bruno Magli, Neiman Marcus, and Saks Fifth Avenue. Stores are open to 6 most nights but to 9 on Monday, Thursday, and Friday. Free buses run twice a day Monday–Saturday from several hotels in Coconut Grove, downtown Miami, and Miami Beach. **Bayside Marketplace** (401 Biscayne Blvd.,

Miami), the 16-acre mall on Biscayne Bay, has 150 specialty shops, entertainment, tour-boat docks, and a food court. It's open late (10 during the week, 11 on Friday and Saturday), but its restaurants stay open even later. A complex of clapboard, coral-rock, and stucco buildings, **Cauley Square** (22400 Old Dixie Hwy., Goulds) was erected in 1907–20 for railroad workers who built and maintained the line to Key West. Crafts, antiques, and clothing shops are here now. The only Sundays that stores are open are from Thanksgiving to Christmas Eve. **Coco Walk** (3015 Grand Ave., Coconut Grove) has three floors of specialty shops that stay open almost as late as the popular restaurants and clubs. The oldest retail mall in the county but always upgrading, **Dadeland** (7535 N. Kendall Dr., Miami) sits at the south side of town close to the Dadeland North and Dadeland South Metrorail stations. Retailers include Florida's largest Burdines, Saks Fifth Avenue, JCPenney, Lord & Taylor, and more than 175 specialty stores plus 17 restaurants. **The Falls** (S.W. 136th St. at U.S. 1, Miami), which derives its name from the several waterfalls inside, is the most upscale mall on the south side of the city. It contains Miami's only Bloomingdale's and Macy's, as well as another 60 specialty stores, restaurants, and theaters. **Mayfair Shops at the Grove** (2911 Grand Ave., Coconut Grove) is a higher-end version of people-friendly CocoWalk, just across the street. **Omni International Mall** (1601 Biscayne Blvd., Miami) rises vertically alongside the atrium of the Crowne Plaza Miami, where the eye-popping feature is an old-fashioned carousel. Among the 85 shops are a JCPenney, many restaurants, and 10 movie screens. The shortest and most elegant shopping arcade in the metropolis, the **Shops at 550** (550 Biltmore Way, Coral Gables) is in the marble halls of the Azteclike 550 Building, three blocks west of Miracle Mile. Shops include the Stones of Venice jewelry store (*see below*), Allure couture, and Habib Oriental rugs. Most shops are open weekdays 10–5, though some close later.

Outdoor Markets

Several farmers markets have set up around Miami since the **Coconut Grove Farmers Market** (Grand Ave., 1 block west of MacDonald Ave. [S.W. 32nd Ave.], Coconut Grove) began in 1977. It still takes place Saturdays 8 to 2 year-round. At the **Farmers Market at Merrick Park** (LeJeune Rd. [S.W. 42nd Ave.] and Biltmore Way, Coral Gables), some 25 produce and plant vendors set up in a little downtown park on Saturdays from 8 to 1, mid-January through March. Gardening workshops, cooking demonstrations, and children's activities are standard features. On Sundays November through March, the **Lincoln Road Farmers Market** (Lincoln Rd. between Meridian and Euclid Aves., Miami Beach) brings some 15 local produce vendors coupled with plant workshops and children's activities. Every weekend since 1984, more than 500 vendors sell a variety of goods at the **Flagler Dog Track** (401 N.W. 38th Ct., Miami) from 9 to 4.

Specialty Shops

ANTIQUES

Alhambra Antiques Center (3640 Coral Way, Coral Gables, ☎ 305/446–1688) is a collection of four antiques dealers selling high-quality decorative pieces from Europe.

BOOKS

Greater Miami's best English-language bookstore, **Books & Books, Inc.** (296 Aragon Ave., Coral Gables, ☎ 305/442–4408; Sterling Bldg., 933 Lincoln Rd., Miami Beach, ☎ 305/532–3222) specializes in books on the arts, architecture, Floridiana, and contemporary and classical literature. Collectors enjoy browsing through the rare-book room upstairs, which doubles as a photography gallery. There are frequent poetry readings and book signings.

CHILDREN'S BOOKS AND TOYS

A Kid's Book Shoppe (1895 N.E. Miami Gardens Dr., North Miami Beach, ☎ 305/937–2665), an excellent children's-book resource, has been at this location since 1984. The friendly staff at **A Likely Story** (5740 Sunset Dr., South Miami, ☎ 305/667–3730) has been helping Miamians choose books and educational toys appropriate to children's interests and stages of development since 1978.

CLOTHING

Allure (550 Biltmore Way, Coral Gables, ☎ 305/444–5252), in the luxurious Shops at 550 mall, sells fine women's wear. **Ninth Street Bizaare** (900 Ocean Dr., Miami Beach, ☎ 305/534–2254) is a trendy Miami Beach minimart with vendors selling clothing and accessories from around the world.

DECORATIVE AND GIFT ITEMS

American Details (3107 Grand Ave., Coconut Grove, ☎ 305/448–6163) sells colorful, trendy crafts items. **Art Deco Welcome Center** (1001 Ocean Dr., Miami Beach, ☎ 305/531–3484) has a gift shop worth checking out for deco-phernalia. The **Indies Company** (101 W. Flagler St., Miami, ☎ 305/375–1492), the Historical Museum of Southern Florida's gift shop, offers interesting artifacts reflecting Miami's history, including some inexpensive reproductions.

JEWELRY

Stones of Venice (550 Biltmore Way, Coral Gables, ☎ 305/444–4474), operated by a three-time winner of the DeBeers Diamond Award for jewelry, sells affordable creations. Customers have included actor Elliott Gould, Pope John Paul II, and film director Barbet Schroeder, among others.

SPORTS AND THE OUTDOORS

Miami's subtropical climate is ideal for active people. Here refugees from the frozen north can enjoy warm-weather outdoor sports, such as boating, swimming, and golf, all year long. During Miami's hot, humid summers, people avoid the sun's strongest rays by playing early or late in the day. Below are listed some of the most popular individual and group sports.

Biking

Dade County has about 100 miles of off-road bicycle trails. A color-coded map outlining Dade's 4,000 miles of roads suitable for bike travel is available for $3.50 from area bike shops and from the **Dade County Bicycle Coordinator** (Metropolitan Planning Organization, 111 N.W. 1st St., Suite 910, Miami 33128, ☎ 305/375–4507). For information on dozens of monthly group rides contact the **Everglades Bicycle Club** (Box 430282, South Miami 33243-0282, ☎ 305/598–3998). Among the best shops for renting bicycles are **Dade Cycle** (3216 Grand Ave., Coconut Grove, ☎ 305/444–5997 or 305/443–6075) and **Gary's Megacycle On the Beach** (1260 Washington Ave., Miami Beach, ☎ 305/534–3306).

Boating

Listed below are the major marinas in Greater Miami. The dock masters at these marinas can provide information on other marine services you may need. Also ask the dock masters for *Teall's Tides and Guides, Miami–Dade County,* and other local nautical publications.

Crandon Park Marina sells bait and tackle. *4000 Crandon Blvd., Key Biscayne,* ☎ *305/361–1281. Office open 7–6.*

Dinner Key Marina has dockage with space for transients and a boat ramp. *3400 Pan American Dr., Coconut Grove,* ☎ *305/579–6980.* ⊙ *Daily 7 AM–midnight.*

Haulover Marine Center offers a bait-and-tackle shop, marine gas station, and boat launch. *10800 Collins Ave., Miami Beach,* ☎ *305/945–3934.* ⊙ *Weekdays 9–5; bait shop and gas station open 24 hrs.*

Miamarina is closed until early 1996, when it is expected to reopen with about 100 slips. *Next to Bayside Marketplace, 401 Biscayne Blvd., Miami, temporary* ☎ *305/579–6955.*

Miami Beach Marina has become the "happening" marina. A multi-million-dollar expansion completed in 1995 has yielded restaurants, charters, boat and vehicle rentals, a complete marine hardware store, dive shop, large grocery store, fuel dock, concierge services, and 400 boat slips accommodating vessels up to 190 feet. New, too, is the Thursday evening Art al Fresco, a sunset celebration with original art, crafts, and music, plus free admission and parking. Facilities include air-conditioned rest rooms, washers and dryers, U.S. Customs clearing, and a heated swimming pool expected in 1996. This is the nearest marina to the South Beach Deco District, about a 15-minute walk away. *300 Alton Rd., Miami Beach,* ☎ *305/673–6000.* ⊙ *Daily 8–6.*

Watson Island Marina will probably become a mega-yacht marina with a boutique hotel before the end of the decade, while maybe keeping a few charter and dive boats operating out of a facility that has become dilapidated from official neglect. Chalk's International Airlines will likely remain, and a new heliport could be added. A potential botanical garden may include a refurbished Japanese Garden. Currently 10 slips are available. *1050 MacArthur Causeway, Miami,* ☎ *305/579–6955. Call for hrs.*

Diving

Summer diving conditions in Greater Miami have been compared to those in the Caribbean. Winter diving can be adversely affected when cold fronts come through. Dive-boat schedules vary with the season and with local weather conditions.

Fowey, Triumph, Long, and Emerald reefs are all shallow 10- to 15-foot dives good for snorkelers and beginning divers. These reefs are on the edge of the continental shelf, ¼ mile from depths greater than 100 feet. You can also paddle around the tangled prop roots of the mangrove trees that line Florida's coastline, peering at the fish, crabs, and other onshore creatures that hide there.

In 1994 a greatly expanded artificial-reef program was begun off the shores of Miami. The first units of 100,000 tons of lime-rock boulders were placed on mostly sand and silt sea bottom where sea life had been destroyed by Hurricane Andrew. Early reports confirm fish life was quickly attracted to the new sites.

Look for instructors affiliated with the Professional Association of Dive Instructors (PADI) or the National Association of Underwater Instructors (NAUI). Dive shops and charter services include:

Bubbles Dive Center is an all-purpose dive shop with PADI affiliation. Its boat, *Divers Dream*, is kept on Watson Island on MacArthur Causeway. *2671 S.W. 27th Ave., Miami,* ☎ *305/856–0565.* ⊙ *Weekdays 10–7, Sat. 9–6.*

Divers Paradise of Key Biscayne has a complete dive shop and diving-charter service, including equipment rental and scuba instruction, with PADI affiliation. *4000 Crandon Blvd., Key Biscayne,* ☎ *305/361–3483.* ⊘ *Weekdays 10–6, weekends 7:30–6.*

The **Diving Locker** is a 24-year-old, PADI-affiliated dive shop that offers three-day and three-week Professional Diving Instructors Corporation certification courses, wreck and reef dives aboard *The Native Diver,* and full sales, service, and repairs. *223 Sunny Isles Blvd., North Miami Beach,* ☎ *305/947–6025.* ⊘ *Weekdays 9–9:30, Sat. 8–9:30, Sun. 8–6.*

Team Divers, a PADI five-star facility in the Miami Beach marina, is the only dive shop in the South Beach area. Daily dives are arranged. *300 Alton Rd.,* ☎ *305/673–0101 or 800/543–7887.* ⊘ *Oct.–Mar., weekdays 10–7, weekends 9–6; Apr.–Sept., weekdays 10–7, weekends 7:30–6.*

Fishing

A few ocean fishing-charter operators sailing out of various parts of town are: *Abracadabra* (4000 Crandon Blvd., Key Biscayne, ☎ 305/361–5625), **Blue Waters Sportfishing Charters** (16375 Collins Ave., Sunny Isles, ☎ 305/944–4531), *Therapy IV* (Haulover Marine Center, 10800 Collins Ave., Miami Beach, ☎ 305/945–1578), and *Reward II* (Miami Beach Marina, 300 Alton Rd., MacArthur Causeway, Miami Beach, ☎ 305/372–9470).

Golf

From the famed "Blue Monster" at the Doral Golf Resort and Spa to the scenic Links at Key Biscayne, overlooking Biscayne Bay, Greater Miami has more than 30 private and public courses. For information contact the appropriate parks-and-recreation department: City of Miami (☎ 305/575–5256), City of Miami Beach (☎ 305/673–7730), or Metro-Dade County (☎ 305/857–6868). Some 18-hole courses open to the public include: **Biltmore Golf Course** (1210 Anastasia Ave., Coral Gables, ☎ 305/460–5364), **Don Shula's Hotel & Golf Club** (7601 Miami Lakes Dr., Miami Lakes, ☎ 305/821–1150), **Doral Golf Resort and Spa** (4400 N.W. 87th Ave., Doral, ☎ 305/592–2000 or 800/713–6725), **Links at Key Biscayne** (6700 Crandon Blvd., Key Biscayne, ☎ 305/361–9129), **Normandy Shores Golf Course** (2401 Biarritz Dr., Miami Beach, ☎ 305/868–6502), **Presidential Country Club** (19650 N.E. 18th Ave., North Miami Beach, ☎ 305/933–5266), and **Williams Island California Club** (20898 San Simeon Way, North Miami Beach, ☎ 305/651–3590), after noon daily.

Jogging

Try these recommended jogging routes: in Coconut Grove, along the pedestrian/bicycle path on South Bayshore Drive, cutting over the causeway to Key Biscayne for a longer run; from the south shore of the Miami River, downtown, south along the sidewalks of Brickell Avenue to Bayshore Drive, where you can run alongside the bay; in Miami Beach, along Bay Road (parallel to Alton Road); and in Coral Gables, around the Riviera Country Club golf course, just south of the Biltmore Country Club. Two good sources of running information are the **Miami Runners Club** (7900 S.W. 40th St., Miami, ☎ 305/227–1500) and **Foot Works** (5724 Sunset Dr., South Miami, ☎ 305/667–9322), a running-shoe store.

Sailing

Dinner Key and the Coconut Grove waterfront remain the center of sailing in Greater Miami, although sailboat moorings and rentals are located along other parts of the bay and up the Miami River. **Easy Sail-**

ing offers a fleet ranging from 19 to 127 feet for rent by the hour or the day. Services include sailboat lessons, scuba-diving lessons and certification, and on-board catering. *Dinner Key Marina, 3360 Pan American Dr., Coconut Grove, ☎ 305/858–4001. Reservation and advance deposit required.* ☉ *Daily 9–sunset.*

Spa
The **Doral Golf Resort and Spa** (4000 N.W. 87th Ave., Miami, ☎ 305/ 592–2000) combines mud baths and other European pampering techniques with state-of-the-art American fitness-and-exercise programs. A one-day sampler is available. Formal Italian gardens contain the spa pool and a hydromassage waterfall. Interiors include architectural elements created in 1920 by French architect Alexandre-Gustave Eiffel and fabricated by artist Edgar Brandt for Paris's Bon Marché department store. There are 48 suites, 26 massage rooms, four exercise studios (two with spring-loaded floors), two pools, David fitness equipment, a beauty salon, and a restaurant.

Tennis
Greater Miami has more than 60 tennis centers, of which over a dozen are open to the public. All public tennis courts charge nonresidents an hourly fee. A sampling around the county includes:

Biltmore Tennis Center has 10 hard courts. *1150 Anastasia Ave., Coral Gables, ☎ 305/460–5360. Nonresident day rate $4.30, night rate $5 per person per hr.* ☉ *Weekdays 8 AM–9 PM, weekends 8–8.*

Flamingo Tennis Center has 19 clay courts. *1000 12th St., Miami Beach, ☎ 305/673–7761. Day rate $2.67, night rate $3.20 per person per hr.* ☉ *Weekdays 8 AM–9 PM, weekends 8–7.*

North Shore Tennis Center has 6 clay courts and 5 hard courts. *350 73rd St., Miami Beach, ☎ 305/993–2022. Day rate $2.67, night rate $3.20 per person per hr.* ☉ *Weekdays 8 AM–9 PM, weekends 8–7.*

Tennis Center at Crandon Park, a new $18 million facility and one of America's best, is the site of the annual Lipton Championships held each March (the only time when the courts are off-limits to the public). Included are two grass, eight clay, and 17 hard courts. Reservations are necessary for night play. *7300 Crandon Blvd., Key Biscayne, ☎ 305/365–2300. Laykold courts: day rate $2, night rate $3 per person per hr; clay courts: $4 per person per hr.* ☉ *Daily 8 AM–10 PM.*

Windsurfing
The safest and most popular windsurfing area in city waters is south of town at Hobie Island and Virginia Key on Key Biscayne. The best windsurfing on Miami Beach is at 1st Street, just north of the Government Cut jetty, and at 21st Street. You can also windsurf at Lummus Park at 10th Street and in the vicinity of 3rd, 14th, and 21st streets. Lifeguards discourage windsurfing from 79th to 87th streets.

Sailboards Miami, on Hobie Island, just past the tollbooth for the Rickenbacker Causeway to Key Biscayne, rents windsurfing equipment. *Key Biscayne, ☎ 305/361–7245. Cost: $17 per hr, $95 for 10 hrs; 2-hr lesson: $39.* ☉ *Daily 10–5:30.*

SPECTATOR SPORTS

Greater Miami boasts franchises in all major-league sports—baseball, basketball, football, and ice hockey—plus top-rated events in boat racing, jai alai, and tennis. In addition to contacting the addresses below directly, you can get tickets to major events from **Ticketmaster** (Dade

County, ☎ 305/358–5885; Broward County, ☎ 305/523–3309; Palm Beach, ☎ 407/839–3900), and charge them to your credit card. Generally you can find daily listings of local sports events in the sports section of the *Miami Herald.* Friday's Weekend section carries detailed schedules and coverage of spectator sports.

Activities of the annual **Orange Bowl** and **Junior Orange Bowl Festival** take place from early November to late February. Best known for its King Orange Jamboree Parade and the Federal Express/Orange Bowl Football Classic, the festival also includes two tennis tournaments: the Rolex–Orange Bowl International Tennis Tournament, for top amateur tennis players 18 and under, and an international tournament for players 14 and under. The Junior Orange Bowl Festival is the world's largest youth festival, with more than 20 events between November and January, including sports, cultural, and performing arts activities. The showcase event is the HealthSouth/Junior Orange Bowl Parade, held in downtown Coral Gables.

Auto Racing
Hialeah Speedway, the Greater Miami area's only independent raceway, holds stock-car races on a ⅓-mile asphalt oval in a 5,000-seat stadium. Five divisions of stock cars run weekly. The Marion Edwards, Jr., Memorial Race for late-model stock cars is held in November. The speedway is on U.S. 27, ¼ mile east of the Palmetto Expressway (Route 826). *3300 W. Okeechobee Rd., Hialeah,* ☎ *305/821–6644.* ☛ *$10 ages over 12, special events $12.* ☉ *Late Jan.–early Dec., Sat.; gates open at 5, racing 7–11.*

The **Toyota Grand Prix of Miami** is typically held in February or March on a 1.9-mile, E-shape track in downtown Miami, south of MacArthur Causeway and east of Biscayne Boulevard. Drivers race for three hours; the driver completing the most laps wins. Contact Miami Motor Sports, Inc. (1110 Brickell Ave., Suite 206, Miami 33131, ☎ 305/379–5660 for information or 305/379–7223 for tickets).

Baseball
The **Florida Marlins** (100 N.E. 3rd Ave., Fort Lauderdale 33301, ☎ 305/626–7400) begin their fourth season in 1996 in the Eastern Division of the National League. Home games are played at Joe Robbie Stadium—also home to the Miami Dolphins (*see* Football, *below*)— which is 16 miles northwest of downtown Miami, accessible from I–95 and Florida's Turnpike. On game days the Metro-Dade Transit Agency (☎ 305/638–6700) runs buses to the stadium.

Basketball
The **Miami Heat** (Miami Arena, 701 Arena Blvd., Miami 33136-4102, ☎ 305/577–4328), Miami's National Basketball Association franchise, plays home games November–April at the Miami Arena, a block east of Overtown Metrorail Station.

Dog Racing
The Biscayne and Flagler greyhound tracks divide the annual racing calendar. Check with the individual tracks for dates.

At the **Biscayne Greyhound Track,** greyhounds chase a mechanical rabbit around illuminated fountains in the track's infield. *320 N.W. 115th St., near I–95, Miami Shores,* ☎ *305/754–3484.* ☛ *$1 table seats and grandstand, $2 sports room, $3 clubhouse; parking: 50¢–$2.*

Flagler Greyhound Track, in the middle of Little Havana, is five minutes east of Miami International Airport off the Dolphin Expressway

(Route 836) and Douglas Road (Northwest 37th Avenue and 7th Street). *401 N.W. 38th Ct., Miami,* ☎ *305/649–3000.* ☛ *$1, $3 clubhouse; parking: 50¢–$2.*

Football

The **Miami Dolphins** of the National Football League play at state-of-the-art Joe Robbie Stadium—JRS, as the fans call it—which has 73,000 seats and a grass playing-field surface with built-in drainage under the sod to carry off rainwater. It's on a 160-acre site 16 miles northwest of downtown Miami, 1 mile south of the Dade–Broward county line, accessible from I–95 and Florida's Turnpike. On game days the Metro-Dade Transit Agency (☎ 305/638–6700) runs buses to the stadium. *Joe Robbie Stadium, 2269 N.W. 199th St., Miami 33056,* ☎ *305/620–2578. Box office open weekdays 10–6, also Sat. during season.*

The **University of Miami Hurricanes** (1 Hurricane Dr., Coral Gables 33146, ☎ 305/284–2655), perennial contenders for top collegiate ranking, play their home games at downtown Orange Bowl Stadium (1400 N.W. 4th St., Miami) September through November.

Horse Racing

Calder Race Course, opened in 1971, is Florida's largest glass-enclosed, air-conditioned sports facility. Calder accordingly has an unusually extended season, from late May to early January—though it's a good idea to call the track for specific starting and wrap-up dates. Each year between November and early January, Calder holds the Tropical Park Derby for three-year-olds. The track is on the Dade–Broward county line near I–95 and the Hallandale Beach Boulevard exit, ¾ mile from Joe Robbie Stadium. *21001 N.W. 27th Ave., Miami,* ☎ *305/625–1311.* ☛ *$2, $4 clubhouse; parking: $1–$3. Gates open at 11, racing 1–5:30.*

A superb setting for thoroughbred racing, **Hialeah Park** has 228 acres of meticulously landscaped grounds surrounding paddocks and a clubhouse built in a classic French-Mediterranean style. Since it opened in 1925, Hialeah Park has survived hurricanes and now seems likely to survive even changing demographics, as the racetrack crowd has steadily moved north and east. Racing dates are usually March–May. The park is open year-round for free sightseeing, during which you can explore the gardens and admire the park's breeding flock of 800 Cuban flamingos. Metrorail's Hialeah Station is on the grounds. *2200 E. 4th Ave., Hialeah,* ☎ *305/885–8000.* ☛ *Weekdays $1 grandstand, $2 clubhouse; weekends $2 grandstand, $4 clubhouse; parking: $1–$4. Gates open at 10:30, racing 1–5:30.*

Ice Hockey

The **Florida Panthers** (Miami Arena, 701 Arena Blvd., Miami 33136-4102, ☎ 305/577–4328), made the playoffs in their inaugural season in the National Hockey League. They play their third season in 1995–96 at the Miami Arena, one block east of Overtown Metrorail Station.

Jai Alai

Built in 1926, the **Miami Jai-Alai Fronton,** a mile east of the airport, is the oldest fronton in America. Each evening it presents 13 games—14 on Friday and Saturday—some singles, some doubles. This game, invented in the Basque region of northern Spain, is the world's fastest. Jai-alai balls, called pelotas, have been clocked at speeds exceeding 170 miles per hour. The game is played in a 176-foot-long court called a fronton. Players climb the walls to catch the ball in a cesta—a woven basket—with an attached glove. You can bet on a team to win or on the order in which teams will finish. Dinner is available. *3500 N.W.*

37th Ave., Miami, ☎ 305/633–6400. ☛ $1, $3 reserved seats, $5
Courtview Club. ☉ Mon., Wed., Fri., Sat. noon–5 and 7–midnight; Tues.,
Thurs., Sun 7–midnight.

Tennis

The **Lipton Championships** (7300 Crandon Blvd., Key Biscayne, ☎
305/442–3367), a 10-day spring tournament at the 64-acre Tennis Center at Crandon Park, is one of the largest in the world in terms of at-
tendance, and, with $4.1 million in prize money in 1995, was fifth largest
in purse. It's played in a new permanent stadium that seats 7,500 for
big events.

BEACHES

Key Biscayne

Two of metro Miami's best beaches are on Key Biscayne. Nearest the
causeway is the 3½-mile county beach in **Crandon Park**, popular with
families and rated among the top 10 beaches in North America by many.
The sand is soft, and parking is both inexpensive and plentiful. At the
north end of the beach, the Marjory Stoneman Douglas Biscayne Nature Center interprets a variety of natural habitats through exhibits and
year-round tours. 4000 Crandon Blvd., ☎ 305/361–5421 or 305/
642–9600 for nature center. ☛ Park: $3 per vehicle; nature center: free.
☉ Daily 8–sunset, nature center hrs vary.

The other nice beach is in the **Bill Baggs Cape Florida State Recreation
Area** (see Tour 6 in Exploring, above), which has a bounty of appealing features.

Miami Beach Area

A sandy, 300-foot-wide beach extends for 10 continuous miles from
the foot of Miami Beach to Haulover Beach Park, with several distinct
sections. Amazingly, it's all man-made. Seriously eroded during the mid-
1970s, the beach was restored by the U.S. Army Corps of Engineers
in a $51.5 million project between 1977 and 1981. Between 23rd and
44th streets, Miami Beach built boardwalks and protective walkways
atop a sand dune landscaped with sea oats, sea grape, and other native plants whose roots keep the sand from blowing away.

The new beach lures residents and visitors alike to swim and stroll—
without question, Miami's favorite activities. Here's a guide to where
kindred spirits gather:

From **1st to 15th streets** senior citizens predominate early in the day.
The section from 5th to 15th, known as **Lummus Park,** lies in the heart
of the Deco District and attracts a mix of perfect-bod types and those
of all ages who can only ogle. Volleyball, in-line skating along the paved
upland path, and a lot of posing go on here, and children's playgrounds make this a popular area for families. Along these beaches,
city officials don't enforce the law against female bathers going topless, as long as everyone on the beach behaves with decorum. Gays like
the beach between 11th and 13th streets. Sidewalk cafés parallel the
entire beach area, which makes it easy to come ashore for everything
from burgers to quiche. At 23rd Street, the boardwalk begins, and no
skates or bicycles are allowed.

French-Canadians frequent the **72nd Street beach** and the area from
Surfside to 96th Street, which is colonized by winter visitors from Québec.

Families and anybody else who likes things quiet prefer **North Beach,**
along Ocean Terrace between 73rd and 75th streets. Metered parking

is ample right behind the dune and on Collins Avenue, a block behind, along a pleasant, old shopping street. The area, however, is slated for redevelopment with the intensity, if not the size, of South Beach.

North Shore State Recreation Area is still more quiet. The 40-acre park is, for a change, backed by lush tropical growth rather than hotels. *Collins Ave. between 79th and 87th Sts., Miami Beach; office: Oleta/North Shore GEOpark, 3400 N.E. 163rd St., North Miami Beach, ☎ 305/940–7439. ☛ $2 plus parking. ⊙ Daily 9–6.*

During the winter, wealthy condominium owners cluster on the beach from **96th to 103rd streets** in Bal Harbour.

Older visitors especially complain about just how wide the beaches have become—feet burn easily on long marches across hot sand before reaching the water. If you want the water closer to the upland, try the beaches from **Haulover Beach Park** north through **Sunny Isles.** The eroded sand was never replaced here, and the strand is mercifully narrow. *Haulover Beach Park: 10800 Collins Ave., Miami, ☎ 305/947–3525. ☛ $3 per vehicle. ⊙ Daily 8–sunset.*

DINING

You can eat your way around the world in Greater Miami, enjoying just about any kind of cuisine imaginable, in every price category. The rich mix of nationalities encourages individual restaurateurs and chefs to retain their culinary roots. Thus Miami offers not just Latin fare but dishes native to Spain, Cuba, Nicaragua, and other Hispanic countries; not just Oriental fare but specialties of China, India, Thailand, Vietnam, and other Asian cultures. And don't neglect American fare. In recent years the city has gained eminence for the distinctive cuisine introduced by chefs who have migrated north from the tropics and here combine fresh, natural foods—especially seafoods—with classically inspired dedication.

American

CORAL GABLES

$$ **Restaurant St. Michel.** The setting is utterly French, the little hotel it's
★   in (*see* Lodging, *below*) is Mediterranean, the town it's in is very Spanish, but the cuisine is American. Stuart Bornstein's window on Coral Gables is a lace-curtained café with sidewalk tables that could be across the street from a railroad station in Avignon or Bordeaux. A sculpted bust here, a circus poster there, newly repainted deco chandeliers, a mirrored mosaic in the shiny shape of palm fronds all create a whimsical, foreign feel, an affair of the imagination as much as the rooms upstairs are affairs of the heart. Among light fare, there's a moist couscous chicken and a pasta primavera, rich with olive oil and garlic, its colorful pepper crescents sautéed al dente. Among the heartier entrées are a plum, soy, and lemon-glazed fillet of salmon; sesame-coated loin of tuna; and local yellowtail snapper. Service is very accommodating. ✕ *162 Alcazar Ave., ☎ 305/444–1666. AE, DC, MC, V.*

DOWNTOWN MIAMI

$$$$ **Le Pavillon.** The mahogany, jade marble, and leather appointments of
★   the dining room exude the conservative bias of an English private club. A guitarist plays, beautiful floral displays enhance the mood, and the attentive staff serves regional American fare from a limited and frequently changing menu, including items low in calories, cholesterol, and sodium. Specialties are char-grilled bluefin tuna fillet, poached yellowtail snapper, panfried corn-fed squab, roasted free-range chicken,

spring lamb, and roasted fillet of milk-fed veal. For dessert, the light cuisine feature could be a red berry soup with vanilla ice cream and on the main menu a crème brûlée or black-and-white chocolatine with light mocha sauce. Count on an extensive wine list. ✗ *100 Chopin Plaza,* ☎ *305/577–1000, ext. 4494 or 4462. Jacket required. AE, DC, MC, V. Closed lunch (except Sun. brunch, noon–3) and Sun. dinner.*

KENDALL (SOUTHWEST SUBURB)

$ **Shorty's Bar-B-Q.** Shorty Allen opened his barbecue restaurant in 1951 in a log cabin, and this place has since become a tradition. Parents bring their teenage children here to show them where Mom and Dad ate on their honeymoon. Many fans circulate fresh air through the single, screened dining room, where meals are served family-style at long picnic tables. On the walls hang cowboy hats, horns, saddles, an ox yoke, and heads of boar and caribou. Specialties include barbecued pork ribs, chicken, and pork steak slow-cooked over hickory logs and drenched in Shorty's own warm, spicy sauce, with side orders of tangy baked beans and big chunks of pork, corn on the cob, and coleslaw. ✗ *9200 S. Dixie Hwy.,* ☎ *305/670–7732; 5989 S. University Dr., Davie,* ☎ *305/680–9900 or 305/944–0348 from Miami. MC, V in Davie. Closed Thanksgiving, Dec. 25.*

MIAMI BEACH

$$–$$$ **Embers.** The Embers was a steak-and-potatoes house on 21st Street when cholesterol was still unpronounceable and gay meant frivolous. A bunch of Beach High kids grew up eating dinner there with their families. Cut to 30 years later, and "kids" Sid Lewis, Steven Polisar, and Larry Schwartz, wealthy from Ocean Drive investments, have put their money where their memories are. The new Embers is five blocks south, around the corner from Lincoln Road. Nostalgia hits you right inside the door: Saucer lights dangle an amber glow from the ceiling, collections of early Beach photos hang on the walls, and black, white, and sepia mute the scene. The steaks are still here, as are the original apple fritters, New York–style basket of bread, and double-baked Embers potato mashed with scallions and baked crisp on top. Pastas and à la carte veggies have been added. Come by and add 30 years to your trip. ✗ *1661 Meridian Ave.,* ☎ *305/538–0997. AE, MC, V. No lunch.*

$$ **Max's South Beach.** This place has a warmer style of deco than Ocean Drive and more affordable gourmet cuisine than Chef Allen's and Mark's Place (*see below,* for both). Famed south Florida restaurateur Dennis Max has extended his bijou collection of eateries to South Beach with celebrity chef Kerry Simon in charge of the kitchen. The result is an immensely popular see-and-be-seen addition to Deco District dining. Packed with locals nightly, the 110-seat restaurant is woody, glass, and bistrolike, with a seating mix of high-top tables, booths, starched white linen, and seats of black leather. Photo displays are from *Rolling Stone,* which helped make a star of Simon by naming him one of 1991's 100 hottest personalities. He dares turn out an authentic meat loaf and mashed potatoes; grilled and roasted veggies with organic grains; and pot roast with garlic, fresh herbs, and slow-cooked veggies. But there's also a salmon tandoori with black beans and cayenne onion rings, a big choice of grills, and baked sea bass with basil, carrots, and a carrot-orange vinaigrette. Desserts include a Butterfinger chocolate cake with banana ice cream and Jack Daniel caramel and old-fashioned strawberry shortcake. ✗ *764 Washington Ave.,* ☎ *305/532–0070. AE, D, DC, MC, V. No lunch.*

$ **News Cafe.** This is the hippest joint on Ocean Drive. Owners Mark Soyka, who trained on the cosmopolitan beach scene in Tel Aviv, and Jeffrey Dispenzieri, from New York, are right on the money. Quick, friendly servers don't hurry guests who have come to schmooze or intellects deep in a Tolstoy novel picked out of the book rack. A raw bar has been added in back with 15 stools, but most visitors prefer sitting outside to feel the salt breeze and look at whom they're not with. Offering a little of this and a little of that—bagels, pâtés, chocolate fondue—the café attracts a big all-the-time crowd, with people coming in for a snack, a light meal, or an aperitif and, invariably, to indulge in the people parade. ✗ *800 Ocean Dr.,* ☎ *305/538–6397. AE, DC, MC, V.* ☉ *24 hrs.*

$ **Van Dyke Cafe.** Mark Soyka's second restaurant has quickly attracted the artsy crowd, just as his News Cafe (*see above*) draws the fashion crowd. Of course, tourists like it, too. It features the same style menu, but instead of facing south, this place, in the restored, 1924 Van Dyke Hotel, faces north and is shadier. Save the News Cafe for winter, the Van Dyke for summer. Three meals are served, and a 15% gratuity is included. ✗ *846 Lincoln Rd.,* ☎ *305/534–3600. AE, DC, MC, V.*

NORTH MIAMI

$$$ **Mark's Place.** Behind the adobe facade lies a stylish, deco-detailed din-
★ ing room, a work of art itself, while in the kitchen, owner-chef Mark Militello cooks regional Florida gourmet fare in a special oak-burning oven imported from Genoa. The menu changes nightly, based on the availability of fresh ingredients (many of the vegetables are organically grown by staffers), but typical selections include appetizers of Australian stir-fry with red-tip crawfish, ginger, lemongrass, chili, and garlic, and pan-seared foie gras with fresh huckleberry. Entrées inevitably include several pizzas and pastas (saffron fettuccine with Maine lobster, black beans, roast corn, chilies, tomato, and cilantro, for instance) and, among the specialties, grilled marinated breast of duck with acorn-squash flan, wilted greens, and dried-fruit sauce. For dessert there may be warm chocolate decadence with chocolate sorbet and blackberry *coulis* (puree). There's a second Mark's Place in Fort Lauderdale (*see* Chapter 4, Fort Lauderdale). ✗ *2286 N.E. 123rd St.,* ☎ *305/893–6888. AE, DC, MC, V. Closed Thanksgiving, Dec. 25. No lunch weekends.*

NORTH MIAMI BEACH

$$$ **Chef Allen's.** In this art deco world of glass block, neon trim, fresh flow-
★ ers, and art from the Gallery at Turnberry, your gaze nonetheless remains riveted on the kitchen. Chef Allen Susser designed it with a picture window 25 feet wide, so you can watch him create new American masterpieces almost too pretty to eat. The menu changes nightly. After a salad of baby greens and warm wild mushrooms or the Caribbean antipasto or rock-shrimp hash with roast corn, consider *orecchiette* pasta with sun-dried tomato, aged goat cheese, spinach, and toasted pine nuts; a half dozen or more fish and seafood items, including swordfish with conch-citrus couscous, macadamia nuts, and preserved lemon; a variety of birds, such as honey-chili roasted duck with stir-fried wild rice and green-apple Armagnac chutney; or a choice of meats, including grilled lamb chops with purple eggplant timbale and a three-nut salsa. A favorite dessert is the double-chocolate soufflé with lots of nuts (order before dinner). A four-course, fixed-price degustation menu with two wine selections is offered nightly. ✗ *19088 N.E. 29th Ave.,* ☎ *305/ 935–2900. AE, DC, MC, V. No lunch.*

WEST DADE

$$–$$$ **Shula's Steak House.** Surrounded by memorabilia of coach Don Shula's perfect 1972 season with the Miami Dolphins, you can drink or dine in this shrine for the NFL-obsessed. The certified Black Angus beef is almost an afterthought to the icons, which include quarterback Earl

Morall's rocking chair, assistant coach Howard Schnellenberger's pipe, and a playbook autographed by President Richard Nixon. Otherwise it's steaks, prime rib, and fish (including dolphin) in a woody, fireplace-cheered, cedar-shingled setting, more like a convivial club than just another steak house. Also for Shula fans, there's Shula's All-Star Cafe, a sports celebrity hangout in Don Shula's Hotel (*see* Lodging, *below*). ✕ *15400 N.W. 77th Ave., Miami Lakes,* ☎ *305/822–2324. AE, DC, MC, V.*

Brazilian
CORAL GABLES

$$ **Rodeo Grill.** Skewers aloft, waiters at the imaginative Rodeo Grill race about (just hope they don't trip!), ready to carve off hunks and slices of 10 kinds of meats. The philosophy at this novel 180-seat restaurant in the heart of downtown Coral Gables seems to be "Eat 'til you drop." The idea comes from *rodizio,* a Portuguese word referring to a continuous feed—"rodeo" is an easy-to-pronounce corruption that makes you think "meat"—and in southern Brazil, where they're big meat eaters, that means beef ribs, chicken, lamb, London broil, pork, sausage, and turkey, with sides of rice, potatoes, fried yucca, and a big salad bar. If you have room for dessert you might want to split an order of *quindim,* a cake-and-custard combination made with coconuts and eggs. Restaurateur Tito Valiente, a native of São Paulo and former owner of the largest electronics store on Flagler Street, and his wife, Teresa, have made the Rodeo Grill a great favorite among the 40,000 Brazilians who live in Dade County, as well as with other locals and hordes of visiting Brazilians. The dining room is filled with mostly whimsical Brazilian art, much of it for sale. ✕ *2121 Ponce de León Blvd.,* ☎ *305/447–6336. AE, D, DC, MC, V. No lunch Sun.*

Chinese
DOWNTOWN MIAMI

$$ **Tony Chan's Water Club.** One of a pair of outstanding new Chinese
★ restaurants on the mainland, this beautiful dining room just off the lobby of the high-rise Grand Prix Hotel looks onto a bayside marina. The long room is filled with art and chrome modern rather than stock Chinese. From the care taken in dispensing food to the delicate flavorings and fresh broccoli, execution is noteworthy. Add to that a menu of more than 100 appetizers and entrées. Start with minced quail tossed with bamboo shoots and mushrooms wrapped in lettuce leaves. Then try a seafood spectacular with shrimp, conch, scallops, fish cake, and crabmeat tossed with broccoli in a bird's nest or pork chops sprinkled with green pepper in a black bean–garlic sauce. ✕ *1717 N. Bayshore Dr.,* ☎ *305/374–8888. AE, MC, V. No lunch weekends.*

SOUTH DADE

$–$$ **Tropical Chinese Restaurant.** This place may be out in the burbs, but
★ it's worth the drive. Everyone who craves authentic Chinese comes here, as evidenced by the rack of Chinese daily *World Journal*s outside, which is sold out by noon, even on Saturday. The big 160-seat, lacquer-free room feels as open and busy as a Chinese railway station. The informed wait staff is a terrific help, since you'll find items on the menu you're not accustomed to—for example, the early spring leaves of snow pea pods, sublimely tender and flavorful. The extensive menu is filled with tofu, chicken, beef, duck, pork, and rice and noodle dishes, as well as lots of conch, squid, sea bass, and flounder. Dim sum, the big attraction for families, features great carts loaded with choices and constantly on a roll. Thirteen chefs prepare everything in the big open kitchen as if for dignitaries. ✕ *7991 S.W. 40th St., Miami,* ☎ *305/262–7576 or 305/272–1552. AE, MC, V. Closed Thanksgiving.*

Continental

COCONUT GROVE

$$$ **Grand Cafe.** Understated elegance is the hallmark of this bilevel room
★   with fanlight windows, brass details, pink tablecloths, and floral bou-
quets—sunbathed by day, intimate with a soft golden cast after dark.
French chef Pascal Oudin creates international cuisine in pleasing pre-
sentations that intrigue the palate. Appetizer specialties include pan-seared
Florida crab cake and chilled home-smoked salmon Bavarian (with Reg-
giano cheese ruffle, crème fraîche, Ikura caviar, and roasted tomato dress-
ing). Among main courses, favorites are the baked macadamia and
ginger–crusted salmon, crusted black-bean seared rare yellowfin tuna,
and grilled double lamb chops. For dessert try the white-chocolate-and-
pistachio mousse with blackberry sauce and Beaujolais essence. ✕ 2669
S. Bayshore Dr., ☎ 305/858–9600. AE, DC, MC, V.

$$ **Cafe Tu Tu Tango.** Local artists set up their easels in the rococo-modern
arcades of this eclectic café-lounge on the second story of the highly pop-
ular CocoWalk. It's as if a bunch of imaginative kids were let loose on
every surface. The end result: You'll be blown away, whether you sit indoors or out. Outside offers some of the best people-watching in the South.
Inside, guests at the more than 250 seats graze on chips, dips, breads,
and spreads. House specials include frittatas, crab cakes, *picadillo em-
panadas* (spicy ground beef served with cilantro sour cream), and chicken
and shrimp orzo paella, all to be enjoyed with some of the best sangria
in the city. A few wines are also available, none of which costs too
much. ✕ 3015 Grand Ave. (CocoWalk), ☎ 305/529–2222. AE, MC, V.

CORAL GABLES

$$$ **Aragon Cafe.** If George Merrick entered the bar at this restaurant in
the Omni Colonnade Hotel (*see* Lodging, *below*), he would see on dis-
play his mother's hand-painted china and silver. Designed to look old
and classy, the café glows with subdued lighting from gaslight-style chan-
deliers and etched-glass wall sconces. The menu now emphasizes lighter
fare as well as fresh Florida seafoods, although it still reflects Merrick's
desire to re-create the best of the Mediterranean in a Florida setting.
Specialties range from pan-roasted fillet of salmon with a nest of wilted
greens and grapes to Mediterranean vegetable risotto with saffron to
filet mignon with pistachio butter. Dessert offerings include a baked
apple tart with pecans, vanilla ice cream, and caramel sauce in addi-
tion to a semisweet chocolate–almond terrine with mocha sabayon.
There's free valet parking. ✕ 180 Aragon Ave., ☎ 305/441–2600. AE,
D, DC, MC, V. Closed Sun., Mon. No lunch.

MIAMI BEACH

$$$ **The Forge.** A new courtyard with seating for 70 has opened as part of
the slow rebuilding of this landmark, which suffered a disastrous fire
in 1991. Often compared to a museum, the Forge still stands behind
a facade of 19th-century Parisian mansions, where an authentic forge
once stood. Each intimate dining salon has its own historical artifacts,
including a 250-year-old chandelier that hung in James Madison's
White House. A fully stocked wine cellar contains an inventory of
380,000 bottles—including more than 500 dating from 1822 (and costing as much as $35,000) and recorked in 1989 by experts from Do-
maines Barons de Rothschild. Specialties include Norwegian salmon
served over fresh garden vegetables with spinach vinaigrette, veal tenderloin roasted Tuscan-style over oak wood and marinated with fresh
blackberries, and free-range Wisconsin duck roasted with black cur-
rants. Desserts are extravagant; try the famous blacksmith pie. ✕ 432
Arthur Godfrey Rd., ☎ 305/538–8533. AE, DC, MC, V. No lunch.

NORTH MIAMI

$$$ La Paloma. Like the Forge (*see above*), this Swiss Continental restaurant offers a total sensory experience: fine food, impeccable service, and the ambience of an art museum. Since 1977, owners Werner and Maria Staub have displayed the ornate European antiques they have collected for decades: Baccarat crystal, Limoges china, Meissen porcelain, and Sèvres clocks. The staff speaks Spanish, French, German, Portuguese, and Arabic. Specialties include fresh local fish and shellfish; Wiener schnitzel; lamb chops coated with bread crumbs, mustard, garlic, and herbs; veal chop with morel sauce; and, for dessert, lemon sherbet with fresh kiwi fruit and vodka. ✕ *10999 Biscayne Blvd.,* ☎ *305/891–0505. AE, MC, V. Closed 2 wks in late summer. No lunch weekends.*

Cuban

CORAL GABLES

$$$ **Yuca.** Top Cuban dining can be had at this bistro-chic restaurant in a
★ storefront on restaurant row. The name stands for the homey potato-like staple of Cuban kitchens as well as for young, urban Cuban-American. Cuban cuisine, like the best of everything in Miami, comes hyphenated. The high standards are first evident in the setting—a trendy blend of blond wood, tile, black-iron rails, track lighting, and modern art. Still more impressive is the follow-through on food: traditional corn tamale filled with conch and a spicy jalapeño and Creole cheese pesto, the namesake yuca stuffed with *mamacita's picadillo* and dressed in wild mushrooms on a bed of sautéed spinach, and plantain-coated dolphin with a tamarind tartar sauce. Featured desserts include classic Cuban rice pudding in an almond basket, and coconut pudding in its coconut. The service matches the style at this 250-seat, yet intimate, two-level restaurant. ✕ *177 Giralda Ave.,* ☎ *305/444–4448. Reservations required. AE, DC, MC, V. Closed Dec. 25, Jan. 1. No lunch Sun.*

LITTLE HAVANA

$$–$$$ **Victor's Cafe.** This big, popular upmarket restaurant draws its inspiration from the traditional Cuban *casona,* the great house of colonial Cuba. The mood is old Havana, with Cuban art and antiques, high ceilings, and a glass-covered fountain courtyard. Owner Victor del Corral, who emigrated from Cuba in 1957, first made his mark in Manhattan before branching out to Miami. Now he works with his daughter Sonia Zaldivar and her son Luis. Come on Friday afternoon, when the tapas (hors d'oeuvres) bar is packed and lunch often lasts through dusk, in true Cuban fashion. The food is filling, well seasoned (although not peppery hot), and makes much use of traditional foods, including many root crops. All entrées are accompanied by rice and black beans. You could make a meal on the hot appetizers, such as a puff pastry filled with aromatically herbed lump crabmeat or a savory cassava turnover filled with Florida lobster. An exceptional entrée is the red-snapper fillet Miralda (marinated in bitter orange juice and garlic, sautéed in olive oil, and served over strips of fire-roasted pimentos, green peppers, and scallions); truly jumbo shrimp are served with yam quenelles in a creamy champagne sauce sprinkled with salmon roe. Very sentimental, romantic music is played nightly. ✕ *2430 S.W. 32nd Ave.,* ☎ *305/445–1313. AE, DC, MC, V.*

$ **Islas Canarias.** Since 1976 this has been a gathering place for Cuban poets, pop-music stars, and media personalities. Wall murals depict a Canary Islands street scene (the grandfather of the current owner, Santiago Garcia, came from Tenerife). The menu includes such Canary Islands dishes as baked lamb, ham hocks with boiled potatoes, and

Miami Area Dining

N

OCEAN

MIAMI BEACH

NORTH MIAMI BEACH

NORTH MIAMI

Miami International

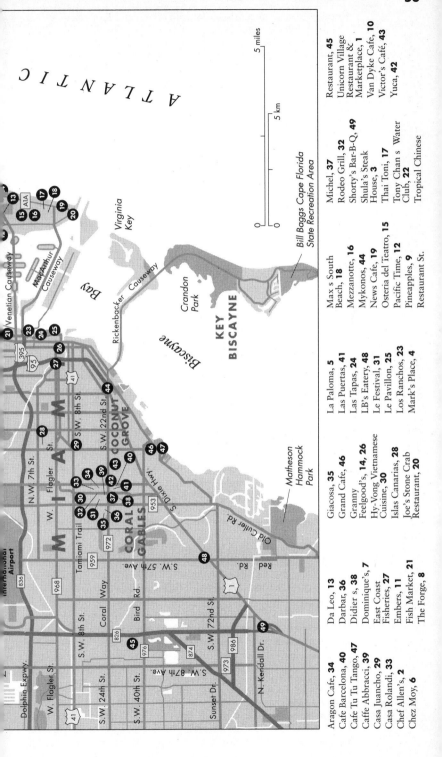

53

ATLANTIC

Bill Baggs Cape Florida
State Recreation Area

Aragon Cafe, **34**
Cafe Barcelona, **40**
Cafe Tu Tu Tango, **47**
Caffe Abbracci, **39**
Casa Juancho, **29**
Casa Rolandi, **33**
Chef Allen's, **2**
Chez Moy, **6**

Da Leo, **13**
Darbar, **36**
Didier s, **38**
Dominique's, **7**
East Coast
  Fisheries, **27**
Embers, **11**
Fish Market, **21**
The Forge, **8**

Giacosa, **35**
Grand Cafe, **46**
Granny
  Feelgood's, **14, 26**
Hy-Vong Vietnamese
  Cuisine, **30**
Islas Canarias, **28**
Joe's Stone Crab
  Restaurant, **20**

La Paloma, **5**
Las Puertas, **41**
Las Tapas, **24**
LB's Eatery, **48**
Le Festival, **31**
Le Pavillon, **25**
Los Ranchos, **23**
Mark's Place, **4**

Max s South
  Beach, **18**
Mezzanotte, **16**
Mykonos, **44**
News Cafe, **19**
Osteria del Teatro, **15**
Pacific Time, **12**
Pineapples, **9**
Restaurant St.

Michel, **37**
Rodeo Grill, **32**
Shorty's Bar-B-Q, **49**
Shula's Steak
  House, **3**
Thai Toni, **17**
Tony Chan s Water
  Club, **22**
Tropical Chinese

Restaurant, **45**
Unicorn Village
  Restaurant &
  Marketplace, **1**
Van Dyke Cafe, **10**
Victor's Café, **43**
Yuca, **42**

tortilla *Española* (Spanish omelet with onions and chorizo), as well as Cuban standards including palomilla steak and fried kingfish. Don't miss the three superb varieties of homemade chips—potato, malanga, and plantain. ✕ *285 N.W. Unity Blvd. (N.W. 27th Ave.),* ☎ *305/649–0440; Coral Way and S.W. 137th Ave., Westchester,* ☎ *305/559–6666. No credit cards. Closes at 6 on Dec. 24 and Dec. 31.*

Family Style
CORAL GABLES
$ **LB's Eatery.** Town and gown meet at this sprout-laden haven a half block from the University of Miami's baseball stadium. Kitschy food-related posters cover the walls, and there are no waiters: You order at the counter and pick up your food when called. Vegetarians thrive on LB's salads and daily meatless entrées, such as lasagna and moussaka. The place is famous for Saturday-night lobster—if you plan to come after 8, call ahead to reserve a lobster. Other specialties include barbecued baby-back ribs, lime chicken, croissant sandwiches, and carrot cake. ✕ *5813 Ponce de León Blvd.,* ☎ *305/661–7091. D, MC, V. Closed Sun., holidays.*

French
CORAL GABLES
$$$ **Le Festival.** The modest canopied entrance to this classical French restaurant belies the elegance within, where decor celebrates Parisian *moderne* with sweeping curves, etched-glass filigree, and posh burgundy, mahogany, and rose-tinted details. A second room, for smokers, is more gilded. An appetizer of lobster in pastry and champagne sauce, for example, prepares the palate for adaptive and traditional French main courses, which include fillet of grouper in bouillabaisse sauce; stuffed quail with grape and red-wine sauce; milk-fed veal sautéed with mushrooms, grapes, and brandy cream sauce; and chateaubriand for two. Desserts comprise various pastries, mousses, and soufflées. The wine list includes 100 selections, many priced less than $30. ✕ *2120 Salzedo St.,* ☎ *305/442–8545. Reservations required for dinner and for lunch parties of 5 or more. AE, D, DC, MC, V. Closed Sun. No lunch Sat.*

$$ **Didier's.** After more than a year's hiatus when the building their restau-
★ rant occupied was sold from under them, the three brothers Colongette have reestablished their corner of Provence in Coral Gables. Didier (the business brother), Olivier (the host), and Thierry (the chef) have re-assembled the elements that earned them their fame. The new restaurant is larger, dividing 120 seats among three rooms with a sunny French style. Flower boxes with seasonal blooms show through the eyelet-cur-tained windows, tulips brighten tables in spring, and floral embellishment continues on menus. Service is informed and attentive. For starters, choose fresh basil soup or snails cooked in clay pots with garlic butter. Follow that up with a seafood entrée, such as bouillabaisse; a free-range chicken marinated in rosemary and served with wild mushrooms and glazed shallots; or roasted rack of lamb with fine herbs and fava beans with a fresh mint sauce. Desserts include crème brûlée, apple tart, and a strawberry with passion-fruit sabayon. All is wonderful and affordable for the quality. ✕ *2530 Ponce de León Blvd.,* ☎ *305/567–2444. AE, DC, MC, V. Closed Sun. No lunch Sat.*

MIAMI BEACH
$$$$ **Dominique's.** Woodwork and mirrors from a Vanderbilt home and other demolished New York mansions create an intimate setting for a unique nouvelle-cuisine experience in either of two enclosed patios, both glass-sided for ocean views. Specialties include exotic appetizers such as buffalo sausage, sautéed alligator tail, and rattlesnake-meat salad;

entrées such as rack of lamb (35% of total sales) and fresh seafood; and an extensive wine list. The restaurant also serves Sunday brunch. ✕ *Alexander Hotel, 5225 Collins Ave.,* ☎ *305/865–6500 or 800/327–6121. AE, DC, MC, V.*

Greek
FIVE POINTS, MIAMI

$ **Mykonos.** A Miami fixture since 1973, this 74-seat restaurant brightens the intersection at Five Points in the Roads section of town with a beautiful mural of the Aegean. That sweet sense of faraway islands carries inside in a sparkling blue-and-white setting dressed up with Greek travel posters. Specialties include gyro, moussaka, marinated lamb and chicken, calamari and octopus sautéed in wine and onions, and sumptuous Greek salads thick with feta cheese and briny olives. Vegetarian moussaka, eggplant roll, lasagna, and a Greek-style omelet are new to the menu. ✕ *1201 Coral Way,* ☎ *305/856–3140. AE, DC, MC, V. Closed July 4, Thanksgiving, Dec. 24–25, Dec. 31, Jan. 1. No lunch Sun.*

Haitian
LITTLE HAITI

$ **Chez Moy.** A fixture in its neighborhood, Chez Moy is utterly without pretense about being anywhere but in an outpost of Haiti. The music is Haitian, the TV in the corner plays Haitian programs, everyone speaks Creole, and the food is as authentic as on the rue Delmas in Port-au-Prince. Seating is outside on a shaded patio or in a pleasant room with oak tables and high-back chairs. Specialties include *grillot* (pork boiled then fried with spices), fried or boiled fish, stewed goat, and conch with garlic and hot pepper. Try a tropical fruit drink such as sweet sop (also called *anon* or *cachiman*) or sour sop (also called *guanabana* or *corrosol*), blended with milk and sugar, and sweet-potato pie for dessert. ✕ *1 N.W. 54th St.,* ☎ *305/757–5056. No credit cards. No smoking.*

Indian
CORAL GABLES

$$ **Darbar.** Owner Bobby Puri's impeccably arranged Darbar (Punjabi for
★ "Royal Court") is the glory of Miami's Indian restaurants. It reigns with authenticity, down to the portraits of turbaned Puri ancestors, kings, and princes. Flavors rise as if in a dance from the *bangan bharta,* a dish of eggplant skinned and mashed with onions, tomatoes, herbs, and spices and baked in a tandoor. The limited menu's focus is on northern Indian or frontier cuisine—various kebabs, tandoori platters, and *tikkas* (chicken or lamb marinated in yogurt and spices and cooked tandoori style)—although there are also curries from different regions and *biryani* specialties prepared with basmati rice and garnished with boiled egg, tomato, nuts, and raisins. Everything, including the unusual Indian breads, is cooked to order. ✕ *276 Alhambra Circle,* ☎ *305/ 448–9691. AE, DC, MC, V. Closed holidays. No lunch Sun.*

Italian
CORAL GABLES

$$$ **Casa Rolandi.** The look is new since 1994: more rustic, less arty. The cuisine is more fully Northern Italian since the departure of highly esteemed chef Fabio Rolandi, whose cuisine tended more to the Swiss. What's still here are the two working brick ovens and the kitchen's earthy commitment to authentic cookery, enhanced by the open beams and weathered village walls. The menu features the expected antipasti and *caldi,* but on the way to the *gelati* and *dolci* you will happily tour through the risottos and pastas—smoky salmon and shrimp bathed in a creamy tomato rice; bow ties combined with ground veal, chicken, onions, and carrots; and a succulent Maine lobster bedded on spaghetti,

fresh tomatoes, and basil—or through such local choices as grouper baked with mushrooms, leeks, and saffron on a bed of arugula. ✕ *1930 Ponce de León Blvd.,* ☎ *305/444–2187. AE, DC, MC, V. Closed Sun., Mon., some holidays. No lunch Sat.*

$$–$$$ **Caffe Abbracci.** Although the kitchen closes at 11 or midnight, the last
★ wave of customers—usually Brazilians—is still partying to the flamenco or salsa music on weekends at 2. The setting is graciously deco, with huge bursts of flowers, frosted glass, gallery lighting, and fresh roses on white linens; lights above each table are on individual dimmers. After the cold and hot antipasti—various carpaccios, porcini mushrooms, calamari, grilled goat cheese, shrimps, mussels—come festive entrées. Most of the pasta is made fresh, so consider sampling two or three, maybe with pesto sauce, Gorgonzola, and fresh tomatoes. The *agnolotti al pesto* are pasta pockets filled with ricotta cheese and spinach; the *dentice alla maggiorana* is red snapper sautéed in white wine, fresh marjoram, and lemon and topped with sliced grilled tomatoes. Room for dessert? The little napoleons are made here daily, as is the tiramisù, and there's always a choice of fresh fruit tarts. ✕ *318 Aragon Ave.,* ☎ *305/441–0700. Reservations required. AE, DC, MC, V. No lunch weekends.*

$$–$$$ **Giacosa.** Named for one of Puccini's librettists, this is another of the
★ superbly evocative—and just plain superb—restaurants in Coral Gables. How does anyone in this town stay thin? The ambience is wonderfully informed—a thickly carpeted room like a smart Venetian salon, fresh flowers, chair cushions inspired by tapestry. The maître d' knows guests by name, and waiters stand as watchful as carabinieri at a bank vault. From putting your napkin in your lap to whisking a tower of airy pita bread with olive oil carafe to the table, the smooth staff is the standard of competence. Parmesan is freshly grated to the plate. A salad *tricolore* imparts the bitter kiss of arugula; pastas, veals, and fresh seafood are all prepared for peak taste. ✕ *394 Giralda Ave.,* ☎ *407/445–5858. AE, DC, MC, V. Closed holidays. No lunch weekends.*

MIAMI BEACH

$$$ **Osteria del Teatro.** This 20-table dining room is the culinary equiva-
★ lent of Pavarotti. Thanks to word of mouth of knowledgeable diner-outers, this Northern Italian restaurant is consistently full, and despite a tiny kitchen, the preparations are just as consistent. Orchids grace the tables in the intimate, low-ceilinged, gray, gray, and gray room with a laced canvas ceiling, deco lamps, and the most refined clink and clatter along this remarkable restaurant row. Everything comes carefully detailed, starting with large, unevenly sliced hunks of homemade bread lightly toasted. Specialties included an appetizer of grilled portobello mushroom topped with fontina cheese and served over a bed of arugula with a green peppercorn–brandy sauce, and among entrées, linguine sautéed with chunks of jumbo shrimp, roasted peppers, capers, black olives, fresh diced tomato, and equally fresh herbs in a tangy garlic–olive oil sauce. Make room for dessert and coffee so you don't feel guilty lingering. ✕ *1443 Washington Ave.,* ☎ *305/538–7850. Reservations required. AE, DC, MC, V. Closed Tues., Dec. 25, Jan. 1. No lunch.*

$$ **Mezzanotte.** Sometime between 6 and 10 each night, the big square room with the square bar in the middle transforms from an empty catering hall to a New Year's Eve party. Trendoids call for their *capellini* with fresh tomato and basil; calamari in clam juice, garlic, and red wine; or scaloppine with mushroom, pepper, and white wine—everything a gift from tomato heaven—and then top it off with their *dolci*: fresh napoleon, chocolate mousse, or tiramisù. Chic but not intimate, Mezzanotte has been known since 1988 for fine food at moderate prices, but watch out for the coffee at $2.25 a pop! ✕ *1200 Washington Ave.,* ☎ *305/673–4343. AE, DC, MC, V. Closed Thanksgiving. No lunch.*

$–$$ **Da Leo.** Tables from this little restaurant spill all over the mall, staying full thanks to consistently good food at prices only half what the trendy places charge. The volume keeps the mood festive and the standards high. You'll be amazed by the art, which so completely covers the walls you might think the canvasses provide structural support. The look is ancient Roman town house (though owner Leonardo Marchini hails from Lucca), with banquettes along one wall and wainscoting along the other. Pastas, a few fish, a couple of veal, and a fowl choice make up most of the entrées. The house salad is shiny with olive oil lavished over fresh garden veggies. ✕ *819 Lincoln Rd. Mall,* ☎ *305/674–0350. AE, DC, MC, V. Closed some holidays. No lunch weekends.*

Mexican
CORAL GABLES

$$ **Las Puertas.** The restaurant row along Giralda Avenue seems touched by magic, and this storefront dining room filled with native arts and crafts is no exception. This is gourmet Mexican, with handsome arches and white tablecloths, redeeming south-of-the-border cuisine from the limits of quick lunch food. The tastes of several Mexican states are represented. The chicken in green *pipian* sauce (breast grilled and poached in a sauce of ground sesame, pumpkin seeds, tomatillos, cilantro, and dark green poblanos chiles) hails from Puebla. Yucatán suckling pig comes baked inside banana leaves, and the red snapper from Veracruz is sautéed with capers, tomatoes, and green olives. Of several desserts you've never seen on franchised Mexican menu boards, the best, when available, is the cheesecake of peaches and cream prepared with fresh peaches. Bring your spirit of adventure. ✕ *148 Giralda Ave.,* ☎ *305/442–0708. AE, D, MC, V. Closed some holidays. No lunch weekends.*

Natural
DOWNTOWN MIAMI

$$ **Granny Feelgood's.** "Granny" is a shrewd gentleman named Irving Field, who caters to health-conscious lawyers, office workers, and cruise-ship crews downtown and to locals and tourists on Lincoln Road on the Beach. Specialties include chicken salad with raisins, apples, and cinnamon; spinach fettuccine with pine nuts; grilled tofu; apple crumb cake; and carrot cake. ✕ *190 S.E. 1st Ave.,* ☎ *305/358–6233; 111 N.W. 1st St.,* ☎ *305/579–2104; 647 Lincoln Rd. Mall, Miami Beach,* ☎ *305/ 673–0408. AE, MC, V. No smoking. Closed Sun. downtown. No lunch.*

MIAMI BEACH

$$ **Pineapples.** Art-filled, tropical pink-and-green café seating occupies half of this popular mid-Beach neighborhood emporium; the other side is a health-foods store. Daily seafood, chicken, and vegetarian specials add variety to longtime favorites lasagna filled with tofu and mushrooms, spinach fettuccine with feta cheese, and salads. Organic wine and beer are new. ✕ *530 Arthur Godfrey Rd.,* ☎ *305/532–9731. AE, MC, V. No smoking.*

NORTH MIAMI BEACH

$$ **Unicorn Village Restaurant & Marketplace.** The top choice in its field
★ in the north end of the city, this 300-seat restaurant caters to vegetarian and nonvegetarian diners. In an outdoor setting of free-form ponds and fountains by a bayfront dock, or in the plant-filled interior under three-story-high wood-beam ceilings, guests enjoy seitan medallions (wheat meat in a mushroom gravy sauce) and a line of homemade organic pizzas. Other favorites include a Tuscan vegetable sauté with Ital-

ian seasonings; grilled honey-mustard chicken; spicy seafood cakes; and the Unicorn's spring roll of uncooked veggies wrapped in thin rice paper with cellophane noodles. Very popular are the early dinner specials—typically eight entrées with soup or salad, basket of rolls, veggies, and coffee—offered 4:30–5:30 for up to $10.95. The nondairy, fat-free chocolate-mocha cake is tasty, and there are organic cappuccinos. The adjacent market is the largest natural-foods source in Florida and features desserts baked on the premises. ✕ *3565 N.E. 207th St.,* ☎ *305/933–8829. AE, MC, V. No smoking.*

Nicaraguan
DOWNTOWN MIAMI

$$ Los Ranchos. Carlos Somoza, owner of this beautiful bayside establishment, is a nephew of Nicaragua's late president Anastasio Somoza. Carlos sustains a tradition begun more than 30 years ago in Managua, when the original Los Ranchos instilled in Nicaraguan palates a love of Argentine-style beef—lean, grass-fed tenderloin with *chimichurri,* a green sauce of chopped parsley, garlic, oil, vinegar, and other spices. Nicaragua's own sauces are a tomato-based marinara and the fiery *cebollitas encurtidas,* with slices of jalapeño pepper and onion pickled in vinegar. Specialties include chorizo, *cuajada con maduro* (skim cheese with fried bananas), and shrimp sautéed in butter and topped with creamy jalapeño sauce. Don't look for veggies or brewed decaf, but you do get live entertainment at lunch and dinner. ✕ *Bayside Marketplace, 401 Biscayne Blvd.,* ☎ *305/375–8188 or 305/375–0666; 125 S.W. 107th Ave., Little Managua,* ☎ *305/221–9367; Kendall Town & Country, 8505 Mills Dr., Kendall,* ☎ *305/596–5353; The Falls, 8888 S.W. 136th St., Suite 303, South Miami,* ☎ *305/238–6867; 2728 Ponce de León Blvd., Coral Gables,* ☎ *305/446–0050. AE, DC, MC, V. Closed Good Fri., Dec. 24, Jan. 1.*

Seafood
DOWNTOWN MIAMI

$$–$$$ Fish Market. If fish are truly running scarce in Florida waters, as some
★ claim, the last of what's available should be reserved for this superior dining room tucked in a corner of the Crowne Plaza Miami lobby. The room is as beautiful as the kitchen staff is fluent in seafood's complexities. Modern chrome and comfortable cushions combine in urban sophistication. Though the menu is limited, whatever's fresh is highlighted daily. Look for seared swordfish with Oriental vinaigrette, broiled Florida lobster with Creole sauce and onion risotto, or sautéed Florida dolphin with roasted peppers in a beurre blanc. All entrées are served with sourdough bread and the vegetable of the day. The chocolate-pecan tart and pistachio-chocolate terrine with orange-cream sauce are two of the featured desserts. There's free valet parking. ✕ *Biscayne Blvd. at 16th St.,* ☎ *305/374–4399. AE, D, DC, MC, V. Closed Sun., holidays. No lunch Sat.*

$$ East Coast Fisheries. This family-owned restaurant and retail fish market on the Miami River features fresh Florida seafood from its own 38-boat fleet in the Keys. From tables along the second-floor balcony, watch the cooks prepare your dinner in the open kitchen below. Specialties include a complimentary fish-pâté appetizer, blackened pompano with owner David Swartz's personal herb-and-spice recipe, lightly breaded fried grouper, and a homemade Key lime pie so rich it tastes like ice cream. ✕ *360 W. Flagler St.,* ☎ *305/373–5515. AE, MC, V. Beer and wine only.*

$$$ **Pacific Time.** This cool California-style restaurant is packed even on
★ nights something special isn't happening, and it's rare that you can get
in without a reservation or a 45-minute wait. The superb 100-seat eatery,
co-owned by chef Jonathan Eismann, has a high blue ceiling and ban-
quettes, accents of mahogany and brass, recessed lights, paddle fans,
plank floors, and an open-windowed kitchen. Entrées include a cedar-
roasted salmon, rosemary-roasted chicken, and shiitake mush-
room–grilled, dry-aged Colorado beef. Rices, potatoes, and vegetables
are à la carte; however, a pre-theater (6–7) prix fixe dinner (a noodle
dish, Szechuan mixed grill, grilled ginger chicken) is more affordable
($20). Desserts (mostly around $7) include baked apricots and fresh
blackberries in phyllo pastry and a warm bittersweet-chocolate bombe.
There's a big California wine list. ✗ *915 Lincoln Rd.,* ☎ *305/534–5979.
AE, DC, MC, V.*

$$ **Joe's Stone Crab Restaurant.** "Before SoBe, Joe Be," touts this fourth-
generation family restaurant, which reopened for the 1996 season with
a chest-puffing facade on Washington Avenue. You go to wait, people-
watch, and finally settle down to an ample à la carte menu. About a ton
of stone-crab claws is served daily, with drawn butter, lemon wedges,
and piquant mustard sauce (recipe available). Popular side orders include
salad with a brisk vinaigrette house dressing, creamed garlic spinach, french-
fried onions, fried green tomatoes, and hash browns. Save room for
dessert—Key lime pie with a graham-cracker crust and whipped cream
or apple pie with a crumb-pecan topping. To minimize the wait, come
for lunch at 11:30, for dinner at 5 or after 9. ✗ *227 Biscayne St.,* ☎
*305/673–0365, 305/673–4611 for takeout, or 800/780–2722 for overnight
shipping. AE, D, DC, MC, V. Closed May 15–Oct. 15.*

Spanish

$$ **Cafe Barcelona.** This high-ceilinged, coral-walled room is highlighted
by gilt-framed art and beautiful, slender ceiling lamps with tiny fluted
green shades that illuminate the food but little else, yielding an ambi-
ence that's part art gallery and part private home. Many of the 25 ta-
bles are typically occupied by friends dining together, their gabble
filling the space with the sophistication of a Continental railway sta-
tion. Exceptional food matches the exceptional mood, and in a city where
fresh fish has gotten priced off the deep end, entrées here range a good
$5 below comparable dishes at first-class restaurants. They do a sea
bass in sea salt for two, a traditional codfish with garlic confit, and a
grouper in a clay pot with seafood sauce as well as lamb, duck, and
several affordable rice dishes, including three versions of a paella. The
crema Catalana is a version of flan not to be missed. ✗ *160 Giralda
Ave.,* ☎ *305/448–0912. AE, D, DC, MC, V. Closed some holidays.
No lunch weekends.*

$$ **Las Tapas.** Overhung with dried meats and enormous show breads, this
popular spot with terra-cotta floors and an open kitchen offers a lot
of imaginative creations. Tapas ("little dishes") give you a variety of
tastes during a single meal. Specialties include *la tostada* (smoked
salmon on melba toast, topped with a dollop of sour cream, baby eels,
black caviar, capers, and chopped onion) and *pincho de pollo a la plancha* (grilled chicken brochette marinated in brandy and onions). Also
available are soups, salads, sandwiches, and standard-size dinners. ✗
Bayside Marketplace, 401 Biscayne Blvd., ☎ *305/372–2737. Reservations required for large parties. AE, D, DC, MC, V.*

$$–$$$ **Casa Juancho.** A meeting place for the movers and shakers of Miami's
★ Cuban community and a haven for lovers of fine Spanish food, Casa
Juancho serves a cross section of Spanish regional cuisines. The exterior is marked by *tinajones,* the huge earthen urns of eastern Cuba,
whereas the interior recalls old Castile: brown brick, rough-hewn dark
timbers, walls hung with hooks of smoked meats and adorned with
colorful Talavera platters. Strolling balladeers (university students
from Spain) will serenade you. Ask for the hake prepared in a fish stock
with garlic, onions, and white wine—it's flown in from Spain and is
usually available—or the *carabineros a la plancha* (jumbo red shrimp
with head and shell on, split and grilled). Other specialties include roast
suckling pig and *parrillada de mariscos* (fish, shrimps, squid, and scallops grilled in a light garlic sauce) from the Pontevedra region of northwest Spain. For dessert, the crema Catalana has a delectable crust of
burnt caramel atop a rich pastry custard. The house features the largest
list of reserved Spanish wines in the United States. ✕ *2436 S.W. 8th
St.,* ☎ *305/642–2452. AE, D, DC, MC, V. Closed Dec. 24.*

Thai

$$ **Thai Toni.** Thai silks, bronze Buddhas, dramatic ceiling drapes, private
dining alcoves, and two raised platforms for those who want to dine
seated on cushions set this exceptional restaurant apart from every-
thing trendy in the neighborhood. The mellow Thai Singha beer com-
plements the spicy jumping squid appetizer with chili paste and hot
pepper or the hot hot pork. Choose from a large variety of inexpen-
sive noodle, fried-rice, and vegetarian dishes or such traditional entrées
as beef and broccoli, basil duck, or hot-and-spicy deep-fried whole snap-
per with basil leaves and mixed vegetables. Desserts are routine, but
the homemade lemonade is distinctly tart. ✕ *890 Washington Ave.,*
☎ *305/538–8424. AE, MC, V. Closed Thanksgiving, Dec. 25. No lunch.*

Vietnamese

$ **Hy-Vong Vietnamese Cuisine.** Beer-savvy Kathy Manning has introduced
★ a half-dozen top brews since taking over in 1989 (Double Grimber-
gen, Moretti, and Spaten, among them), and magic continues to pour
forth from the tiny kitchen of this plain little restaurant. Come before
7 to avoid a wait. Favorites include spring rolls (a Vietnamese version
of an egg roll, with ground pork, cellophane noodles, and black mush-
rooms wrapped in homemade rice paper), whole fish panfried with *nuoc
man* (a garlic-lime fish sauce), and thinly sliced pork, barbecued with
sesame seeds and fish sauce, served with bean sprouts, rice noodles,
and slivers of carrots, almonds, and peanuts. ✕ *3458 S.W. 8th St.,*
*305/446–3674. No credit cards. No smoking. Closed Mon., Ameri-
can and Vietnamese/Chinese New Years, 2 wks in Aug. No lunch.*

LODGING

Few urban areas can match Greater Miami's diversity of accommoda-
tions. The area has hundreds of hotels and motels with lodgings in all
price categories, from $8 for a night in a dormitory-style hostel to $2,000
for a night in the luxurious presidential suite atop a posh downtown hotel.
As recently as the 1960s many hotels in Greater Miami opened only in
winter to accommodate Yankee snowbirds. Now all hotels stay open all
year. In summer they cater to European and Latin American vacation-
ers, who find Miami congenial despite the heat, humidity, and intense
afternoon thunderstorms.

Although some hotels (especially on the mainland) have adopted year-round rates, many still adjust their rates to reflect the ebb and flow of seasonal demand. The peak occurs in winter, with a dip in summer (prices are often more negotiable than rate cards let on), when families with school-age children take vacation. You'll find the best values between Easter and Memorial Day (a delightful time in Miami but a difficult time for many people to travel) and in September and October (the height of hurricane season).

Major conventions have left Miami Beach with complaints about service, housekeeping, and, frequently, staff who, at least to complainants, seem to be speaking foreign languages all the time, leaving guests feeling alien. Individual travelers may not encounter the same service problems. In recent years, those who stayed in South Beach hotels had to learn to put up with small rooms and less-than-professional service, problems of where to park, and noise. South Beach is finally attracting professional operators, however, and a few new choices—some of Miami's best places to stay—have solved all but the parking problem.

Coconut Grove

$$$$ **Grand Bay Hotel.** Combining the classical and flawless elegance of
★ Greece, a stepped facade that feels vaguely Aztec, a hint of the South, and a brush of the tropical, this hotel is like no other in south Florida—distinctive in look and supremely restful. Detailed moldings and burnished finishes are highlights inside, where artwork and fresh flowers enhance the beautiful lobby symmetry. Guest rooms are filled with superb touches: a canister of sharpened pencils giving off the fresh aroma of shaved wood, an antique sideboard that holds house phones, and matched woods, variously inlaid and fluted. The piano in 814 is tuned when Pavarotti is in residence, but your needs will be met equally well. After all, standards are standards. Rooms at the northeast corner have the best views, looking out on downtown Miami. An afternoon tea is served. ☎ 2669 S. Bayshore Dr., 33133, ☎ 305/858–9600 or 800/327–2788, FAX 305/858–1532. 132 rooms, 49 suites. Restaurant, bar, lounge, pool, beauty salon, hot tub, massage, saunas, health club. AE, DC, MC, V.

$$$$ **Mayfair House.** This European-style luxury hotel sits within Mayfair Shops at the Grove, an exclusive open-air shopping mall. Public areas have Tiffany windows, polished mahogany, marble walls and floors, and imported ceramics and crystal. Also impressive is the glassed-in elevator that whisks you to the corridor on your floor; a balcony overlooks the mall's central fountains and walkways. All rooms are suites (22 for nonsmokers), with outdoor terraces facing the street, screened from view by vegetation and wood latticework. Each has a Japanese hot tub on the balcony or a Roman tub in the suite; otherwise, each room is individually furnished. The Sunset (Room 505) is one of 50 suites with antique pianos. Other luxury touches: All bathrooms have double sinks, makeup lights, and scales, and all closets are lighted. An added bonus is a rooftop recreation area. Revival of the Mayfair mall has also led to the reopening of the hotel's nightclub, Ensign Bitters. You'll want to ask to make sure you get a quiet suite. ☎ 3000 Florida Ave., 33133, ☎ 305/441–0000 or 800/433–4555, FAX 305/447–9173. 182 suites. Snack bar, pool, sauna. AE, D, DC, MC, V.

Coral Gables

$$$$ **Biltmore Hotel.** This is Miami's grand boom-time hotel, one of a hand-
★ ful in Florida that recapture an era of uncompromising elegance. Now part of the Westin chain, the Biltmore was built in 1926 as the centerpiece of George Merrick's "city beautiful," and it rises like a sienna-color wedding cake in the heart of the Coral Gables residential district.

A championship golf course, tennis courts, and waterway surround the hotel. The lobby is spectacularly vaulted with hand-painted rafters on a background sky of twinkling blue; travertine marble, Oriental rugs, and palms in blue porcelain pots set the tone that continues through the fountain patio and opulent ballrooms. Guest rooms are twice as large as they were when the hotel was built but may still appear small by today's grand hotel standards. They were completely modernized in a restrained Moorish style during a $55 million overhaul in 1986, when the hotel reopened after decades of neglect. A second, $5 million renovation, after its acquisition by Westin in 1992, brought a fitness center and spa with three workout areas in a 15,000-square-foot facility. Historical tours of the property take place Sunday at 1:30, 2:30, and 3:30. ☎ *1200 Anastasia Ave., 33134,* ☎ *305/445–1926 or 800/445–2586,* FAX *305/442–9496. 237 rooms, 38 suites. Restaurant, coffee shop, lounge, pool, sauna, spa, 18-hole golf course, 10 lighted tennis courts. AE, DC, MC, V.*

$$$$ **Hyatt Regency Coral Gables.** In keeping with historic Gables style, the
★ exterior of this Hyatt makes an overt Spanish statement, courtesy of tile roofs, white-frame casement windows, and pink stucco. Spanish influences in the interiors, newly redone, are more subliminal: traces in the headboard design, a stair-stepped outline at guest information, the styling of antique furniture, and the fall browns and blonds that evoke peninsular Spain. The staff is savvy and helpful, as befits a business-oriented hotel. Yet the mood remains comfortable and residential. The large meeting facilities are all to the side, so vacationers don't feel they've stumbled into the corporate world they're trying to get away from. There are no bad views, but the best look onto the pool. ☎ *50 Alhambra Plaza, 33134,* ☎ *305/441–1234,* FAX *305/443–7702. 192 rooms, 50 suites. Restaurant, lounge, pool, sauna, steam rooms, health club. AE, D, DC, MC, V.*

$$$$ **Omni Colonnade Hotel.** The twin 13-story towers of this $65 million
★ hotel, office, and shopping complex dominate the heart of Coral Gables. Architectural details echo the adjoining two-story Corinthian-style rotunda on Miracle Mile, from which 1920s developer George Merrick sold lots in his fledgling city. Merrick's family provided old photos, paintings, and other heirlooms that are on display throughout the hotel. The oversize rooms come in 26 floor plans, each with a sitting area, built-in armoires, and traditional furnishings of mahogany. The hospitality bars feature marble counters and gold-plated faucets with 1920s-style ceramic handles. The pool on a 10th-floor terrace looks south toward Biscayne Bay. Ask for a room with a private balcony. Rooms for nonsmokers and people with disabilities and 24-hour room service are available. ☎ *180 Aragon Ave., 33134,* ☎ *305/441–2600 or 800/533–1337,* FAX *305/445–3929. 157 rooms, 17 bilevel suites. 2 restaurants, pool, 2 saunas, exercise room. AE, DC, MC, V.*

$$$ **David William Hotel.** Easily the most affordable of the top Gables hotels, the DW (as aficionados call it) was the first high-rise of Miami's modern era, standing 13 stories tall with a distinctive waffled facade. That dates it from the 1960s, but the DW has been kept in top shape. The hotel is solidly built, like a fort, so the rooms are very private and very quiet. Guest rooms are large, with marble baths; all those facing south (the sunnier exposure) have balconies. Many rooms have kitchens, and some are no-smoking. The decor features new furniture trimmed with braids of varicolored wood, upholstered in tan and blue. The lobby is a bit tacky, with tables outside the elegant Chez Vendôme, a popular traditional French restaurant. The excellent desk staff is more concerned with helping guests than with maintaining airs. Rooftop cabana guest rooms are the best bargains. ☎ *700 Biltmore Way, 33134,*

☎ *305/445–7821 or 800/327–8770 outside FL,* FAX *305/445–5585. 70 rooms, 54 suites. Restaurant, bar, pool. AE, DC, MC, V.*

$$$
★

Hotel Place St. Michel. Art nouveau chandeliers suspended from vaulted ceilings grace the public areas of this intimate jewel in the heart of downtown. The historic low-rise hotel, built in 1926 and restored from 1981 to 1986, is filled with the scent of fresh flowers, circulated by the paddle fans hanging from the ceilings. Each room has its own dimensions, personality, and imported antiques from England, Scotland, and France. A complimentary Continental breakfast is served. ⌖ *162 Alcazar Ave., 33134,* ☎ *305/444–1666 or 800/247–8526,* FAX *305/529-0074. 24 rooms, 3 suites. Restaurant, lounge. AE, DC, MC, V.*

Downtown Miami

$$$$
★

Hotel Inter-Continental Miami. Stand outside on the fifth-floor pool deck for the best view of downtown. You see only the clean upper stories of the city, nothing of the ragtag street—the view Miami likes best of itself, with its Disneyesque Metromover, the booming port, the beautiful bay. The marble grain in the lobby of this 34-story landmark matches that in *The Spindle,* a massive centerpiece sculpture by Henry Moore. With all that marble, the lobby could easily look like a mausoleum— and did before the addition of palm trees and oversize wicker chairs and tables. Atop a five-story atrium, a skylight lets in the afternoon sun. Guest rooms are traditional with a Latin flavor—in grays and beige and the darkest imaginable chintz. Bathrooms are travertine. The Inter-Con, as guests call it, is altogether the most manorial property in the city—as well as, it happens, the most committed to waste reduction and recycling. ⌖ *100 Chopin Plaza, 33131,* ☎ *305/577–1000 or 800/327–0200,* FAX *305/577–0384. 644 rooms, 34 suites. 3 restaurants, lounge, pool, spa, jogging. AE, DC, MC, V.*

$$$$

Hyatt Regency Miami. By 1996, a $9 million renovation will have brought this centrally located, 24-story convention hotel a new sophisticated style, adapting the deco of South Beach to the deeper, less frivolous character of an essentially business hotel. The blend of leisure and business should position the Hyatt well for the downtown renaissance likely to follow the opening of the new Miami Avenue Bridge later in 1996. Public spaces are to be more colorful than the more businesslike, but no less distinctive, guest rooms, done in unusual avocado, beige, and blond and yielding views of the river or port. The best are on upper floors. The James L. Knight International Center (*see* Tour 2 *in* Exploring, *above*) is accessible without stepping outside, as is the downtown Metromover, with its Metrorail connection, and there's a free shuttle to Coconut Grove. ⌖ *400 S.E. 2nd Ave., 33131,* ☎ *305/358–1234 or 800/233–1234,* FAX *305/358–0529. 615 rooms, 25 suites. 2 restaurants, lounge, pool. AE, D, DC, MC, V.*

$$

Miami River Inn. Preservationist Sallye Jude has restored these five 1904 clapboard buildings, the oldest continuously operating inn south of St. Augustine and the only concentration of houses in Miami remaining from that period. The inn is an oasis of country hospitality in a working-class neighborhood—one of Miami's safest even if it doesn't look that way—at the edge of downtown. The heart of the city is only a 10-minute walk across the 1st Street Bridge, and José Martí Park, one of the city's prettiest but lately a haven for the homeless, is only a few hundred feet from the inn gates. There are 40 antiques-filled rooms (some with tub only), a room with breakfast area, small meeting space, outdoor pool and patio, and an oval lawn. Guests receive a complimentary Continental breakfast and have use of a refrigerator. The best rooms look over and down the river from the second and third stories. Avoid the tiny rooms in Building D with a view of the stark condo to the west. As part of the same property—officially designated the Riverside Historic District—four modified-deco mid-century masonry buildings house long-term renters. ☎ *118 S.W. South River Dr., 33130,* ☎ *305/325–0045 or 800/468–3589,* FAX *305/325–9227. 40 rooms (2 with shared bath). Pool. AE, D, DC, MC, V.*

Key Biscayne

$$$$ **Sonesta Beach Hotel & Tennis Club.** This 1969 hotel is again the newest
★ in Miami, its eight stories entirely rebuilt since Hurricane Andrew. The Sonesta was always one of Miami's best and now is more tropical than ever, with reef pastels and stunning views of the sea, at least from those rooms facing east. Two villas are actually three-bedroom homes with full kitchen and screened pool. Don't miss the displays of museum-quality modern art by prominent painters and sculptors, especially Andy Warhol's drawings of rock star Mick Jagger in the hotel's disco bar, Desires. The 750-foot beach, one of Florida's best, has a big variety of recreational facilities. ☎ *350 Ocean Dr., 33149,* ☎ *305/361–2021 or 800/766–3782,* FAX *305/365–2096. 284 rooms, 14 suites, 2 villas. 3 restaurants, bar, snack bar, pool, massage, steam rooms, 9 tennis courts (3 lighted), aerobics, health club, beach, windsurfing, children's program. AE, DC, MC, V.*

Miami Beach

$$$$ **Alexander Hotel.** Located amid the high-rises of the mid-Beach district,
★ this 16-story hotel represents the elegance for which the Beach was once famous. It has immense suites furnished with antiques and reproductions, each with a terrace affording ocean or bay views, each with a living and dining room. Everything is understated, from the marquetry-paneled and landscaped lobby to the oceanfront dining rooms. Service is of the highest standard and includes twice-daily maid service. ☎ *5225 Collins Ave., 33140,* ☎ *305/865–6500 or 800/327–6121,* FAX *305/864–8525. 158 1- and 2-bedroom suites with 2 baths and kitchen. Restaurant, coffee shop, 2 pools, spa, beach, boating. AE, D, DC, MC, V.*

$$$$ **Casa Grande.** This was the first of the new top-flight hotels in South
★ Beach, and it's still the best. Luxurious suites capture the fashionable air of the street out front, yet in classical, fine taste. The lobby has been designed with a baffle that smartly sets it apart from the hyperactive street. Teak, tile, and recessed lighting create a warm, burnished look, welcoming and relaxing. There's nothing showy here, just liberal gifts of space. Corridors are handsome and wide; suites of museumlike quality are done in teak and mahogany, with dhurrie rugs and beautiful Indonesian fabrics and artifacts, two-poster beds with ziggurat turns, full electric kitchens equipped with fine European utensils, and large baths—absolutely unheard of in the Deco District—clad in green decorator tiles. There are lots of goodies, too, from a daily newspaper at your door and in-room coffee service to fresh flowers, complete TV/VCR/CD/radio entertainment stations, and evening turndown with Italian chocolates. You will have to book well in advance for peak periods, but it's worth it. One can even imagine scalpers outside dealing rooms in the busy season. ☎ *834 Ocean Dr., 33139,* ☎ *305/672–7003 or 800/688–7678,* FAX *305/673–3669. 32 suites. Café, laundry service and dry cleaning, concierge. AE, DC, MC, V.*

$$$$ **Doral Ocean Beach Resort.** Of the great Miami Beach hotels, this 18-
★ story glass tower that opened in 1962 remains a standout. It boasts the only rooftop restaurant in town (Alfredo, the Original of Rome), the only rooftop ballroom (with 8,000 twinkling ceiling lights), two presidential suites designed in consultation with the Secret Service, an FAA-licensed helipad, and the kind of service that's kept the Beach going through the

years. (Waitresses call guests in the coffee shop "honey" and declare anybody who comes in twice "my favorite customer.") Some of the staff have worked here for 20 or 30 years, and the hotel remembers hospitality as it was before voice mail. The Doral has all the amenities—from aqua sports when you want the sun, to lobby-level shops when you want to be out of it—as well as meeting space, workout space, and disco space. Guest rooms are done in warm colors reminiscent of Italy: blues and tans reflecting sea and beach, mauve, and palest peach. Adding to rooms' completeness are good nonobjective art and lots of details: a small fridge; three sets of drapes, including blackout curtains; big closets; and in the bath, high-quality toiletries, two lavatories, a magnifying mirror, and a sliding door between toilet and shower-bath. Free transportation to Doral Golf Resort and Spa (*see below*) is provided. ☎ *4833 Collins Ave., 33140,* ☎ *305/532–3600 or 800/223–6725,* FAX *305/534–7409. 293 rooms, 127 suites. 3 restaurants, 4 lounges, pool, 2 lighted tennis courts, exercise room, beach, helipad. AE, DC, MC, V.*

$$$$ **Fontainebleau Hilton Resort and Towers.** This is the Grand Central of Miami area hotels—the busiest, the biggest, and the showiest. Its convention facilities rank second only to the city's own mammoth space. The place is constantly being renovated; most recently, a $4.7 million makeover of the 126 tower units has produced a very upscale look and the feel of a luxe hotel within a hotel. Tower rooms are now country in spirit, light and flowery, yet come with traditional amenities and the added security of special elevator keys. The Continental breakfast is more like a banquet, and the smashing view extends halfway to the Azores. Decor in the other wings varies: You can request a '50s look or one that's contemporary. Even the smallest rooms are large. ☎ *4441 Collins Ave., 33140,* ☎ *305/538–2000 or 800/548–8886,* FAX *305/531–9274. 1,146 rooms, 60 suites. 12 restaurants, 4 lounges, 2 pools, saunas, 7 lighted tennis courts, health club, volleyball, beach, windsurfing, boating, parasailing, children's programs. AE, DC, MC, V.*

$$$$ **Hotel Impala.** It seems there's nothing more routine on South Beach than
★ a crack house transformed into a sybarite's playpen. The difference here, at the former La Flora, built in the '30s, is that the style is tropical Georgian, rather than deco. Iron, mahogany, and stone on the inside are in sync with the sporty white-trimmed ocher exterior. Rooms, though small, come across as complete and elegantly comfortable. It's all very European—from mineral water and orchids to Mediterranean-style armoires, wrought-iron furniture, Italian fixtures, tab draperies hung from heavy ornamental rods, and Spanish surrealist art above the white-on-white, triple-sheeted, modified Eastlake sleigh beds. (Not surprisingly, a Continental breakfast is included.) Wastebaskets in the unusually large baths are galvanized fire buckets, and everything from towels to toilet paper is of exceptional quality. ☎ *1228 Collins Ave., 33139,* ☎ *305/673–2021 or 800/646–7252,* FAX *305/673–5984. 17 rooms, 3 suites. Restaurant, lounge. AE, DC, MC, V.*

$$$$ **La Voile Rouge.** So thoroughly does the Red Sail (as the name trans-
★ lates) immerse you in Continental style and service, you might imagine yourself transported to your favorite French watering place (complete with the highest prices on the Beach). The boutique-size hotel is blessed with the only beachfront setting among the luxury properties of South Beach, and with astonishing facilities considering its few rooms. (The property survives financially on memberships in the resort club, which, not surprisingly, makes for a busy, clubby, party atmosphere.) Tropical gardens, two pools, outdoor bars, and decks are secluded behind high iron gates. Inside, the Piano Bar, the Cozy Bar, and Mimosa Dining Room glow with crystal-reflected mahogany beneath coffered ceilings and walls hung with exquisite reproductions of the past century's

masterpieces. The oversize suites, some with private terrace and Jacuzzi, all have king-size beds and immense baths. Each comes with hand-painted vases, floral arrangements, robes and slippers for padding about hard-wood floors, Evian water, and a theme—Art Deco, Marbella, Proven-cale, Santa Fe. Morocco, for example, lays out beneath a blue sky with gold stars and moon. Its bed linens are silk, bedside lamps Arabic, and art Moorish. A separate bath compartment contains toilet and bidet. Continental breakfast is included in the rate. ⊞ *455 Ocean Dr., 33139,* ☎ *305/535–0099 or 800/528–6453,* ℻ *305/532–4442. 8 suites. Restaurant, bars, 2 pools, beach. AE, DC, MC, V.*

$$$$ **Marlin Hotel.** If it isn't the Casa Grande, it's the Marlin—the best in
★   the Deco District, that is. However, they're utterly different. The Mar-lin is so Jamaican that it could be Jamaica's cultural showcase. It's deco danced to the intense rhythms of Saturday night reggae. Just off the lobby is the "cookshack" Shabeen, the brilliant bar/café version of a north coast beach shack exploding in color. Suites were put together of rooms from the hotel's previous 1930s incarnation. Jamaican art complements striking hand-painted furniture, woven grass rugs, batik-like shades, and rattan and mahogany furniture. Every room is different, some with pungent accents of ocher and plum, some with pale sky blue, but all complete in their detailing. Even the studio suites, with rattan sitting areas, are sizeable; larger suites hint at villas. There are only 11 in all, so you might want to come back 10 times. ⊞ *1200 Collins Ave., 33139,* ☎ *305/673–8770,* ℻ *305/673–9609. 11 suites (studio to 2-bedroom). Bar-café. AE, D, DC, MC, V.*

$$$$ **Pelican.** Dazzling, brilliant spaces that combine acid humor with Deco-inspired frivolity have turned still one more tired Ocean Drive home for the elderly into pop-eyed digs for the hip. Rooms, with names like Leafforest, Best Whorehouse, People from the 50s, and Cubarrean, are all different. What they have in common are small Deco dimensions in the sleeping chambers with bathrooms tripled in size and outfitted with outrageously industrial piping. You'll be too busy checking out the details to sleep. Best Whorehouse, for example, envelops you in thoroughly red flocked wallcoverings flecked with gold, and gilt, black silk, and silver are everywhere. Ornaments are bordello extravagant: a heart-shape red velvet chair, hideously aqua night tables, whorish art, and griffins with voluptuous mammaries. (You can imagine a former but now displaced elderly tenant muttering only a plaintive "Oy!") Each room comes with its own cylindrical entertainment center. The ground floor of this four-story hotel has its own restaurant and sidewalk café. You'd almost think it was normal up above, as opposed to paranor-mal. Hey, it's the Beach! ⊞ *826 Ocean Dr., 33139,* ☎ *305/673–3373 or 800/773–5422,* ℻ *305/673–3255. 25 units, penthouse. Restau-rant, bar, concierge. AE, MC, V.*

$$$–$$$$ **Park Central.** Across the street from the glorious beach, this seven-story Deco hotel—painted blue, with wraparound corner windows—makes all the right moves to stay in the forefront of the Art Deco revival. Most of the fashion models visiting town come to this property, which dates from 1937. Black-and-white photos of old beach scenes, hurricanes, and familiar faces attest to its longevity. Stylishly, rooms are decorated with Philippine mahogany furnishings—originals that have been re-stored. Newly incorporated in the property, the Imperial Hotel next door has an additional 36 rooms. The Barocco Beach restaurant of three years ago, which became Le Zebre, has now become Burt Reynolds's Backstage, assuming that if you can't count on trendy Ital-ian or French-Continental, you ought to be able to count on Ameri-can. ⊞ *640 Ocean Dr., 33139,* ☎ *305/538–1611 or 800/727–5236,*

FAX *305/534–7520. 121 rooms. Restaurant, bar, espresso bar, pool, exercise room. AE, DC, MC, V.*

$$$ **Essex House.** This was one of the premier lodgings of the Art Deco era, now painted in cool pastel gray with sulphur-yellow trim. They got it right from the start: designed by architect Henry Hohauser, Everglades mural by Earl LaPan. Here are the ziggurat arches, the hieroglyph-style ironwork, etched-glass panels of flamingos under the palms, 5-foot rose-medallion Chinese urns. Hallways have recessed showcases with original Deco sculptures. The 66 rooms from 1938 are now 60, including petite and grand suites. Amenities include designer linens and towels, feather-and-down pillows and sofa rolls, and individually controlled air-conditioning and central heat plus ceiling fans. The rooms are sound-proofed from within (otherwise unheard of in beach properties of the '30s), and rooms to the east have extra-thick windows to reduce the band noise from a nearby hotel. The smallest rooms are yellow-themed and face north. Continental breakfast is free. ⌧ *1001 Collins Ave., 33139,* ☎ *305/534–2700 or 800/553–7739,* FAX *305/532–3827. 51 rooms, 9 suites. Breakfast room. AE, DC, MC, V.*

$$–$$$ **Bay Harbor Inn.** Here you'll find down-home hospitality in the most affluent zip code in the county. Retired Washington lawyer Sandy Lankler operates this 38-unit lodging in two sections, two moods. Townside is the oldest building in Bay Harbor Islands, vaguely Georgian in style but dating from 1940. Behind triple sets of French doors under fan windows, the lobby is full of oak desks, hand mills, grandfather clocks, historical maps, and potted plants. Rooms are antique-filled, and no two are alike. Along Indian Creek the inn incorporates the former Albert Pick Hotella, a shipshape tropical-style set of rooms on two floors, off loggias surrounded by palms, with all rooms facing the water. The decor here is mid-century modern, with chintz. A complimentary Continental breakfast and the *Miami Herald* are provided. The popular Miami Palm restaurant is located townside and B.C. Chong's Seafood Garden creekside, with the London Bar serving the best ½-pound hamburger in the city. ⌧ *9660 E. Bay Harbor Dr., Bay Harbor Islands 33154,* ☎ *and* FAX *305/868–4141. 25 rooms, 12 suites, penthouse. 2 restaurants, lounge, pool. AE, DC, MC, V.*

$$–$$$ **Dorchester Hotel.** It's wonderful that such good-value, untrendy places
★ remain in the Deco District. Here you'll find an older Miami Beach, from the pre-Disney era when all you had to do was offer good lodgings and service, even if not directly on the beach, and the family trade was yours. This hotel maintains those standards at affordable rates any time of year. Moreover, it's set back from the avenue for peace and quiet. Also appealing are a big pool in a tropical garden, a large lobby, and a dining room for inexpensive breakfasts. Guest rooms are spacious, carpeted, outfitted with a fridge, and furnished with rattan and floral bedcovers—all the usuals of traditional hotel rooms, here done in pink and green. The best buys are rooms with a kitchenette, only $5 more per night. ⌧ *1850 Collins Ave., 33139,* ☎ *305/534–6971, 305/531–5745, or 800/327–4739,* FAX *305/673–1006. 94 rooms, 6 suites. Breakfast room, grills, pool, Ping-Pong, billiards, free parking. AE, DC, MC, V.*

$$ **Mermaid Guest House.** Shazam! Lightning in the form of a long-haired former investment banker transformed a Collins Avenue fleabag into this delightful guest house that goes by the name Mermaid. Part Caribbean hideaway, part Bohemian youth hostel, the place oozes the same kind of exuberance that early on sparked the birth of the Deco District. Everything is framed in color: a back-of-the-house patio set in a jungle waiting to burst loose and retake Miami Beach; dresser drawers, each painted

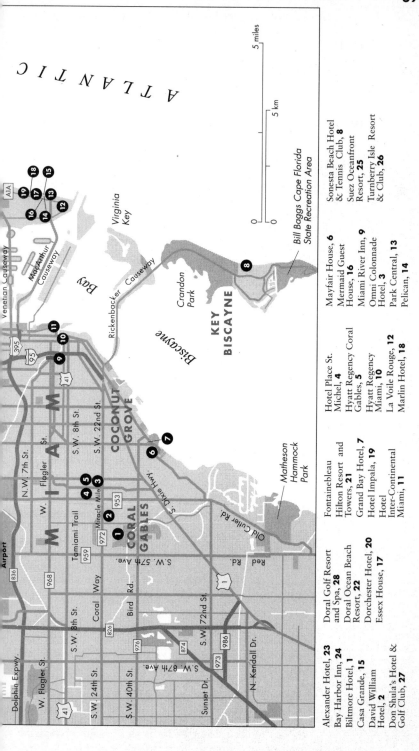

ATLANTIC

Bill Baggs Cape Florida
State Recreation Area

Virginia
Key

Crandon
Park

Rickenbacker Causeway

Biscayne
Bay

KEY
BISCAYNE

Matheson
Hammock
Park

MacArthur Causeway
Venetian Causeway

MIAMI
CORAL GABLES
COCONUT GROVE

5 miles
5 km

Sonesta Beach Hotel
& Tennis Club, **8**
Suez Oceanfront
Resort, **25**
Turnberry Isle Resort
& Club, **26**

Mayfair House, **6**
Mermaid Guest
House, **16**
Miami River Inn, **9**
Omni Colonnade
Hotel, **3**
Park Central, **13**
Pelican, **14**

Hotel Place St.
Michel, **4**
Hyatt Regency Coral
Gables, **5**
Hyatt Regency
Miami, **10**
La Voile Rouge, **12**
Marlin Hotel, **18**

Fontainebleau
Hilton Resort and
Towers, **21**
Grand Bay Hotel, **7**
Hotel Impala, **19**
Hotel
Inter-Continental
Miami, **11**

Doral Golf Resort
and Spa, **28**
Doral Ocean Beach
Resort, **22**
Dorchester Hotel, **20**
Essex House, **17**

Alexander Hotel, **23**
Bay Harbor Inn, **24**
Biltmore Hotel, **1**
Casa Grande, **15**
David William
Hotel, **2**
Don Shula's Hotel &
Golf Club, **27**

a different, vivid color; and louvered shutters outlined in bold graphics that bring the outdoor garden in. Beds are shrouded in mosquito netting, though rooms have air-conditioning (but not phones or TV), and small deco baths have tub-showers. There's a shared kitchen outside and a pay phone in the garden. A Continental breakfast is included, and frequent BYOB guest cookouts add to the family-style climate. A youthful and young-at-heart clientele adores this place. ⊠ *909 Collins Ave., 33139,* ☎ *305/538–5324. 10 units. MC, V.*

\$\$ **Suez Oceanfront Resort.** They call this Miami Beach, and though it is on the beach, it's several miles north of the municipality of Miami Beach, in the section called Sunny Isles—more popularly referred to as Motel Row. This is affordable Miami Beach, chockablock with fancy motels but few of distinction. The carousel-stripe Suez, however, stands out; generous with space, it has been family run since the 1960s. Get past the tacky sphinx icons, walk upstairs in the main building, and you're in a quiet, gardenlike rattan-and-palm lounge. A landscaped palm courtyard leads to the beach, where you find a popular bar and beachside restaurant, two pools, a tennis court, and playground. Rooms are done with matched chinois furniture and dazzling color that counteracts the generally small spaces. The 46 rooms in the north wing are the smallest and the least expensive; they have views of the parking lot. Modified American Plan dining, fridges in all the rooms and kitchens in some, and special kids' rates make this an especially good value. Free laundry service is a bonus. ⊠ *18215 Collins Ave., 33160,* ☎ *305/932–0661 or 800/327–5278; in FL, 800/432–3661;* FAX *305/937–0058. 196 rooms. Restaurant, bar, freshwater and saltwater pools, wading pool, lighted tennis court, shuffleboard, volleyball, beach, playground, laundry service. AE, D, DC, MC, V.*

North Dade

\$\$\$\$ **Turnberry Isle Resort & Club.** Finest of the Miami-area grand resorts, ★   Turnberry sits on 300 superbly landscaped acres by the bay, and it's recently been done over with an \$80 million three-wing Mediterranean-style annex. Guests can also choose from the intimate Marina Hotel, the Yacht Club on the Intracoastal Waterway, or the Mizner-style Country Club Hotel, beside one of the two Robert Trent Jones–designed golf courses. Interiors of the oversize rooms feature light woods and earth tones, large curving terraces, Jacuzzis, honor bar, and in-room safes. The marina has moorings for 117 boats up to 150 feet, and there's free shuttle service from the hotel to the beach club and the Aventura Mall. ⊠ *19999 W. Country Club Dr., Aventura 33180,* ☎ *305/932–6200 or 800/327–7028,* FAX *305/933–6560. 300 rooms, 40 suites. 6 restaurants, 5 lounges, 4 pools, saunas, spa, steam rooms, 2 18-hole golf courses, 24 tennis courts (18 lighted), health club, jogging, racquetball, beach, dive shop, windsurfing, boating, helipad. AE, DC, MC, V.*

West Dade

\$\$\$\$ **Don Shula's Hotel & Golf Club.** This low-rise suburban resort is part of a planned town developed by Florida senator Bob Graham's family about 14 miles northwest of downtown Miami. The golf resort opened in 1962 and added two wings in 1978; facilities include a championship course, a lighted executive course, and a golf school. Its decor is English-traditional throughout, rich in leather and wood. All rooms have balconies. The hotel opened in 1983 with a typically Florida-tropics look—light pastels and furniture of wicker and light wood. In both locations the best rooms are near the lobby for convenient access; the worst are near the elevators. ⊠ *6840 Main St., Miami Lakes 33014,* ☎ *305/821–1150 or 800/247–4852,* FAX *305/879–8298. 269 rooms, 32 suites. 3 restaurants, 2 lounges, 2 pools, saunas, steam rooms, 2*

18-hole golf courses, 9 lighted tennis courts, aerobics, basketball, health club, racquetball, volleyball. AE, D, DC, MC, V.

$$$$ **Doral Golf Resort and Spa.** Millions of airline passengers annually peer down upon this 2,400-acre jewel of an inland golf-and-tennis resort while fastening their seat belts. It's 4 miles west of Miami International Airport and consists of eight separate three- and four-story lodges nestled beside the golf links (four championship and three executive courses). The entire resort has been undergoing a $17 million renovation since 1994, with half the rooms expected to be redone by 1996. Given the resort's division into separate lodges, guests are in no way inconvenienced by the rebuilding, which takes on a lodge at a time. Restaurants have been redesigned, adding Champions Bar & Grill, across from the pro shop, and Terraza, an informal Italian trattoria, as well as a lobby bar. The Provare Restaurant has become the more elegant Windows, specializing in seafood, with views of four golf courses. Outdoors, the famed Blue Monster course has been redesigned, as will the remaining courses by 1997. The resort is site of the annual Doral-Ryder Open Tournament, one of the most popular on the PGA tour. Transportation to the beach is provided. ☎ 4400 N.W. 87th Ave., Doral 33178-2192, ☎ 305/592–2000 or 800/223–6725, FAX 305/594–4682. 592 rooms, 102 suites. 4 restaurants, 3 lounges, pool, spa, 7 golf courses, 15 tennis courts (4 lighted), health club, jogging, fishing, bicycles, pro shop. AE, DC, MC, V.

THE ARTS AND NIGHTLIFE

For information on what's happening around town, Greater Miami's English-language daily newspaper, the *Miami Herald*, publishes reliable reviews and comprehensive listings in its Weekend section on Friday and in the Lively Arts section on Sunday. Call ahead to confirm details.

If you read Spanish, check *El Nuevo Herald* (a Spanish version of the *Miami Herald*) or *Diario Las Américas* (the area's largest independent Spanish-language paper) for information on the Spanish theater and a smattering of general performing-arts news.

Another good source of information on the performing arts and nightspots is the calendar in *Miami Today,* a free weekly newspaper available each Thursday in downtown Miami, Coconut Grove, and Coral Gables. The best, most complete source is the *New Times,* a free weekly distributed throughout Dade County each Wednesday. Various tabloids reporting on Deco District entertainment and society come and go on Miami Beach. *Wire* reports on the gay community; *Ocean Drive* out-glosses everything else.

The free *Greater Miami Calendar of Events* is published twice a year by the Dade County Cultural Affairs Council (111 N.W. 1st St., Suite 625, Miami 33128, ☎ 305/375–4634).

Guide to the Arts/South Florida is a pocket-size publication produced 10 times a year ($2 per issue, $15 per year) that covers all the cultural arts in Dade, Broward, and Palm Beach counties and is available from Kage Publications (3800 S. Ocean Dr., Hollywood 33019, ☎ 305/456–9599).

Real Talk/WTMI (93.1 FM) provides classical concert information on its **Cultural Arts Line** (☎ 305/358–8000, ext. 9398), as well as on-air reports three times daily at 7:30 AM and 12:50 and 6:30 PM. WLVE (93.9 FM) sponsors an **Entertainment Line** (☎ 305/654–9436) with information on touring groups of all kinds except classical. **Blues Hot Line**

(☎ 305/666–6656) lists local blues clubs and bars. **Jazz Hot Line** (☎ 305/382–3938) lists local jazz programs.

The Arts

Performing-arts aficionados in Greater Miami will tell you they survive quite nicely, despite the area's historic inability to support a county-based professional symphony orchestra. In recent years this community has begun to write a new chapter in its performing-arts history.

The New World Symphony, a unique advanced-training orchestra, begins its ninth season in 1996. The Miami City Ballet has risen rapidly to international prominence in its 10-year existence. The Florida Grand Opera ranks among America's largest and best, and a venerable chamber-music series brings renowned ensembles here to perform. Several churches and synagogues run classical-music series with international performers. In theater, Miami offers English-speaking audiences an assortment of professional, collegiate, and amateur productions of musicals, comedy, and drama. Spanish theater also is active. In the cinema world, the Miami Film Festival attracts more than 45,000 people annually to screenings of new films from all over the world—including some made here.

To order tickets for performing-arts events by telephone, call **Ticketmaster** (Dade County, ☎ 305/358–5885; Broward County, ☎ 305/523–3309; Palm Beach, ☎ 407/839–3900) and charge tickets to a major credit card.

Performing-Arts Centers

Colony Theater (1040 Lincoln Rd., Miami Beach 33139, ☎ 305/674–1026), once a movie theater, has become a 465-seat, city-owned performing-arts center featuring dance, drama, music, and experimental cinema.

Dade County Auditorium (2901 W. Flagler St., Miami 33135, ☎ 305/545–3395) satisfies patrons with 2,498 comfortable seats, good sight lines, and acceptable acoustics. Opera, concerts, and touring musicals are usually on the schedule.

Gusman Center for the Performing Arts (174 E. Flagler St., Miami 33131, ☎ 305/372–0925), in downtown Miami, has 1,739 seats seemingly made for sardines—and the best acoustics in town. Concerts, ballet, and touring stage productions are seen here. An ornate former movie palace, the hall resembles a Moorish courtyard. Lights twinkle, starlike, from the ceiling.

Jackie Gleason Theater of the Performing Arts (TOPA) (1700 Washington Ave., Miami Beach 33139, ☎ 305/673–7300) has finally brought its acoustics and visibility up to par for all 2,750 seats. The Broadway Series each year presents five or six major productions (or other performances); contact the box office (505 17th St., Miami Beach 33139, ☎ 305/673–8300).

Theater

Acapai (6161 N.W. 22nd Ave., Miami 33142, ☎ 305/758–3534), whose name stands for African Caribbean American Performing Artists, Inc., mounts productions year-round at various area stages.

Acme Acting Company (955 Alton Rd., Miami Beach 33139, ☎ 305/372–9077) presents thought-provoking, on-the-edge theater by new playwrights in its winter and summer seasons.

Actor's Playhouse (280 Miracle Mile, Coral Gables 33134, ☎ 305/444–9293) is a nine-year-old professional Equity company. Late in 1995, it moved into the renovated Miracle Theater but still presents adults' and children's productions year-round.

Area Stage (645 Lincoln Rd., Miami Beach 33139, ☎ 305/673–8002) performs provocative off-Broadway-style productions throughout the year.

Coconut Grove Playhouse (3500 Main Hwy., Coconut Grove 33133, ☎ 305/442–4000 for box office or 305/442–2662 for administrative office) stages Broadway-bound plays and musical reviews and experimental productions in its 1,100-seat main theater and 100-seat cabaret-style Encore Room. Parking is $2 in the day, $4 evenings.

The **Florida Shakespeare Festival** (2304 Salzedo Ave., Coral Gables 33134, ☎ 305/446–1116) performs classic and contemporary theater with one Shakespeare production a year at the 200-seat Carrusel Theater (235 Alcazar Ave., Coral Gables).

Gold Coast Mime Company (905 Lincoln Rd., Miami Beach 33139, ☎ 305/538–5500) performs an October–June season in the studios of the Miami City Ballet.

New Theatre (65 Almeria St., Coral Gables 33134, ☎ 305/443–5909) showcases contemporary and classical plays.

Ring Theater (1380 Miller Dr., Coral Gables 33146, ☎ 305/284–3355) is the 311-seat hall of the University of Miami's Department of Theatre Arts, where eight plays a year are performed.

SPANISH THEATER

Spanish theater prospers, although many companies have short lives. About 20 Spanish companies perform light comedy, puppetry, vaudeville, and political satire. To locate them, read the Spanish newspapers. When you call, be prepared for a conversation in Spanish—few box-office personnel speak English.

Prometeo (Miami-Dade Community College, New World Center Campus, 300 N.E. 2nd Ave., Miami 33132, ☎ 305/237–3263), in its 23rd year, produces two major plays and holds many workshop productions. Admission is free.

Teatro de Bellas Artes (2173 S.W. 8th St., Miami 33135, ☎ 305/325–0515), a 255-seat theater on Calle Ocho, Little Havana's main commercial street, presents eight Spanish plays and musicals year-round.

Music

Concert Association of Florida (555 Hank Meyer Blvd. [17th St.], Miami Beach 33139, ☎ 305/532–3491), a not-for-profit organization directed by Judith Drucker, is the South's largest presenter of classical artists.

Friends of Chamber Music (44 W. Flagler St., Miami 33130, ☎ 305/372–2975) presents an annual series of chamber concerts by internationally known guest ensembles, such as the Beaux Arts Trio, the Tokyo Quartet, and the Juilliard String Quartet.

Gusman Concert Hall (1314 Miller Dr., Coral Gables 33146, ☎ 305/284–2438), a 600-seat concert hall on the University of Miami's Coral Gables campus, has good acoustics and plenty of room. Parking is a problem when school is in session.

New World Symphony (541 Lincoln Rd., Miami Beach 33139, ☎ 305/673–3331 for box office or 305/673–3330 for main office), conducted by Michael Tilson Thomas, performs October–May. Greater

Miami has no resident symphony orchestra, and this group helps fill the void. Musicians ages 22–30 who have finished their academic studies perform here before moving on to other orchestras.

Opera

Florida Grand Opera (1200 Coral Way, Miami 33145, ☎ 305/854–7890, box office open weekdays 10–4) is south Florida's leading opera company. It presents five operas each year in the Dade County Auditorium, featuring the Florida Philharmonic Orchestra (James Judd, artistic director). The annual series brings such luminaries as Placido Domingo and Luciano Pavarotti. (Pavarotti made his American debut with the company in 1965 in *Lucia di Lammermoor.*) All operas are sung in the original language, with subtitles in English projected onto a screen above the stage.

Dance

The **Miami City Ballet** (905 Lincoln Rd., Miami Beach 33139, ☎ 305/532–7713 or 305/532–4880) is Florida's first major, fully professional, resident ballet company. Edward Villella, the artistic director, was a principal dancer of the New York City Ballet under George Balanchine. Now the Miami City Ballet re-creates the Balanchine repertoire and introduces new works of its own during its September–March season. Performances are held at TOPA in Miami Beach; at the Broward Center for the Performing Arts; Bailey Concert Hall, also in Broward County; the Raymond F. Kravis Center for the Performing Arts; and at the Naples Philharmonic Center for the Arts. Demonstrations of works in progress take place at the 800-seat Lincoln Theater in Miami Beach. Villella narrates the children's and works-in-progress programs.

Film

The **Alliance Film/Video Project** (Sterling Building, Suite 119, 927 Lincoln Rd. Mall, Miami Beach 33139, ☎ 305/531–8504) presents cutting-edge cinema from around the world, with special midnight shows.

The **Miami Film Festival** (444 Brickell Ave., Suite 229, Miami 33131, ☎ 305/377–3456) screens new films from all over the world for 10 days every February, in the Gusman Center for the Performing Arts.

Nightlife

Greater Miami has found a new concentration of nightspots in South Beach along Ocean Drive, Washington Avenue, and most recently along Lincoln Road Mall. Other nightlife centers on Little Havana, Coconut Grove, and on the fringes of downtown Miami.

Individual clubs offer jazz, reggae, salsa, various forms of rock, and Top-40 sounds on different nights of the week. Some clubs refuse entrance to anyone under 21; others set the age limit at 25. On South Beach, where the sounds of jazz and reggae spill into the streets, fashion models and photographers frequent the lobby bars of small Art Deco hotels. Throughout the Greater Miami area, bars and cocktail lounges in larger hotels operate discos nightly, with live entertainment on weekends. Many hotels extend their bars into open-air courtyards, where patrons dine and dance under the stars throughout the year. It's a good idea to inquire in advance about cover charges. Policies change frequently.

Bars and Lounges

COCONUT GROVE

Hungry Sailor (3064½ Grand Ave., ☎ 305/444–9359), with two bars, serves up Jamaican-English food, British beer, and music Wednesday to Saturday. **Taurus Steak House** (3540 Main Hwy., ☎ 305/448–0633) is an unchanging oasis in the trendy Grove. The bar, built in 1922 of native cypress, draws an over-30 singles crowd nightly that drifts outside to a patio. A band plays Wednesday through Saturday.

CORAL GABLES

In a building that dates from 1926, **Stuart's Bar-Lounge** (162 Alcazar Ave., ☎ 305/444–1666) was named one of the best new bars of 1987 by *Esquire*; nine years later, locals still favor it. The style is fostered by beveled mirrors, mahogany paneling, French posters, pictures of old Coral Gables, and art nouveau lighting. It's closed Sunday.

KEY BISCAYNE

Sundays on the Bay (5420 Crandon Blvd., ☎ 305/361–6777) is a classic Miami over-the-water scene on Key Biscayne with an upscale menu. The clientele includes lots of Latins who love Miami the way it was. There's a disco nightly and live entertainment Friday–Sunday ($5–$10 cover).

MIAMI

Tobacco Road (626 S. Miami Ave., ☎ 305/374–1198), opened in 1912, holds Miami's oldest liquor license. Upstairs, in space occupied by a speakeasy during Prohibition, local and national blues bands perform nightly. There's excellent bar food and a dinner menu.

MIAMI BEACH

Bash (655 Washington Ave., ☎ 305/538–2274) has bars inside and out and dance floors with music—sometimes reggae, sometimes Latin, plenty of loud disco, and world-beat sounds in the garden, where there are artsy benches. Inside it's grottolike. Not quite SoBe, **Blue Steel** (2895 Collins Ave., ☎ 305/672–1227) is a cool but unpretentious hangout with pool tables, darts, live music, comfy old sofas, and beer paraphernalia. Open-mike night is Friday, and there's a jam on Monday. **Mac's Club Deuce** (222 14th St., ☎ 305/673–9537) is a South Beach gem where top international models pop in to have a drink and shoot some pool. All you get late at night are minipizzas, but the pizzazz lasts. Up in a nondescript motel row with nudie bars, baby stores, bait-and-tackle shops, and bikini warehouse stores, **Molly Malone's** (166 Sunny Isles Blvd., ☎ 305/948–9143) is the only cool, down-to-earth spot that thrives in this neighborhood. The Irish pub, a big local fave, has live Irish music Friday, acoustic sounds Saturday, and poetry readings Thursday. **Rose's Bar & Lounge** (754 Washington Ave., ☎ 305/532–0228) features the best in local bands from Hendrix-style rock and rap/funk to jazz jams and Afro-Cuban/world beat, with the occasional national act. Though it doesn't take credit cards, there is an ATM. It's open seven nights, but it's packed Wednesday through Saturday. **Shabeen Cookshack and Bar** (Marlin Hotel, 1200 Collins Ave., ☎ 305/673–8770) is Jamaican all the way—brilliant island decor and upbeat Caribbean music. **Union Bar** (653 Washington Ave., ☎ 305/672–9958), like Bash with bare concrete floors, features progressive/alternative music. It comes complete with pool table, informal dining area, strobe lighting, an unusual bubble fish tank in back-to-back rooms, and an immense dog sculpture.

Discos and Rock Clubs

COCONUT GROVE

Baja Beach Club (3015 Grand Ave., CocoWalk, ☎ 305/445–0278), the number-one party place in the Grove, has waiters and waitresses dressed in beach attire.

Stefano's of Key Biscayne (24 Crandon Blvd., ☎ 305/361–7007) is a
northern Italian restaurant cum disco; the music's live Tuesday–Sunday.

Amnesia (136 Collins Ave., ☎ 305/531–5535), open Thursday–Sunday, feels like a luxurious amphitheater in the tropics, complete with
rain forest, what used to be called go-go dancers, and frenzied dancing in the rain when showers pass over the open-air ground-level club.
The full-service Portobello restaurant, on an upper level, has picture
windows for taking in the scene without the decibels. **Bermuda Bar &
Grille** (3509 N.E. 163rd St., ☎ 305/945–0196) plays LOUD MUSIC
for disco dancing. Male bartenders wear knee-length kilts whereas the
female BTs dress in miniskirt kilts. The atmosphere and crowd, though,
are stylish island casual, and there's a big tropical forest scene, booths
you can hide in, and six bars and pool tables, too. One drawback is
there's no draft brew. It's closed Monday. **Glam Slam** (1235 Washington
Ave., ☎ 305/672–4858) is where Club Z, 1235, and Paragon all hit
the heights of fashion before falling out of favor. The artist formerly
known as Prince has dressed the place up with his motorcycle from
Purple Rain in the foyer, and there's a secret passage for his celeb pals.
Theme nights include Southern Fried Soul, Glamour Girls, Gay Night,
and Saturday's wild, packed Disco Party Time. It's open Wednesday
through Sunday. **Ruby's** (300 Alton Rd., Miami Beach Marina, ☎
305/673–3444), open Thursday–Sunday, was dreamed up for a more
mainstream, yuppie crowd, who may be less hip but still wants to be
seen. The ritzy disco is filled with overstuffed seating, wall-to-wall trop-
ical-print carpeting, and a fortune in A/V gear. It sits to the side of Nick's
Miami Beach Restaurant and attracts the same stylish dressers.

Jazz Club
MoJazz Cafe (928 71st St., ☎ 305/865–2636) arrived on the scene in
1993 with its easy neighborhood style, combining a local café with real
(nonfusion) jazz. It's in the Normandy Isle section—a long overlooked
neighborhood just right for hosting the occasional national name, like
Mose Allison, and the national attention–deserving local talents of Ira
Sullivan, Little Nicky, Joe Donato, and a stellar roster of Miami's
longtime jazz best. A nightly happy hour, food from the country
kitchen, and late-night breakfast are all on tap.

Nightclubs
Les Violins Supper Club (1751 Biscayne Blvd., ☎ 305/371–8668) is a reliable standby owned for 35 years by the Cachaidora-Currais family, who
ran a club and restaurant in Havana. There's a live dance band and a
wood dance floor. Reservations are advised; the cover charge is $15.

Club Tropigala at La Ronde (Fontainebleau Hilton, 4441 Collins Ave.,
☎ 305/672–7469)—lately discovered by such stars as Sylvester Stallone, Madonna, and Elton John—is a four-tier round room decorated
with orchids, banana leaves, philodendrons, cascading waterfalls, and
a dancing fountain, creating the effect of a tropical jungle. The band
plays standards as well as Latin music for dancing on the wood floor.
Reservations are advised.

MIAMI ESSENTIALS

Arriving and Departing

BY PLANE

Miami International Airport (MIA), 6 miles west of downtown Miami, is Greater Miami's only commercial airport. With a daily average of 1,450 flights, it handled 30.2 million passengers in 1994, 43% of them international travelers. (It's also the nation's busiest airport for air cargo.) Altogether 149 airlines serve 188 cities around the world with nonstop or one-stop service. MIA has 118 aircraft gates and eight concourses; the newest, Concourse A, opened in late spring of 1995.

Anticipating continued growth, the airport has begun an over $3 billion expansion program that will require much of the decade to complete. Passengers will mainly notice rebuilt and expanded gate and public areas, which should reduce congestion.

A greatly underused convenience for passengers who have to get from one concourse to another in this long, horseshoe-shape terminal is the cushioned Moving Walkway, on the skywalk level, with access points at every concourse. Also available on site is the 263-room **Miami International Airport Hotel** (Concourse E, upper level, ☎ 305/871–4100), which has the Top of the Port restaurant on the seventh floor and Port Lounge on the eighth. MIA, the first to offer duty-free shops, now boasts 14, carrying liquors, perfumes, electronics, and various designer goods.

When you fly out of MIA, plan to check in 55 minutes before departure for a domestic flight and 90 minutes before departure for an international flight. Services for international travelers include 24-hour multilingual information and paging phones and foreign-currency conversion booths throughout the terminal. There is an information booth with a multilingual staff and 24-hour currency exchange at the entrance of Concourse E on the upper level. Other tourist information centers are available at the customs exit, Concourse E, lower level, 5 AM–11 PM; customs exit, Concourse B, lower level, 11–7; Concourse G, lower level, 11–7; Concourse D, lower level, 11–11; and Satellite Terminal, 11–7.

Airlines that fly into MIA include **ACES** (☎ 305/265–1272), **Aero Costa Rica** (☎ 800/237–6274), **Aeroflot** (☎ 800/995–5555), **Aerolineas Argentinas** (☎ 800/333–0276), **Aeromexico** (☎ 800/237–6639), **AeroPeru** (☎ 800/777–7717), **Air Aruba** (☎ 800/882–7822), **Air Canada** (☎ 800/776–3000), **Air France** (☎ 800/237–2747), **Air Guadeloupe** (☎ 800/522–3394), **Air Jamaica** (☎ 800/523–5585), **Air South** (☎ 800/247–7688), **Airways International** (☎ 305/887–2794), **Alitalia** (☎ 800/223–5730), **ALM** (☎ 800/327–7230), **American** and **American Eagle** (☎ 800/433–7300), **American TransAir** (☎ 800/225–2995), **APA** (☎ 305/599–1299), **Avensa** (☎ 800/428–3672), **Avianca** (☎ 800/284–2622), **Aviateca** (☎ 800/327–9832), **Bahamasair** (☎ 800/222–4262), **British Airways** (☎ 800/247–9297), **BWIA** (☎ 305/371–2942), **Caribbean Airlines** (☎ 305/594–3232), **Carnival** (☎ 800/437–2110), **Cayman Airways** (☎ 800/422–9626), **Comair** (☎ 800/354–9822), **Continental** (☎ 800/525–0280), **Copa** (☎ 800/359–2672), **Delta** (☎ 800/221–1212), **Dominicana** (☎ 800/327–7240), **El Al** (☎ 800/223–6700), **Faucett** (☎ 800/334–3356), **Finnair** (☎ 800/950–5000), **Gulfstream International** (☎ 800/871–1200), **Guyana Airways** (☎ 800/242–4210), **Haiti Trans Air** (☎ 800/394–5313), **HANAIR** (☎ 305/757–7247), **Iberia** (☎ 800/772–4642), **LAB** (☎ 800/327–7407), **Lacsa** (☎ 800/225–2272), **Ladeco** (☎ 305/670–3066), **Lan Chile** (☎ 800/735–5526), **LAP** (☎ 800/677–7677), **Lauda Air** (☎ 800/645–3880), **LTU** (☎ 800/888–0200), **Lufthansa** (☎ 800/645–3880),

Martinair Holland (☎ 800/366–4655), **Mexicana** (☎ 800/531–7921), **Nica** (☎ 800/831–4396), **Northwest** (☎ 800/225–2525), **Paradise Island** (☎ 800/432–8807), **Saeta** (☎ 800/827–2382), **Sahsa** (☎ 800/327–1225 or 800/432–9818 in FL), **Servivensa** (☎ 800/428–3672), **South African Airways** (☎ 800/722–9675), **Surinam Airways** (☎ 800/432–1230), **Taca** (☎ 800/535–8780), **Tower Air** (☎ 800/348–6937), **Transbrasil** (☎ 800/872–3153), **TWA** (☎ 800/221–2000), **United** (☎ 800/241–6522), **USAir** and **USAir Express** (☎ 800/842–5374), **ValuJet** (☎ 800/825–8538), **Varig** (☎ 800/468–2744), **VASP** (☎ 800/732–8277), **Viasa** (☎ 800/468–4272), **Virgin Atlantic** (☎ 800/862–8621), and **Zuliana** (☎ 800/223–8780).

BETWEEN THE AIRPORT AND CENTER CITY

By Bus: The county's **Metrobus** (☎ 305/638–6700) still costs $1.25, though equipment has improved. From the airport you can take Bus 7 to downtown (weekdays every 40 minutes 5:30 AM–9 PM; weekends 6:30–7:30), Bus 37 south to Coral Gables and South Miami (every 30 minutes 6 AM–11:30 PM) or north to Hialeah (every 30 minutes 5:30 AM–11:30 PM), Bus J south to Coral Gables (every 30 minutes 6 AM–12:30 AM) or east to Miami Beach (every 30 minutes 4:30 AM–11:30 PM), and Bus 42 to Coconut Grove (hourly 5:40 AM–7 PM).

By Taxi: Except for the flat-fare trips described below, cabs cost $1.70 per mile plus a $1 toll for trips originating at MIA or the Port of Miami. Approximate fares from MIA include $10 to Coral Gables, $15–$20 to downtown Miami, and $25–$30 to Key Biscayne. Newly established flat fares to the beaches are $38 to Golden Beach and Sunny Isles, north of Haulover Beach Park; $32 from Surfside through Haulover Beach Park; $27 between 63rd and 87th streets; and $22 from 63rd Street south to the foot of Miami Beach. These fares are per trip, not per passenger, and include tolls and $1 airport surcharge but not tip. The flat fare between MIA and the Port of Miami, in either direction, is $15.75.

For taxi service to destinations in the immediate vicinity, ask a uniformed county taxi dispatcher to call an **ARTS (Airport Region Taxi Service)** cab for you. These special blue cabs offer a short-haul flat fare in two zones. An inner-zone ride is $5.60; the outer-zone fare is $9. The area of service is north to 36th Street, west to the Palmetto Expressway (77th Avenue), south to Northwest 7th Street, and east to Douglas Road (37th Avenue). Maps are posted in cab windows on both sides.

By Van: SuperShuttle (☎ 305/871–2000 from MIA, 305/764–1700 in Broward [Fort Lauderdale], or 800/874–8885 from elsewhere) vans transport passengers between MIA and local hotels, the Port of Miami, and even individual residences on a 24-hour basis. The company's service area extends from Palm Beach to Monroe County (including the Lower Keys). Drivers provide narration en route. Service from MIA is available around the clock, on demand, but for the return it's best to make reservations 24 hours in advance, although the firm will try to arrange pickups within Dade County on as little as four hours' notice. The cost from MIA to downtown hotels is about $8. Additional members of a party pay a lower rate for many destinations, and children under four ride free with their parents. There's a pet transport fee of $5 for animals in kennels.

By Limousine: Miami, where it seems everyone is on stage, has more than 100 limousine services, though they're frequently in and out of business. If you rely on the Yellow Pages, look for a company with a street address, not just a phone. One of the oldest companies in town is **Vintage Rolls Royce Limousines of Coral Gables** (4501 Monserrate

St., Coral Gables 33146, ☎ 305/662–5763), which operates a 24-hour reservation service and provides chauffeurs for privately owned cars.

By Rental Car: Six rental-car firms—**Avis** (☎ 800/831–2847), **Budget** (☎ 800/527–0700), **Dollar** (☎ 800/800–4000), **Hertz** (☎ 800/654–3131), **National** (☎ 800/227–7368), and **Value** (☎ 800/468–2583)—have booths near the baggage-claim area on MIA's lower level.

By Car

The main highways into Greater Miami from the north are Florida's Turnpike (a toll road) and I–95. From the northwest take I–75 or U.S. 27 into town. From the Everglades to the west, use I–75 or the Tamiami Trail (U.S. 41), and from the south use U.S. 1 and the Homestead Extension of Florida's Turnpike. Continuous reconstruction of I–95 forever slows traffic one place or another in south Florida. A $400 million, 46-mile widening project between Miami and West Palm Beach was completed in 1995, and the huge plate of spaghetti known as the Golden Glades interchange, north of downtown, which carries between 300,000 and 400,000 vehicles a day, has a new nine-story-high, $32 million car-pool overpass. On the flip side, a three- to four-year repaving project will keep I–95 from operating at peak capacity through most of the decade. The new Brickell Avenue Bridge, from the south into downtown, is scheduled to open during 1996; meanwhile, drivers must cross the Miami River on the Miami Avenue twin bridges, across I–95, or on the Southwest 3rd Avenue Bridge. On the other hand, driving across the newly widened MacArthur Causeway, which connects downtown with Miami Beach, has become easier, thanks to a new high-rise span that eliminates frequent openings for boat traffic.

By Train

Amtrak (☎ 800/872–7245) runs two trains daily between New York City and Miami (8303 N.W. 37th Ave., ☎ 305/835–1221 for recorded arrival and departure information or 305/835–1222 for shipping); the *Silver Meteor* and *Silver Star* make different stops along the way. The thrice-weekly *Sunset Limited* operates between Miami and Los Angeles, stopping in Jacksonville and Pensacola and other Florida towns en route.

The seven-year-old **Tri-Rail** (1 River Plaza, 305 S. Andrews Ave., Suite 200, Fort Lauderdale, ☎ 305/728–8445 or 800/874–7245) commuter train system connects Miami with Broward and Palm Beach daily.

By Bus

Greyhound (☎ 800/231–2222) buses stop at five bus terminals in Greater Miami (700 Biscayne Blvd., Miami; 4111 N.W. 27th St., Miami; 16250 Biscayne Blvd., North Miami; 7101 Harding Ave., Miami Beach; and 5 N.E. 3rd Rd., Homestead). There are no reservations.

By Boat

If you're entering the United States along Florida's Atlantic Coast south of Sebastian Inlet, you must call the **U.S. Customs Service** (☎ 800/432–1216). Customs clears by phone most boats of less than 5 tons, but you may be directed for further inspection to one or another marina.

Getting Around

Greater Miami resembles Los Angeles in its urban sprawl and traffic congestion. You'll need a car to visit many of the attractions and points of interest listed in this book, though some are accessible via the public transportation system, run by a department of the county government—the **Metro-Dade Transit Agency.** It consists of almost 600 **Metrobuses** on 71 routes, the 21-mile **Metrorail** elevated rapid-transit system, and the **Metromover,** an elevated light-rail system. Free maps, schedules, and a "First-Time Rider's Kit" are available. *Government Center Station, 111 N.W. 1st St., Miami 33128; Maps by Mail, ☎ 305/654–6586; route information, ☎ 305/638–6700 weekdays 6 AM–10 PM, weekends 9–5.*

By Car
In general, Miami traffic is the same as in any big city, with the same rush hours and the same likelihood that parking garages will be full at peak times. The large immigrant population creates additional problems, however, introducing a different cultural attitude toward traffic laws. Many drivers who don't know their way around turn and stop suddenly, and you may often find drivers dropping off passengers where they shouldn't. Some drivers are short-tempered and will assault those who cut them off or honk their horn.

Motorists need to be careful even when their driving behavior is beyond censure, however, especially in rental cars. Despite the removal of identifying marks, cars piled with luggage or otherwise showing signs that a tourist is at the wheel remain prime targets for thieves. Longtime residents know that reports of crime against tourists are blown way out of proportion by the media and that Miami is more or less as safe for a visitor as any American city its size. Still, before setting off on any drive, make sure you know where you're going and carry a map. Ask where you rent your car or at your hotel if there are any areas between your point of departure and your destination that you should especially avoid. A new system indicates the main tourist routes in a series of red sunbursts on special directional signs. You can't miss them. Keep your doors locked, and ask questions only at toll booths, gas stations, or other obviously safe locations. Don't stop if your car is bumped from behind or if you're asked for directions. One hesitates to foster rude behavior, but at least for now the roads are too risky to stop any place you're not familiar with (other than as traffic laws require).

By Train
Elevated **Metrorail** trains run from downtown Miami north to Hialeah and south along U.S. 1 to Dadeland, daily 5:30 AM–midnight. Trains run every five minutes in peak hours, every 15 minutes at other times. The fare is $1.25. Transfers, which cost 25¢, must be bought at the first station entered. Parking at train stations costs $1.

Metromover has two loops that circle downtown Miami, linking major hotels, office buildings, and shopping areas (*see* Tour 2 *in* Exploring, *above*). The system has been expanded from 1.9 miles to 4.4 miles, including the 1.4-mile Omni extension, with six stations to the north, and the 1.1-mile Brickell extension, with six stations to the south. Service runs daily every 90 seconds, 6 AM–midnight. The fare is 25¢. Transfers to Metrorail are $1.

By Bus
Metrobus (☎ 305/638–6700) stops are marked by blue-and-green signs with a bus logo and route information. The frequency of service varies widely, so call in advance to obtain specific schedule information. The fare is $1.25 (exact change), transfers 25¢; 60¢ with 10¢ transfers for people with disabilities, senior citizens (65 and older), and students. Some express routes carry surcharges of $1.50. Reduced-fare tokens sold 10 for $10 are now available from Metropass outlets. Lift-

equipped buses for people with disabilities are available on 16 routes, including one from the airport that links up with many routes in Miami Beach as well as Coconut Grove, Coral Gables, Hialeah, and Kendall. All but four of these routes connect with Metrorail. Those unable to use regular transit service should call **Special Transportation Services** (☎ 305/263–5400) for information on such services as curb-to-curb van pickup.

By Taxi

One cab "company" stands out immeasurably above the rest. It's actually a consortium of drivers who have banded together to provide good service, in marked contrast to some Miami cabbies, who are rude, unhelpful, unfamiliar with the city, or dishonest, taking advantage of visitors who don't know the area. To plug into this consortium—they don't have a name, simply a number—call the dispatch service (☎ 305/888–4444). If you have to use another company, try to be familiar with your route and destination.

Since 1974 fares have been $1.75 per mile, 25¢ a minute waiting time, and there's no additional charge for extra passengers, luggage, or tolls. Taxis can be hailed on the street, although you may not always find one when you need one—it's better to call for a dispatch taxi or have a hotel doorman hail one for you. Some companies with dispatch service are **Central Taxicab Service** (☎ 305/532–5555), **Diamond Cab Company** (☎ 305/545–5555), **Metro Taxicab Company** (☎ 305/888–8888), **Miami-Dade Yellow Cab** (☎ 305/633–0503), **Miami Springs Taxi** (☎ 305/888–1000), **Society Cab Company** (☎ 305/757–5523), **Speedy Cab** (☎ 305/861–9999), **Super Yellow Cab Company** (☎ 305/888–7777), **Tropical Taxicab Company** (☎ 305/945–1025), and **Yellow Cab Company** (☎ 305/444–4444). Many now accept credit cards; inquire when you call.

By Water Taxi

The service inaugurated in 1987 in Fort Lauderdale began Miami area operations in 1994 and expanded service between Miami Beach Marina and the Eden Rock Hotel in 1995. Canopied boats, 28 feet and longer, connect Miami Beach, Coconut Grove, and Key Biscayne from Bayside Marketplace. Routes cover downtown and Miami Beach hotels and restaurants and the Watson Island airboat station. Taxis operate daily 10 AM–2:30 AM. One-way fares around downtown Miami are $3, longer runs $7. For information, call 305/858–6292.

Guided Tours

Special-Interest Tours

AIR TOURS

Air Tours of Miami (1470 N.E. 123rd St., Suite 602, Miami, ☎ 305/893–5874) flies over Miami, the Everglades, and nearby waters in a one-hour sightseeing tour on a Piper Seneca II six-seater. Tours depart from Opa-Locka Airport (ask for directions), and the cost is $75 adults, $50 children, with a minimum of three adults. Reservations are required.

Chalk's International Airlines (1000 MacArthur Causeway, Miami, ☎ 305/371–8628 or 800/424–2557, ℻ 305/359–5240) has seaplane tours that depart from Watson Island every Saturday at 1:45. They last 25 minutes and include the Vizcaya Museum and Gardens, Miami Seaquarium, Fisher Island/Star Island, the Art Deco District, and Orange Bowl Stadium. The fee is $39.50 adults, $29.50 children 2–11.

BOAT TOURS

Heritage of Miami II offers sightseeing cruises on board a two-mast, 85-foot topsail schooner. Tours start and end at Bayside Marketplace (401 Biscayne Blvd., ☎ 305/442–9697). One-hour sails cost $5 per person, and two-hour sails are $10; children under 12 are half price. Tours loop through lower Biscayne Bay with views of the Vizcaya Museum and Gardens, movie-star homes, Cape Florida Lighthouse, the Port of Miami, and several residential islands.

Island Queen, Island Lady, and *Pink Lady* are 150-passenger double-decker tour boats docked at Bayside Marketplace (401 Biscayne Blvd., ☎ 305/379–5119). They go on daily 90-minute narrated tours of the Port of Miami and Millionaires' Row, costing $10 adults, $5 children under 13.

ECOTOURS

EcoTours Miami (Box 22, Miami 33256-0022, ☎ 305/232–5398), consisting of longtime environmentalist Ginni Hokanson and friends, conduct customized interpretive tours of the Everglades, Big Cypress Swamp, Fackahatchee Strand, Florida Bay, and wherever else in south Florida's native environment visitors want to explore. Tour guides—environmental educators and natural history specialists—are available who speak German, Italian, Portuguese, and Spanish. Price quotes are given on request.

HISTORIC TOURS

Art Deco District Tour (1001 Ocean Dr., Miami Beach, ☎ 305/672–2014), operated by the Miami Design Preservation League, is a 90-minute guided walking tour departing from the league's welcome center at the Ocean Front Auditorium at 10:30 AM Saturday. Private group tours can be arranged with advance notice. A two-hour bike tour at 10:30 Sunday leaves from Cycles on the Beach (713 5th St., Miami Beach, ☎ 305/673–2055). The walking tour costs $6; the bike tour is $10 with a rental bike, $5 with your own bike.

Deco Tours Miami Beach (420 Lincoln Rd., Suite 412, Miami Beach, ☎ 305/531–4465) also offers walking tours of the Art Deco District. These 90-minute tours, which cost $10, depart from various locations and take in Lincoln Road, Washington Avenue, Espanola Way, Ocean Drive, Lummus Park, and the Art Deco Welcome Center.

Professor Paul George (1345 S.W. 14th St., Miami, ☎ 305/858–6021), a history professor at Miami-Dade Community College and past president of the Florida Historical Society, leads a variety of walking tours as well as boat tours and tours that make use of Metrorail and Metromover. Tours generally last about two hours and 20 minutes. Covering downtown and other historic neighborhoods, they start Saturday at 10 and Sunday at 11 at various locations, depending on the tour. Call for each weekend's schedule and for additional tours by appointment. The fee is $10 adults.

RICKSHAW TOURS

Majestic Rickshaw (75 N.E. 156 St., Biscayne Gardens, ☎ 305/256–8833) has two-person rickshaws along Main Highway in Coconut Grove's Village Center, nightly 8 PM–2 AM. It's $3 per person for a 10-minute ride through Coconut Grove or $6 per person for a 20-minute lovers' moonlight ride to Biscayne Bay.

SELF-GUIDED TOURS

The **Junior League of Miami** (2325 Salzedo, Coral Gables 33134, ☎ 305/443–0160) publishes excellent self-guiding tours to architectural

and historical landmarks in downtown Miami, the northeast, and
south Dade. Coconut Grove and Coral Gables tours are out of print
but can sometimes still be found at bookstores. Each costs $3.

The **Miami Design Preservation League** (Bin L, Miami Beach 33139,
☎ 305/672–2014) sells the *Art Deco District Guide,* a book of six detailed walking or driving tours of the Art Deco District, for $10.

Important Addresses and Numbers

Emergencies
Dial 911 for **police** or **ambulance.** You can dial free from pay phones.

AMBULANCE
Randle Eastern Ambulance Service Inc. (35 S.W. 27th Ave., Miami 33135,
☎ 305/642–6400) operates at all hours.

HOSPITALS
The following hospitals have 24-hour emergency rooms:

In Miami Beach: **Miami Heart Institute** (4701 N. Meridian Ave., Miami
Beach, ☎ 305/672–1111; physician referral, ☎ 305/674–3004), **Mt.
Sinai Medical Center** (off Julia Tuttle Causeway, I–195 at 4300 Alton
Rd., Miami Beach, ☎ 305/674–2121; emergency, ☎ 305/674–2200;
physician referral, ☎ 305/674–2273), and **South Shore Hospital &
Medical Center** (630 Alton Rd., Miami Beach, ☎ 305/672–2100).

In the north: **Golden Glades Regional Medical Center** (17300 N.W. 7th
Ave., North Miami, ☎ 305/652–4200; no physician referral).

In central Miami: **Coral Gables Hospital** (3100 Douglas Rd., Coral
Gables, ☎ 305/445–8461), **Jackson Memorial Medical Center** (1611 N.W.
12th Ave., near Dolphin Expressway, Miami, ☎ 305/585–1111; emergency, ☎ 305/585–6901; physician referral, ☎ 305/547–5757), **Mercy
Hospital** (3663 S. Miami Ave., Coconut Grove, ☎ 305/854–4400;
emergency, ☎ 305/285–2171; physician referral, ☎ 305/285–2929), and
Pan American Hospital (5959 N.W. 7th St., Miami, ☎ 305/264–1000;
emergency, ☎ 305/264–6125; physician referral, ☎ 305/264–5118).

In the south: **Baptist Hospital of Miami** (8900 N. Kendall Dr., Miami,
☎ 305/596–1960; emergency, ☎ 305/596–6556; physician referral, ☎
305/596–6557) and **South Miami Hospital** (6200 S.W. 73rd St., South
Miami, ☎ 305/661–4611; emergency, ☎ 305/662–8181; physician referral, ☎ 305/633–2255).

DOCTORS
Dade County Medical Association (1501 N.W. North River Dr., Miami,
☎ 305/324–8717) is open weekdays 9–5 for medical referral.

DENTISTS
East Coast District Dental Society (420 S. Dixie Hwy., Suite 2E, Coral
Gables, ☎ 305/667–3647) is open weekdays 9–4:30 for dental referral. Services include general dentistry, endodontics, periodontics, and
oral surgery.

LATE-NIGHT PHARMACIES
Eckerd Drug (1825 Miami Gardens Dr. NE, at 185th St., North Miami
Beach, ☎ 305/932–5740; 9031 S.W. 107th Ave., Miami, ☎ 305/274–
6776). **Terminal Rexall Pharmacy** (Concourse F, Miami International
Airport, Miami, ☎ 305/876–0556). **Walgreen** (500–B W. 49th St., Palm
Springs Mall, Hialeah, ☎ 305/557–5468; 12295 Biscayne Blvd., North
Miami, ☎ 305/893–6860; 5731 Bird Rd., Miami, ☎ 305/666–0757;

1845 Alton Rd., Miami Beach, ☎ 305/531–8868; 791 N.E. 167th St., North Miami Beach, ☎ 305/652–7332).

Services for People with Hearing Impairments

Fire, police, medical, rescue (TDD ☎ 305/595–4749).

Operator and directory assistance (TDD ☎ 800/855–1155).

Deaf Services of Miami (9100 S. Dadeland Blvd., Suite 104, Miami 33156, voice ☎ 305/670–9099) operates 24 hours year-round.

Florida Relay Service (voice ☎ 800/955–8770, TDD ☎ 800/955–8771).

Tourist Information

Greater Miami Convention & Visitors Bureau (701 Brickell Ave., Suite 2700, Miami 33131, ☎ 305/539–3063 or 800/283–2707). Satellite tourist information centers are located at Bayside Marketplace (401 Biscayne Blvd., Miami 33132, ☎ 305/539–2980), Miami Beach Chamber of Commerce (*see below*), and South Dade Visitor Information Center (160 U.S. 1, Florida City 33034, ☎ 305/245–9180 or 800/388–9669, FAX 305/247–4335).

Coconut Grove Chamber of Commerce (2820 McFarlane Rd., Coconut Grove 33133, ☎ 305/444–7270, FAX 305/444–2498). **Coral Gables Chamber of Commerce** (50 Aragon Ave., Coral Gables 33134, ☎ 305/446–1657, FAX 305/446–9900). **Florida Gold Coast Chamber of Commerce** (1100 Kane Concourse, Suite 210, Bay Harbor Islands 33154, ☎ 305/866–6020) serves the beach communities of Bal Harbour, Bay Harbor Islands, Golden Beach, North Bay Village, Sunny Isles, and Surfside. **Greater Miami Chamber of Commerce** (1601 Biscayne Blvd., Miami 33132, ☎ 305/350–7700, FAX 305/374–6902). **Greater South Dade/South Miami Chamber of Commerce** (6410 S.W. 80th St., South Miami 33143-4602, ☎ 305/661–1621, FAX 305/666–0508). **Key Biscayne Chamber of Commerce** (Key Biscayne Bank Bldg., 95 W. McIntyre St., Key Biscayne 33149, ☎ 305/361–5207). **Miami Beach Chamber of Commerce** (1920 Meridian Ave., Miami Beach 33139, ☎ 305/672–1270, FAX 305/538–4336). **North Miami Chamber of Commerce** (13100 W. Dixie Hwy., North Miami 33181, ☎ 305/891–7811, FAX 305/893–8522). **Surfside Tourist Board** (9301 Collins Ave., Surfside 33154, ☎ 305/864–0722 or 800/327–4557, FAX 305/861–1302).

3   The Everglades

Created in 1947, this national park in the southernmost extremity of the peninsula preserves a portion of the slow-moving "river of grass"—a 50-mile-wide stream that flows through marshy grassland en route to Florida Bay. Biscayne National Park, nearby, is the largest national park in the continental United States with living coral reefs.

Updated by
Herb Hiller

MIAMI IS THE ONLY metropolitan area in the United States with two national parks—Everglades and Biscayne—in its backyard. Everglades National Park, created in 1947, was meant to preserve the slow-moving "River of Grass"—a freshwater river 50 miles wide but only 6 inches deep, flowing from Lake Okeechobee through marshy grassland into Florida Bay. Biscayne National Park, established as a national monument in 1968 and 12 years later expanded and upgraded to park status, is the nation's largest marine park and the largest national park in the continental United States with living coral reefs. A small portion of the park's almost 274 square miles consists of mainland coast and outlying islands, but 96% is under water, much of it in Biscayne Bay.

Unfortunately, Miami's "backyard" is being threatened by the suburban sprawl that has long characterized metro area development. Added to the mix is the presence nearby, between the suburbs and the parks, of one of the most productive, albeit shrinking, agricultural districts in the eastern United States. What results is competition between environmental, agricultural, and development interests—for land, for government money, and for rules to govern this one-of-a-kind region's future.

The biggest issue is control of water. Originally, the natural cycle of alternating floods and dry periods in the Everglades maintained wildlife habitat and regulated the quality and quantity of water that flowed into Florida Bay. The brackish seasonal flux sustained a remarkably vigorous bay, including the most productive shrimp beds in American waters and thriving mangrove fringes and coral reefs at its Atlantic edge. The system nurtured both sea life and recreationists, who flocked to the region for fishing and diving. Starting in the 1930s, however, a giant flood-control system began diverting water to canals that run to the Gulf and the Atlantic. As you travel Florida's north–south routes, you cross this network of canals, symbolized by a smiling alligator that represents the South Florida Water Management District, "Protector of the Everglades."

Ironically, the unintended result of flood control has been devastation in the wilderness that lies within the boundaries of Everglades National Park, the Big Cypress National Preserve, and a series of water-conservation areas to the northeast. Park visitors decry diminished bird counts (a 90% reduction over 50 years), the black bear has been eliminated, and the Florida panther nears extinction. Exotic plants once imported to drain the Everglades and feral pigs released for hunting are crowding out indigenous species. In 1995 the nonprofit group American Rivers again ranked the Everglades among the most threatened rivers of North America. Meanwhile in Florida Bay, the loss of all that fresh water has made the bay more salty, creating dead zones where pea-green algae has replaced sea grasses and sponges, devastating sea-life breeding grounds.

Luckily, priorities change, and new policies, still largely on paper, hold promise for an ecosystem that continues to diminish. Tourism and fishing industries, preservationists, and aggressive park management have pushed for improvement. The federal and state governments are now working together to advance environmental protection toward the top of water-management priorities. Congressional appropriations to study restoration of the Everglades have increased. The state has acquired the Frog Pond, some 1,800 acres of critical farmland to the east of the Everglades, in order to allow more natural flooding. Passage in

1994 of Florida's Everglades Forever Act mandates creation of 40,000 acres of filtration marshes to remove nutrients before they enter the protected wetlands. Within the next decade, farming must sharply reduce its phosphorus runoff, and the U.S. Army Corps of Engineers, which maintains Florida's flood-control system, proposes restoring a more natural flow of water into the Everglades and its related systems. Although the future of the natural system hangs uncertainly in this time of transition, these are certainly promising signs.

Much like Florida Bay, Biscayne Bay functions as a lobster sanctuary and a nursery for fish, sponges, and crabs. Manatees and sea turtles frequent its warm, shallow waters, and the ocean east of the islands harbors the northernmost sections of Florida's tropical reef. At the park's boundary, the continental shelf runs to 60 feet deep; farther east, the shelf falls rapidly away to a depth of 400 feet at the edge of the Gulf Stream. Lamentably, this bay, too, is under assault from forces similar to those in Florida Bay, and coral is additionally damaged by boat anchors and commercial ships that run off course onto the reefs.

The farm towns of Homestead and Florida City provide the closest visitor facilities to the two parks. They date from early in the century, when Henry Flagler extended his railroad to Key West but decided that farming in South Dade would do more for rail revenues than would passengers. Although both towns were devastated by Hurricane Andrew in 1992, both have fully recovered. Homestead Air Force Base is becoming a civil air facility with commercial development. Downtown Homestead has become a preservation-driven Main Street city and has attracted a number of antiques stores. The area's better restaurants are here, whereas the best choices for overnighting are in Florida City. Farms, including U-pick fields, extend west to the edge of Everglades National Park, and a vast network of almost 200 miles of bicycle and hiking trails is under development along the banks of flood-control canals. Routes are likely to connect the two national parks before 2000.

Another way to see the Everglades is via a 15-mile probe that extends south from the Tamiami Trail (U.S. 41) between Miami and Naples. Miccosukee Indians in the area operate a range of cultural attractions and restaurants. The remaining entrance to the park is Everglades City, 35 miles southeast of Naples just off the Tamiami Trail. This community, around since the late 19th century, offers lodgings, restaurants, and guided tours.

EXPLORING

The best way to experience the real Everglades is to get your feet wet— but most visitors won't do that. Boat tours at Everglades City and Flamingo, a tram ride at Shark Valley, and boardwalks along the main park road allow you to see the park with dry feet.

Winter is the best time to visit Everglades National Park. Temperatures and mosquito activity are moderate. Low water levels concentrate the resident wildlife around sloughs that retain water all year. Migratory birds swell the avian population. Winter is also the busiest time in the park. Make reservations and expect crowds at the most popular visitor service areas—Flamingo, the Main Visitor Center, and Royal Palm.

In spring the weather turns increasingly hot and rainy, and tours and facilities are less crowded. Migratory birds depart, and you must look harder to see wildlife. Be especially careful with campfires and matches;

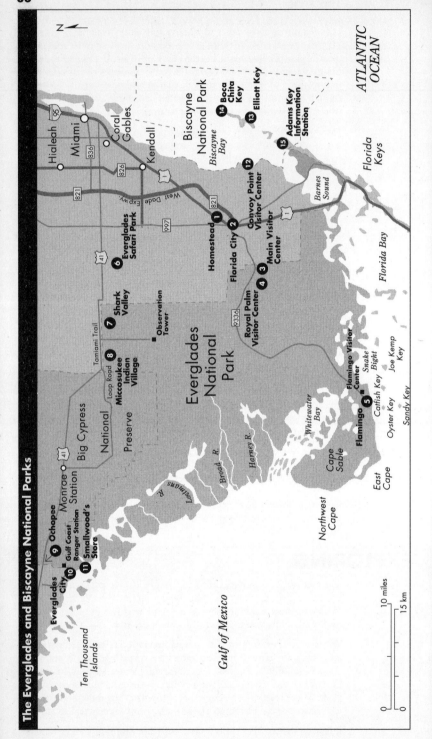

The Everglades and Biscayne National Parks

this is when the wildfire-prone saw-grass prairies and pinelands are most vulnerable.

Summer brings intense sun and billowing clouds that unleash torrents of rain almost every afternoon; water levels rise and wildlife disperses. Mosquitoes hatch, swarm, and descend on you in voracious clouds. It's a good time to stay away. Europeans constitute 80% of the summer visitors.

In mid-October, the first cold front sweeps through. The rains diminish, water levels start to fall, and the ground begins to dry out. Wildlife moves toward the sloughs. Flocks of migratory birds and tourists swoop in, as the cycle of seasons builds once more.

Biscayne National Park includes 18 miles of mainland coast and 45 barrier islands 7 miles to the east across Biscayne Bay. The islands (called keys) are fossilized coral reefs that emerged from the sea when glaciers trapped much of the world's water supply during the Ice Age. Today a tropical hardwood forest grows in their rocky crevices. From December through April, when the mosquito population is relatively quiescent, you can comfortably explore several of the keys by boat, either your own or the park concessionaire's.

East of the keys another 3 miles lies the park's main attraction: living coral reefs, some the size of a student's desk, others as large as a football field. Once again, you must take a boat ride to see this underwater wonderland, and you really have to snorkel or scuba dive to appreciate it fully. A diverse population of colorful fish—angelfish, gobies, grunts, parrot fish, pork fish, wrasses, and many more—flits through the reefs. Fortunately, Hurricane Andrew did the reefs only minor damage and, scientists now believe, may actually have helped regenerate them.

Tour 1: The Everglades—Florida City to Flamingo

Numbers in the margin correspond to points of interest on the Everglades and Biscayne National Parks map.

❶ Before going to Everglades National Park, you might want to stop off in **Homestead** and view a portion of a historic photo collection at the restored 1917 **City Hall** (43 N. Krome Ave., ☎ 305/247–2332), which also houses the chamber of commerce. More of the collection is displayed in a storefront across the street.

❷ In **Florida City,** you can visit the **Florida Pioneer Museum** (826 N. Krome Ave., ☎ 305/246–9531), that is if it's reopened. In this former station agent's house, you could, until Hurricane Andrew, pore over a collection of articles from daily life that evoke the homestead period of the area, on the last frontier of mainland America. Items recall a time when Henry Flagler's railroad vaulted the development of the Florida Keys all the way to Key West, and Homestead and Florida City were briefly the take-charge supply outposts. Another part of the museum, the old East Coast Railway Station, was demolished by Hurricane Andrew, but its caboose, which was tumbled on its side, has since been righted.

❸ Enter the park at the **Main Visitor Center,** where a full range of interpretive materials is to be displayed in the new, more cracker-style park headquarters, expected by mid-1996. The new structure replaces a temporary facility with limited materials, which in turn replaced a structure destroyed by Hurricane Andrew. *11 mi west of Homestead on Rte.*

9336, ☎ 305/242–7700. ☞ *Park: $5 per car; $3 per person on foot, bicycle, or motorcycle; free for U.S. citizens over 62 with Golden Age Passport ($10, good for life).* ☉ *Visitor center: daily 8–5.*

❹ At the **Royal Palm Visitor Center** (4 mi west on Rte. 9336 and south on a side road), you can stroll along the Anhinga Trail boardwalk or follow the Gumbo Limbo Trail through a hardwood hammock (a tree island). The visitor center has an interpretive display, a bookstore, and vending machines and is open 8–noon and 1–4:30.

★ The main **Everglades park road** (Route 9336) travels 38 miles from the Main Visitor Center to Flamingo, across a cross section of the park's eight distinct ecosystems: hardwood hammock, freshwater prairie, pineland, freshwater slough, cypress, coastal prairie, mangrove, and marine/estuarine. Highlights of the trip include a dwarf cypress forest, the ecotone (transition zone) between saw grass and mangrove forest, and a wealth of wading birds at Mrazek and Coot Bay ponds. Boardwalks and trails along the main road and several short spurs allow you to see the Everglades on dry land.

❺ At the far end, **Flamingo** offers access to Florida Bay; tour boats and fishing guides leave from here. A visitor center provides an interpretive display, and you can also make use of a lodge, restaurant, lounge, gift shop, marina, and campground. ☎ *305/242–7700 (Park Service),* ☎ *305/253–2241 (Flamingo Lodge).* ☉ *Visitor center: daily 8–5.*

Tour 2: The Everglades—Along the Tamiami Trail

Another way to visit the Everglades is to follow the Tamiami Trail (U.S. 41) for the scenic 83 miles between Miami and Naples. The following tour runs east to west (keep in mind that the sun will be in your eyes after noon), but you can just as easily drive in the opposite direction.

❻ From Homestead, go north on Krome Avenue (Route 997) to the Tamiami Trail, and head west for 9 miles. Turn left to **Everglades Safari Park.** This commercial attraction includes an airboat ride, jungle trail, observation platform, alligator wrestling, wildlife museum, gift shop, and restaurant. *Tamiami Trail,* ☎ *305/226–6923 or 305/223–3804, FAX 305/554–5666.* ☞ *$14 adults, $6 children under 12.* ☉ *Daily 8:30–5.*

❼ Continue on to **Shark Valley,** site of a park entrance and a visitor center, which has rotating exhibits and a bookstore. From here you can walk along a ¼-mile boardwalk, follow hiking trails, or take one of

★ the **Shark Valley Tram Tours** (*see* Guided Tours *in* Everglades Essentials, *below*), which visits a 50-foot observation tower built on the site of an oil well drilled in the 1940s. From atop the tower you can view the Everglades' vast river of grass sweeping south toward the Gulf of Mexico. *Visitor center: Tamiami Trail,* ☎ *305/221–8776.* ☞ *Park: $4 per car; $2 per person on foot, bicycle, or motorcycle; free for U.S. citizens over 62 with Golden Age Passport.* ☉ *Visitor center: daily 8:30–5.*

★ ❽ Near the Shark Valley entrance, the Miccosukee tribe operates the **Miccosukee Indian Village** as a tourist attraction. You can watch Miccosukee families cooking and making clothes, dolls, beadwork, and baskets and then buy their very unusual crafts, as you can at the nearby **Everglades Shark Valley Crafts Center** (*see* Shopping, *below*). You'll also see an alligator-wrestling demonstration. The village has a boardwalk and a museum. **Buffalo Tiger's Florida Everglades Airboat Ride** (*see* Guided Tours *in* Everglades Essentials, *below*) departs from here. *Tamiami Trail, mile marker 75.5, Shark Valley,* ☎ *305/223–8380.*

☛ *$5 adults, $3.50 children 5–12.* ⊘ *Daily 9–5, last guided tour at 4, last airboat ride and alligator-wrestling show at 4:30.*

Continuing west on the Tamiami Trail, you'll drive through the **Big Cypress National Preserve,** with its variegated pattern of wet prairies, ponds, marshes, sloughs, and strands. Just west of the Miccosukee Indian Reservation, turn onto Route 94, the 29-mile **Loop Road.** It starts out paved, turns to dirt, and traverses deep, clear cypress swamps of rare beauty. Be sure to keep car windows rolled up when you stop, especially in summer, because mosquitoes can be a severe problem; lather on repellent if you leave the car. Walk silently and you may see gators, deer, rabbits, and other wildlife, as well as orchids and bromeliads. The road returns to the Tamiami Trail at Monroe Station, midway between the Miccosukee Indian Reservation and Everglades City.

⑨ Just before you reach Route 29, you'll pass through **Ochopee,** site of the smallest post office in North America. Buy a picture postcard of the little one-room shack and mail it to a friend, thereby helping to keep this picturesque post office in business.

⑩ To reach the Everglades' western entrance, turn south onto Route 29, and drive 3 miles to **Everglades City** and the **Gulf Coast Ranger Station.** The visitor center here offers exhibits and a gift shop, and backcountry campers can pick up the required free permits. This station offers access to the Ten Thousand Islands region along the Gulf of Mexico, but there are no roads from here to other sections of the park. *Rte. 29,* ☏ *941/695-3311.* ☛ *Free.* ⊘ *Nov.–Apr., daily 7–4:30; reduced hrs May–Oct.*

★ Stop at the **Rod and Gun Club** (200 Riverside Dr., ☏ 941/695–2101), and take a time-warp trip back to the '20s, when wealthy hunters, anglers, and yachting parties from all over the world came here for the winter season. Founded in 1889, the inn (*see* Dining and Lodging, *below*) is built on the foundations of the first house on the south bank of the Barron River. Sit on the screened porch, have a beer, and watch the yachts and the fishing boats go by.

★ ⑪ Three miles from Everglades City across a free causeway is **Smallwood's Store,** a perfectly restored old trading post that dates from 1906. Ted Smallwood pioneered this last American frontier deep in the Everglades and built a 3,000-square-foot pine store raised on pilings in Chokoloskee Bay. Smallwood's granddaughter Lynn McMillin reopened it in 1989, after it had been closed several years, and installed a small museum and gift shop. *360 Mamie St., Chokoloskee Island,* ☏ *941/695-2989.* ☛ *$2.50 ages over 12, $2 senior citizens.* ⊘ *Dec. 1–May 1, daily 10–5; May 2–Nov. 30, Fri.–Tues. 10–4.*

Tour 3: Biscayne National Park

⑫ Though a new park headquarters was opened in 1993, a replacement for the **Convoy Point Visitor Center,** which was badly damaged in Hurricane Andrew, will not open until the last half of 1996. A temporary visitor center offers books for sale, limited exhibits, an eight-minute slide orientation, and an 18-minute video on Hurricane Andrew's effects on the park. A short trail and boardwalk lead to a jetty, boat dock, and launch ramp. *9700 S.W. 328th St., Homestead,* ☏ *305/230–7275.* ☛ *Free.* ⊘ *Park: daily 8–sunset; visitor center: weekdays 8:30–4:30 (to 5:30 June–Aug.), weekends 8:30–5. By 1996, park may resume its pre-hurricane closing hr of sunset.*

The visitor centers on the park's remote islands, which already attracted fewer visitors than they deserved, were the worst hit by the hurricane.

None are now open. Happily, a new park concessionaire, **Biscayne National Underwater Park, Inc.** (*see* Guided Tours *in* Everglades Essentials, *below*), is offering glass-bottom boat trips to the keys as well as reef tours.

⑬ On **Elliott Key,** the harbor and campground, for which there are neither fees nor reservations, are open. The only access is by boat (on your own or by special arrangement with the concessionaire). Outdoor exhibits at ground level under the ranger station are planned for 1996.

⑭ Just north at **Boca Chita Key,** which was once owned by Mark C. Honeywell, former president of Minneapolis's Honeywell Company, most of the historical structures have been repaired and stabilized. Revegetation, harbor repair, and rest room construction are expected to be complete by 1996, at which time the island will be reopened to the public. Overnight docking and camping is to be allowed. Access will be by private boat only.

⑮ On **Adams Key,** rest rooms and a picnic shelter are scheduled for 1996, at which time the island will be reopened for day use (camping to follow later). A public dock and nature trail will be available. Here, too, access will be by private boat.

SHOPPING

For the sheer fun as well as the bargain, you can't beat a stint in any of the local fields that welcome you to pick your own produce. The season runs from November to April, and you can expect to find strawberries for maybe $2 a pound, corn at $1.25 a dozen ears, and tomatoes for 50¢ a pound. Drive and look for signs—in season they're everywhere among the fields—or call the **South Dade Visitor Information Center** (*see* Important Addresses and Numbers *in* Everglades Essentials, *below*). You can also buy fresh-picked produce at stands that border fields, but you won't save quite as much.

Florida City

Florida Keys Factory Shops (250 E. Palm Dr.) offers discount shopping at some 50 stores plus a small food court. **Robert Is Here** (19200 Palm Dr. [S.W. 344th St.], ☎ 305/246–1592) is a remarkable fruit stand that sells vegetables, milk shakes, and, seasonally, some 40 kinds of tropical fruits, including carambola, egg fruit, litchis, monstera, sapodilla, soursop, sugar apple, and tamarind, as well as fresh juices. It's open 8–7 every day of the year.

Homestead

In addition to Homestead Boulevard (U.S. 1) and Campbell Drive (Southwest 312th Street and Northeast 8th Street), **Krome Avenue** (Route 997) is a popular street for shopping. In the heart of old Homestead, it has a new brick sidewalk and many antiques stores.

Shark Valley

The larger of two Miccosukee-run crafts depots, **Everglades Shark Valley Crafts Center** (Tamiami Trail, mile marker 76, Shark Valley, ☎ 305/223–5055) carries a broad selection of interesting Native American crafts and, in addition, offers airboat rides. Some of the most unusual crafts found in south Florida are the beadwork, dolls, baskets, and patchwork dresses and jackets sold at the **Miccosukee Indian Village** (*see* Tour 2 *in* Exploring, *above*), ½ mile east of the Everglades Shark Valley Crafts Center.

SPORTS AND THE OUTDOORS

Most of the sports and recreational opportunities in Everglades and Biscayne national parks are related in some way to water or nature study, or both. Even on land, be prepared to get a bit damp on the region's marshy hiking trails. In summer, save your outdoor activities for early or late in the day to avoid the sun's strongest rays, and use a sunscreen. Carry mosquito repellent at any time of year.

Biking and Hiking

In the Everglades, there are several nice places to ride or hike. Take the Shark Valley Loop Road, 15 miles round-trip, or ask a ranger for a copy of "Foot and Canoe Trails of the Flamingo Area," a leaflet that also lists bike trails. Inquire about water levels and insect conditions before you go. Bike rentals are available from **Flamingo Lodge Marina & Outpost Resort** for $12 a day, $7 per half day, or $2.50 an hour; **North American Canoe Tours**, in Everglades City, for $3 per hour; and **Shark Valley Tram Tours** for $3.25 per hour, 8:30–3 (*see* Guided Tours *in* Everglades Essentials, *below,* for all).

In Biscayne National Park, rangers lead informal nature walks on **Elliott Key.** You can walk the length of the 7-mile key on your own along a rough path locally referred to as the "spite highway," which developers bulldozed before the park was created.

Boating

Bring aboard the proper *NOAA Nautical Charts* before you cast off to explore the waters of the parks. The charts run $15–$15.95 at many marine stores in south Florida, at the Convoy Point Visitor Center in Biscayne National Park, and at Flamingo Marina.

Waterway Guide (southern regional edition) is an annual publication that many boaters use as a guide to these waters. Bookstores all over south Florida sell it, or you can order it directly from the publisher (Argus Business, Book Department, 6151 Powers Ferry Rd., Atlanta, GA 30339, ☎ 800/233–3359) for $33.95 plus $3 shipping and handling.

MARINAS

Listed below are the major marinas serving the two parks. Dock masters can provide information on other marine services.

Black Point Park is a 155-acre Metro-Dade County Park with a hurricane-safe harbor basin. Although badly mauled by Hurricane Andrew, it reopened in 1993. **Black Point Marina's** facilities include storage racks for 300 boats, 178 wet slips, 10 ramps, fuel, a bait-and-tackle shop, canoe-launching ramp, powerboat rentals from Marine Management, and the Tugboat Annie Restaurant, serving lunch and dinner with a full bar. From Florida's Turnpike, exit at Southwest 112th Avenue, go two blocks north, turn east on Coconut Palm Drive (Southwest 248th Street), and drive to the end. *24777 S.W. 87th Ave., Miami,* ☎ *305/258–3500.* ⊙ *Office: daily 8:30–5 (later in summer); park: daily 6–sunset.*

Homestead Bayfront Park, just 5 miles south of Black Point Park, has a marina with a dock and 173 wet slips, 60 dry slips, fuel, bait and tackle, ice, boat hoist, and ramp; the park also has a tidal swimming area and concessions. *9698 S.W. 328th St., Homestead,* ☎ *305/230–3033.* ☛ *$3 per car, $5 for boat ramp, $10 for hoist.* ⊙ *Daily 7–sunset.*

Flamingo Lodge Marina & Outpost Resort (1 Flamingo Lodge Hwy., Flamingo, ☎ 305/253–2241 from Miami or 941/695–3101 from Gulf

Coast) has a 50-slip marina that rents more than 40 canoes, 10 power skiffs, and seven houseboats; several private boats are also available for charter. There are two ramps, one for Florida Bay, the other for Whitewater Bay and the backcountry. The hoist across the plug dam separating Florida Bay from the Buttonwood Canal can take boats up to 26 feet long. A small marina store sells food, camping supplies, bait and tackle, and car and boat fuel.

Camping

In **Biscayne National Park,** you can camp free on designated keys 7 miles offshore at primitive sites or in the backcountry. Carry all your food, water, and supplies onto the keys, and carry all trash off when you leave. Bring plenty of insect repellent. Inquire at the park concessionaire office about boats to the keys, as there are no regular ferries or boats for rent. No reservations are made, but for backcountry camping, you need to get a free permit from rangers at Convoy Point, Elliott Key, or, when it reopens, Adams Key.

Everglades National Park includes three developed campsites with drinking water, sewage dump station, and rest rooms. **Long Pine Key** offers 108 campsites. **Flamingo** contains 235 drive-in sites, 60 walk-in sites, and cold showers. **Chekika** has 20 sites plus a group site for up to 20, and additionally offers both hot and cold showers. Primitive campgrounds are located throughout the park but offer no water or electricity. Come early to get a good site, especially in winter, and bring plenty of insect repellent. ☛ *$8 per site in winter, free in summer except for walk-in sites at Flamingo, which are $4. Stay limited to 14 days Nov.–Apr. Check-out time 10* AM. *Register at campground.* ☉ *All year.*

There are 48 designated **Everglades National Park Backcountry Sites** deep in the park. Two are accessible by land, the others only by canoe; 15 have chickees (raised wood platforms with thatch roofs). All have chemical toilets, including the 18 beach sites and 15 inland sites. Four chickee sites and nine of the ground sites are within an easy day's canoeing of Flamingo; five of the ground sites are within an easy day's canoeing of Everglades City. Carry all your food, water, and supplies in; carry out all trash. You'll need a free permit, issued for a specific site. Capacity and length of stay are limited, and sites are available on a first-come, first-served basis. For information on handicap accessibility, updates, and permits, contact the **Flamingo** or **Gulf Coast Ranger Station** (*see* Important Addresses and Numbers *in* Everglades Essentials, *below,* for both).

Everglades Gator Park, on the Tamiami Trail, has an RV park with full hookups for up to 80 RVs, in addition to conducting Everglades airboat tours for sightseeing, hunting, and fishing. *24050 S.W. 8th St., Miami (mailing address: 13800 S.W. 8th St., Box 107, Miami 33184),* ☎ *305/559–2255 or 800/559–2205. Year-round rates $25 per night, $100 per wk, $365 per month. MC, V.*

Canoeing

The subtropical wilderness of southern Florida is a mecca for flat-water paddlers. You'll find the best canoeing in winter, when temperatures are moderate, rainfall is minimal, and the mosquitoes are tolerable. You don't need a permit for day trips, as you do for camping, but tell someone where you're going and when you expect to return. Getting lost out here is easy, and spending the night without proper gear can be unpleasant, if not dangerous.

At Biscayne, you can explore five creeks through the mangrove wilderness within 1½ miles of park headquarters at Convoy Point.

Everglades has six well-marked canoe trails in the Flamingo area, including the southern end of the 99-mile Wilderness Trail from Flamingo to Everglades City. **North American Canoe Tours** (*see below*) provides shuttle service between Everglades City and Flamingo for canoes or vehicles but not for people alone.

The vendors listed below all rent aluminum canoes. Most have 17-foot Grummans. Bring your own cushions.

Biscayne National Underwater Park, Inc. (Convoy Point, Biscayne National Park, ☎ 305/230–1100, FAX 305/230–1120) rents canoes for $7 an hour, $20 for four hours, $25 per day. It's open daily 9–5:30.

Everglades National Park Boat Tours (Gulf Coast Ranger Station, Everglades City, ☎ 941/695–2591 or 800/445–7724 in FL) rents canoes for $15 per half day, $20 per full day. It's open daily 8:30–5.

North American Canoe Tours (Ivey House, 107 Camellia St., Box 5038, Everglades City 33929, ☎ 941/695–4666), open daily 7 AM–9 PM, is an established source for canoes, sea kayaks, and guided Everglades trips (November–April) approved by the National Park Service. Canoes cost $20 the first day, $18 for every day after. Kayaks are $35–$45 per day. Car shuttles for canoeists paddling the 99-mile Wilderness Trail from Chokoloskee (Everglades City) to Flamingo are $135 with NACT canoe ($150 with your own) plus $5 park entrance fee. Reservations are required.

Diving
Biscayne National Underwater Park, Inc., is the official concessionaire for Biscayne National Park. It rents and sells equipment and conducts trips aboard *Boca Chita,* a 43-foot dedicated snorkel and scuba boat. Trips include 1¼ hours on the reefs. The resort course and private instruction lead to full certification, and group charters can also be arranged. *Convoy Point, Box 1270, Homestead 33090, ☎ 305/230–1100, FAX 305/230–1120. Cost: $27.95 snorkeling, $34.50 scuba. ☼ Office: daily 9–5:30; trips daily 1:30–5.*

Fishing
The rangers in the two parks enforce all state fishing laws and a few of their own. Ask at each park's visitor center for that park's specific regulations.

Skydiving
Skydive Miami offers jumps above Homestead General Aviation Airport. All first jumps start with an hour of classroom instruction, leading to an aerial flight to altitude and a tandem dive with an instructor. *Homestead General Aviation Airport, 28700 S.W. 217th Ave., Homestead, ☎ 305/759–3483. Cost: $129; discounts for groups of 5 or more, 5% surcharge for credit cards. Jumps weekends 7–sunset with 1-hr notice for more than 2 people, weekdays by appointment with 24-hrs notice.*

SPECTATOR SPORTS

Auto Racing
The first events at the 343-acre **Homestead Motorsports Complex** (1707 S.E. 43rd Ave., Homestead, temporary ☎ 305/247–1801) are slated for late 1995. The state-of-the-art facility has a 1½-mile quad-oval, 8-degree banked-turn track resembling the Indianapolis Motor Speedway. The oval is the key element of the 2.21-mile road course. A schedule of year-round manufacturer and race-team testing, club rac-

ing, and other events climaxes with IndyCar Grand Prix racing and the season-ending NASCAR Busch Series Grand National Division event.

BEACHES

Elliott Key has a 30-foot-wide sandy beach (the only beach in Biscayne National Park); boaters like to anchor off it for a swim. It's about a mile north of the harbor on the west (bay) side of the key.

Homestead Bayfront Park has a saltwater atoll pool, adjacent to Biscayne Bay, which is flushed by tidal action. It's popular with local families and teenagers. Highlights include a "tot-lot" playground, ramps for people with disabilities (including a ramp that leads into the swimming area), and four barbecues in the picnic pavilion. *9698 S.W. 328th St., Homestead, ☎ 305/230–3034. ☛ $3 per car. ☉ Daily 7–sunset.*

DINING AND LODGING

Dining

Although the two parks are wilderness areas, there are restaurants within a short drive of all park entrances: between Miami and Shark Valley along the Tamiami Trail (U.S. 41), in the Homestead–Florida City area, in Everglades City, and in the keys along the Overseas Highway (U.S. 1). The only food service in either park is at Flamingo in the Everglades, but many of the independent restaurants listed below will pack picnic fares to take to the parks. (You can also find fast-food establishments with carryout service on the Tamiami Trail and in Homestead–Florida City.)

Lodging

Southwest of Miami, Homestead has become a bedroom community for both parks. You'll find well-kept older properties and shiny new ones, chain motels, and independents. Prices tend to be somewhat lower than in the Miami area.

Everglades City

DINING

$–$$ **Oyster House.** An established local favorite, this rustic seafood house
★ is accented by mounted swampcats, gator heads, deer, crabs, nets, shells, and anchor chains. Lanterns from the A-frame ceiling burnish plank walls. You sit at booths and tables set without cloths. They'd serve on the porch, too, but the insects can get too pesty—though in winter, when the bugs relent, guests sit outside with a drink from the bar to wait for a table. Fresh oysters are shucked daily, and main-course favorites include the broiled or grilled pompano, black-tip shark, frogs' legs, gator tail, and custom-cut steaks. Desserts include a homemade Key lime pie, carrot cake, and Black Forest cake. ✕ *Rte. 29 (Chokoloskee Causeway), ☎ 941/695–2073. MC, V. Closed Thanksgiving, Dec. 25.*

$ **Susie's Station.** Susie Olson fell in love with Everglades City and made good here, opening this 85-seat restaurant in 1992 and running it until a car accident carried her away. Now her longtime sweetheart, Biss Williams, runs it exactly the way Susie did. You'd swear the place dates from Everglades City's heyday, with its white-balustered screened porch, the gas station memorabilia, and the 1898 horse-drawn oil tanker. Replica '20s lamps are strung over booths set with beige cloths. There are three dining areas, one with original area art by Camille Baumgartner, another fixed up like an old general store, and the third on the screened porch. Biss serves stone crabs in season, a cold seafood plate with lobster salad, seafood, steaks, and pizzas. The best buy is the nightly dinner special—maybe lasagna, baked chicken, or Salisbury steak. The homemade Key lime pie sells out daily (whole pies to go cost $14). ✗ *103 S.W. Copeland Ave.,* ☎ *941/695–2002. No credit cards. Closed Thanksgiving, Dec. 25. Beer and wine only.*

LODGING

$$ **Rod and Gun Club.** Hurricane Donna in 1960 did more damage than Andrew in 1992, but the pool and veranda were quickly restored at this landmark inn on the banks of the Barron River. With dark cypress and a nautical theme, the Rod and Gun is a vestige of backwoods glory days when imperial developer Barron Collier greeted U.S. presidents, Barrymores, and Gypsy Rose Lee here for days of leisurely fishing. Most of them flew in to the private landing strip; in the evenings they were fed by one of Collier's big catches, a chef who once worked for Kaiser Wilhelm. The old guest rooms, upstairs from the restaurant and bar, aren't open anymore, but you can stay in comfortable cottages (basic, with the standard amenities except room phone). The food is more than passable. Breakfast, lunch, and dinner are still served in the original dining room or on the wide veranda, and, as in days of yore, if you catch a "keeper" fish, the chef will prepare it for your dinner. ⌂ *200 Riverside Dr., 33929,* ☎ *941/695–2101. 25 rooms. Restaurant, lounge, pool, tennis courts. No credit cards.*

$ **Ivey House.** It's clean, homey, friendly, and a bargain, run by the folks who operate North American Canoe Tours. New manager Catlin Maser is a B&B-style innkeeper, and there are always adventure travelers around in the big living room—and lots of chatter over breakfast. The house is trailerlike, set upon blocks, and was a popular boardinghouse when workers were building the Tamiami Trail. Earl and Agnes Ivey ran it from 1928 to 1974. There was nothing at all fancy about it then, or now. Baths are down the hall, but the rooms are private. ⌂ *107 Camellia St., 33929,* ☎ *941/695–3299. 10 rooms with shared baths. Bicycles, recreation room, library. MC, V. Closed May–Oct.*

Flamingo

DINING

$$ **Flamingo Restaurant.** The grand view, convivial lounge, and casual style are great. Big picture windows on the visitor center's second floor overlook Florida Bay, revealing variously soaring eagles, gulls, pelicans, terns, and vultures. Dine at low tide, and you get to see the birds flock to the sandbar just offshore. Less satisfying is the food itself. All the seafood comes frozen—unless it's your own catch, which the kitchen will prepare after you've cleaned it at the marina. Otherwise look for pastas and a few grills. Service is limited to buffets in summer, though the snack bar at the marina store stays open all year to serve pizza, sandwiches, and salads, and you can always order a picnic basket. ✗ *Flamingo Lodge, 1 Flamingo Lodge Hwy.,* ☎ *305/253–2241 from Miami or 941/695–3101 from Gulf Coast. AE, D, DC, MC, V.*

LODGING

$$ **Flamingo Lodge Marina & Outpost Resort.** This plain low-rise motel offers the only lodging inside Everglades National Park. Accommodations are basic but well kept, and an amiable staff with a sense of humor helps you adjust to the alligators who sometimes bellow in the sewage-treatment pond down the road, raccoons roaming the pool enclosure at night, and the flock of ibis grazing on the lawn. Rooms have carpeting, wood-paneled and plaster walls, contemporary furniture, flo-

ral bedspreads, and art prints of bird life. Bathrooms are tiny. All motel rooms face Florida Bay but don't necessarily overlook it. The cottages, in a wooded area on the margin of a coastal prairie, have kitchenettes and accommodate six people, except for the two units accessible to people with disabilities, which accommodate four. Ask about reserving tours, skiffs, and canoes when you make reservations. ⌕ *1 Flamingo Lodge Hwy., 33034,* ☎ *305/253–2241 from Miami, 941/695–3101 from Gulf Coast, or 800/600–3813. 101 motel rooms, 24 cottages. Restaurant, lounge, snack bar, pool, coin laundry. AE, D, DC, MC, V.*

Florida City

DINING

$$ **Mutineer Restaurant.** Former Sheraton Hotels builder Allan Bennett built this upscale roadside restaurant with its indoor-outdoor fish and duck pond at a time (1980) when Florida City was barely on the map. Bi-level dining rooms are divided by sea scenes in etched glass, and there's striped velvet chairs, stained glass, and a few portholes, but no excess. The Wharf Lounge behind its solid oak doors is imaginatively decorated with a magnified aquarium and nautical antiques, including a crow's nest with stuffed crow, gold parrot, and treasure chest. The big menu features 18 seafood entrées plus another half dozen daily seafood specials, as well as game, ribs, and steaks. Favorites include barbecued baby back ribs, whole Dungeness crab, and snapper Oscar (topped with crabmeat and asparagus). Enjoy live music Thursday–Saturday evenings. ✕ *11 S.E. 1st Ave.,* ☎ *305/245–3377. AE, D, DC, MC, V.*

$-$$ **Richard Accursio's Capri Restaurant** and **King Richard's Room.** One
★ of the oldest family-run restaurants in Dade County—since 1958— this is where locals dine out: business groups at lunch, the Rotary Club each Wednesday at noon, and families at night. Specialties include pizza with light, crunchy crusts and ample toppings; mild, meaty conch chowder; mussels in garlic-cream or marinara sauce; Caesar salad with lots of cheese and anchovies; antipasto with a homemade, vinegary Italian dressing; pasta shells stuffed with rigatoni cheese in tomato sauce; yellowtail snapper française; and Key lime pie with plenty of real Key lime juice. A choice of six early-bird entrées is offered 4:30–6:30 for $7.95, including soup or salad and potato or spaghetti. ✕ *935 N. Krome Ave.,* ☎ *305/247–1544. AE, D, MC, V. Closed Dec. 25, Sun. except Mother's Day.*

LODGING

$$ **Best Western Gateway to the Keys.** New at the end of 1994, this two-story motel sits well back from the highway and contains such amenities as full closets, a heat lamp in the bathroom, and complimentary Continental breakfast. More expensive rooms come with wet bar, fridge, microwave, and coffeemaker. Otherwise it's a standard modern motel with floral prints and twin reading lamps. ⌕ *1 Strano Blvd., 33034,* ☎ *305/246–5100,* 𝖥𝖠𝖷 *305/242–0056. 114 units. Pool, spa, laundry. AE, D, DC, MC, V.*

$$ **Hampton Inn.** This two-story motel just off the highway has good clean rooms (including a post–Hurricane Andrew wing) and public-friendly policies, including free Continental breakfast, local calls, and movie channel. All rooms have at least two upholstered chairs, twin reading lamps, and a desk and chair. Units are color-coordinated and carpeted. Baths have tub-showers. ⌕ *124 E. Palm Dr., 33034,* ☎ *305/247–8833 or 800/426–7866,* 𝖥𝖠𝖷 *305/247–8833. 122 units. Pool. AE, D, DC, MC, V.*

Homestead

DINING

$ El Toro Taco. The Hernandez family came to the United States from San
★ Luis Potosí, Mexico, to pick crops. In 1976 they opened this area institution, where they make their own salt-free tortillas and nacho chips
with Texas corn that they grind themselves. The cilantro-dominated
salsa is mild, for American tastes; if you like more fire on your tongue,
ask for a side dish of minced jalapeño peppers to mix in. Specialties
include *chile rellenos* (green peppers stuffed with ground beef and
topped with cheese) and chicken fajitas. ✗ *1 S. Krome Ave.,* ☎ *305/
245–8182. MC, V. BYOB.*

$ Potlikker's. This southern country-style restaurant takes its name from
the broth—pot liquor—left over from the boiling of greens. Plants dan-
gle from the sides of open rafters in the lofty pine-lined dining room.
Specialties include a lemon-pepper chicken breast with lemon sauce,
fresh-carved roast turkey with homemade dressing, and at least 11 different vegetables to serve with lunch and dinner entrées. For dessert,
try Key lime pie—4 inches tall and frozen; it tastes great if you daw-
dle while it thaws. ✗ *591 Washington Ave.,* ☎ *305/248–0835. AE,
MC, V. Closed Dec. 25.*

$ Tiffany's. This country-French cottage with shops and a restaurant under
a big banyan tree looks like a converted pioneer house with its high-
pitched roof and lattice. That's because fourth-generation Miamian Rebecca DeLuria, who built it in 1984 with her husband, Robert, wanted
a place that reminded her of the Miami she remembered. Teaberry-color
tables, satinlike floral place mats, marble-effect floor tiles, fresh flowers on each table, and lots of country items lend to the tearoom style
found here. Featured entrées include hot crabmeat au gratin, aspara-
gus supreme (rolled in ham with hollandaise sauce), and quiche of the
day. Homemade desserts are to die for: old-fashioned (very tall) carrot cake, strawberry whipped-cream cake, and a harvest pie with double crust that layers apples, cranberries, walnuts, raisins, and a caramel
topping. There's also a Sunday brunch. ✗ *22 N.E. 15th St.,* ☎
305/246–0022. MC, V. Closed Mon., Dec. 25, Jan. 1. No dinner.

Nearby Miami

DINING

$ Coopertown Restaurant. In 1995 Jesse and Sally Kimmon celebrated
50 years of running their rustic 30-seat restaurant just into the Everglades, west of Miami. They've added a chickee that can accommodate another 40 diners outdoors, but otherwise this still has Old Florida
style—filled with alligator skulls, stuffed alligator heads, and gator accessories (belts, key chains, and the like). Specialties include alligator
and frogs' legs, breaded and deep-fried in vegetable oil, available for
breakfast, lunch, or dinner. ✗ *22700 S.W. 8th St.,* ☎ *305/226–6048.
MC, V. Beer and wine only.*

$ Pit Bar-B-Q. The intense aroma of barbecue and blackjack-oak smoke
will overwork your salivary glands. Order at the counter; then come
when called to pick up your food. Specialties include barbecued chicken
and ribs with a tangy sauce, french fries, coleslaw, and a fried biscuit
as well as catfish, frogs' legs, and breaded shrimp deep-fried in vegetable oil. ✗ *16400 S.W. 8th St.,* ☎ *305/226–2272. MC, V. Beer only.
Closed Thanksgiving, Dec. 25.*

Shark Valley

DINING

$ Miccosukee Restaurant. Murals depict Native American women cook-
ing and men engaged in a powwow. Specialties include catfish and frogs'
legs breaded and deep-fried, Indian fry bread (a flour-and-water dough

deep-fried), pumpkin bread, Indian burger (ground beef browned, rolled in fry bread dough, and deep-fried), and Indian tacos (fry bread with chili, lettuce, tomato, and shredded Cheddar cheese on top). ✕ *Tamiami Trail, near Shark Valley park entrance,* ☎ *305/223–8380, ext. 332. No credit cards.*

LODGING

$ **Everglades Tower Inn.** If you're overnighting in Shark Valley, odds are you just need a plain, serviceable, and affordable room, and that's just what you get here. This Miccosukee family-run lodging is 1 mile west of the Shark Valley entrance to Everglades National Park. Rooms have double doubles and baths but no phones. Next door are the Gator Hut Cafe, for affordable meals, and the Everglades Shark Valley Crafts Center. ⌂ *Tamiami Trail, mile marker 70, SR Box E–4910, Ochopee 33943,* ☎ *305/559–7779 or 800/423–6218 in FL. 20 rooms. MC, V.*

EVERGLADES ESSENTIALS

Arriving and Departing

By Plane

Miami International Airport (MIA) is the closest commercial airport to the Everglades and Biscayne national parks. It's 34 miles from Homestead and 83 miles from the Flamingo resort in Everglades National Park.

BETWEEN THE AIRPORT AND TOWNS

SuperShuttle (☎ 305/871–2000) operates 11-passenger air-conditioned vans to Homestead. Service from MIA is available around the clock, on demand; booths are located outside most luggage areas on the lower level. For the return to MIA, a 24-hour advance reservation is requested. The cost is $40 for the first person, $12 for each additional person at the same address.

Airporter (☎ 800/830–3413) runs shuttle buses three times daily off-season, four times daily in winter, that stop at the Hampton Inn in Florida City on their way between MIA and the Florida Keys. Shuttle service, which takes approximately an hour, runs 6:10 AM–5:20 PM from Florida City, 7:30 AM–6 PM from the airport, but reservations must be made in advance. Pickups can be arranged for all baggage-claim areas. The cost is $20 one-way.

Metrobus Route 1A runs from Homestead to MIA only during peak weekday hours: 6:30–9 AM and 4–6:30 PM.

Greyhound Lines operates three buses daily in each direction between the Homestead bus stop (5 N.E. 3rd Rd., ☎ 305/247–2040) and Miami's Greyhound depot (4111 N.W. 27th St., ☎ 305/871–1810), from which it's about a $5 cab ride to MIA. You can take a blue ARTS (Airport Region Taxi Service) car from MIA to the Greyhound depot for about $5.

By Car

From Miami, the main highways to Homestead–Florida City are U.S. 1, the Homestead Extension of Florida's Turnpike, and Krome Avenue (Route 997/old U.S. 27).

To reach the western gateway to Everglades National Park, take the Tamiami Trail (U.S. 41). From Naples, it's 35 miles east to Everglades City's Gulf Coast Ranger Station and 70 miles to the Shark Valley Information Center. From Miami, it's 40 miles west to Shark Valley and 83 miles to Everglades City.

To reach Biscayne National Park, take the turnpike extension from Miami to the Tallahassee Road (Southwest 137th Avenue) exit, turn left, and go south. Turn left at North Canal Drive (Southwest 328th Street), go east, and follow signs to park headquarters at Convoy Point. The park is about 30 miles from downtown Miami.

By Boat

If you're entering the United States by boat, you must phone **U.S. Customs** (☎ 800/432–1216) either from a marine phone or on first arriving ashore. At its option, customs will direct you to Dodge Island Seaport (Miami), will otherwise rendezvous with you, or will clear you by phone.

Getting Around

By Car

If you don't have your own car, you'll want to rent one to get from Homestead–Florida City to the parks. Agencies in the area include **A&A Auto Rental** (30005 S. Dixie Hwy., Homestead 33030, ☎ 305/246–0974), **Enterprise Rent-a-Car** (30428 S. Federal Hwy., Homestead 33030, ☎ 305/246–2056), and **Thrifty Car Rental** (406 N. Krome Ave., Homestead 33030, ☎ 305/245–8992).

To reach Everglades National Park's Main Visitor Center and Flamingo, turn right (west) onto Route 9336 in Florida City, and follow signs to the park. From Homestead, the Main Visitor Center is 11 miles, and Flamingo is 49 miles.

To get to the south end of Everglades National Park in the Florida Keys, take U.S. 1 south from Homestead. It's 27 miles to the Key Largo Ranger Station (between mile markers 98 and 99, BS, Overseas Hwy.), which is not always staffed but has maps and information.

To reach Biscayne National Park from Homestead, take U.S. 1 or Krome Avenue to Lucy Street (Southeast 8th Street), and turn east. Lucy Street becomes North Canal Drive (Southwest 328th Street). Follow signs for about 8 miles to the park headquarters.

By Taxi

The local cab company is **New Taxi** (☎ 305/247–7466). Others servicing the area include **Action Express Taxi** (☎ 305/743–6800) and **South Dade Taxi** (☎ 305/256–4444).

Guided Tours

Tours of Everglades and Biscayne national parks typically focus on native wildlife, plants, and park history. Concessionaires operate tram tours in the Everglades and boat cruises in both parks. In addition, the National Park Service organizes a variety of free programs at Everglades National Park. Ask a ranger for the daily schedule.

Orientation Tours

All Florida Adventure Tours (8263-B S.W. 107th Ave., Miami 33173-3729, ☎ 305/270–0219) operates from one-day to two-week custom tours and standard 10-day tours for groups, emphasizing nature, history, and ecology.

Special-Interest Tours

AIR TOURS

Everglades Air Tours (Homestead General Aviation Airport, 28790 S.W. 217th Ave., Homestead, ☎ 305/248–7754) gives narrated, bird's-eye tours of the Everglades and Florida Bay that last 50 minutes and cost $55 per person.

AIRBOAT TOURS

In Everglades City, **Florida Boat Tours** (200 Rte. 29, ☎ 941/695–4400 or 800/282–9194 in FL) run 30- to 40-minute backcountry tours aboard custom-designed jet airboats. The cost is $11.95 adults and $5.50 children 7–12; one-hour tours for a maximum of six people are $30 adults and $15 children under 13. **Swampland Airboat Tours** (Box 619, 33929, ☎ 941/695–2740 or 800/344–2740) offer personalized tours of the Everglades or the Big Cypress National Preserve. The cost is $60 per hour for up to six persons. Reservations are required. **Wooten's Everglades** (Wooten's Alligator Farm, Tamiami Trail, ☎ 941/695–2781 or 800/282–2781) runs a variety of airboat and swamp-buggy tours through the Everglades. (Swamp buggies, giant tractorlike vehicles with oversize rubber wheels, can take up to 20 people at a time.) Tours of approximately 30 minutes cost $12 for ages seven and over; younger children are free.

Southwest of Florida City near the entrance to Everglades National Park, **Everglades Alligator Farm** (40351 S.W. 192nd Ave., ☎ 305/247–2628) runs a 4-mile, 30-minute tour of the River of Grass with departures 20 minutes after the hour. The tour includes free hourly alligator shows and feedings. Costs are $11 adults, $10 senior citizens, and $6 children 4–12 for the tour and show, or $5 adults and senior citizens, $3 children for the show only. No reservations are necessary.

From Shark Valley, **Buffalo Tiger's Florida Everglades Airboat Ride** (12 mi west of Krome Ave., 20 mi west of Miami city limits on Tamiami Trail, ☎ 305/559–5250) is led by a former chairman of the Miccosukee tribe. The 35- to 40-minute trip through the Everglades includes a stop at an old Native American camp. Tours cost $10 adults and $5 children under 10 (family rates available) and operate Monday through Thursday and Saturday 10–sunset and Sunday 11–sunset. Reservations are not required. **Coopertown Airboat Ride** (5 mi west of Krome Ave. on Tamiami Trail, ☎ 305/226–6048) operates the oldest airboat rides in the Everglades (since 1945). The 30- to 35-minute tour through the Everglades saw grass visits two hammocks (subtropical hardwood forests) and alligator holes. The charge is $9 ages 7 and over, with a $22 minimum for the boat. **Everglades Gator Park** (12 mi west of Florida's Turnpike on Tamiami Trail, ☎ 305/559–2255) offers free tours of a Native American village and 45-minute airboat tours. Rates (including tax) are $12 adults and $6.50 children 6–12. A gift shop and restaurant are also on the premises.

BOAT TOURS

From Everglades City, **Everglades National Park Boat Tours** (Gulf Coast Ranger Station, Rte. 29, ☎ 941/695–2591 or 800/445–7724 in FL) carry 40 to 140 passengers (the two largest boats have food and drink concessions) on three separate 14-mile tours through the Ten Thousand Islands region along the Gulf of Mexico on the western margin of the park. The cost is $11 adults and $5.50 children 6–12. **Majestic Tours** (Box 241, 33929, ☎ 941/695–2777) are led by exceptionally well-informed guides, Frank and Georgia Garrett. The 3½- to four-hour trips, on a 24-foot pontoon boat, depart from Glades Haven, just shy of a mile south of the circle in Everglades City; take in the Ten Thousand Islands; and visit the Watson Place, site of a turn-of-the-century wilderness plantation run by a fearsome outlaw. Tours are limited to six passengers and include brunch or afternoon snacks. The cost is $60 per person, $30 children under 12.

At **Flamingo Lodge Marina & Outpost Resort** (TW Recreational Services Inc., Everglades National Park, 1 Flamingo Lodge Hwy., Flamingo

33034, ☎ 305/253–2241 or 941/695–3101, FAX 941/695–3921), a number of services are offered, including help in arranging for individualized tours given by charter fishing-boat captains. The cost is $265 a day for up to two people, $25 each additional person. **Back Country Tour** gives two-hour cruises aboard a 40-passenger catamaran. The cost (including tax) is $12 adults and $6 children 6–12. **Florida Bay Cruise** runs 90-minute tours of Florida Bay aboard *Bald Eagle*, a 90-passenger catamaran. It costs $8.50 adults and $4.50 children 6–12 (including tax).

★ Tours at Biscayne National Park are now run by people-friendly **Biscayne National Underwater Park, Inc.** (Convoy Point, east end of North Canal Dr. [S.W. 328th St.], Box 1270, Homestead 33090, ☎ 305/230–1100, FAX 305/230–1120). Daily trips (10–1) explore the park's living coral reefs 10 miles offshore on *Reef Rover IV*, a 53-foot glass-bottom boat that carries up to 49 passengers. On days when the weather is unsuitable for reef viewing, an alternative two-hour, ranger-led, interpretive tour visits Elliott Key. Reservations are recommended, especially in summer. The cost is $16.50 adults, $15.50 senior citizens, and $8.50 children under 13.

CANOE AND KAYAK TOURS
North American Canoe Tours (Ivey House, 107 Camellia St., Box 5038, Everglades City 33929, ☎ 941/695–4666 or 941/695–3299; May–Sept. 203/739–0791; FAX 941/695–4155) leads one-day to six-night Everglades tours November–April for up to 10 participants. Highlights include bird and gator sightings, mangrove forests, no-man's-land beaches, relics of the hideouts of infamous and just plain reclusive characters, and spectacular sunsets. Included in the cost of extended tours ($450–$750) are canoes, all necessary equipment, a guide, meals, and lodging for the first and last nights at the Ivey House B&B in Everglades City. Day trips cost $40, and one-day bicycling and hiking tours are also offered.

TRAM TOURS
In Flamingo, **Wilderness Tram Tour** (Flamingo Lodge, ☎ 305/253–2241 or 941/695–3101) visits Snake Bight, an indentation in the Florida Bay shoreline, aboard a 42-passenger screened tram. This two-hour tour passes through a mangrove forest and a coastal prairie to a 100-yard boardwalk over the mud flats at the edge of the bight. The cost (including tax) is $7.95 adults, $4 children 6–12.

Starting at the Shark Valley visitor center off the Tamiami Trail, **Shark Valley Tram Tours** (Box 1729, Tamiami Station, Miami 33144, ☎ 305/221–8455) follow a 15-mile loop road into the interior, stopping at a 50-foot observation tower especially good for viewing gators in winter. Tours cost $8 adults, $7.20 senior citizens, and $4 children under 13. Reservations are recommended December–March.

Important Addresses and Numbers

Emergencies
Dial 911 for **police** or **ambulance**. In the national parks, rangers answer police, fire, and medical emergencies. Phone the park switchboards: **Biscayne** (☎ 305/230–1144) or **Everglades** (☎ 305/242–7700). **Florida Marine Patrol** (☎ 305/325–3346), a division of the Florida Department of Natural Resources, maintains a 24-hour telephone service for reporting boating emergencies and natural resource violations. **Miami Beach Coast Guard Base** (100 MacArthur Causeway, Miami Beach, ☎ 305/535–4300 or 305/535–4314, VHF-FM Channel 16) responds to local marine emergencies and reports of navigation hazards. The National

Weather Service supplies local forecasts through its **National Hurricane Center** (Tamiami Trail Campus of Florida International University, ☎ 305/665–0429). Call for information on a new 24-hour recording and hurricane advisories June–November.

HOSPITALS
SMH Homestead Hospital (160 N.W. 13th St., Homestead, ☎ 305/248–3232; physician referral, ☎ 305/633–2255).

Tourist Information
South Dade Visitor Information Center (160 U.S. 1, Florida City 33034, ☎ 305/245–9180 or 800/388–9669, FAX 305/247–4335). **Biscayne National Park:** Convoy Point Visitor Center (9700 S.W. 328th St., Box 1369, Homestead 33090-1369, ☎ 305/230–7275). **Everglades City Chamber of Commerce** (Rte. 29 and Tamiami Trail, Everglades City 33929, ☎ 941/695–3941). **Everglades National Park:** Main Visitor Center (40001 Rte. 9336, Florida City 33034-6733, ☎ 305/242–7700), Gulf Coast Ranger Station (Rte. 29, Everglades City 33929, ☎ 941/695–3311), Flamingo Ranger Station (1 Flamingo Lodge Hwy., Flamingo 33034-6798, ☎ 941/695–2945). **Homestead–Florida City Chamber of Commerce** (43 N. Krome Ave., Homestead 33030, ☎ 305/247–2332).

4 Fort Lauderdale

Once known for its wild spring breaks, this southern Florida city on the east coast is newly chic. Just as the beach has renewed itself, so has downtown—with residential construction and an emerging cultural arts district.

By Herb Hiller

WITH ITS REJUVENATED beachfront and downtown like balanced weights on the ends of a barbell, Fort Lauderdale has bench-pressed its way out of a reputation for rowdy spring breaks, and urban renewal has replaced scantily clad collegians as the most-talked-about attraction of vacationing here. You can drive between beach and town along beautiful Las Olas Boulevard, ride the free midweek trolley, or—the best bet for experiencing this canal-laced city—cruise aboard the city's water taxi. All these, plus the new expressway system that connects city and airport (including Florida's only vehicular tunnel), make getting around Fort Lauderdale, unlike elsewhere in congested Florida, remarkably hassle-free.

Also unlike elsewhere, where gaudy tourist zones stand aloof from workaday downtowns, Fort Lauderdale exhibits uncommon consistency at both ends of the 2-mile Las Olas corridor. The sparkling new look results from a decision to thoroughly improve both beachfront and downtown rather than focus design integrity in town and let the beachfront fall prey to design by T-shirt retailers. Fort Lauderdale also differs from other Florida coastal resorts in its long stretch of unbuilt-upon beachfront. For 2 miles beginning just north of the new welcome center and the big Radisson Bahia Mar Beach Resort, strollers and café goers along Atlantic Boulevard enjoy clear views, typically across rows of colorful beach umbrellas, to the sea and ships passing in and out of nearby Port Everglades. Those on the beach can look back to an exceptionally graceful promenade.

Pedestrians rank ahead of cars in Fort Lauderdale. Broad walkways line both sides of the shore road, and traffic has been trimmed to two gently curving northbound lanes, where in-line skaters dance alongside the slow-moving cars. On the beach side, a low masonry wall, which serves as an extended bench, edges the promenade with wavelike curls. Where side streets reach the shore road, the wave crests and then breaks for pedestrian access to the beach. At night, the wall is wrapped in ribbons of fiber-optic color. On the upland side of Atlantic Boulevard, the 17-story Beach Place residential, retail, and entertainment complex is under construction two blocks north of Las Olas. Otherwise there are mostly low-rise hotels plus a defining row of smart cafés, restaurants, bars, and shops that seem to have sprung up overnight.

North of the redesigned beachfront are another 2 miles of open and natural upland and seaside. Much of the way parallels the Hugh Taylor Birch State Recreation Area, which preserves a patch of primeval Florida.

As lovely as the renewed beach is, the downtown area along the New River, site of a new arts and entertainment district, is equally attractive. Where drug deals went down less than five years ago, pricey tickets now sell for *Miss Saigon* and other touring Broadway shows at the riverfront Broward Center for the Performing Arts. Clustered within a five-minute walk are the Museum of Discovery and Science with its Blockbuster IMAX Theater, the expanding Fort Lauderdale Historical Society Museum, and the Museum of Art with its leading collection of 20th-century CoBrA works. Restaurants, sidewalk cafés, delis, and blues, folk, jazz, reggae, and rock clubs flourish. Brickell Station, along several blocks once owned by pioneers William and Mary Brickell, is expected to open its multistory entertainment stages, restaurants, and shops in 1996. A year later will bring the $40 million New World

Aquarium, and, in 1998, a living-history complex called Old Fort Lauderdale, with reenactments and docents in pioneer dress centered on the Museum of History.

Tying this district together is the Riverwalk, which extends a mile along the river's north bank and a half mile along the south. Tropical gardens with benches and interpretive displays fringe the walk on one side, boat landings on the other. East along Riverwalk is Stranahan House, where, in the late 19th century, beloved Frank Stranahan ran a pioneer trading post. A block away, Las Olas attractions begin. Tropical landscaping sets off fine shops, restaurants, and popular nightspots. From here it's five minutes by car or 30 minutes by water taxi back to the beach.

Broward County is named for Napoleon Bonaparte Broward, Florida's governor from 1905 to 1909, whose drainage schemes around the turn of the century opened much of the marshy Everglades region for farming, ranching, and settlement (in retrospect an environmental disaster). Fort Lauderdale's first known white settler, Charles Lewis, established a plantation along the New River in 1793. Major William Lauderdale built a fort at the river's mouth in 1838 during the Seminole Indian wars—hence the name.

Incorporated in 1911, with just 175 residents, Fort Lauderdale grew rapidly during the Florida boom of the 1920s. Today the city has a population of 150,000, while its suburban areas keep growing and growing—1.3 million in the county. New homes, offices, and shopping centers have filled in the gaps between older communities along the coastal ridge. Now they're marching west along I–75, I–595, and the Sawgrass Expressway. Broward County is blessed with near-ideal weather, with some 3,000 hours of sunshine a year. The average temperature is about 66°F–77°F in winter, 84°F in summer. Once a home for retirees, the county today attracts younger, working-age families, too. It's always been known as a sane and pleasant place to live. Now it's also becoming one of Florida's most diverse and dynamic places to vacation.

EXPLORING

The metro area is laid out in what is essentially a grid system. Streets run east–west, as do roads, courts, and drives, whereas avenues, terraces, and ways run north–south.

Tour 1: Downtown Fort Lauderdale

Numbers in the margin correspond to points of interest on the Fort Lauderdale Area map.

❶ This tour begins, appropriately enough, at **Stranahan House,** home of pioneer businessman Frank Stranahan and the oldest standing structure in Fort Lauderdale. Stranahan arrived in 1892 and with his wife Ivy befriended the Seminoles, traded with them, and taught them "new ways." In 1901 he built a store and later made it his home. Now it's a museum with many of his furnishings on display. *1 Stranahan Pl. (S.E. 6th Ave. at Las Olas Blvd.),* ☎ *305/524–4736.* ☛ *$5 adults, $2 children under 12.* ☉ *Wed.–Sat. 10–4, Sun. 1–4.*

Go north on Southeast 6th Avenue to **Las Olas Boulevard.** Between Southeast 6th and Southeast 11th avenues, Las Olas is an upscale shopping street with Spanish-Colonial buildings housing high-fashion boutiques, jewelry shops, and art galleries. If you drive east on Las Olas, you'll ❷ cross into **The Isles,** Fort Lauderdale's most expensive and prestigious

Fort Lauderdale Area

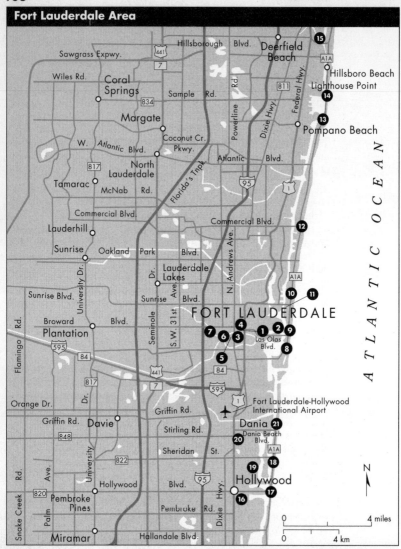

Art and Culture
Center of
Hollywood, **16**

Arts and Science
District, **6**

Bonnet House, **11**

Broadwalk, **17**

Broward County
Main Library, **4**

Deerfield Island
Park, **15**

Fort Lauderdale
beachfront, **9**

Graves Museum of
Archeology &
Natural History, **20**

Hillsboro Light, **14**

Hollywood North
Beach Park, **18**

Hugh Taylor Birch
State Recreation
Area, **10**

International
Swimming Hall of
Fame Museum and
Aquatic Complex, **8**

The Isles, **2**

John U. Lloyd Beach
State Recreation
Area, **21**

Lauderdale-by-
the-Sea, **12**

Museum of Art, **3**

Pompano Beach, **13**

Riverwalk, **5**

Sailboat Bend, **7**

Stranahan House, **1**

West Lake Park, **19**

neighborhood, where the homes line a series of canals with large yachts beside the seawalls.

★ ❸ Return west on Las Olas to Andrews Avenue, turn right, and park in one of the municipal garages while you walk around downtown Fort Lauderdale. First stop is the **Museum of Art,** which features a major collection of works from the CoBrA (Copenhagen, Brussels, and Amsterdam) movement, plus Native American, pre-Columbian, West African, and Oceanic ethnographic art. Edward Larabee Barnes designed the museum building, which opened in 1986. The museum has a notable collection of works by celebrated Ashcan School artist William Glackens and other early 20th-century American painters. *1 E. Las Olas Blvd.,* ☎ *305/525–5500.* ☞ *$5 adults, $4 senior citizens, $3 students over 12.* ⊘ *Tues. 11–9, Wed.–Sat. 10–5, Sun. noon–5.*

❹ Walk one block north to the **Broward County Main Library,** in a distinctive building designed by Marcel Breuer. On display here are many works from Broward's Art in Public Places program, including a painting by Yaacov Agam; a wood construction by Marc Beauregard; an outdoor, aluminum-and-steel sculpture by Dale Eldred; and ceramic tile by Ivan Chermayeff. (Art in Public Places displays more than 200 works—painting, sculpture, photographs, weaving—by nationally renowned and Florida artists. Works are located at 13 major sites, including the main bus terminal and the airport (*see* Arriving and Departing *in* Fort Lauderdale Essentials, *below*). Productions from theater to poetry readings are presented in a 300-seat auditorium. *100 S. Andrews Ave.,* ☎ *305/357–7444 or 305/357–7457 for self-guided Art in Public Places walking tour brochure.* ☞ *Free.* ⊘ *Mon.–Thurs. 9–9, Fri.–Sat. 9–5, Sun. noon–5:30. Closed holidays.*

★ ❺ Go west on Southeast 2nd Street to Southwest 2nd Avenue, turn left, and head toward palm-lined **Riverwalk,** a lovely, paved promenade on the north bank of the New River. (SunBank sponsors a jazz brunch along Riverwalk the first Sunday of every month.) By the late 1990s, it will extend 2 miles on both sides of the beautiful urban stream, connecting
★ ❻ a cluster of new facilities collectively known as the **Arts and Science District.** The district includes the outdoor **Esplanade,** which features several exhibits, including a hands-on display of the science and history of navigation.

The major science attraction is the $30 million **Museum of Discovery and Science,** opened in 1992. It contains a 55-foot-by-71-foot screen in the Blockbuster IMAX Theater, which has six-channel sound and interactive exhibits on ecology, health, and outer space. Many displays focus on the local environment, including a replica of an oak forest complete with mosses, lichens, and air plants, which grow without soil. Another unusual exhibit offers a cutaway of an Indian shell mound. *401 S.W. 2nd St.,* ☎ *305/467–6637 for museum or 305/463–4629 for IMAX.* ☞ *Museum: $6 adults, $5 senior citizens and children over 3; IMAX: $5 adults, $4 senior citizens and children over 3; both: $8 adults, $7 senior citizens and children over 3.* ⊘ *Weekdays 10–5, Sat. 10–8:30, Sun. noon–5.*

The adjacent **Broward Center for the Performing Arts** (201 S.W. 5th Ave., ☎ 305/462–0222), a massive glass-and-concrete structure by the river, opened in 1991.

East of the Esplanade along the Riverwalk is the **Fort Lauderdale Historical Society Museum,** which by 1997 is expected to expand into several historic buildings, including the King-Cromartie House and the old New River Inn, adjacent to its longtime site. The museum surveys the city's history from the Seminole era to World War II. A model in the lobby depicts old Fort Lauderdale. The building also houses a research library and a bookstore. *219 S.W. 2nd Ave.,* ☎ *305/463–4431.* ☛ *$2 adults, $1 students and children 6–12.* ☉ *Tues.–Sat. 10–4, Sun. 1–4.*

For a look at one of Fort Lauderdale's reviving, historic residential districts, go five blocks west along Las Olas Boulevard to Southwest 7th Avenue and the entrance to **Sailboat Bend.** Between Las Olas and the river, as well as just across the river, lies a neighborhood with much the character of Old Town in Key West and historic Coconut Grove in Miami. No shops or services are located here. You can return to the start of the tour by traveling east along Las Olas Boulevard.

Tour 2: North on Scenic A1A

Go east on Southeast 17th Street across the **Brooks Memorial Causeway** over the Intracoastal Waterway and bear left onto Seabreeze Boulevard (Route A1A). You will pass through a neighborhood of older homes set in lush vegetation before emerging at the south end of Fort Lauderdale's beachfront strip. On your left at the newly renovated **Radisson Bahia Mar Beach Resort** (801 Seabreeze Blvd., ☎ 305/764–2233 or 800/327–8154) novelist John McDonald's fictional hero, Travis McGee, is honored with a plaque at marina slip F-18, where he docked his houseboat.

★ ⑧ Three blocks north, visit the **International Swimming Hall of Fame Museum and Aquatic Complex,** which celebrates its 31st anniversary in 1996. It contains two 10-lane, 50-meter pools and an exhibition building featuring photos, medals, and other souvenirs from major swimming events around the world, as well as a theater that shows films of onetime swimming stars Johnny Weismuller and Esther Williams. *1 Hall of Fame Dr.,* ☎ *305/462–6536 for museum or 305/468–1580 for pool.* ☛ *Museum: $3 adults; $1 senior citizens, children 6–12, and military personnel; $5 family. Pool: $3 adults; $2 nonresident senior citizens and students; $1.50 resident senior citizens and students and military personnel.* ☉ *Museum and pro shop: daily 9–7. Pool: weekdays 8–4 and 6–8, weekends 8–4; closed mid-Dec.–mid-Jan.*

★ ⑨ As you approach Las Olas Boulevard, you will see the lyrical new styling that has given a distinctly European flavor to the **Fort Lauderdale beachfront.** A wave theme unifies the setting—from the low, white wave wall between the beach and widened beachfront promenade to the widened and bricked inner promenade in front of shops, restaurants, and hotels. Alone among Florida's major beachfront resorts, Fort Lauderdale Beach remains open and unbuilt-upon, and throughout the beach area, you'll see distinctive signs and street furniture. More than ever, the boulevard is worth promenading.

⑩ Turn left off Route A1A at Sunrise Boulevard, then right into **Hugh Taylor Birch State Recreation Area.** Amid the 180-acre park's tropical greenery, you can stroll along a nature trail, visit the Birch House Museum, picnic, play volleyball, pitch horseshoes, and paddle a canoe. *3109 E. Sunrise Blvd.,* ☎ *305/564–4521.* ☛ *$3.25 per vehicle with up to 8 people.* ☉ *8–sunset; ranger-guided nature walks Fri. at 10:30.*

★ ⑪ Cross Sunrise Boulevard and visit the **Bonnet House.** Closed in winter, when Evelyn Fortune Bartlett (now 107) is in residence, this charming mansion, built by Mrs. Bartlett's late husband, artist Frederic Clay Bartlett, stands on land he was given by his first father-in-law, Hugh Taylor Birch. The house and its subtropical 35-acre estate contain original works of art, whimsically carved animals, a swan pond, and, most of all, tranquillity. *900 N. Birch Rd.,* ☎ *305/563–5393.* ☛ *$8 adults; $6 senior citizens, students over 6, and military personnel (by reserved tour only).* ☼ *May–Nov., Tues.–Thurs. 10 and 1:30, Sun. 1:30.*

North of Birch Park, Route A1A edges back from the beach through a section known as the **Galt Ocean Mile,** marked by beach-blocking high-rises. The pattern changes again in **Lauderdale-by-the-Sea,** a low-rise family resort town. Construction over three stories is banned, and dozens of good restaurants and shops are nearby, so vacationers don't bother to use their cars. One block east of Route A1A, you can drive along lawn-divided El Mar Drive, lined by garden-style motels.

TIME OUT Where Commercial Boulevard meets the ocean, you can walk out onto **Anglin's Fishing Pier,** stretching 875 feet into the Atlantic. Stop in at the coffee shop or at any of the popular restaurants clustered around the seafront plaza. **Aruba Beach Cafe** (☎ 305/776–0001) is your best bet. A big beachside barn of a place, always crowded, always fun-loving, it serves large portions of Caribbean conch chowder, Cuban black-bean soup, fresh tropical salads, burgers, sandwiches, and seafood.

North of Lauderdale-by-the-Sea, Route A1A enters **Pompano Beach,** where the high-rise procession begins again. Take Atlantic Boulevard east to the beach road, which is first called Pompano Beach Boulevard and then again A1A. Behind a low coral rock wall, a park extends north and south of **Fisherman's Wharf** along the road and beach. The road swings back from the beach, and then returns to it crossing **Hillsboro Inlet.** To your right across the inlet you can see **Hillsboro Light,** the brightest light in the Southeast. The light is on private property and is inaccessible to the public.

Route A1A now enters onto the so-called **Hillsboro Mile** (actually more than 2 miles), which only a few years ago was one of Florida's outstanding residential corridors—a millionaire's row. Changes in zoning laws, however, have altered it; except for sections in the south and north, the island seems destined to sink under the weight of its massive condominiums. The road runs along a narrow strip of land between the Intracoastal Waterway and the ocean, with bougainvillea and oleanders edging the way and yachts docked along both banks. In winter, the traffic often creeps at a snail's pace along here, as vacationers and retirees gawk at the views.

Turn left on Hillsboro Boulevard (Route 810). Make a sharp right just over the bridge onto Riverview Road, and park at the Riverview Restaurant to take a free boat ride to **Deerfield Island Park.** This 8½-acre island, officially designated an urban wilderness area, resulted from the dredging of the Intracoastal Waterway and from construction of the Royal Palm Canal. Its mangrove swamp provides a critical habitat for gopher tortoises, gray foxes, raccoons, and armadillos. *1 Deerfield Island, Deerfield Beach,* ☎ *305/360–1320.* ☛ *Free.* ☼ *Wed., Sat. 8:15–sunset.*

At this point you're not far from the Palm Beach County line (*see* Chapter 5, Palm Beach and the Treasure Coast). You can return to Fort Lauderdale along Route A1A or turn west and head south along U.S. 1 or I–95.

Tour 3: Hollywood

Begin exploring at the junction of U.S. 1 and Hollywood Boulevard, called Young Circle after Joseph W. Young, a California real estate developer who in 1921 began developing the community of **Hollywood** from the woody flatlands. Just east of here, you can visit the **Art and Culture Center of Hollywood.** A visual and performing arts center, it is set in a 1924 Mediterranean-style residence, typical of its era, and by 1996 will have expanded to 3,500 square feet. Facilities include an art reference library, outdoor sculpture garden, arts school, and museum store. *1650 Harrison St.,* ☎ *305/921–3274.* ☛ *$3 Wed.–Sat., $5 Sun. (including a classical or jazz concert); donations welcome Tues.* ☉ *Tues.–Sat. 10–4, Sun. 1–4.*

Drive east along wide Hollywood Boulevard, a reminder of the glory of the Young era. Cross the Intracoastal Waterway in front of the **Hollywood Beach Resort Hotel** (101 N. Ocean Dr., ☎ 305/921–0990), opened by Young in 1922 and now filled with time-share condominiums and some available by the night. To the rear of the hotel is the separately operated retail and entertainment mall **Oceanwalk**—a good idea that only inconsistently achieves the right execution.

Take the ramp north onto Route A1A. The Intracoastal Waterway parallels it to the west, and the beach and ocean lie just on the other side of the 2.2-mile **Broadwalk.** A paved promenade since 1924, it's popular with pedestrians and cyclists. Expect to hear French spoken, especially during the winter; Hollywood Beach has been a favorite winter getaway for Québecois ever since Joseph Young hired French-Canadians to work here in the 1920s.

TIME OUT   One-half mile north on the left is **Le Tub** (1100 N. Ocean Dr., ☎ 305/ 921–9425), formerly a Sunoco gas station and now a quirky waterside saloon with an affection for clawfoot bathtubs. Hand-painted tubs are everywhere, under ficus, sea grape, and palm trees. Le Tub is highly favored by locals for affordable food, mostly shrimp and barbecue.

The Broadwalk ends at **Hollywood North Beach Park.** No high-rises overpower the scene, nothing hip or chic, just a laid-back old-fashioned place for enjoying sun, sand, and sea. *Rte. A1A and Sheridan St.,* ☎ *305/926–2444.* ☛ *Free; parking: $5 until 2, $3 after.* ☉ *Daily 8–6.*

Turn west onto Sheridan Street and proceed ½ mile. On your left, enter 1,400-acre **West Lake Park.** By early 1996, Broward County's outstanding new resource-preserving nature facility and its wide range of recreational and interpretive attractions should be up and running. Canoes, kayaks, and boats with electric motors (no fossil fuels allowed in the park) will be available, and more than $1 million in nature exhibits will be on display at the Anne Kolb Nature Center, where a shop is expected to carry a large stock of books on the region's environment. Extensive boardwalks will traverse a mangrove community, and a 65-foot observation tower will yield views of the entire park and miles of contrasting development. *1200 Sheridan St.,* ☎ *305/926–2410.* ☛ *Fees and hrs to be determined.*

Drive west to Federal Highway (U.S. 1), turn right (you have now entered **Dania**), and continue past one of Florida's largest antiques districts (*see* Specialty Stores *in* Shopping, *below*) to the **Graves Museum of Archaeology & Natural History.** After 15 years of using makeshift facilities in various locations, the museum has settled into a 50,000-square-foot permanent home. Exhibits include collections of pre-

Columbian art and underwater artifacts from St. Thomas harbor as well as displays of Greco-Roman materials, a 3-ton quartz crystal, and dioramas of Tequesta Indian life and jaguar habitat. A 9,000-square-foot dinosaur hall and additional wildlife dioramas are expected in late 1996. Monthly lectures, conferences, field trips, and a summer archaeological camp are offered, and the museum bookstore is one of the best in Florida. *481 S. Federal Hwy.,* ☎ *305/925–7770,* FAX *305/925–7064.* ☛ *$5 adults, $4 senior citizens on Tues. only, $3 children 4–12.* ☉ *Tues.–Wed. and Fri.–Sat. 10–4, Thurs. 10–8, Sun. 1–4.*

★ ㉑ Continue north to Dania Beach Boulevard (Route A1A), turn right, and drive to the beach. Just before turning left to enter the **John U. Lloyd Beach State Recreation Area,** you'll find the Dania Pier (*see* Fishing *in* Sports and the Outdoors, *below*) and the colorful SeaFair, a small collection of shops and diversions yet to hit their stride. The recreation area has a pleasant pine-shaded beach and a jetty pier where you can fish, and it offers good views, north almost to Palm Beach County and south to Miami Beach. From the road, look west across the waterway to Port Everglades, with its deepwater freighters and cruise ships. *6503 N. Ocean Dr.,* ☎ *305/923–2833.* ☛ *$3.25 per vehicle with up to 8 people.* ☉ *8–sunset.*

From here return via A1A and Hollywood Boulevard to where you began, or take Dania Beach Boulevard north into Fort Lauderdale.

What to See and Do with Children

Butterfly World is a screened-in aviary in a tropical rain forest on 2.8 acres of land. Thousands of caterpillars, representing up to 150 species, pupate and emerge as butterflies. *3600 W. Sample Rd., Coconut Creek,* ☎ *305/977–4400.* ☛ *$8.95 adults, $7.95 senior citizens, $5 children 3–12.* ☉ *Mon.–Sat. 9–5, Sun. 1–5.*

Flamingo Gardens has gators, crocodiles, river otters, birds of prey, a 23,000-square-foot walk-through aviary, a plant house, and an Everglades Museum in the pioneer Wray Home. Admission includes a half-hour guided tram ride through a citrus grove and wetlands area. *3750 Flamingo Rd., Davie,* ☎ *305/473–0010.* ☛ *$8 adults, $6.40 senior citizens, $4.50 children 4–12.* ☉ *Daily 9–5.*

Museum of Discovery and Science (*see* Tour 1, *above*).

Sawgrass Recreation Park is on the site of a 16½-acre former fish camp at the edge of the Everglades. Here you can rent fishing boats, get bait and tackle, and enjoy a 90-minute series of three tours in one that includes an airboat ride, a tour of a Native American village replica, and an educational live reptile exhibit with alligators and caimans. A snack and gift shop is also available. *2 mi north of I–75 on U.S. 27,* ☎ *305/389–0202 or 800/457–0788. Tour package: $13.40 adults, $12.40 senior citizens, $6.50 children 4–12. Tours daily 9–5; shop open daily 6–6.*

Seminole Native Village (4150 N. Rte. 7, Hollywood, ☎ 305/961–5140 for recording or 305/961–3220 for information) is a reservation where Seminole Indians sell arts and crafts. (The village also features a high-stakes bingo parlor and low-stakes poker tables, but these are not open to kids.) On the other side of Stirling Road, which separates Hollywood from Fort Lauderdale, is the **Anhinga Indian Museum and Art Gallery** (5791 S. Rte. 7, Fort Lauderdale, ☎ 305/581–0416). Here Joe Dan and Virginia Osceola display a collection of artifacts from the Seminoles and other tribes and sell contemporary Native American art and craft objects. Both the village and the museum and gallery are open daily 9–5. Ask at either site for directions to the Ah-Tha-Thi-Ki ("a place to remember") Seminole Museum in the Big Cypress Swamp, due to open in 1996.

Spykes Grove & Tropical Gardens, in operation since 1944, has discontinued its tram tours but still allows visitors to walk through the gardens and visit the minizoo with alligators, a bear born in captivity, peacocks, and roosters. *7250 Griffin Rd., Fort Lauderdale,* ☎ *305/583–0426.* ☛ *Free.* ☉ *Oct.–June, daily 9–5:30.*

Young at Art Children's Museum teaches kids to work in paint, graphics, sculpture, and crafts according to themes that change three times a year. Visitors can view work hung, mounted on pedestals, and even in motion. *801 S. University Dr., in the Fountains Shoppes, Plantation,* ☎ *305/424–0085.* ☛ *$3 ages over 2.* ☉ *Tues.–Sat. 11–5, Sun. noon–5.*

SHOPPING

Malls

Broward Mall (8000 W. Broward Blvd., at University Dr., Plantation), the county's largest shopping center, features such stores as Burdines, JCPenney, and Sears. A three-level, 669,000-square-foot, landscaped, glass-enclosed facility, **Fashion Mall** (University Dr., just north of Broward Blvd., Plantation) counts Macy's and Lord & Taylor among its 150 shops, boutiques, and restaurants. **Galleria Mall** (2414 E. Sunrise Blvd., just west of the Intracoastal Waterway, Fort Lauderdale) occupies more than 1 million square feet and includes Neiman-Marcus, Lord & Taylor, Saks Fifth Avenue, and Brooks Brothers. **Pompano Square** (2001 N. Federal Hwy., Pompano Beach) has 110 shops with three department stores and food stalls. **Sawgrass Mills Mall** (Flamingo Rd. and Sunrise Blvd., Sunrise) is a 2 million-square-foot, candy-color, Disney-style discount mall containing restaurants and entertainment activities in addition to 250 stores that include Loehmann's, JCPenney, Ann Taylor, Alfred Angelo Bridal, Levi's, TJ Maxx, and Donna Karan, Saks, and Spiegel's outlets. On weekdays, two shuttle buses run: One calls at major beach hotels between 8:55 and 9:30 AM, arrives at the huge mall around 10, and returns at 2:30, while the other leaves between 11:30 and 12:15 and returns just past 5. To schedule a pickup, call 305/846–2350 or 800/356–4557. The charge is $4 each way and includes a coupon book for use at the mall.

Flea Market

Some 600 vendors set up at the **Festival Flea Market** (2900 W. Sample Rd., at Florida's Turnpike, Pompano Beach). The largest market of its type in the county, it's open Tuesday–Friday 9:30–5, weekends to 6.

Specialty Stores

ANTIQUES

More than 75 dealers line Federal Highway (U.S. 1) in **Dania,** ½ mile south of the Fort Lauderdale airport and ½ mile north of Hollywood. Take the Stirling Road or Griffin Road East exits off I–95.

UPSCALE BOUTIQUES

If only for a stroll and some window-shopping, don't miss the **Shops of Las Olas** (a block off the New River just east of U.S. 1, Fort Lauderdale). The city's best boutiques plus top restaurants (many affordable) and art galleries line a beautifully landscaped street.

SPORTS AND THE OUTDOORS

Biking

Cycling is popular in Broward County, though the bad news is that metro Fort Lauderdale is one of the most dangerous places to bike in Florida. The good news is that you can ride the 330-meter **Brian Piccolo Park velodrome** (Sheridan St. and N.W. 101st Ave., Cooper City) in western Broward County. For a schedule of public hours and spectator events, as well as a copy of the new "Bicycling in Fort Lauderdale" brochure, contact the **County Bicycle Coordinator** (115 S. Andrews Ave., Fort Lauderdale 33301, ☎ 305/357–6661). Another safe cycling option is along the 2.2-mile **Broadwalk** on Hollywood Beach. Between April 16 and November 15, the cycling lane can be used at all hours. Other times of the year, use of the lane is restricted to between sunrise and 8 AM and between 4 PM and sunset. Otherwise, the most popular routes include Route A1A and Bayview Drive, especially early in the morning before traffic builds; the 7-mile bike path that parallels Route 84 and the New River and leads to Markham Park, which has mountain bike trails; a 4-mile loop that connects Pompano City Park, the Goodyear blimp hangar, and shopping in the vicinity of Copans Road and Federal Highway; and plenty of roads in the southwest and northwest sections of the county. Many shops along the beach rent bikes. A map for cycling Broward's streets is available in bike stores or from the county bicycle coordinator.

Diving

Good diving can be enjoyed within 20 minutes of the shore along Broward County's coast. Among the most popular of the county's 80 dive sites is the 2-mile-wide, 23-mile-long **Fort Lauderdale Reef,** the product of Florida's most successful artificial reef–building program. The project began in 1984 with the sinking of a 435-foot freighter donated by an Oklahoma marine electronics manufacturer. Since then more than a dozen houseboats, ships, and oil platforms have been sunk in depths of 10 to 150 feet to provide a habitat for fish and other marine life, as well as to help stabilize beaches. The most famous sunken ship is the 200-foot German freighter *Mercedes,* which was blown onto Palm Beach socialite Mollie Wilmot's pool terrace in a violent Thanksgiving storm in 1984; the ship has now been sunk a mile off Fort Lauderdale beach. For more information, contact the Greater Fort Lauderdale Convention & Visitors Bureau (*see* Important Addresses and Numbers *in* Fort Lauderdale Essentials, *below*). Dive shops and charter boats include:

Force E (2700 E. Atlantic Blvd., Pompano Beach, ☎ 305/943–3483; 2160 W. Oakland Park Blvd., Oakland Park, ☎ 305/735–6227) stores rent scuba and snorkeling equipment, provide instruction at all skill levels, and run charters.

Lauderdale Diver (1334 S.E. 17th St. Causeway, Fort Lauderdale, ☎ 305/467–2822 or 800/654–2073), which is PADI affiliated, arranges dive charters throughout the county. Dive trips typically last four hours. Nonpackage reef trips are also open to divers for $35, to snorkelers for $25; scuba and snorkel gear are extra.

Pro Dive (Radisson Bahia Mar Beach Resort, 801 Seabreeze Blvd., Fort Lauderdale, ☎ 305/761–3413 or 800/772–3483), a PADI five-star facility, is the area's oldest diving operation and offers packages with Radisson Bahia Mar Beach Resort, from where its 60-foot boat departs. Snorkelers can go out for $25 on the four-hour dive trip or $20 on the two-hour snorkeling trip, which includes snorkel equipment but not scuba gear. Scuba divers pay $35 using their own gear or $85 with all rentals included.

Fishing

Four main types of fishing are available in Broward County: bottom or drift-boat fishing from party boats, deep-sea fishing for large sport fish on charters, angling for freshwater game fish, and dropping a line off a pier.

For bottom fishing, party boats typically charge between $20 and $22 per person for up to four hours, including rod, reel, and bait. Three operators are **Captain Bill's** (south dock, Radisson Bahia Mar Beach Resort, 801 Seabreeze Blvd., Fort Lauderdale, ☎ 305/467–3855), **Fish City Pride** (Fish City Marina, 2621 N. Riverside Dr., Pompano Beach, ☎ 305/781–1211), and **Sea Leg's III** (5400 N. Ocean Dr., Hollywood, ☎ 305/923–2109).

Two primary centers for saltwater charter boats are **Radisson Bahia Mar Beach Resort** (801 Seabreeze Blvd., Fort Lauderdale, ☎ 305/764–2233) and the **Hillsboro Inlet Marina** (2629 N. Riverside Dr., Pompano Beach, ☎ 305/943–8222). Half-day charters for up to six people now run up to $325, six-hour charters up to $495, and full-day charters (eight hours) up to $595. Skipper and crew, plus bait and tackle, are included. Split parties can be arranged at a cost of about $85 per person for a full day.

Among marinas catering to freshwater fishing are **Sawgrass Recreation** (U.S. 27 north of I–595, ☎ 305/426–2474) and **Everglades Holiday Park** (21940 Griffin Rd., ☎ 305/434–8111). For $47.50 for five hours, you can rent a 14-foot, flat-bottom John boat (with a 9.9-horsepower Yamaha outboard) that carries up to four people. A rod and reel rent for $9 a day, and bait is extra. For two people, a fishing guide for a half day (four hours) is $110, for a full day (eight hours) $170; a third person adds $25 for a half day, $50 for a full day. You can also buy a freshwater fishing license (mandatory) here.

Fishing piers draw anglers for pompano, amberjack, bluefish, snapper, blue runners, snook, mackerel, and Florida lobsters. Pompano Beach's **Fisherman's Wharf** (☎ 305/943–1488) extends 1,080 feet into the Atlantic. The cost is $2.65 for adults, $1.06 for children under 10; rod-and-reel rental is $10.07 (including admission and initial bait). **Anglin's Fishing Pier** (☎ 305/491–9403), in Lauderdale-by-the-Sea, reaches 876 feet and is open for fishing 24 hours a day. Fishing is $3 for adults and $2 for children up to 12, tackle rental is an additional $10 (plus $10 deposit), and bait averages $2. Newly reopened in 1995 after complete rebuilding following Hurricane Andrew, the 920-foot **Dania Pier** (☎ 305/927–0640), in Dania, is open around the clock. Fishing is $3 for adults (including parking), tackle rental is $6, bait's about $2, and spectators pay $1. A snack bar is to open by mid-1996.

Golf

In addition to having a tropical climate that's perfect for playing almost every day of the year, Broward County features great golf bargains. More than 50 courses, public and private, green the landscape in metro Fort Lauderdale, including famous championship links. Off-season (May–October) greens fees range $15–$45, whereas peak-season (November–April) charges run $25–$65. Fees can be trimmed by working through **Next Day Golf** (☎ 305/772–2582), which customizes hotel-golf packages as well as providing 10%–25% discounts to golfers willing to wait until after 5 PM to book tee times for next-day play. Some private clubs even provide access to nonmembers through the service.

Members of the general public usually can arrange to play at: **Bonaventure Country Club** (200 Bonaventure Blvd., Fort Lauderdale, ☏ 305/389–2100 or 800/327–8090), 36 holes; **Broken Woods Country Club** (9000 Sample Rd., Coral Springs, ☏ 305/752–2270), 18 holes; **Colony West Country Club** (6800 N.W. 88th Ave., Tamarac, ☏ 305/726–8430), 36 holes; **Diplomat Resort & Country Club** (501 Diplomat Pkwy., Hallandale, ☏ 305/457–2082), 18 holes; **Emerald Hills** (4100 Hills Dr., Hollywood, ☏ 305/961–4000), 18 holes; **Jacaranda Golf Club** (9200 W. Broward Blvd., Plantation, ☏ 305/472–5855), 18 holes; **Oaks Golf & Racquet Club** (3701 Oaks Clubhouse Dr., Pompano Beach, ☏ 305/978–1737), 36 holes; **Rolling Hills** (3501 Rolling Hills Circle, Davie, ☏ 305/475–3010), 27 holes; **Sabal Palms Golf Course** (5101 W. Commercial Blvd., Fort Lauderdale, ☏ 305/731–2600), 18 holes; and **Sunrise Country Club** (7400 N.W. 24th Pl., Sunrise, ☏ 305/742–4333), 18 holes.

Spas

If you watch *Lifestyles of the Rich and Famous* on TV, you'll recognize the names of Greater Fort Lauderdale's two world-famous spas, the Bonaventure Resort & Spa and Palm-Aire Spa Resort. At each resort, women comprise 75%–80% of the spa clientele. Both resorts offer single-day spa privileges to nonguests, including body massage, exercise classes, facials, herbal wraps, spa-cuisine lunches, and other spa facilities and services. Price and availability of services vary with seasonal demand; resort guests have priority. Bring your own sneakers and socks—the spa provides everything else you'll need. Each spa will help you design a personal exercise-and-diet program tied to your lifestyle at home. If you already have an exercise program, bring it with you. If you have a medical problem, bring a letter from your doctor.

Bonaventure Resort & Spa (250 Racquet Club Rd., Fort Lauderdale, ☏ 305/389–3300 or 800/327–8090, FAX 305/384–0563) offers complimentary caffeine-free herbal teas in the morning and fresh fruit in the afternoon. The staff nutritionist follows American Heart Association and American Cancer Society guidelines and can accommodate macrobiotic and vegetarian diets. The full-service beauty salon is open to the public. In addition, there are 500 luxury guest rooms and suites, four restaurants, two lounges, two 18-hole championship golf courses, 24 tennis courts, five swimming pools, a Saddle Club, indoor roller-skating, bowling, a gift shop, and a boutique.

Palm-Aire Spa Resort (2601 Palm-Aire Dr. N, Pompano Beach, ☏ 305/972–3300 or 800/272–5624) is a 191-room, 750-acre health, fitness, and stress-reduction spa offering exercise activities, personal treatments, and calorie-controlled meals. It's 15 minutes from downtown Fort Lauderdale.

Less elaborate facilities are available at **Spa LXVI of the Hyatt Regency Pier Sixty-Six** (2301 S.E. 17th St., Fort Lauderdale, ☏ 305/525–6666 or 800/327–3796). The 22-acre site on the Intracoastal Waterway is minutes from the beach.

Tennis

Some 20 sites offer public courts throughout the county. Best known to Broward Countians (and largest) is **Holiday Park** (701 N.E. 12th Ave., Fort Lauderdale, ☏ 305/761–5378), which has 18 clay (14 lighted) and three hard-surface courts in the downtown area, 10 minutes from the beach. This is where former tennis pro Jimmy Evert taught his daughter Chris.

Waterskiing

A unique waterskiing cableway, which pulls water-skiers across the water, is found at **Quiet Waters Park,** just north of the Pompano Harness Track. **Ski Rixen** operates the waterskiing, which includes skis and life vests. *Power Line Rd., Pompano Beach,* ☎ *305/360–1315 for park or 305/ 429–0215 for Ski Rixen.* ☛ *Park: free weekdays, $1 per person week-ends. Waterskiing: $12 for 1 hr, $14 for 2 hrs.* ☉ *Park: daily 8–6:30, waterskiing daily 10–6.*

SPECTATOR SPORTS

In addition to contacting the addresses below directly, you can get tick-ets to major events from **Ticketmaster** (☎ 305/523–3309).

Dog Racing

Hollywood Greyhound Track has plenty of dog-racing action during its season, from December 26 to April 26. There is a clubhouse din-ing room. *831 N. Federal Hwy., Hallandale,* ☎ *305/454–9400.* ☛ *50¢–$1 box seats, $1 grandstand, $2 clubhouse, senior citizens free at matinees. Racing Tues., Thurs., Sat. at 12:30, 7:30; Sun., Mon., Wed., Fri. at 7:30.*

Horse Racing

Gulfstream Park Race Track is the home of the Florida Derby, one of the Southeast's foremost horse-racing events. The park greatly im-proved its facilities during the past two years: Admission costs have been lowered, time between races shortened, and the paddock ring elevated for better viewing by fans. Racing is held January–mid-March. *901 S. Federal Hwy., Hallandale,* ☎ *305/454–7000.* ☛ *$3 general admission (including parking and program), $5 clubhouse plus $2 for reserved seat or $1.75 for grandstand. Racing daily at 1.*

Pompano Harness Track, Florida's only harness track, was sold in early 1995 to Casino America. However, since Florida doesn't allow casino gambling, this 327-acre facility continues to operate as a har-ness track 11 months of the year. The Top o' the Park restaurant over-looks the finish line. *1800 S.W. 3rd St., Pompano Beach,* ☎ *305/ 972–2000.* ☛ *$1 grandstand, $2 clubhouse. Racing Mon., Wed.–Sat. at 7:30.*

Jai Alai

Dania Jai-Alai Palace offers one of the fastest games on the planet. Games are held year-round. *301 E. Dania Beach Blvd., Dania,* ☎ *305/428–7766.* ☛ *$1 general admission, $1.50–$7 reserved seats, senior citizens free 11:30–noon. Games Tues., Thurs., Sat. at noon, 7:15; Wed., Fri. at 7:15. Closed Wed. in June.*

Rodeo

Davie Arena for Rodeo holds rodeos throughout the year, but you have to call for the dates. For five-star rodeos, show up at 6:30, when gates open, and you can pay to get into the very popular country barbecue that precedes events. *6591 S.W. 45th St. (Orange Dr.), Davie,* ☎ *305/797–1145.* ☛ *Jackpot events: $5 adults, $2 children; five-star rodeo: $9 adults, $5 children.*

Rugby

The **Fort Lauderdale Knights** play September–April on the green at Crois-sant Park. *S.W. 17th St. at 2nd Ave., Fort Lauderdale,* ☎ *305/561–5263 for recording.* ☛ *Free. Games Sat. at 2.*

Soccer

In their 12th season of play, the **Fort Lauderdale Strikers** will host 12 games, April to September, at 9,500-seat Lockhart Stadium (next door to the team's office). The Strikers play against U.S. and Canadian squads in the eight-team American Professional Soccer League. *5301 N.W. 12th Ave., Fort Lauderdale, ☎ 305/771–5677.* ☛ *$8 adults, $4 children under 17. Most games at 7 or 7:30, occasional weekend day games.*

BEACHES

Fort Lauderdale's beachfront extends for miles without interruption, although the character of the communities behind the beach changes. For example, in Hallandale at far south Broward County, the beach is backed by towering condominiums; in Hollywood, by motels and the hoi-polloi Broadwalk; and just north of there—blessedly—there's nothing at all.

The most crowded portion of beach is along **Ocean Boulevard,** between Las Olas Boulevard and Sunrise Boulevard in Fort Lauderdale. This is the onetime "strip" famed from *Where the Boys Are* and the era of spring-break madness, now but a memory. Parking is readily available, often at parking meters.

Dania, Lauderdale-by-the-Sea, Pompano Beach, and **Deerfield Beach** each have piers where you can fish in addition to beaches.

John U. Lloyd Beach State Recreation Area (*see* Tour 3 *in* Exploring, *above*) is the locals' favorite beach area. It offers a beach for swimmers and sunners but also 251 acres of mangroves, picnic facilities, fishing, and canoeing. *6503 N. Ocean Dr., Dania, ☎ 305/923–2833.* ☛ *$3.25 per vehicle with up to 8 people.* ☉ *8–sunset.*

DINING

American

$$$ **Burt & Jack's.** Situated at the far end and most scenic lookout of Port Everglades, this trencherman's favorite has been operated by veteran restaurateur Jack Jackson and fronted by actor Burt Reynolds since 1984. Signs pointing the way through the port maze are few and far between, as if the entire complex were only a movie set, but diners manage to find their way, driven on by a romantic urge as much as a hunger for food. Behind the heavy mission doors and bougainvillea, guests are rewarded with Maine lobster, steaks, and chops. The two-story gallery of haciendalike dining rooms surrounded by glass has stunning views of the Intracoastal Waterway and John U. Lloyd Beach State Recreation Area. Come Saturday or Sunday in early evening for cocktails (served from 4:30, dinner from 5) and watch the cruise ships steam out. The dining area is nonsmoking. ✗ *Berth 23, Port Everglades, Fort Lauderdale, ☎ 305/522–2878 or 305/525–5225. Jacket required. AE, D, DC, MC, V. Closed Dec. 25. No lunch.*

$$$ **Cafe Maxx.** New-wave epicurean dining had its south Florida start here
★ in the early '80s, and Cafe Maxx remains very popular among regional gourmets. The setting, in a little strip of stores, is ordinary to the extreme, but inside there's a holiday glow year-round. From the open kitchen to booths that rim the boxy dining room, guests and the culinary staff under chef Oliver Saucy engage in ritual devotion to the preparation of fine cuisine and the pleasure of polishing it off. A menu that changes nightly showcases foods from the tropics: jumbo stone crab

claws with honey-lime mustard sauce, Florida lobster with *salsa verde,* and black-bean and banana pepper chili with Florida avocado. Desserts, too, reflect a tropical theme, from praline macadamia mousse over chocolate cake with butterscotch sauce to candied ginger with Sekel pears poached in muscatel and sun-dried cherry ice cream. More than 200 wines are offered by the bottle, another 20 by the glass. ✕ *2601 E. Atlantic Blvd., Pompano Beach,* ☎ *305/782–0606. AE, D, DC, MC, V. Closed Super Bowl Sun., July 4. No lunch.*

\$\$\$ Mark's Las Olas. New in late 1994, Mark's is an expansion of the ac-
★   claimed Mark's Cafe in north Dade. At his new restaurant, chef Mark Militello introduces several practices to Fort Lauderdale that other gourmet establishments will have to consider: lunch service six days a week and rounded-dollar pricing. (Instead of \$15.95 or \$22.95, a dish would cost \$16 or \$23.) Although it adds pennies to the bill, it reflects a move toward pricing restraint. Though Mark is applying Manhattan standards of cuisine, they don't come with Manhattan prices. In the dining room, tables are close together in a long, almost officelike row, lacking only the cubicles. Metallic finishes bounce the upscale hubbub around the room, making conversation difficult. The menu is easier to take, long on that mix of nouvelle and tropical cuisine that south Floridians now regard as American. Typical choices include Gulf shrimp, dolphin, yellowtail snapper, grouper, swordfish, Florida lobster, and vegetables like callaloo (a West Indian spinach variety), chayote (cho-cho on Mark's menu), ginger, jicama, and plantain, all brilliantly presented and combined in sauces that tend to the low fat. Dollar-saving pastas and full-size dinner pizzas are thoughtful offerings. ✕ *1032 E. Las Olas Blvd., Fort Lauderdale,* ☎ *305/463–1000. AE, DC, MC, V. Closed Thanksgiving, Dec. 25. No lunch Sun.*

Argentinian

\$\$ Las Brisas. There's a wonderful bistro atmosphere here, fostered by Mexican tiles, blue-and-white checked tablecloths beneath paddle fans, and a size that's small enough to always feel crowded. Right next to the beach, Las Brisas offers eating inside or out (protected by a plastic canopy), and food is Argentinian with an Italian flair. Antipasto salads are prepared for two, the roasted vegetables crunchy and flavorful. A small pot sits on each table filled with *chimichurri* (a paste made of oregano, parsley, olive oil, salt, garlic, and crushed pepper) for spreading on steaks so juicy they almost squirt to the knife. Grilled or deep-fried fish are favorites, as are pork chops, chicken, and pasta entrées. Desserts include a rum cake, a flan like *mamacita* used to make served with Chantilly cream, and a *dulce con leche* (a sweet milk pudding). The wine list is predominantly Argentine. ✕ *600 N. Surf Rd., Hollywood,* ☎ *305/923–1500. AE, MC, V. Closed Mon. No lunch.*

Continental

\$\$\$ Cafe Arugula. Large portions of perfectly prepared dishes are the hall-
★   mark of this intimate, 34-table paean to "cuisines of the sun." Former adman–turned–chef Dick Cingolani draws upon the culinary traditions of warm climates from Italy to the American Southwest. The decor, too, blends southwestern with Mediterranean looks—mauve velvet booths beneath steamboat-wheel windows surrounds and an entire wall of chili peppers, corn, cactus, and garlic cloves around the display kitchen. A frequently changing menu may include a succulent fresh hogfish with capers and shaved almonds over fettuccine or a free-range loin of venison with juniper–wild mushroom sauce, quesadilla, and stir-fried vegetables. Though expensive, prices here are generally \$3–\$5 lower than at restaurants serving comparable cuisine. ✕ *3110 N. Federal Hwy.,*

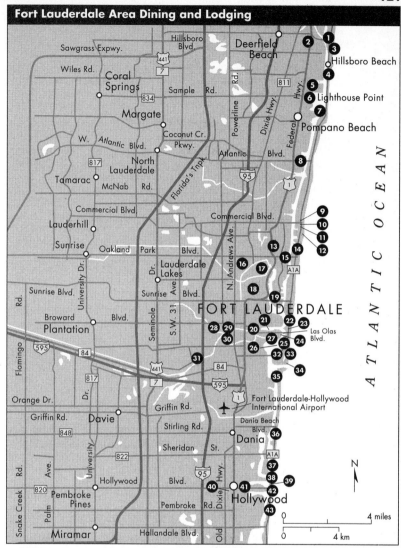

Fort Lauderdale Area Dining and Lodging

Lodging

Bahia Cabana Beach Resort, **25**

Banyan Marina Apartments, **21**

Blue Seas, **11**

Carriage House Resort Motel, **4**

Driftwood on the Ocean, **43**

Hyatt Regency Pier Sixty-Six, **32**

Lago Mar Resort Hotel & Club, **34**

Lauderdale Colonial, **26**

A Little Inn by-the-Sea, **10**

Maison Harrison, **41**

Manta Ray Inn, **42**

Marriott's Harbor Beach Resort, **33**

Nina Lee Motel, **24**

Ocean Terrace Suites, **3**

Pier Pointe Resort, **12**

Riverside Hotel, **27**

Royal Flamingo Villas, **1**

Sea Downs, **37**

Tropic Seas Resort Inn, **9**

Dining

Brooks, **2**

Burt & Jack's, **35**

Cafe Arugula, **6**

Cafe Grazia, **5**

Cafe Maxx, **8**

Cap's Place, **7**

Down Under, **15**

Evangeline, **23**

Good Planet Cafe, **29**

Istanbul, **38**

Juice Extractor, **28**

La Coquille, **18**

Las Brisas, **39**

Mark's Las Olas, **20**

Martha's, **36**

Mistral, **22**

Old Florida Seafood House, **17**

Primavera, **16**

Rustic Inn Crab-house, **31**

Sage, **13**

Sea Watch, **14**

Shirttail Charlie's, **30**

Studio One French Bistro, **19**

Sushi Blues Cafe, **40**

Lighthouse Point, ☎ *305/785–7732. AE, D, DC, MC, V. Closed Super Bowl Sun., Dec. 25. No lunch.*

$$$ Down Under. When Leonce Picot and the late Al Kocab opened Down
★   Under in 1968, the Australian government sent them a boomerang as
a gift. The name actually describes the restaurant's location, below a
bridge approach at the edge of the Intracoastal Waterway. This was the
first in a Gold Coast cluster of Kocab and Picot dining rooms combin-
ing gourmet cuisine with gracious old-house settings. Over the years the
number has dwindled to a precious two: this and La Vieille Maison in
Boca Raton (*see* Chapter 5, Palm Beach and the Treasure Coast), still
drawing their devoted following. The Down Under is styled with an-
tique brick deliberately laid off-plumb and an open-air upstairs. Spe-
cials might include a sautéed, Florida farm–raised striped bass with fennel
and broth, spinach flan, tomato strips, and potatoes; a classic duck con-
fit with crunchy red cabbage, roasted new potatoes, and truffle sauce;
or one of many grills, from a hot spicy Jamaican jerked roast pork ten-
derloin with Calvados apples to a trio of lamb chops, thick-cut USDA
choice prime rib, and a prime 12-ounce sirloin or steak au poivre.
Desserts include a classic Key lime pie, raspberry tiramisù (a creamy lay-
ered dessert), fresh-fruit cobbler, and a Grand Marnier sabayon with
fresh seasonal berries. ✕ *3000 E. Oakland Park Blvd., Fort Lauderdale,*
☎ *305/563–4123. AE, D, DC, MC, V.*

$$$ Martha's. Situated on the Intracoastal across from a 417-acre mangrove
preserve, just below the Dania Boulevard Bridge, the restaurant is
dressy downstairs—tables adorned with orchid buds, fanned napery,
etched-glass dividers, brass, rosewood, and an outdoor patio surrounded by a wildly floral mural. Here piano music accompanies dinner, and later a band plays for dancing, setting a supper-club mood.
The upstairs was enclosed in 1993 but keeps its more informal look;
the menu now features chiefly Florida seafoods. Either up or down you
can expect outstanding seafood preparations: flaky dolphin in a court
bouillon; shrimp dipped in a piña colada batter, rolled in coconut, pan-
fried with orange mustard sauce; and snapper prepared 17 ways. Upstairs, an assortment of rolls and banana bread comes with entrées. For
dessert, try fresh sorbet and vanilla and chocolate ice cream topped with
meringue and hot fudge brandy sauce. ✕ *6024 N. Ocean Dr., Hollywood,* ☎ *305/923–5444. Reservations advised. AE, D, DC, MC, V.*

$$ Brooks. This is one of the city's best and most affordable restaurants
★   thanks to a French perfectionist, Bernard Perron, born in Poitiers.
Meals are served in a series of brilliantly set rooms, filled with replicas
of Old Masters, cut glass, antiques, and tapestrylike floral wallpapers,
though the shedlike dining room still feels very Florida. The secret is
fresh ingredients, which translate into a distinctly Floridian cuisine. Main
courses include red snapper in papillote, broiled fillet of pompano with
seasoned root vegetables, and a sweet lemongrass linguine with bok
choy and julienne of crisp vegetables. Desserts include pecan pie with
banana ice cream, a filo purse filled with chocolate ganache and straw-
berries, and rum-basted bananas with coconut ice cream and toasted
macadamia nuts. ✕ *500 S. Federal Hwy., Deerfield Beach,* ☎
305/427–9302. AE, D, MC, V. Closed Super Bowl Sun., Dec. 25.

$$ Mistral. This first of the gourmet cafés along the dreamily restyled beach
★   drive demonstrates how fun and dining combine. As part of a novelty
dinner, limited to 25, you can board a choo-choo replica for a progressive
dinner that includes Mistral's two sister restaurants: Evangeline, just
down the oceanfront walk, and Sage, in town. The price is $55, in-
cluding tax, tip, and all wines. Novelty dinners start from Mistral at
6:30 on the first Tuesday of the month. For those less whimsically in-

clined, go no further than Mistral. The open-air restaurant rates high
for both taste and looks. About 75 can sit inside surrounded by tropical art and pottery, with another 35 on the wave-theme sidewalk. The
kitchen staff is knowledgeable about pastas, turning out a hearty *primavera* redolent with garlic and herbs and *tagliolini* (an angel-hair pasta)
with prosciutto, pine nuts, and tomato. Other favorites from the sun-
drenched cuisine are grilled shrimp and black-bean cakes as well as pan-
seared dolphin. Pizzas, big salads, and a strong selection of affordable
wines, including by the glass, are also served. ✗ *201 Rte. A1A, Fort
Lauderdale,* ☎ *305/463–4900. AE, D, DC, MC, V.*

Creole

$$$ Evangeline. Set inside and out on the ocean drive just south of its sis-
ter restaurant Mistral (*see above*), 225-seat Evangeline celebrates Aca-
dian Louisiana in decor and food. The mood is set with paneled
wainscoting and plank floors—a tankard and tavern look—highlighted
by verse from Longfellow's legendary poem inscribed along the turn
of the ceiling. Traditional favorites include oyster and artichoke pie,
smoked rabbit gumbo with andouille sausage, a crawfish Caesar salad,
jambalaya (clams, mussels, shrimp, and chicken andouille with a Cre-
ole sauce), sautéed alligator in a meunière sauce topped with flash-fried
oysters, and crisp roasted duckling with poached plums and prunelle
brandy. There's music nightly, and a Dixieland band plays weekends,
including Sunday afternoon. ✗ *211 Rte. A1A, Fort Lauderdale,* ☎
305/522–7001. AE, D, DC, MC, V.

French

$$ La Coquille. Already providing excellent French fare in a country-
French setting, La Coquille enhanced its ambience measurably in 1995
with the opening of a new tropical garden—walled, tiled, and with fountain. The restaurant sits at the edge of busy Sunrise Boulevard yet worlds
apart thanks to French doors, pastel coral and green, faux open beams,
and 18 tables set with double white covers and topped by carnations
and baby's breath. Service is friendly, helpful, and with a delightful French
accent, and the cuisine is equally authentic: Dubonnet and vermouth
cassis aperitifs lead to escargots Provençal and various pâtés, followed
by seared sea scallops with spring vegetables in a glazed citrus sauce,
honey-glaze duckling with lingonberry sauce and wild rice, sweet-
breads in a morel and truffle sauce, or veal *picatta* with shallots and
sweet bell peppers. There's always a soufflé among the desserts and a
dinner-savings special, such as a four-course dinner for two with bottle of wine for $47.50 (excluding tax and tip and not valid Saturday
or holidays). ✗ *1619 E. Sunrise Blvd., Fort Lauderdale,* ☎
*305/467–3030. AE, MC, V. Beer and wine only. Closed Sun. and Mon.
June–Sept., Aug., some holidays. No lunch Sat.–Thurs.*

$ Sage. This joyous, country-French café presents a country-American
setting: exposed brick walls, captain's chairs, lace curtains, herbal art,
and baskets of dried grains and flowers. The menu is a happy mix of
very affordable quiches and pâtés, savory and dessert crepes, salads,
and main-course specialties. Entrées include coq au vin, beef bour-
guignonne, cassoulet *à l'Armagnac* (layers of duck and garlic sausage
with white beans), and a platter of fresh vegetables that's a veritable
garden of legumes. Early-bird dinners (weekdays 4:30–6) feature four
courses for $12.50. There are good selections of beers and wines by
the glass. ✗ *2378 N. Federal Hwy., Fort Lauderdale,* ☎ *305/565–2299.
AE, D, MC, V.*

$ Studio One French Bistro. As if one great bargain French restaurant
★ weren't enough, Fort Lauderdale offers a second. More like a gallery
of art—intimate, black-and-white, mirrored—this restaurant serves

up bountiful portions at ridiculously low prices. Food is thoughtfully presented, from high-gluten breads through a dozen or so appetizers, dinner-size salads, and entrées that include a grilled salmon in puff pastry with lobster sauce, Camembert-stuffed chicken breast with French cranberry sauce, and crispy roasted duckling with vanilla sauce. For dessert try the mildly sweet custard apple tart. Chef Bernd Asendorf now has charge of the kitchen, and his wife, Roberta, carries on the tradition of greeting by name the locals who return time and again, often bringing out-of-town guests. ✕ *2447 E. Sunrise Blvd., Fort Lauderdale,* ☎ *305/565–2052. AE, DC, MC, V. Closed Mon. mid-May–mid-Dec. No lunch.*

Italian

$$–$$$ **Primavera.** Night becomes brilliant Tuscan day in this creamy setting
★   of etched-glass dividers, statuary, figureheads, gorgeous planters, balusters, and pilasters. Taste redeems the lavish display of thematic decor—taste and larger than usual tables set with double covers, burgundy napkins, and fresh flowers, placed generously apart from each other atop thick, sound-muffling carpet. There's no piped-in music either, just the hum of content. Waiters do not merely recite the evening's specials but guide guests through the subtleties of the various pastas, risottos, and scaloppines. Among pasta choices are a green-and-white pasta in a pink sauce with baby peas and ham and a linguine with clam sauce or seafood. A fresh catch is prepared with sun-dried tomato sauce and topped with fried leeks. Veal is served in wine with oregano and tomato, with mushrooms and sun-dried tomato, or with apples and peppers in a light curry sauce. Desserts are rich yet delicate. Consider sun-dried mangoes and banana in filo pastry, baked with a touch of passion fruit, coulis (a puree) of raspberry, and kiwi fruit under whipped cream. ✕ *840 Plaza, Oakland Park Blvd., Oakland Park,* ☎ *305/564–6363. AE, D, DC, MC, V. Closed Mon. except after holidays, Thanksgiving, Dec. 25, Jan. 1, 3 wks in Aug., Sept.*

$–$$ **Cafe Grazia.** This happy green-red-and-white recollection of an Ital-
★   ian garden is so close to the highway that its bar glasses jiggle to the passing of 18-wheelers. Not to worry—exuberance is what really shakes the scene. Chef Ace Gonzalez and his wife Estelita have created a happy case of the best for less: dinners on the low side of moderate and downright inexpensive if you come between 4:30 and 5:30 for the early-bird specials, a choice of three-course dinners priced at $6.95–$9.95 year-round. Pocketbook-pleasing, too, are the regular menu's 15 pasta selections, including penne pasta with hot chilies, vodka, tomatoes, and cream, and fresh pasta rosettes with fontina cheese, smoked ham, and spinach in a blush cream sauce. Other entrées include fowl, veal, and grills. ✕ *3850 N. Federal Hwy., Lighthouse Point,* ☎ *305/942–7206. AE, MC, V. No lunch weekends.*

Japanese

$–$$ **Sushi Blues Cafe.** First-class Japanese food, accompanied by live music Thursday through Saturday evenings, is served up in a cubicle setting that's always so jammed you wonder where this hip group goes by day. Chef Yozo Masuda prepares conventional and macrobiotic-influenced dishes that range from a variety of sushi and rolls (California, tuna, and the "Yozo roll" with snapper, *masago* [flying-fish eggs], asparagus, and Japanese mayonnaise) to steamed veggies with tofu and steamed snapper with miso sauce. There's no MSG, no additives, and nothing microwaved. Also available are a few wines by the glass or bottle, a selection of Japanese beers, and some very un-Japanese desserts—fried banana and Swiss chocolate mousse cake. ✕ *1836 S.*

Young Circle, Hollywood, ☎ *305/929–9560. No credit cards. Closed Sun. No lunch.*

Natural

$ **Juice Extractor.** Three guys from Pittsburgh, Philadelphia, and New York have made a splash in the arts district's Himmarshee Village with their inexpensive, deli-style organic foods and Champion-blended juices. Frothy and light, juices are made from fresh apples, pears, strawberries, citrus, and veggies and can be enjoyed with bagels, whitefish salads, and homemade breads for breakfast. Lunch features dairy-free veggie burgers, pita sandwiches, and organic salads (at least three pasta versions). Free-range chicken prepared with mushrooms and vegetables, marinated in lemon and honey with veggies, or served with organic pasta and red sauce; steamed salmon; bison steaks, whole or ground; and a vegetarian choice with brown rice and beans are just some of the dinner platters, which come with a choice of soup or salad. There are 28 seats inside (nonsmoking) and 32 outside at this restaurant in among five shops with imported art and crafts. ✗ *320 S.W. 2nd St., Fort Lauderdale,* ☎ *305/524–6935. D, MC, V. Beer and wine only. Closed Thanksgiving, Dec. 25, Jan. 1.*

Seafood

$$–$$$ **Cap's Place.** On an island that was once a bootlegger's haunt, this restau-
★ rant is reached by launch and has served such luminaries as Winston Churchill, Franklin D. Roosevelt, and John F. Kennedy. "Cap" was Captain Theodore Knight, born in 1871, who, with partner-in-crime Al Hasis, floated a derelict barge to the area in the 1920s. Today the rustic restaurant, built on the barge, is run by descendants of Hasis, who make freshness and excellence a priority. Baked wahoo steaks are lightly glazed and meaty, the long-cut french fries arouse gluttony, hot and flaky rolls are baked fresh several times a night, and tangy lime pie is the finishing touch. Turn east off Federal Highway onto Northeast 24th Street (two blocks north of Pompano Fashion Square); follow the double yellow line to the launch. ✗ *Cap's Dock, 2765 N.E. 28th Ct., Lighthouse Point,* ☎ *305/941–0418. AE, MC, V. No lunch.*

$$ **Old Florida Seafood House.** Owner Bob Wickline has run this traditional seafood restaurant since 1978 with a West Virginian's eye toward giving value for money: It's plain on atmosphere and friendly on price, with nothing frozen and nothing portion-controlled. He'll bring out a whole swordfish to show that it's fresh. Try the veal Gustav (sautéed veal topped with a lobster tail) or a snapper New Orleans (sautéed with mushrooms and artichokes, laced with a light brown sauce). There's usually a 30-minute wait weekends. ✗ *1414 N.E. 26th St., Wilton Manors,* ☎ *305/566–1044; 4535 Pine Island Rd., Sunrise,* ☎ *305/572–0444; 9980 Pines Blvd., Pembroke Pines,* ☎ *305/436–0200. AE, MC, V. Closed Thanksgiving, Dec. 25. No lunch weekends.*

$$ **Rustic Inn Crabhouse.** Wayne McDonald started with a cozy one-room roadhouse saloon in 1955, when this was a remote service road just west of the little airport. Now, the plain, rustic place seats 700. Steamed crabs seasoned with garlic and herbs, spices, and oil are served with mallets on tables covered with newspapers; peel-and-eat shrimp are served either Key West–style (with garlic and butter) or spiced and steamed with Old Bay seasoning. The big menu includes other seafood items as well. Pies and cheesecakes are offered for dessert. ✗ *4331 Ravenswood Rd., Fort Lauderdale,* ☎ *305/584–1637. AE, D, DC, MC, V. Closed Thanksgiving.*

$$ **Sea Watch.** It's back from the road and easy to miss—but not missed by many. Waiting for a table, you're likely to hear announced, "Party

of 47, your tables are ready!" After more than 20 years, this nautical-theme restaurant by the sea stays packed during lunch and dinner. Waits can be as long as 30 minutes, but the time passes quickly in the sumptuous upstairs lounge with its comfy sofas and high-back rattan chairs. The menu has all the right appetizers: oysters Rockefeller, Florida Gulf shrimp, clams casino, and Bahamian conch fritters. Typical daily specials might be sautéed yellowtail snapper, oat-crusted with roasted red bell pepper sauce and basil, or a charbroiled dolphin fillet marinated with soy sauce, garlic, black pepper, and lemon juice. Desserts include a Granny Smith apple crisp cheesecake, cappuccino brownie, and strawberries Romanoff. Good early-bird specials are offered May–mid-December. ✕ *6002 N. Ocean Blvd., Fort Lauderdale,* ☎ *305/781–2200. AE, MC, V. Closed Dec. 25.*

$$ **Shirttail Charlie's.** Overlooking the New River, you can watch the world go by from the outdoor deck or upstairs dining room of this restaurant, named for a yesteryear Seminole Indian who wore his shirts in the traditional way with the tails out. Diners may take a free 30- to 40-minute after-dinner cruise on *Shirttail Charlie's Express,* which chugs upriver past an alleged Al Capone speakeasy or across the river to and from the Broward Center. Charlie's is built to look old, with a 1920s tile floor that leans toward the water. Florida-style seafood offerings include an alligator-tail appetizer served with tortuga sauce (a béarnaise with turtle broth and sherry), conch served four ways, crab balls, blackened tuna with Dijon mustard sauce, crunchy coconut shrimp with a not-too-sweet piña colada sauce, three fresh catches nightly, and a superbly tart Key lime pie with graham-cracker crust. ✕ *400 S.W. 3rd Ave., Fort Lauderdale,* ☎ *305/463–3474. AE, D, MC, V.*

Southwestern

$–$$ **Good Planet Cafe.** A half block from the Florida East Coast Railroad track in a neighborhood that's turned from rundown to trendy, thanks to the Broward Center for the Performing Arts and all the nearby museums, this 50-seat eatery has primed the scene for food. Modeled after the Last Ditch Cafe in Silver City, New Mexico, run by sister Julie, the Good Planet is run by the Good family, especially brother Jonathan. Mom and pop handle the contracting and pick out the thrift shop furniture that, with local art on the walls, creates a feel of hand-me-down chic. Most of the long list of entrées are served with *posole* (a corn chowder) or rice and beans. Try the bite-size chunks of lean pork marinated in red chili and fruit juices with a fresh mango-pineapple salsa, the Last Ditch pasta *pollo verde* (chicken chunks with diced green chili and fresh tomato tossed in a cream sauce with fettuccine), or the Szechuan scallop and shrimp angel hair. There are lots of vegetarian choices, and everything comes in big portions. ✕ *214 S.W. 2nd St., Fort Lauderdale,* ☎ *305/527–4663. AE, MC, V. Closed Sun., Thanksgiving, Dec. 25. No lunch Sat.*

Turkish

$ **Istanbul.** So there you are on the beach—hungry, without a picnic basket, but not yet ready to pack it in. Leave your significant other on the blanket and go grab a take-out order from this Turkish fast-food place. Actually fast food is a misnomer, since everything is prepared from scratch: hummus, tabouli, *adana* kebab (partially grilled, chopped lamb on skewers on a bed of yogurt-soaked pita squares, oven finished with hot butter sauce), pizza, salads, soups, and filo pie fingers filled with spinach, chicken, or meat. The creamy rice pudding, baklava, and pastries are equally transportable. To be sure, you can also sit and eat at one of the few tables, but how often do you get to lounge on the beach with a reasonably priced Turkish picnic? ✕ *707 N. Broadwalk, Hollywood,* ☎ *305/921–1263. No credit cards.*

LODGING

In Fort Lauderdale, Pompano Beach, and the Hollywood–Hallandale area, dozens of hotels face the Atlantic Ocean beaches. In much of Fort Lauderdale, however, lodgings are limited to the upland side of the beach roads and in much of Hollywood to the upland side of the Broadwalk, leaving the beaches open to pedestrians and motorists. Lodgings range from economy motels—in particular the affordable buys along much of the Hollywood beachfront and back of the beach in Fort Lauderdale— to a few opulent beachfront and canalfront resorts in Fort Lauderdale. Good choices are found, too, in Lauderdale-by-the-Sea, graced with an accessible cultural life and high standards. Inland, the major chain hotels along I–95 north and south of the airport cater primarily to business travelers and overnight visitors en route to somewhere else.

An innovative Superior Small Lodging program, set up by the Greater Fort Lauderdale Convention & Visitors Bureau and administered by the hospitality department of Broward County's Nova University, has led to substantial upgrading of many smaller properties, many of which charge modest rates.

Wherever you plan to stay in Broward County, reservations are a good idea throughout the year. Tourists from the northern United States and Canada fill up the hotels from Thanksgiving through Easter. In summer, southerners and Europeans create a second season that's almost as busy.

Deerfield Beach

$$$–$$$$ **Ocean Terrace Suites.** This four-story motel is in one of the quieter sections of north Broward, just south of Boca Raton, across the narrow shore road from the beach. Large units—efficiencies and one- and three-bedroom apartments—all have big balconies overlooking the sea. Colors are from shore washed to bright; pink and green pastels tint the bedrooms. The furniture is rattan, and units are clean and neat but lack attention to detail. Art is throwaway, flowers are artificial, and materials are bargain quality. Still for size, location, and price this is a good buy. 🏠 *2080 E. Hillsboro Blvd., 33441,* ☎ *305/427–8400,* 𝖥𝖠𝖷 *305/427–0555. 30 units. Grill, pool. AE, D, DC, MC, V.*

$$–$$$ **Carriage House Resort Motel.** Very clean and tidy, this good beachfront motel sits one block from the ocean. Run by a French-American couple (who speak German and some Spanish as well), the two-story, black-shuttered white Colonial-style motel is actually two buildings connected by a second-story sundeck. Steady improvements have been made to the facility, including the addition of Bahama beds that feel and look like sofas. Kitchenettes are equipped with good-quality utensils. Rooms are self-contained and quiet and have walk-in closets and room safes. 🏠 *250 S. Ocean Blvd., 33441,* ☎ *305/427–7670,* 𝖥𝖠𝖷 *305/428–4790. 6 rooms, 14 efficiencies, 10 apartments. Pool, shuffleboard, coin laundry. AE, MC, V.*

Fort Lauderdale: Beach

$$$$ **Lago Mar Resort Hotel & Club.** No one steadily upgrades resort prop-
★ erty like Walter Banks. No sooner had he opened a new signature wing in 1993 as part of an ambitious $5 million project than he turned to renovating older hotel rooms, adding suitelike areas, balconies, and new furniture. The sprawling Lago Mar has been owned by the Banks

family since the early 1950s. The lobby is luxurious, with fanlight surrounds, a coquina-rock fireplace, and an eye-popping saltwater aquarium behind the registration desk. Allamanda trellises and bougainvillea plantings edge the swimming lagoon, and guests have the use of the broadest beach in the city. Lago Mar is less a big resort than a small town—still a family-run operation after all these years and, in its way, a slice of Old Florida. ☎ *1700 S. Ocean La., 33316, ☎ 305/523–6511 or 800/524–6627, ℻ 305/524–6627. 32 rooms, 123 1-bedroom suites, 15 2-bedroom suites. 4 restaurants, 2 pools, miniature golf, 4 tennis courts, shuffleboard, volleyball. AE, DC, MC, V.*

$$$$ Marriott's Harbor Beach Resort. This sprawling resort, built in 1984, is the resort of the Surplus Age. No other hotel gives you so much to take advantage of. Located south of the big public beach, it's a property of imperial dimensions—16 acres on the sea. Seen at night from upper stories (14 in all), the grounds, with their waterfall-pool beset by tall palms, shimmer like a jewel. The spacious guest rooms were refurbished in 1994 and 1995 with more tropical colors, lively floral prints, rattan, wicker, and wood. Each has a balcony facing either the ocean or the Intracoastal Waterway. There are in-room minibars and rooms for nonsmokers and people with disabilities. Sheffield's, one of five restaurants, is one of the city's top spots. ☎ *3030 Holiday Dr., 33316, ☎ 305/525–4000 or 800/228–6543, ℻ 305/766–6152. 588 rooms, 36 suites. 5 restaurants, 3 lounges, pool, massage, saunas, 5 tennis courts, fitness center, beach, windsurfing, boating, parasailing, children's program (ages 5–12). AE, DC, MC, V.*

$$$ Bahia Cabana Beach Resort. *Boating Magazine* ranks the waterfront bar and restaurant here among the 10 best in the world. It's far enough from guest rooms so that the nightly entertainment is not disturbing. Rooms are spread among five buildings furnished in tropical-casual style, last redone with new carpets, paint, tiles, landscaping, and patio furniture in 1992–93. Added at the same time was a video bar with a sweeping view of the marina. Rooms in the 500 Building are more motel-like and overlook the parking lot, but rates here are lowest. ☎ *3001 Harbor Dr., 33316, ☎ 305/524–1555 or 800/922–3008; in FL, 800/232–2437; ℻ 305/764–5951. 52 rooms, 37 efficiencies, 10 suites. Restaurant, 2 bars, café, 3 pools, hot tub, saunas, shuffleboard. AE, D, DC, MC, V.*

$$$ Lauderdale Colonial. The city's miles of canal shoreline offer afford-
★ able waterfront lodgings off the beach, but as close as a one- or two-minute walk away. This 1950 resort motel, consisting of two two-story buildings with good overhangs, occupies as good a location as there is, right where the New River empties into the Intracoastal Waterway, 600 yards from the beach. The setting keeps it from feeling commercial, and the views are spectacular. At sunset, the waterway shimmers orange with that distinctive shiver of heat of Florida's winters. After dark, yachts make the stealthy moves of wealth playing its unseen hand. Every unit—motel rooms, efficiencies, and one- and two-bedroom apartments—has a view of the water, and the best ones have full views. Most are large, done in tropical rattan and mock French provincial: whites, pastels, chintz, and stripes. Even the small motel rooms are desirable, since the space is used well; each has an alcove with an eight-drawer double dresser, so the double bed isn't squeezed in. Motel rooms have a coffee pot and small fridge, while other units have full kitchens. ☎ *3049 Harbor Dr., 33316–2491, ☎ 305/525–3676, ℻ 305/463–3787. 14 units. Pool, dock, fishing, laundry. MC, V.*

$$ Nina Lee Motel. This is typical of the modest, affordable 1950s-style lodgings that can be found within a block or two of the ocean along the Fort Lauderdale shore. Be prepared for plain rooms—homey and clean, but not tiny, with at least a toaster, coffee pot, and fridge; efficiencies have gas kitchens, large closets, and tub-showers. The pool is set in a garden, and the entire property is just removed enough from the beach causeway so that it's quiet. ☎ *3048 Harbor Dr., 33316, ☎ 305/524–1568. 14 units. Pool. MC, V.*

Fort Lauderdale: Downtown and Beach Causeways

$$$$ **Hyatt Regency Pier Sixty-Six.** This flagship of Fort Lauderdale's resort
★ hotels entered 1995 with new Hyatt management, while the previous year's $4 million renovation, including the 350-seat, multilevel, upscale waterfront California Cafe Bar & Grill alongside the 142-slip luxury yacht marina, still feels nearly new. The trademark of this high-rise resort, however, remains its rooftop Pier Top Lounge, which revolves every 66 minutes and is reached by an exterior elevator. The 17-story tower dominates a 22-acre spread that includes the complete LXVI Spa. Tower and lanai lodgings are tops from the ground up. In the early evening, guests try to perch at the Pelican Bar; at 6:06 a cannon is shot off, and anybody who's around the bar gets a drink on the house. ☎ *2301 S.E. 17th St., 33316, ☎ 305/525–6666 or 800/327–3796, FAX 305/728–3541. 380 rooms, 8 suites. 3 restaurants, 3 lounges, pool, hot tub, spa, 2 tennis courts, snorkeling, boating, parasailing, waterskiing, fishing. AE, DC, MC, V.*

$$$ **Banyan Marina Apartments.** French doors have been added to guest
★ quarters, further fine-tuning these already outstanding waterfront apartments on a residential island just off Las Olas Boulevard. Imaginative landscaping includes a walkway through the upper branches of a banyan tree. Luxurious units with leather sofas, springy carpets, real potted plants, sheer curtains, custom drapes, high-quality art, and jalousies for sweeping the breeze in make these apartments as comfortable as any first-class hotel—but for half the price. Also included are a full kitchen, dining area, water view, beautiful gardens, dock space for eight yachts, and exemplary housekeeping. This is Florida the way you want it to be. ☎ *111 Isle of Venice, 33301, ☎ 305/524–4430, FAX 305/764–4870. 10 rooms, 1 efficiency, 4 1-bedroom apartments, 2 2-bedroom apartments. Pool. MC, V.*

$$$ **Riverside Hotel.** This six-story hotel, on Fort Lauderdale's most fashionable shopping thoroughfare, was built in 1936 and has been steadily upgraded since 1987. Expected for 1996, a sidewalk café will front Bob Jenny's tropical murals, one of which is a New Orleans–style work that stretches across 725 square feet of the hotel's facade. An attentive staff includes many who have been with the hotel for two decades or more. Each room is distinctive, with antique oak furnishings, framed French prints on the walls, in-room refrigerators, and European-style baths. The best rooms face south, overlooking the New River; the least desirable are the 36 series, where you can hear the elevator. Rooms for nonsmokers are available. ☎ *620 E. Las Olas Blvd., 33301, ☎ 305/467–0671 or 800/325–3280, FAX 305/462–2148. 103 rooms, 7 suites. 2 restaurants, bar, pool, volleyball, dock. AE, DC, MC, V.*

Hillsboro Beach

$$$–$$$$ **Royal Flamingo Villas.** This small community of houselike villas, built in the 1970s, reaches from the Intracoastal Waterway to the sea. The roomy and comfortable one- and two-bedroom villas are all condominium owned, so they're fully furnished the way owners want them. All are so quiet that you hear only the soft click of ceiling fans and kitchen clocks. Some living rooms have tile floors, but there's carpet in the bedrooms. The development is wisely set back a bit from the beach, which is eroded anyway, though enjoyable at low tide. Lawns are so lushly landscaped you might trip. If you don't need lavish public facilities, this is your upscale value choice. ☎ *1225 Hillsboro Mile (Rte. A1A), 33062,* ☎ *305/427–0669, 305/427–0660, or 800/241–2477,* FAX *305/427–6110. 40 villas. Pool, putting green, shuffleboard, beach, dock, boating, coin laundry. D, MC, V.*

Hollywood

$$–$$$ **Sea Downs.** This three-story lodging directly on the Broadwalk is a good choice for efficiency or apartment living (one-bedroom apartments can be joined to make two-bedroom units). Views vary from full on the beach to rear-of-the-house prospects of neighborhood motels, and luck of the draw determines what you get. All units are comfortably done in chintz, however, with blinds, no drapes. Kitchens are fully equipped and most units have tub-showers and closets. Every room has a ceiling fan, and of course everything is air-conditioned with TV and phone. Housekeeping is provided once a week. In between, guests receive fresh towels daily and sheets on request, but they make their own beds. Bougainvillea on the Beach (2813 N. Surf Rd., ☎ 305/925–1368), under the same ownership, also has efficiencies and one-bedroom apartments. Guests here are welcome to use the Sea Downs pool, and those at Sea Downs can enjoy Bougainvillea's gardens. A block off the beach and with decor a slim notch below its sister, Bougainvillea units are lower priced. ☎ *2900 N. Surf Rd., 33019-3704,* ☎ *305/923–4968,* FAX *305/923–8747. 5 efficiencies, 8 1-bedroom apartments. Pool. No credit cards.*

$$ **Driftwood on the Ocean.** This attractive 36-year-old resort motel faces the beach at the secluded south end of Surf Road. The setting is what draws guests, but attention to maintenance and frequent refurbishing are what add value for the money. Most units have a kitchen, one-bedroom apartments have a daybed, and standard rooms have a queen-size Murphy bed. All have balconies. ☎ *2101 S. Surf Rd., 33019,* ☎ *305/923–9528,* FAX *305/922–1062. 10 rooms, 39 efficiencies. Pool, shuffleboard, beach, bicycles, laundry. AE, MC, V.*

$$ **Maison Harrison.** This house feels very much like the '20s and '30s, when developer Joseph Young planned and built Hollywood as if overnight. As a result, it feels comfortable but a little dated. Living-room lighting is all by floor lamp—more suggestive than illuminating. The sunporch, where breakfast is served, overlooks the street, which, as was customary for the time, is extraordinarily wide even though houses are cheek by jowl. The building originally housed Young's salesmen, so bedrooms have private baths. Today Millie Poole competently manages it in a style that's as much commercial as engaging; it's good for those who want neither a sterile motel nor that sense of obligation that sometimes comes with doting hosts. Rooms are complete if a little fussy (various swags, poufs, and an enormous canopy). Here and there a closet or bathroom-cabinet door doesn't quite close, or unplugged screw holes remain where a towel rack once hung. Beds are firm, there's plenty of hot water, and a couple of rooms have usable balconies. Furnishings are mostly traditional, with much upholstery and Oriental-style rugs. An expanded Continental breakfast is included. ☎ *1504 Harrison St., 33020,* ☎ *305/922–7319. 4 rooms. V.*

$$ **Manta Ray Inn.** Canadians Donna and Dwayne Boucher run this ex-
★   emplary two-story lodging on the beach, keeping the place immaculate and the rates affordable. Dating from the 1940s, the inn offers the casual, comfortable beachfront vacationing Hollywood is famous for. Nothing's fussy—white spaces with burgundy trim and rattan furniture—and everything's included. Kitchens are equipped with pots, pans, and mini-appliances that make housekeeping convenient. All apart-

ments have full closets, and except for second baths with stalls in two-bedroom units, baths have tub-showers. ☎ *1715 S. Surf Rd., 33019,* ☏ *305/921–9666,* ℻ *305/929–8220. 12 units. Grills, beach. No credit cards.*

Lauderdale-by-the-Sea

$$$–$$$$ **Tropic Seas Resort Inn.** It's only a block off A1A, but it might as well be a mile. It's a million-dollar location—directly on the beach, two blocks from municipal tennis courts. Built in the 1950s, units are plain but clean and comfortable, with tropical rattan furniture and ceiling fans. Managers Sandy and Larry Lynch tend to the largely repeat family-oriented clientele. Added features include a complimentary Sunday brunch and weekly wiener roast and rum swizzle party—good opportunities to mingle with other guests. ☎ *4616 El Mar Dr., 33308,* ☏ *305/772–2555 or 800/952–9581,* ℻ *305/771–5711. 16 rooms, 6 efficiencies, 7 apartments. Pool, beach. AE, D, DC, MC, V.*

$$$ **A Little Inn by-the-Sea.** In 1992 former owners took a pair of old motels and completely renovated them to create one of the better lodgings in this low-rise town. Today it's maybe even a little better. New owners (since 1994) have added balconies to units that didn't have them. Room themes reflect much of what Florida is about: shells and boats and birds and fish. All floors are newly tiled, and all rooms have at least a fridge, if not complete kitchens. Plantings surround the pool, and the furniture can be taken onto the beach. The entire fountain lobby, where a complimentary Continental breakfast is served, is given over to guest use. A daily newspaper is provided. ☎ *4546 El Mar Dr., 33308,* ☏ *305/772–2450 or 800/492–0311,* ℻ *305/938–9354. 10 rooms, 13 efficiencies, 6 apartments. Pool, hot tub, beach, bicycles. AE, D, DC, MC, V.*

$$$ **Pier Pointe Resort.** Built in the 1950s, this oceanfront resort, located a block off the main street (Route A1A) and a block from the fishing pier, is reminiscent of the Gold Coast 40 years ago. The aqua-color canopied entry opens onto two- and three-story buildings set among brick pathways on cabbage palm lawns. The attractive wood pool deck is set off by sea grapes and rope-strung bollards. Rooms are plain and comfortable and have balconies; most have kitchens. There's a complimentary barbecue on Wednesday. ☎ *4320 El Mar Dr., 33308,* ☏ *305/776–5121 or 800/331–6384,* ℻ *305/491–9084. 40 suites, 31 efficiencies, 27 apartments. 3 pools, volleyball, beach, coin laundry. AE, D, DC, MC, V.*

$–$$ **Blue Seas.** Bubbly innkeeper Cristie Furth runs this one- and two-story motel with her husband, Marc, and small as it is, they keep investing their future in it. Newly added are lattice fencing and gardens of cactus and impatiens in front, so there's more privacy around the brick patio and garden-set pool. Guest quarters feature kitchenettes, terracotta tiles, bright Haitian and Peruvian art, and generally Tex-Mex and Danish furnishings, whose woody textures work well together. Handmade painted shutters and indoor plants add to the look. This remains an excellent buy in a quiet resort area just a block from the beach. ☎ *4525 El Mar Dr., 33308,* ☏ *305/772–3336. 13 units. Pool, coin laundry. MC, V.*

THE ARTS AND NIGHTLIFE

For the most complete weekly listing of events, read the "Showtime!" entertainment insert and events calendar in the Friday *Fort Lauderdale News/Sun Sentinel.* "Weekend" in the Friday edition of the *Herald,* the Broward edition of the *Miami Herald,* carries similar listings.

The weekly *XS* is principally an entertainment and dining paper with a relic "underground" look. A 24-hour **Arts & Entertainment Hotline** (☎ 305/357–5700) provides updates on art, attractions, children's events, dance, festivals, films, literature, museums, music, opera, and theater.

Tickets are sold at individual box offices and through **Ticketmaster** (☎ 305/523–3309).

The Arts

Bailey Concert Hall (Central Campus of Broward Community College, 3501 S.W. Davie Rd., Davie, ☎ 305/475–6884) is a popular place for classical music concerts, dance, drama, and other performing arts activities, especially October–April.

Broward Center for the Performing Arts (201 S.W. 5th Ave., Fort Lauderdale, ☎ 305/462–0222) is the waterfront centerpiece of Fort Lauderdale's new cultural arts district. More than 500 events a year are scheduled at the performing arts center, including Broadway musicals, plays, dance, symphony and opera, rock, film, lectures, comedy, and children's theater.

Sunrise Musical Theatre (5555 N.W. 95th Ave., Sunrise, ☎ 305/741–8600) stages Broadway musicals, a few dramatic plays with name stars, and concerts by well-known singers throughout the year. The theater is 14 miles west of Fort Lauderdale Beach via Commercial Boulevard.

Theater

Parker Playhouse (707 N.E. 8th St., Holiday Park, Fort Lauderdale, ☎ 305/763–2444) features Broadway plays, musicals, drama, and local productions.

Vinnette Carroll Repertory Company (503 S.E. 6th St., Fort Lauderdale, ☎ 305/462–2424), a multiethnic theater company housed in a renovated church, has mounted productions of such Broadway hits as *Your Arms Too Short to Box with God* and *Don't Bother Me I Can't Cope.*

Music

The **Florida Philharmonic Orchestra** (3401 N.W. 9th Ave., Fort Lauderdale, ☎ 305/561–2997), south Florida's only fully professional orchestra, is Broward-based but performs in six locations in Broward, Dade, and Palm Beach counties.

Opera

Florida Grand Opera (221 S.W. 3rd Ave., Fort Lauderdale, ☎ 305/728–9700), formed in 1994 by the merger of the Opera Guild of Fort Lauderdale and the Greater Miami Opera, is now the 10th-largest opera company in the United States. It presents five productions a season at the Broward Center for the Performing Arts.

Nightlife

As an alternative to designated drivers, Fort Lauderdale's famous water taxi offers a Tuesday and Thursday evening "pub crawl" from 7 to midnight except holidays. The price is about $30 per person, including visits to three clubs with a drink at each. For pickup and drop-off points, call 305/565–5507.

Bars and Lounges

Baja Beach Club (Coral Ridge Mall, 3200 N. Federal Hwy., Fort Lauderdale, ☎ 305/561–2432) offers trendy entertainment: karaoke, lip sync, virtual reality, performing bartenders, temporary tatoos—plus a 40-

No matter where you go, travel is easier when you know the code.^{SM}

dial 1 8 0 0
C A L L
A T T®

Dial 1 800 CALL ATT
and you'll always get
through from any phone
with any card* and you'll
always get AT&T's best
deal.** It's the one number
to remember when calling
away from home.

*Other long distance company calling cards excluded.
**Additional discounts available.

AT&T
Your True Choice

©1995 AT&T

foot free buffet. There are free drinks for women Wednesday night. **Bloody Mary's** (101 N. Beach Rd., Dania, ☎ 305/922–5600), a canal-front bar just across from the John U. Lloyd Beach, is popular on winter weekends, when live acts perform. **Cheers** (941 E. Cypress Creek Rd., Fort Lauderdale, ☎ 305/771–6337) is a woody nightspot with two bars and a dance floor. Every night has something special. Local favorite **Club M** (2037 Hollywood Blvd., Hollywood, ☎ 305/925–8396) features live blues, dancing, and every kind of paraphernalia that starts with the letter M. **Confetti** (2660 E. Commercial Blvd., Fort Lauderdale, ☎ 305/776–4080) is a high-energy "in" spot for adults up to 50. **Crocco's** (3339 N. Federal Hwy., Oakland Park, ☎ 305/566–2406) is the action place for singles. Women drink free Wednesday and Sunday nights from 8 to 11. A long-running venue for the best of blues, jazz, rock-and-roll, and reggae performers, **Musicians Exchange** (729 W. Sunrise Blvd., Fort Lauderdale, ☎ 305/764–1912) has a new Italian-American café. Events include national acts on weekends and a Monday blues jam. **O'Hara's Pub & Sidewalk Cafe** (722 E. Las Olas Blvd., Fort Lauderdale, ☎ 305/524–2801) features live jazz and blues nightly. It's packed for TGIF, though usually by the end of each day the trendy crowd spills onto this prettiest of downtown streets. The **Parrot Lounge** (911 Sunrise La., Fort Lauderdale., ☎ 305/563–1493) is a loony feast for the eyes, with a very casual, friendly, local crowd. Fifteen TVs and frequent sing-alongs add to the fun. A jukebox jams all night. **Squeeze** (401 S. Andrews Ave., Fort Lauderdale, ☎ 305/522–2068) welcomes a wide-ranging clientele—hard-core new-wavers to yuppie types. Along with serving great Japanese food (*see* Dining, *above*), **Sushi Blues Cafe** (1836 S. Young Circle, Hollywood, ☎ 305/929–9560) hosts live music Thursday through Saturday evenings.

Comedy Clubs
The **Comic Strip** (1432 N. Federal Hwy., Fort Lauderdale, ☎ 305/565–8887) headlines stand-up comedians from New York and nationally touring comics, performing among framed old newspaper funnies. **Uncle Funny's Comedy Club** (9160 Rte. 84, Davie, ☎ 305/474–5653) features national and local comics in two shows Friday and Saturday.

Country-and-Western Clubs
Desperado (2520 S. Miami Rd., Fort Lauderdale, ☎ 305/463–2855) features a mechanical bull and free line-dance lessons.

FORT LAUDERDALE ESSENTIALS

Arriving and Departing

By Plane
Fort Lauderdale–Hollywood International Airport (FLHIA) (☎ 305/359–6100), 4 miles south of downtown Fort Lauderdale and just off U.S. 1, is Broward County's major airline terminal and becoming one of Florida's busiest—more than 10 million arrivals and departures a year, a figure that's expected to triple within 20 years. FLHIA is especially favored by new low-cost carriers. Scheduled airlines include **Airways International** (☎ 305/887–2794), **American** (☎ 800/433–7300), **Bahamasair** (☎ 800/562–7661), **Carnival Air Lines** (☎ 305/359–7886), **Chalk's International** (☎ 800/424–2557), **Comair** (☎ 800/354–9822), **Continental** (☎ 800/525–0280), **Delta** (☎ 800/221–1212), **Eagle Air** (☎ 800/332–4533), **Icelandair** (☎ 305/359–2735), **Martinair** (☎ 800/366–4655), **Midwest Express** (☎ 800/452–2022), **Northwest** (☎ 800/225–2525), **Paradise Island** (☎ 800/432–8807), **TWA** (☎ 800/221–

2000), **United** (☎ 800/241–6522), **USAir** (☎ 800/842–5374), and **Valujet** (☎ 800/825–8538).

BETWEEN THE AIRPORT AND CENTER CITY

Broward Transit (☎ 305/357–8400) operates bus route No. 1 between the airport and its main terminal at Broward Boulevard and Northwest 1st Avenue in the center of Fort Lauderdale. Service from the airport begins daily at 5:40 AM; the last bus from the downtown terminal to the airport leaves at 9:30 PM. The fare is 85¢. **Gray Line** (☎ 305/561–8886) provides limousine service to all parts of Broward County. Fares to most Fort Lauderdale beach hotels are in the $6–$10 range.

Rental-car agencies located in the airport include **Avis** (☎ 305/359–3255), **Budget** (☎ 305/359–4700), **Dollar** (☎ 305/359–7800), **Hertz** (☎ 305/359–5281), and **National** (☎ 305/359–8303). In season you'll pay about $120–$130 by the week; the collision-damage waiver adds about $11 per day.

By Car

Access to Broward County from the north or south is via Florida's Turnpike, I–95, U.S. 1, or U.S. 441. I–75 (Alligator Alley) connects Broward with Florida's west coast and runs parallel to Route 84 within the county.

By Train

Amtrak (☎ 800/872–7245) provides daily service to the Fort Lauderdale station (200 S.W. 21st Terr., ☎ 305/463–8251) as well as to the other Broward County stops, Hollywood and Deerfield Beach.

Tri-Rail (☎ 305/728–8445) operates train service daily, 5 AM–11 PM (more limited on weekends) through coastal Broward, Dade, and Palm Beach counties. There are six stations in Broward County, all of them west of I–95.

By Bus

Greyhound Lines (☎ 800/231–2222) buses stop in Fort Lauderdale (515 N.E. 3rd St., ☎ 305/764–6551).

Getting Around

By Car

Except during rush hour, Broward County is a fairly easy place to drive. East–west I–595 runs from westernmost Broward County and links I–75 with I–95 and U.S. 1, providing handy access to Fort Lauderdale–Hollywood International Airport. The scenic but slow Route A1A generally parallels the beach.

By Bus and Trolley

Broward County Mass Transit (☎ 305/357–8400) serves the entire county. The fare is 85¢ (40¢ senior citizens, people with disabilities, and students), plus 10¢ for a transfer. Service on all beach routes starts before 6 AM and continues past 10 PM except on Sunday. Call for route information. Special seven-day tourist passes, which cost $8, are good for unlimited use on all county buses. These are available at some hotels, at Broward County libraries, and at the main bus terminal (Broward Blvd. at N.W. 1st Ave.).

Supplementary bus and trolley services include the expanding free **Downtown Trolley,** which operates weekdays 7:30–5:30 on the Red Line (Courthouse Line) and 11:30–2:30 on the Green (Arts & Science to Las Olas) and Blue (Las Olas to Courthouse) lines. The wait is rarely more than 10 minutes. The lines connect major tourist sites in the Arts and Science District, offices, banks, and government and academic buildings to water taxi stops along the Riverwalk and to the main bus terminal. Along the beach, the **Wave Line Trolley** (☎ 305/527–5600) costs $1 and operates daily every hour 10:15–8:15 except half-hourly 4:45–6:15. It runs along Route A1A from the Galleria Mall on Sunrise Boulevard in the north to close by the Hyatt Regency Pier Sixty-Six in the south.

By Taxi

It's difficult to hail a cab on the street. Sometimes you can pick one up at a major hotel. Otherwise, phone ahead. Fares are not cheap; meters run at a rate of $2.45 for the first mile and $1.75 for each additional mile; waiting time is 25¢ per minute. The major company serving the area is **Yellow Cab** (☎ 305/565–5400).

By Water Taxi

Water Taxi (☎ 305/565–5507) provides service along the Intracoastal Waterway between Port Everglades and Commercial Boulevard 10 AM–1 AM and between Atlantic Boulevard and Hillsboro Boulevard in Pompano Beach noon–midnight. The boats stop at more than 30 restaurants, hotels, shops, and nightclubs; the fare is $6 one-way, $14 ($8 for children under 12) for an all-day pass, and $45 ($25 for children) weekly.

Guided Tours

Carrie B. (Riverwalk at S.E. 5th Ave., ☎ 305/768–9920), a 300-passenger day cruiser, gives 90-minute tours up the New River and Intracoastal Waterway.

Jungle Queen III and IV (Radisson Bahia Mar Beach Resort, 801 Seabreeze Blvd., ☎ 305/462–5596) are 155-passenger and 578-passenger tour boats that take day and night cruises up the New River, through the heart of Fort Lauderdale.

Las Olas Horse and Carriage (600 S.E. 4th St., ☎ 305/763–7393) operates in-town tours and transportation to and from the performing arts center.

Marine Sciences Under Sails School of Environmental Education (2514 Hollywood Blvd., Suite 400, Box 222145, Hollywood 33020-2145, ☎ 305/983–7015, FAX 305/923–2585), a not-for-profit organization, conducts dry-land field trips throughout south Florida and one-day, overnight, and longer boat tours as part of its Science & Sailing program. Sailing trips can accommodate as few as two people (about $100 per person for a day, $114 overnight) or families for customized itineraries in the coastal zone. Unaccompanied children can sometimes be accommodated at lower cost in under-subscribed school trips, on both land and water. Call in advance for availability.

Professional Diving Charters (Radisson Bahia Mar Beach Resort, 801 Seabreeze Blvd., ☎ 305/467–6030) operates the 60-foot glass-bottom boat ***Pro Diver II.*** On Tuesday through Saturday mornings and Sunday afternoon, two-hour sightseeing trips take in offshore reefs, and snorkeling can be arranged.

River and Walking Tours (219 S.W. 2nd Ave., ☎ 305/463–4431), cosponsored by the Fort Lauderdale Historical Society, trace the New River by foot and by boat.

Waterway Tours (Intracoastal Waterway immediately north of the International Swimming Hall of Fame, ☎ 305/943–8738) operates daily

90-minute tours of Millionaires' Row and various waterways on a 26-foot, Bimini-topped catamaran that carries up to six passengers.

Important Addresses and Numbers

Emergencies
Dial 911 for **police** or **ambulance**.

Florida Poison Information Center (☎ 800/282–3171).

HOSPITALS
The following hospitals have a 24-hour emergency room: **Broward General Medical Center** (1600 S. Andrews Ave., Fort Lauderdale, ☎ 305/355–4400; physician referral, ☎ 305/355–4888), **Coral Springs Medical Center** (3999 Coral Hills Dr., Coral Springs, ☎ 350/344–3000; physician referral, ☎ 305/355–4888), **Hollywood Medical Center** (3600 Washington St., Hollywood, ☎ 305/985–6274; physician referral, ☎ 800/237–8701), **Holy Cross Hospital** (4725 N. Federal Hwy., Fort Lauderdale, ☎ 305/492–5753; physician referral, ☎ 305/776–3223), **Imperial Point Medical Center** (6401 N. Federal Hwy., Fort Lauderdale, ☎ 305/776–8500; physician referral, ☎ 305/355–4888), **North Broward Medical Center** (201 E. Sample Rd., Pompano Beach, ☎ 305/941–8300; physician referral, ☎ 305/355–4888), **Plantation General Hospital** (401 N.W. 42nd Ave., Plantation 33317, ☎ 305/797–6470; physician referral, ☎ 305/472–8879), and **Universal Medical Center in Plantation** (6701 W. Sunrise Blvd., Plantation, ☎ 305/581–7800; physician referral, ☎ 305/581–0448).

LATE-NIGHT PHARMACIES
Eckerd Drug (1385 S.E. 17th St., Fort Lauderdale, ☎ 305/525–8173; 1701 E. Commercial Blvd., Fort Lauderdale, ☎ 305/771–0660; 154 University Dr., Pembroke Pines, ☎ 305/432–5510). **Medical Associates Plaza Pharmacy** (3700 Washington St., Hollywood, ☎ 305/963–2008 or 800/793–2008). **Walgreen** (2855 Stirling Rd., Fort Lauderdale, ☎ 305/981–1104; 5001 N. Dixie Hwy., Oakland Park, ☎ 305/772–4206; 289 S. Federal Hwy., Deerfield Beach, ☎ 305/481–2993).

Tourist Information
Chamber of Commerce of Greater Fort Lauderdale (512 N.E. 3rd Ave., Fort Lauderdale 33301, ☎ 305/462–6000). The walk-up, official **Visitors Information Center** (600 Seabreeze Blvd.), on the beach three blocks south of Las Olas Boulevard, is an excellent source for maps, transportation schedules, and events information; it's open Monday–Saturday 9–6, Sunday 11–6.

Dania Chamber of Commerce (100 W. Dania Beach Blvd., Dania 33004, ☎ 305/927–3377). **Greater Deerfield Beach/North Broward Chamber of Commerce** (1601 E. Hillsboro Blvd., Deerfield Beach 33441, ☎ 305/427–1050). **Greater Fort Lauderdale Convention & Visitors Bureau** (200 E. Las Olas Blvd., Suite 1500, Fort Lauderdale 33301, ☎ 305/765–4466 or 800/227–8669 for brochures). **Hollywood Chamber of Commerce** (2410 Hollywood Blvd., Hollywood 33019, ☎ 305/923–4000). **Latin Chamber of Commerce of Broward County** (4000 Hollywood Blvd., Hollywood 33021, ☎ 305/966–0767). **Lauderdale-by-the-Sea Chamber of Commerce** (4201 N. Ocean Dr., Lauderdale-by-the-Sea 33308, ☎ 305/776–1000). **Pompano Beach Chamber of Commerce** (2200 E. Atlantic Blvd., Pompano Beach 33062, ☎ 305/941–2940).

5 Palm Beach and the Treasure Coast

For 100 years, high society has made headlines along south Florida's Atlantic shore from Palm Beach south to Boca Raton—part of the Gold Coast. The coast north of Palm Beach County, called the Treasure Coast, is also worth exploring. Comprising Martin, St. Lucie, and Indian River counties, it's dotted with nature preserves, fishing villages, and towns with active cultural scenes.

By Herb Hiller

AFTER A CENTURY, the Flagler influence finally wanes. Henry Flagler, railroad and real-estate magnate, *created* Palm Beach. Before him, it was an island of fisherfolk and coconut planters, premodern pioneers who lived escapist lives and traveled by boat over sea and inland lagoon because there was no road. Then, suddenly, 100 years ago, the piney woods echoed with the whistle of Flagler's trains. He extended his railroad from Jacksonville and St. Augustine and connected south Florida to New York and the world. In the blink of history's eye, the area exchanged wilderness for luxury. It became the playground of Vanderbilts and Rockefellers, and the Gold Coast was born.

At the same time, West Palm Beach began as the scullery of Palm Beach. Flagler ousted the workers who were helping build his New World Riviera, relocating them across Lake Worth to his freight yards. Palm Beach was for society. West Palm was for servants. Nevertheless, West Palm would have its day. In the '20s the town roared. Then after World War II, suburbs spread in all directions (except east, where Palm Beach remained apart). As recently as a decade ago, West Palm had the most boarded-up downtown in Florida, and one-third of everything standing—77 acres' worth—was torn down and scraped bare.

But failure finally brought action. A strong administration and solid planning have brought new ideas about good downtown living. Residents are returning to live above storefronts; job-skills programs are being underwritten by a consortium of philanthropies; big projects, such as the $124 million County Judicial Center and Courthouse and the $60 million Kravis Center for the Performing Arts, have meant jobs; and a mix of cultural and entertainment organizations and facilities has taken root.

From Flagler's time through the '20s, everything came from the north, but today's prevailing influences come from the south. Fort Lauderdale reinvented its downtown a few years ago. Miami Beach's Deco District set the standard for south Florida nightlife. Now it's West Palm's turn to get caught up in the action. Latin influence grows, too, as Palm Beach County absorbs rich and poor from South and Central America (now 10%–12% of a county population of nearly a million).

What all this means for visitors is a treasury of arts attractions; downtown preservation; and a beautifully landscaped Clematis Street with boutique shopping, good restaurants, and exuberant nightlife that mimics South Beach. There's a free downtown shuttle by day, free on-street parking at night and on weekends. West Palm Beach, born as an afterthought, has become the cultural, entertainment, and business center of the county and of the region to the north.

Elsewhere in Palm Beach County, the arts also flourish. From Boca Raton in the south to Jupiter in the north, there's a profusion of museums, galleries, and theaters and towns committed to historic preservation.

As for Palm Beach, socialites and celebrities still flock here. They attend charity galas at The Breakers. They browse in the stores along Worth Avenue, still one of the world's classiest shopping districts. They swim on secluded beaches that are nominally public but lack convenient parking and access points. They pedal the world's most beautiful bicycle path beside Lake Worth. And what they do, *you* can do—if you can afford it. But despite its prominence and affluence, the town of Palm Beach occupies far less than 1% of the land area of the remarkably diverse political jurisdiction that Palm Beach County has become.

Also worth exploring is the region just north of Palm Beach County; called the Treasure Coast, it encompasses Martin, St. Lucie, and Indian River counties. Remote and sparsely populated as recently as the late 1970s, the Treasure Coast lost its relative seclusion in 1987, when I–95's missing link from Palm Beach Gardens to Fort Pierce was completed. Now malls crowd corridors between I–95 and the beaches from Palm Beach north to Vero Beach. Martin and Indian River counties are known for their high environmental standards (though not St. Lucie County in between). Stuart, the Martin County seat, has revived its downtown with restaurants and shops, while Vero Beach, the Indian River County seat, is a hub of Treasure Coast arts. On the beach just north of Vero, Disney has completed phase one of its first resort outside a theme park.

Inland, the Treasure Coast is largely devoted to citrus production, with cattle ranching in rangelands of pine-and-palmetto scrub. Along the coast, the broad tidal lagoon called the Indian River separates the barrier islands from the mainland. It's a sheltered route for boaters on the Intracoastal Waterway, a nursery for many saltwater game fish, and a natural radiator keeping frost away from the tender orange and grapefruit trees that grow near its banks. Sea turtles come ashore at night from April to August to lay their eggs on the beaches, and you can join organized turtle-watches run by local conservation groups, chambers of commerce, and resorts.

EXPLORING

Tour 1: Palm Beach

Numbers in the margin correspond to points of interest on the Gold Coast and Treasure Coast and the Palm Beach and West Palm Beach maps.

❶ **Palm Beach** is an island community 12 miles long and no more than ¼ mile across at its widest point. Three bridges connect Palm Beach to West Palm Beach and the rest of the world.

Begin at Royal Palm Way and County Road in the center of Palm Beach.
❷ Go north on County Road to Episcopal **Bethesda-by-the-Sea,** built in 1927 by the first Protestant congregation in southeast Florida. Spanish-Gothic design and ornamental gardens mark the site. *141 S. County Rd.,* ☎ *407/655–4554.* ☯ *Gardens: daily 8–5; services Sept.–May, Sun. at 8, 9, and 11* AM; *June–Aug., Sun. at 8 and 10; call for weekday schedule.*

★ ❸ Continue north on County Road past **The Breakers** (*see* Dining and Lodging, *below*), an ornate Italian renaissance hotel built in 1926 by Henry M. Flagler's widow to replace an earlier hotel, which had burned twice.

❹ Farther up County Road, at Royal Poinciana Way, go inside the **Palm Beach Post Office** to see the murals depicting Seminole Indians in the Everglades and royal and coconut palms. *95 N. County Rd.,* ☎ *407/ 832–0633 or 407/832–1867.* ☯ *Lobby: 24 hrs.*

Continue 3.9 miles on North County Road/North Ocean Boulevard, past the very private Palm Beach Country Club and a neighborhood of expansive (and expensive) estates. Among these, at 1095 North Ocean Boulevard, is the former home of the Kennedy family, unoccupied, decaying,
❺ and lately for sale. You must turn around at **East Inlet Drive,** the northern tip of the island, where a dock offers a view of Lake Worth Inlet. Observe the no-parking signs; Palm Beach police will issue tickets.

140

Gold Coast and Treasure Coast

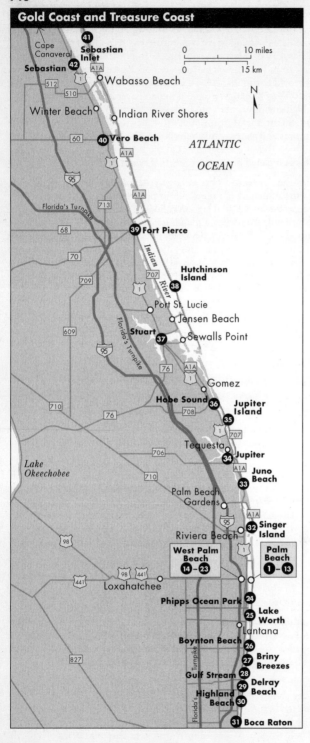

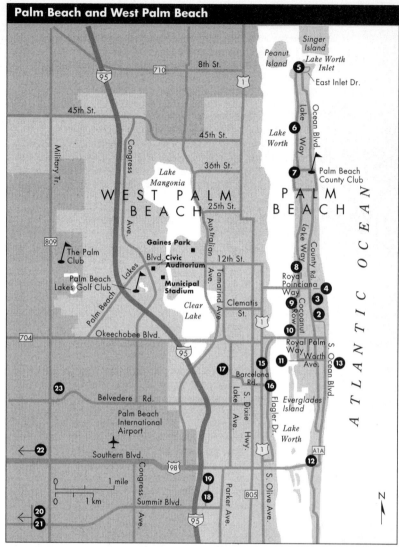

Palm Beach and West Palm Beach

Ann Norton
Sculpture
Gardens, **16**

Armory Art
Center, **17**

Bethesda-by-
the-Sea, **2**

The Breakers, **3**

Canyon of Palm
Beach, **7**

Dreher Park Zoo, **18**

East Inlet Drive, **5**

Lion Country
Safari, **22**

Mar-A-Lago, **12**

Mounts Horticultural
Learning Center, **23**

Norton Gallery
of Art, **15**

Okeeheelee Nature
Center, **21**

Palm Beach Bicycle
Trail, **6**

Palm Beach Biltmore
Hotel, **8**

Palm Beach Post
Office, **4**

Pine Jog
Environmental
Education Center, **20**

Public beach, **13**

Society of the Four
Arts, **10**

South Florida Science
Museum, **19**

Whitehall, **9**

Worth Avenue, **11**

Turn south and make the first right onto Indian Road, then the first left onto Lake Way. You'll return to the center of town through an area of newer mansions, past the posh, private Sailfish Club. Along the shoreline of Lake Worth, the **Palm Beach Bicycle Trail,** a palm-fringed path through the backyards of some of the world's priciest homes, parallels Lake Way.

Lake Way runs into Country Club Road, which takes you through the **Canyon of Palm Beach,** a road cut about 25 feet deep through a ridge of sandstone and oolite limestone.

As you emerge from the canyon, turn right onto Lake Way and continue south. Lake Way becomes Bradley Place. You'll pass the **Palm Beach Biltmore Hotel,** now a condominium. Another flamboyant landmark of the Florida boom, it cost $7 million to build and opened in 1927 with 543 rooms.

As you cross Royal Poinciana Way, Bradley Place becomes Cocoanut Row. Stop at **Whitehall,** the palatial 73-room mansion that Henry M. Flagler built in 1901 for his third wife, Mary Lily Kenan. In 1960 Flagler's granddaughter, Jean Flagler Matthews, bought the building. She turned it into a museum, with many of the original furnishings on display. In addition to an art collection, the house features a 1,200-pipe organ and exhibits on the history of the Florida East Coast Railroad. Flagler's personal railroad car, "The Rambler," is parked behind the building. A tour by well-informed guides takes about an hour. *Cocoanut Row at Whitehall Way,* ☎ *407/655–2833.* ☛ *$7 adults, $3 children 6–12.* ☉ *Tues.–Sat. 10–5, Sun. noon–5.*

Continue south on Cocoanut Row to Royal Palm Way. Turn right and then right again onto the grounds of the **Society of the Four Arts.** This 60-year-old cultural and educational institution is privately endowed and incorporates an exhibition hall for art, concerts, films, and lectures; a library open without charge; 13 distinct gardens; and the Philip Hulitar Sculpture Garden. *Four Arts Plaza,* ☎ *407/655–7226.* ☛ *$3 suggested donation. Concert and lecture tickets for nonmembers may be purchased 1 wk in advance; tickets for Fri. films available at time of showing.* ☉ *Exhibitions and programs: Dec.–mid-Apr., Mon.–Sat. 10–5, Sun. 2–5; library and children's library: weekdays 10–5, also Sat. 9–1 Nov.–Apr.; gardens: Mon.–Sat. 10–5, also Sun. 2:30–5 Jan.–Apr. 15.*

Return to Royal Palm Way and County Road, where we began this tour. Now go south on County Road, until you reach **Worth Avenue** (*see* Shopping, *below*), one of the world's finest shopping streets.

County Road runs south along a mansion row fronted by thick stands of palm trees and high hedges, some hedgerows higher than 20 feet. You will see de rigueur barrel tile roofs on the houses. After a mile, County Road joins Ocean Boulevard to become the shore road (now officially designated A1A). A low wall separates the road from the sea and hides the badly eroded beach. Here and there where the seaside strand deepens a bit, homes have been built directly on the beach.

Grandest of homes along this road is **Mar-A-Lago** (1100 S. Ocean Blvd.), its Italianate towers silhouetted against the sky. Mar-A-Lago, the former estate of breakfast-food heiress Marjorie Meriweather Post, has lately been owned by real-estate magnate Donald Trump, who has turned it into a membership club. The property curves for ⅓ mile along the road.

Rather than cross the bridge to the mainland, turn back along Ocean Boulevard, heading north along one of Florida's most scenic drives. The road follows the dune top, with some of Palm Beach's most opulent mansions on your left. As you approach Worth Avenue, the **public beach** begins. Parking meters along Ocean Boulevard between Worth Avenue and Royal Palm Way signify the only stretch of beach in Palm Beach with convenient public access.

Tour 2: West Palm Beach

Royal Palm Way runs across the Royal Palm Bridge from Palm Beach into **West Palm Beach.** Okeechobee Boulevard leads west from here to downtown, past the **Kravis Center for the Performing Arts** (*see* The Arts and Nightlife, *below*). Besides the Kravis Center, which opened in 1992, new buildings on the skyline include the mammoth $124 million Palm Beach County Judicial Center and Courthouse and the State Administrative Building, both opened in 1993.

Rather than drive into downtown, however, once you have reached the mainland side of the bridge turn left onto Flagler Drive. Running along the west shore of Lake Worth, the body of water that separates Palm Beach from the mainland, Flagler Drive has been spruced up with a $4.2 million waterfront restoration project.

One-half mile south of the bridge, turn right onto Actaeon Street, which leads to the **Norton Gallery of Art.** Founded in 1941 by steel magnate Ralph H. Norton, the Norton Gallery boasts an extensive permanent collection of 19th- and 20th-century American and European paintings with emphasis on 19th-century French Impressionists, Chinese bronze and jade sculptures, a sublime outdoor patio with sculptures on display in a tropical garden, and a library housing more than 3,000 art books and periodicals. Visitors in 1996 will find a new wing under construction, expected to open in 1997. *1451 S. Olive Ave.,* ☎ *407/832–5194.* ☛ *$5 suggested donation.* ☉ *Tues.–Sat. 10–5, Sun. 1–5.*

Return to Flagler Drive, go ½ mile south to Barcelona Road, and turn right again. You're at the entrance to the **Ann Norton Sculpture Gardens,** a monument to the late American sculptor Ann Weaver Norton, second wife of Norton Gallery founder Ralph H. Norton. In three distinct areas of the 3-acre grounds, the art park displays seven granite figures and six brick megaliths. Plantings were designed by Norton, an environmentalist, to attract native bird life. *253 Barcelona Rd.,* ☎ *407/832–5328.* ☛ *$3 ages over 12.* ☉ *Tues.–Sat. 10–4 (call first because schedule is not always observed) or by appointment.*

Continue west on Barcelona Road to Lake Avenue, turn right, and go three blocks to Park Place and the former Palm Beach County National Guard Armory, now the **Armory Art Center.** Designed as a WPA project in 1939, the armory today serves as a complete visual-arts center with exhibitions, classes, workshops, and special events. *1703 S. Lake Ave.,* ☎ *407/832–1776.* ☛ *Free.* ☉ *Weekdays 9–5.*

Head back on Lake Avenue to Southern Boulevard (U.S. 98). Turn right and go west one block, turn left onto Parker Avenue, and go south about a mile. Turn right onto Summit Boulevard, and at the next stoplight you'll find the **Dreher Park Zoo.** The 22-acre zoo has more than 500 animals representing more than 100 species, including an endangered Florida panther. *1301 Summit Blvd.,* ☎ *407/533–0887 or 407/547–9453 for a recording.* ☛ *$5.50 adults, $5 senior citizens, $4.50 children 3–12; boat rides: $1.* ☉ *Daily 9–5 (to 7 on spring and summer weekends); boat rides every 15 min.*

⑲ About ¼ mile from the zoo is the **South Florida Science Museum.** Here you'll find hands-on exhibits, aquarium displays with touch-tank demonstrations, planetarium shows, and a chance to observe the heavens Friday night through the most powerful telescope in south Florida (weather permitting). *4801 Dreher Trail N,* ☎ *407/832–1988.* ☛ *$5 adults, $4.50 senior citizens, $3 students 13–21, $2 children 4–12; Aldrin Planetarium: $1.75 extra, laser show $2 extra.* ☺ *Sat.–Thurs. 10–5, Fri. 10–10.*

Leaving the science museum, head west on Summit Boulevard to the **⑳** **Pine Jog Environmental Education Center.** The 150-acre site is mostly undisturbed Florida pine flatwoods. There are now two self-guided ½-mile trails, and formal landscaping around the five one-story buildings features an array of native plants. Dioramas and displays show native ecosystems. *6301 Summit Blvd.,* ☎ *407/686–6600.* ☛ *Free.* ☺ *Weekdays 9–5, weekends 1–4; closed holidays.*

Continuing west on Summit, turn left (south) on Jog Road and right on Forest Hill Boulevard; a mile farther is another regional environmental **㉑** resource, the **Okeeheelee Nature Center.** Here you can explore 5 miles of trails through 90 acres of native pine flatwoods and wetlands. A spacious visitor center/gift shop has hands-on exhibits. *7715 Forest Hill Blvd.,* ☎ *407/233–1400.* ☛ *Free.* ☺ *Visitor center: Tues.–Fri. 1–4:45, Sat. 8:15–4:45; trails open daily.*

Continue west on Forest Hill Boulevard, turn right on U.S. 441 and take it for about 15 miles (as it bears west and joins Southern Boule- **㉒** vard) to **Lion Country Safari.** Here you drive (with car windows closed) on 8 miles of paved roads through a 500-acre cageless zoo where 1,000 wild animals roam free. Lions, elephants, white rhinoceroses, giraffes, zebras, antelopes, chimpanzees, and ostriches are among the species in residence. *Southern Blvd. W,* ☎ *407/793–1084.* ☛ *$11.95 adults, $8.55 senior citizens, $9.95 children 3–16; car rental: $5 per hr.* ☺ *Daily 9:30–5:30.*

Returning east on Southern Boulevard, turn left on Military Trail, which runs alongside the western perimeter of Palm Beach International Airport. On the right just north of Belvedere Road (less than 2 miles) **㉓** is the 14-acre **Mounts Horticultural Learning Center,** where you can walk among displays of tropical and subtropical plants. Free guided tours are given. *531 N. Military Trail,* ☎ *407/233–1749.* ☛ *Free.* ☺ *Mon.–Sat. 8:30–5, Sun. 1–5; tours Sat. at 11, Sun. at 2:30.*

Okeechobee Boulevard, the next cross street north, will take you back to anywhere in the Palm Beaches, to Florida's Turnpike, or to I–95.

Tour 3: South to Boca Raton

★ This tour carries you along the coast of south Palm Beach County, nearly 40 miles along **Route A1A** through an almost uninterrupted realm of the rich and famous that has earned the sobriquet "the Gold Coast." Little commuter traffic occurs, but the route all the way is two-lane and slow-moving in winter. Watch for cyclists and joggers.

Starting from the center of Palm Beach, on Royal Palm Way, head south on County Road. It soon joins Ocean Boulevard and proceeds south, **㉔** as Route A1A, along the barrier island. On the left is **Phipps Ocean Park** with a Palm Beach County landmark: the Little Red Schoolhouse, which dates from 1886, the first schoolhouse in what was then Dade County. (Dade County today is metropolitan Miami, but at one time it extended all the way to Lake Okeechobee.) *Rte. A1A, Palm Beach. Parking: 25¢ for 20 mins, quarters only.* ☺ *8–6.*

㉕ Below the Palm Beach Golf Club you enter the town of **Lake Worth.** Turn right at the causeway into Casino Park (also known as Lake Worth Municipal Park).

TIME OUT About the only time the line lets up at **John G's** (Lake Worth Casino, ☎ 407/585–9860) is when the restaurant closes at 3 PM. The menu is as big as the crowd: eggs every which way, including a United Nations of ethnic omelets; big fruit platters; sandwich-board superstars; grilled burgers; and seafood. The Greek shrimp (seven at recent count) come on fresh linguine topped by feta cheese.

Go through the little towns of **Manalapan** and, across Boynton Inlet, **Ocean Ridge.** The Ritz-Carlton Hotel is on the left in Manalapan; then pass the Ocean Club Golf Course to the west, its villas and beach club ㉖ to the east. The little **Boynton Beach** city park, **Oceanfront Park** (*see* Beaches, *below*), has a good swimming beach but a prohibitive parking fee for nonresidents.

Just below the crossing of Route 804 (East Ocean Avenue), a niche road ㉗ (Old Ocean Boulevard) cuts off directly along the beach to enter **Briny Breezes,** a wonderful old blue-collar town, 42 acres directly on the sea. It's an incongruous neighbor in these precincts of the high and mighty, but here it has been, incorporated since 1963.

Beyond this you'll pass another anomaly in this ritzy area—a row of mildly ramshackle houses, with overgrown yards full of rusting gear— ㉘ and then come to the beautiful little community of **Gulf Stream.** You'll pass the very private St. Andrews Country Club and the bougainvillea-topped walls of the Gulfstream Club, part of the Addison Mizner legacy, where a private police officer may come onto the road to halt traffic for the moment it takes a golfer to cross in his or her cart.

㉙ **Delray Beach,** which began as an artists' retreat and a small settlement of Japanese farmers, recently won the title of All-American City. At the edge of town, across Northeast 8th Street (George Bush Boulevard), begins a lovely pedestrian way along the big broad swimming beach that extends north and south of Atlantic Avenue. This avenue, Delray's main street, has revived retailing thanks to historic preservation and pedestrian friendliness. The chief landmark along the 12 mostly store-lined blocks leading west from the ocean is the Mediterranean-revival **Colony Hotel** (525 E. Atlantic Ave., ☎ 407/276–4123), still open only for the winter season as it has been for more than 60 years. Just off Atlantic Avenue, the **Old School Square Cultural Arts Center** (51 N. Swinton Ave., ☎ 407/243–7922) houses several museums, notably the **Cornell Museum of Art & History,** and a performing arts center in restored school buildings dating from 1913 and 1926. On the next street north is **Cason Cottage** (5 N.E. 1st St., ☎ 407/243–0223), a home that dates from about 1915 and that now serves as offices of the Delray Beach Historical Society.

TIME OUT A block south of the Old School Square, the charmingly old-fashioned **Sundy House** (106 S. Swinton Ave., ☎ 407/278–2163 or 407/ 272–3270) has a restaurant, which serves lunch and a traditional afternoon tea; antiques trove; and gift shop. Flagler foreman John Shaw Sundy, who became the first mayor of Delray, and his family lived here. The house has beautiful gardens and five gingerbread gables that complement Delray's finest wraparound porch.

Apart from downtown, the main tourist attraction in Delray Beach is ★ the **Morikami Museum and Japanese Gardens,** a 200-acre cultural and recreational facility. Some programs and exhibits are in the lakeside museum building and theater; an earlier building, modeled after a Japanese imperial villa, houses a permanent exhibition detailing the history of the Yamato Colony, an agricultural community of Japanese, which dated from 1905. The grounds include a nature trail, picnic pavilions, a library and audiovisual center on Japanese culture, museum shop, snack bar/café, and various gardens, including the only collection known to exist of bonsai Florida plants. *4000 Morikami Park Rd.,* ☎ *407/495–0233.* ☛ *$4.25 adults, $3.75 senior citizens, $2 children 6–18, free Sun. 10–noon.* ☉ *Park: daily sunrise–sunset; museum: Tues.–Sun. 10–5, closed Jan. 1, Easter, July 4, Thanksgiving, Dec. 25.*

㉚ South of Linton Boulevard the beachfront character changes, becoming more high-rise. You enter the town of **Highland Beach,** which has been completely developed from bare dune in the last 25 years. Today the shoreside is packed with condominiums, and across the Intracoastal Waterway, mansions. The road here is called South Ocean Boulevard.

㉛ Where the road rises along the dune, you enter **Boca Raton.** This visionary city, developed by architect Addison Mizner in the 1920s, had barely made it off the drawing board when the Depression hit. For half a century after, Boca grew along the beach and along U.S. 1 without a town center. Off to the right ahead you will see the peachy plum–color Boca Tower of the **Boca Raton Resort & Club** (*see* Dining and Lodging, *below*); alongside it, lower to the ground, is the nucleus of the hotel, the original Cloister Inn built by Mizner. To the left is the Boca Beach Club, a newer part of the same property.

Cross the drawbridge over Boca Inlet and drive onto Camino Real, a six-lane boulevard with a double row of Malaysian dwarf palms down the center. Cross Federal Highway (U.S. 1), and just before Dixie Highway, turn left into the parking lot of **Addison's Flavor of Italy** (2 E. Camino Real, ☎ 407/391–9800). Built in 1925 by the Mizner Development Corporation to house the city administration, this building shows Mizner's characteristic Spanish-revival architectural style: pecky cypress, wrought-iron grills, a barrel tile roof, and handmade tiles around the courtyard.

Turn right onto South Dixie Highway. Immediately on your left is the restored **Boca Raton Florida East Coast Railroad Station,** now used for small community meetings.

As you continue north on Dixie Highway, on your right notice the distinctive Boca look: buildings in pink and burnt sienna, all with barrel tile roofs, many with canopies and iron balconies. One block past Palmetto Park Road, turn right onto Boca Raton Road; on your right is the gold-domed **Old Town Hall,** built in 1927 to a Mizner design. A gift shop with unusual Boca items, especially good books and prints, is located in the original mayor's office. Historical exhibits rotate in the hall gallery. *71 N. Federal Hwy.,* ☎ *407/395–6766.* ☛ *Free.* ☉ *Weekdays 10–4.*

Turn left on North Federal Highway, and at Northeast 3rd Street you'll find **Mizner Park** (*see* Shopping, *below*), the new heart of downtown Boca Raton, with its shopping promenade, apartments, and offices. This successful development has quickly given the community the focal point it sorely needed. A potential blockbuster, the **International Museum of Cartoon Art,** long championed by *Beetle Bailey* artist Mort Walker, is expected to open here before the end of 1996.

Exit Mizner Park across Northeast 2nd Street and continue west across the railroad tracks. The new **Boca Raton City Hall** is on your left, designed in the style of the original and set among enormous banyan trees.

Return to Palmetto Park Road and continue west to visit the **Boca Raton Museum of Art,** with its whimsical metal sculptures outdoors on the lawn. The museum's permanent collection includes works by Picasso, Degas, Matisse, Klee, and Modigliani as well as notable pre-Columbian art. *801 W. Palmetto Park Rd.,* ☎ *407/392–2500.* ☛ *Free.* ⊘ *Weekdays 10–4, weekends noon–4.*

The residential area behind the museum is **Old Floresta,** developed by Addison Mizner starting in 1925 and landscaped with many varieties of palms and cycads. The houses are mainly Mediterranean style, many with upper balconies supported in the Mizner style by exposed wood columns.

Tour 4: The Treasure Coast

This tour takes you north from Palm Beach along the coast as far as Sebastian, but you can break away at any intermediate point and return to Palm Beach on I–95. From downtown West Palm Beach, take U.S. 1 about 5 miles north to Blue Heron Boulevard (Route A1A) in
❸❷ Riviera Beach, turn right, and cross the Jerry Thomas Bridge onto **Singer Island.** Continue on Route A1A as it turns north onto Ocean Boulevard, past hotels and high-rise condominiums to **John D. MacArthur State Park,** which offers almost 2 miles of beach and interpretive walks to a mangrove estuary along the upper reaches of Lake Worth. *10900 Rte. A1A, North Palm Beach,* ☎ *407/624–6950 for office or 407/624–6952 for nature center.* ☛ *$3.25 per vehicle with up to 8 people.* ⊘ *8–sunset; nature center open Wed.–Mon. 9–5.*

North of MacArthur State Park, Route A1A rejoins U.S. 1, then veers
❸❸ east again 1½ miles north at **Juno Beach.** Take Route A1A north to Donald Ross Road, west to U.S. 1, and north immediately to enter **Loggerhead Park Marine Life Center of Juno Beach,** established by Eleanor N. Fletcher, "the turtle lady of Juno Beach." Museum displays interpret the sea turtles' natural history. Also on view are displays of coastal natural history, sharks, whales, and shells. *1200 U.S. 1 (entrance on west side of park),* ☎ *407/627–8280. Donations welcome.* ⊘ *Tues.–Sat. 10–4, Sun. noon–3.*

❸❹ From Juno Beach north to **Jupiter,** Route A1A runs for almost 4 miles atop the beachfront dunes. At Jupiter Beach Road, turn right and immediately left onto Dubois Road. At its end in **Dubois Park** is the **Dubois Home,** a modest pioneer home that dates from 1898. The house, with design features that include Cape Cod as well as "cracker," sits atop an ancient Jeaga Indian mound 20 feet high, looking onto Jupiter Inlet. Even if you arrive when the house is closed, the park is worth the visit for its lovely beaches around swimming lagoons. *Dubois Rd.,* ☎ *407/747–6639.* ☛ *Donations welcome.* ⊘ *Sun. 1–4.*

Return to A1A, turn right to U.S. 1, and then turn left (south) for ⅓ mile. On the east side of the highway, in Burt Reynolds Park, is the **Florida History Center and Museum.** Permanent exhibits review Seminole, steamboat-era, and pioneer history on the Loxahatchee River; shipwrecks; railroads; and modern-day development. *805 N. U.S. 1,* ☎ *407/747–6639.* ☛ *$3 adults, $2 senior citizens, $1 children 6–18.* ⊘ *Tues.–Sat. 10–4, Sun. 1–5.*

③⑤ Return north on U.S. 1 and cross the Loxahatchee River onto **Jupiter Island;** just across the Jupiter Inlet Bridge, pick up Route 707 (Beach Road). On your right is the **Jupiter Inlet Light Station,** a redbrick Coast Guard navigational beacon that has operated here since 1866. The 105-foot structure is open Sunday through Wednesday 10–4. Tours of the lighthouse and a visit to a small museum cost $5, used for restoring the property.

Head north on Route 707 and stop at the Nature Conservancy's 73-acre **Blowing Rocks Preserve.** Within the preserve you'll find plant communities native to beachfront dune, coastal strand (the landward side of the dunes), mangrove, and hammock (tropical hardwood forest). The best time to visit is when high tides and strong offshore winds coincide, causing the sea to blow spectacularly through holes in the eroded outcropping. Park in the lot; Jupiter Island police will ticket cars parked along the road shoulder. *Rte. 707,* ☎ *407/575–2297 for office or 407/747–3113 for preserve.* ☛ *$3 donation requested.* ⊙ *Daily 6–5.*

Continue north through the town of Jupiter Island, a carefully laid-out community with estates screened from the road by dense vegetation. At the north end of town, **Hobe Sound National Wildlife Refuge** has a 3½-mile beach where turtles nest and shells wash ashore. High tides and strong winds have severely eroded the beach; during winter high tides only a sliver of beach remains to walk along. *Beach Rd., off Rte. 707,* ☎ *407/546–6141.* ☛ *$4 per vehicle.* ⊙ *Sunrise–sunset generally.*

③⑥ To visit the refuge headquarters and the **Elizabeth W. Kirby Interpretive Center,** return to the mainland, pass through the town of **Hobe Sound,** turn left on U.S. 1, and travel approximately 2½ miles. An adjacent ½-mile trail winds through a forest of sand pine and scrub oak—one of Florida's most unusual and endangered plant communities. *13640 S.E. Federal Hwy.,* ☎ *407/546–6141.* ☛ *Free.* ⊙ *Trail: sunrise–sunset; nature center: weekdays 9–11 and 1–3, call for Sat. hrs; group tours by appointment.*

From the interpretive center, go south 2½ miles to the entrance to **Jonathan Dickinson State Park.** Follow signs to Hobe Mountain, an ancient dune topped with a tower, from which you have a panoramic view across the park's 10,285 acres of varied terrain. Here the Loxahatchee River, part of the federal government's wild and scenic rivers program, is populated by manatees in winter and alligators all year. The park has bicycle and hiking trails, a campground, and a snack bar, and it's a great place to canoe (*see* Sports and the Outdoors, *below*) or to take a narrated river cruise (*see* Guided Tours *in* Palm Beach and the Treasure Coast Essentials, *below*). *16450 S.E. Federal Hwy.,* ☎ *407/546–2771.* ☛ *$3.25 per vehicle with up to 8 people.* ⊙ *Daily 8–sunset.*

③⑦ Return to U.S. 1 and proceed north. Quality of life is important in **Stuart**—the Martin County seat—a one-time fishing village that has become a magnet for sophisticates who want to live and work in a small-town atmosphere. Strict architectural and zoning standards ★ guide civic renewal projects in the **historic downtown,** which now claims eight antiques shops, nine restaurants, and more than 50 specialty shops within a two-block area. The old courthouse has become the **Court House Cultural Center** (80 E. Ocean Blvd., ☎ 407/288–2542), which features art exhibits. The Old Stuart Feed Store has become the **Stuart Heritage Museum** (161 S.W. Flagler Ave., ☎ 407/220–4600). The **Lyric Theatre** (59 S.W. Flagler Ave., ☎ 407/220–1942) has been revived for performing and community events (and recently listed on the National Register of Historic Places), and a new gazebo features free music performances. For information on downtown, contact the **Stuart Main Street Office** (151 S.W. Flagler Ave., 34994, ☎ 407/ 286–2848).

TIME OUT In an old bank building, the **Jolly Sailor Pub** (1 S.W. Osceola St., ☎ 407/221–1111) is owned by a retired 27-year British Merchant Navy veteran, which may account for the endless ship paraphernalia. A veritable Cunard museum, it has a model of the *Brittania*, prints of 19th-century side-wheelers, and a big bar painting of the *QE2*. There's a wonderful brass-railed wood bar, a dartboard, and such pub grub as fish-and-chips, cottage pie, and bangers (sausage) and mash, with Guinness and Double Diamond ales on tap.

❸❽ Continue north on Route A1A to **Hutchinson Island.** At Indian River Plantation, turn right onto MacArthur Boulevard, and go 1½ miles to the **House of Refuge Museum,** built in 1875. It's the only one remaining of nine such structures erected by the U.S. Life Saving Service (a predecessor of the Coast Guard) to aid stranded sailors. Exhibits include antique lifesaving equipment, maps, artifacts from nearby wrecks, and boat-making tools. *301 S.E. MacArthur Blvd., Stuart, ☎ 407/ 225–1875.* ☛ *$2 adults, 50¢ children 6–13.* ☉ *Tues.–Sun. 11–4; closed holidays.*

Return to Route A1A and go ³⁄₁₀ mile north to the pastel-pink **Elliott Museum,** built in 1961 in honor of Sterling Elliott, inventor of an early automated addressing machine and a four-wheel bicycle. In addition, the museum features antique automobiles, dolls and toys, and fixtures from an early general store, blacksmith shop, and apothecary shop. *825 N.E. Ocean Blvd., Stuart, ☎ 407/225–1961.* ☛ *$4 adults, 50¢ children 6–13.* ☉ *Daily 11–4.*

Across the road is the **Coastal Science Center** (890 N.E. Ocean Blvd., Stuart, ☎ 407/225–0505) of the Florida Oceanographic Society. Its nearly 44-acre site combines a coastal hardwood hammock and mangrove forest. A 2,000-square-foot visitor center opened at the end of 1994, with aquariums, an auditorium, research laboratory, and permanent library to follow.

Continue up Route A1A as far as the Jensen Beach Bridge. Cut back to the mainland and turn right on Indian River Drive (Route 707). This scenic road full of curves and dips follows the course of early 20th-century pineapple plantations. At Midway Road (Route 712), 14 miles **❸❾** north of Jensen Beach in **Fort Pierce,** turn left and go ½ mile to the **Savannahs Recreation Area.** This 550-acre site was once a reservoir but has been allowed to return to its natural state. Today it's semiwilderness with campsites, a petting zoo, botanical garden, boat ramps, and trails. *1400 E. Midway Rd., ☎ 407/464–7855.* ☛ *$1 per vehicle.* ☉ *Daily 8 AM–9 PM.*

Return to Route 707 and continue north to Savannah Road, turn left, go ⁸⁄₁₀ mile, and turn right immediately after Heathcote Road to **Heathcote Botanical Gardens.** A self-guided tour takes in a palm walk, Japanese garden, and subtropical foliage. *210 Savannah Rd., ☎ 407/ 464–4672.* ☛ *Donations welcome.* ☉ *Tues.–Sat. 9–5, also Sun. 1–5 Nov.–Apr.*

A mile farther on Route 707, visit the **A. E. "Bean" Backus Gallery,** home of the Treasure Coast Art Association. Beanie Backus was Florida's foremost landscape artist until his death in 1990 at age 84. Many of his masterpieces are displayed here. The gallery also mounts changing exhibits and offers exceptional buys on locally produced art.

500 N. Indian River Dr., ☎ *407/465–0630.* ☛ *Donations welcome.* ☻ *Tues.–Sun. 1–5.*

Turn right over the South Beach Causeway Bridge. On the east side, take the first road left onto the grounds of the **St. Lucie County Historical Museum.** Among its exhibits are historic photos, early 20th-century memorabilia, vintage farm tools, a restored 1919 American La France fire engine, replicas of a general store and the old Fort Pierce railroad station, and the restored 1905 Gardner House. *414 Seaway Dr.,* ☎ *407/468–1795.* ☛ *$2 adults, $1 children 6–11.* ☻ *Tues.–Sat. 10–4, Sun. noon–4.*

From here, backtrack to the mainland, turn north (right) on U.S. 1, and then take your pick of two routes to Vero Beach. To proceed along the coast, head east across North Beach Causeway. Just before Route A1A turns north, turn south instead into the southern section of the **Fort Pierce Inlet State Recreation Area.** This section of the park offers swimming, surfing, and a self-guiding nature trail. *905 Shorewinds Dr.,* ☎ *407/468–3985.* ☛ *$3.25 per vehicle with up to 8 people.* ☻ *Daily 8–sunset.*

Follow Route A1A north to Pepper Park and the **UDT-Seal Museum,** beside the beach where more than 3,000 Navy frogmen trained during World War II. In 1993 exhibit space was tripled (further expansions are planned through the decade). Numerous patrol boats and vehicles constitute an outdoor exhibit area. *3300 N. Rte. A1A,* ☎ *407/595–1570.* ☛ *$2 adults, $1 children 6–12.* ☻ *Tues.–Sat. 10–4, Sun. noon–4.*

About 1 mile north of Pepper Park, turn left to the parking lot for the 958-acre **Jack Island Wildlife Refuge,** accessible only by footbridge. The 1½-mile Marsh Rabbit Trail across the island traverses a mangrove swamp to a 30-foot observation tower overlooking the Indian River. Trails cover 4⅓ miles altogether. *Rte. A1A,* ☎ *407/468–3985.* ☛ *Free.* ☻ *8–sunset.*

Back on Route A1A, go north to Vero Beach. If you'd rather take the mainland route from Fort Pierce, continue north from there along Route 707, which becomes Old Dixie Highway (Route 605). Just after the intersection of Immokalee Road (Route 608), turn right into **St. Lucie Village.** This is one of Florida's rare old settlements, largely left to change at its own pace. Old houses with screened porches behind broad lawns face the Indian River Lagoon across a narrow shore road. Some once served as lodgings for prominent northerners, including President William McKinley, who around the turn of the century enjoyed winter hunting and fishing here.

Continue north on Route 605 to the **Harbor Branch Oceanographic Institution,** a diversified research and teaching facility with a staff of some 200 and an international reputation. Its fleet of research vessels— particularly its two submersibles—operates around the world for NASA, NOAA, and NATO, among other contractors. Visitors can take a 90-minute tour of the 500-acre facility, which contains submersibles; aquariums of sea life indigenous to the Indian River Lagoon; exhibits of marine technology; learning facilities; lifelike and whimsical bronze sculptures created by founder J. Seward Johnson, Jr.; and a gift shop of imaginative items related to the sea. *5600 Old Dixie Hwy.,* ☎ *407/465–2400.* ☛ *$5 adults, $3 students. Tours Mon.–Sat. at 10, noon, 2, except Thanksgiving, Dec. 25.*

From here Old Dixie Highway continues north through a generally rural and otherwise ungussied landscape of small farms, residential areas, and commerce into downtown **Vero Beach.** Vero is an affluent city of about 30,000 (retirees make up half the winter population), with a strong commitment to the environment and the arts. At 17th Street, turn east, cross the 17th Street Bridge, and head for the beach, where you can turn north onto A1A. In the exclusive Riomar Bay section, north of the 17th Street Bridge, "canopy roads" are shaded by massive live oaks.

At Beachland Boulevard, turn left (west), and after less than a mile, just east of the new high-rise Merrill Barber Bridge, is Riverside Park. Here you'll find the **Civic Arts Center,** a cluster of cultural facilities that includes theaters (*see* The Arts and Nightlife, *below*) and the **Center for the Arts** (3001 Riverside Park Dr., ☎ 407/231–0707). In its ninth season, the center presents a full schedule of exhibitions, art movies, lectures, workshops, and other events, with a focus on Florida artists.

Return to Route A1A and continue north past the John's Island development. Turn left onto Old Winter Beach Road, where the pavement turns to hard-packed dirt as the road curves north, indicating the old **Jungle Trail.** For nearly 9 miles the trail meanders through largely undeveloped forestland across from Pelican Island, which harbors the first national wildlife refuge established in the United States, dating from 1903. State agencies are creating a buffer for the trail to shield it from sight of further development and are stabilizing its surface for improved recreational use.

Turn left where the trail rejoins A1A, and visit the **McLarty Museum,** a National Historical Landmark site. Its displays are dedicated to the 1715 hurricane that sank a fleet of Spanish treasure ships. *13180 N. Rte. A1A, Sebastian,* ☎ *407/589–2147.* ☛ *$1 ages over 6.* ☯ *Daily 10–4:30.*

At the northern end of Orchid Island is **Sebastian Inlet,** where a high bridge offers spectacular views. Along the sea is a dune area that's part of the **Archie Carr National Wildlife Refuge,** a haven for sea turtles and other protected Florida wildlife. The 587-acre **Sebastian Inlet State Recreation Area,** on both sides of the bridge, is the best-attended park in the Florida state system because of the inlet's highly productive fishing waters. *9700 S. Rte. A1A, Melbourne Beach,* ☎ *407/984–4852 or 407/589–9659 for camping.* ☯ *Bait and tackle shop: daily 7:30–6; concession stand: 8–5.*

Backtrack along Route A1A to Wabasso Beach Road and turn right. On the south side of the road you'll see the finished first phase of the **Disney Vacation Club at Vero Beach,** the first Disney resort separate from a theme park. Completed so far are a 115-room inn and 60 of the 320 planned vacation villas.

Cross the bridge to the mainland, and immediately turn left and follow the signs to the **Environmental Learning Center.** The outstanding 51-acre facility has a new wet lab with aquariums filled with Indian River Lagoon life in addition to its preexisting 600-foot boardwalk through mangrove shore and 1-mile canoe trail. *255 Live Oak Dr., Vero Beach,* ☎ *407/589–5050.* ☛ *Free.* ☯ *Weekdays 9–5, weekends 1–4.*

Take Wabasso Beach Road west and U.S. 1 north for 4½ miles, just past Route 512, to the little fishing village of **Sebastian.** At **Mel Fisher's Treasure Museum,** you can view some of the recovery from the treasure ship *Atocha* and its sister ships of the 1715 fleet. *1322 U.S. 1,* ☎

407/589–9874. ☞ *$5 adults, $4 senior citizens, $1.50 children 6–12.* ⊙ *Mon.–Sat. 10–5, Sun. noon–5.*

To return to Palm Beach, take Route 512 (Fellsmere Road) west for approximately 6 miles to I–95 south.

What to See and Do with Children

At the **Burt Reynolds Ranch and Film Studio Tours,** a 160-acre working horse ranch owned by the famous actor, visitors can take a 1½-hour tour by air-conditioned bus, with stops that include movie sets, a chapel, tree house, petting farm, and wherever else filming may be in progress. *16133 Jupiter Farms Rd. (2 mi west of I–95 at Exit 59-B), Jupiter,* ☎ *407/747–5390.* ☞ *Petting farm: free; tour: $10 adults, $5 children.* ⊙ *Daily 10–4:30; closed holidays.*

Children's Museum of Boca Raton at Singing Pines is a learning center featuring hands-on exhibits, workshops, and special programs, such as introductions to Florida Philharmonic performances. There are five changing exhibits each year. *498 Crawford Blvd., Boca Raton,* ☎ *407/ 368–6875.* ☞ *$1.* ⊙ *Tues.–Sat. noon–4.*

Children's Science Explorium features some 40 hands-on exhibits and workshops on special themes that change quarterly, such as computers, electricity, oceans, and weather. *Royal Palm Plaza, Suite 15, 131 Mizner Blvd., Boca Raton,* ☎ *407/395–8401.* ☞ *$2 ages over 3.* ⊙ *Tues.–Sat. 10–5, Sun. noon–5.*

Gumbo Limbo Nature Center lets children view four 20-foot-diameter saltwater sea tanks, stroll a 1,628-foot boardwalk through a dense tropical forest, and climb a 50-foot tower to overlook the tree canopy. The center's staff leads guided turtle walks to the beach to see nesting females come ashore and lay their eggs. *1801 N. Ocean Blvd., Boca Raton,* ☎ *407/338–1473.* ☞ *Donations welcome; turtle tour: $3 (tickets must be obtained in advance).* ⊙ *Mon.–Sat. 9–4, Sun. noon–4; turtle tours late May–mid-July, Mon.–Thurs. 9 PM–midnight.*

Hoffman's Chocolate Shoppe lets you look through windows to see chocolate being made. The Hoffman Garden Railroad, a 500-foot scale model railroad with 17 switches controlling six trains, operates through Candyland. *5190 Lake Worth Rd., Greenacres,* ☎ *407/967–2213 or 800/ 545–0094.* ☞ *Free.* ⊙ *Mon.–Sat. 9–6, Sun. noon–6.*

If your kids love orange juice, what better place to visit than the **Indian River Citrus Museum.** Displays, which include photos, farm tools, and videos, tell about when oxen hauled the crop to the railroads, when family fruit stands dotted the roadsides, and when gorgeous packing labels made every crate arriving up north an enticement to visit the Sunshine State. You can also book free citrus tours in actual groves. *2140 14th Ave., Vero Beach,* ☎ *407/770–2263.* ☞ *Donations welcome.* ⊙ *Tues.–Sat. 10–4, Sun. 1–4.*

Knollwood Groves dates from the 1930s, when it was planted by the partners of the "Amos and Andy" radio show. Activities include a 30-acre tram tour through groves and a processing plant and a visit to the Hallpatee Seminole Indian Village, with its alligator exhibit and crafts shop. *8053 Lawrence Rd., Boynton Beach,* ☎ *407/734–4800.* ☞ *$5 adults, $3 children.* ⊙ *Daily 8:30–5:30.*

Morikami Museum and Japanese Gardens (*see* Tour 3, *above*).

Puppetry Arts Center provides shows and educational programs from the home of the Gold Coast Puppet Guild. *Cross County Mall, 4356*

*Okeechobee Blvd. and Military Trail, West Palm Beach, ☎ 407/
687–3280. Shows: $2.50; generally Fri. evening, Sat. morning (call for
schedule).*

Riverside Children's Theatre offers a series of professional touring and
local productions as well as acting workshops at the Agnes Wahlstrom
Youth Playhouse in Riverside Park, Vero's cultural arts center. *3280
Riverside Park Dr., Vero Beach, ☎ 407/234–8052. Professional shows:
$6–$20; local shows: $4–$6. Performances Sept.–July; professional
shows typically over a long weekend at 11, 2, 7; local shows over 2
consecutive weekends at noon, 7.*

SHOPPING

Boca Raton

Mizner Park (Federal Hwy. between Palmetto Park Rd. and Glades Rd.),
a 30-acre shopping village within the city of Boca Raton, debuted in
1991. Since then, apartments and town houses have added a residential atmosphere to the gardenlike spaces that already made for distinctive shopping. There are some three dozen retail stores to choose among,
including the excellent Liberties Fine Books & Music, a Jacobson's specialty department store, seven restaurants with sidewalk cafés, and eight
movie screens. **Town Center** (6000 W. Glades Rd.) combines a business park with high-gloss shopping and some of the city's best restaurants. Major retailers include Bloomingdale's, Burdines, Lord & Taylor,
Saks Fifth Avenue, and Sears—187 stores and restaurants in all.

Delray Beach

Unlike many cities along this resort coast, Delray Beach has a thriving old-fashioned downtown with hundreds of shops and restaurants,
centered on a mile of east–west **Atlantic Avenue,** which ends at the oceanfront.

Fort Pierce

One of Florida's best discount malls, the **Manufacturer's Outlet Center** (Rte. 70, off I–95 at Exit 65) contains 41 stores offering such brand
names as American Tourister, Jonathan Logan, Aileen, Polly Flinders,
Van Heusen, London Fog, Levi Strauss, and Geoffrey Beene.

Palm Beach

One of the world's showcases for high-quality shopping, **Worth Avenue** runs ¼ mile east–west across Palm Beach, from the beach to Lake
Worth. The street has more than 250 shops, and many upscale stores
(Cartier, Gucci, Hermès, Pierre Deux, Saks Fifth Avenue, and Van
Cleef & Arpels) are represented, their merchandise appealing to the
discerning tastes of the Palm Beach clientele. Most merchants open at
9:30 or 10 and close at 5:30 or 6. The six blocks of **South County Road**
north of Worth Avenue also have appealing stores. For specialty items
(out-of-town newspapers and health foods in particular), try the shops
along the north side of **Royal Poinciana Way.**

Stuart

More than 60 shops and restaurants featuring antiques, art, and fash-
ions have opened along **Osceola Street** in the restored downtown,
with hardly a vacancy.

Vero Beach

Along **Ocean Drive** near Beachland Boulevard, a specialty shopping area
includes art galleries, antiques shops, and upscale clothing stores.

West Palm Beach

Good as the malls are, they're sterile compared to the in-the-midst-of-things excitement—the mix of food, art, performance, landscaping, and retailing—that has renewed downtown West Palm around **Clematis Street.** Shopping per se is still the weakest part of the mix, but new water-view parks, outdoor performing areas, and attractive plantings and lighting—including fanciful palm tree sculptures—add to the pleasure of shopping and window shopping. Retailers sell art, books, flowers, jewelry, sporting goods, and stylish men's and women's apparel. For those single-mindedly bent on mall shopping, West Palm offers the **Palm Beach Mall** (Palm Beach Lakes Blvd. at I–95), with Burdines, JCPenney, Lord & Taylor, and Sears. In Palm Beach Gardens, **The Gardens** (3101 PGA Blvd.) contains Bloomingdale's, Burdines, Macy's, Saks Fifth Avenue, and Sears.

SPORTS AND THE OUTDOORS

Biking

Bike lanes are marked by stripes on Palm Beach streets. Two good rides for less experienced cyclists include a 10-mile path bordering Lake Worth in Palm Beach, from the Flagler Bridge to the Lake Worth Inlet, and a 5-mile ride along Flagler Drive on the Intracoastal Waterway, in West Palm Beach. Both rides are almost completely free of cross streets. Parks with bicycling trails include Dreher (where the zoo is), John Prince, and Okeeheelee. Bicycle lanes are going in along U.S. 1 in downtown Boynton Beach, Delray Beach, and Hypoluxo. Much of redone Okeechobee Boulevard through downtown West Palm Beach now has marked bike lanes. For on-the-road rides, group rides, and schedules of longer rides and general cycling savvy, contact Wendell Phillips, the **Palm Beach County Bicycle Coordinator** (☎ 407/684–4170), who can put you in touch with the **West Palm Beach Bicycle Club.** Other contacts are Susan Kenney, the **Juno Beach Bicycle Coordinator** (☎ 407/626–1122), and Jeff Borick, the **Boca Raton Bicycle Coordinator** (☎ 407/393–7797). Rentals, including mopeds and Rollerblades, are available at **Palm Beach Bicycle Trail Shop** (223 Sunrise Ave., Palm Beach, ☎ 407/659–4583).

Canoeing

Bill Rogers Outdoor Adventures (1541 DeWitt La., Sebastian, ☎ 407/388–2331) outfits canoe trips down the Sebastian River, along Indian River Lagoon, through Pelican Island Wildlife Refuge, and for more distant locations.

Canoe Outfitters of Florida (4100 W. Indiantown Rd., Jupiter, ☎ 407/746–7053) runs trips along the Loxahatchee River, Florida's only designated wild and scenic river.

Arthur R. Marshall Loxahatchee National Wildlife Refuge (☎ 407/734–8303) and **Jonathan Dickinson State Park** (☎ 407/546–2771) are good spots for canoeing. **Jonathan Dickinson's River Tours** (16450 S.E. Federal Hwy., Hobe Sound, ☎ 407/746–1466), a concessionaire, rents canoes at the park.

Diving

You can drift dive or anchor dive along Palm Beach County's 47-mile Atlantic Coast. Drift divers take advantage of the Gulf Stream's strong currents and proximity to shore—sometimes less than a mile. A group of divers joined by nylon line may drift across coral reefs with the current; one member of the group carries a large, orange float that the charter-boat captain can follow. Drift diving works best from Boynton Beach north. South of Boynton Beach, where the Gulf Stream is farther from shore, diving from an anchored boat is more popular. Among the more intriguing artificial reefs in the area is a 1967 Rolls-Royce Silver Shadow in 80 feet of water off Palm Beach.

Ocean Reef Park (3860 N. Ocean Dr., Riviera Beach, ☎ 407/966–6655) is attractive for snorkeling because the reefs are close to shore in shallow water. You may see angelfish, sergeant majors, rays, robin fish, and occasionally a Florida lobster (actually a species of saltwater crayfish). Wear canvas sneakers and cloth gloves.

Some 200 yards from shore ¼ mile north of the UDT Seal Museum on North Hutchinson Island in Fort Pierce lies the **Urca de Lima Underwater Archaeological Preserve.** Here you can dive to the remnant of a flat-bottom, round-bellied storeship that was part of a treasure fleet bound for Spain from Havana but destroyed by hurricane.

In **Vero Beach,** snorkelers and divers can swim out to explore reefs 100–300 feet off the beach. Summer offers the best diving conditions. At low tide you can see the boiler and other remains of an iron-screw steamer, *Breconshire,* which foundered on a reef just south of Beachland Boulevard in 1894.

Scuba and snorkeling equipment can be rented from longtime, family-owned **Force E** (1399 N. Military Trail, West Palm Beach, ☎ 407/471–2676; 155 E. Blue Heron Blvd., Riviera Beach, ☎ 407/845–2333; 11911 U.S. 1, Suite 101-G, North Palm Beach, ☎ 407/624–7136; 877 E. Palmetto Park Rd., Boca Raton, ☎ 407/368–0555; 7166 Beracasa Way, Boca Raton, ☎ 407/395–4407; 660 Linton Blvd., Delray Beach, ☎ 407/276–0666). All stores have PADI affiliation and provide instruction at all skill levels; dive-boat charters are also available.

Fishing

Palm Beach County and the Treasure Coast are anglers' heaven, from deep-sea strikes in "sailfish alley," where the Gulf Stream is nearer shore than anywhere else, to the bass, speckled perch, and bluegill of Lake Okeechobee (*see* Excursion to Lake Okeechobee, *below*). In between are numerous fishing piers, bridges, and waterways where pompano, sheepshead, snapper, and grouper are likely catches. The best inlet fishing is at Sebastian Inlet State Recreation Area, where the catch includes bluefish, flounder, jack, redfish, sea trout, snapper, snook, and Spanish mackerel.

To request a free Palm Beach County "Fish Finder Kit," with information on artificial reefs, boat ramps, charters, fish camps, marinas, tides, and tournament schedules, write to the **West Palm Beach Fishing Club** (c/o Fish Finder, Box 468, West Palm Beach 33402).

For deep-sea fishing in the southern part of the region, try **B-Love Fleet** (314 E. Ocean Ave., Lantana, ☎ 407/588–7612); a half day costs $20 per person ($16 for senior citizens on weekdays), including rod, reel, and bait. In the northern end of the region, try *Miss Sebastian* (Sembler Dock, ½ block north of Capt. Hiram's, Sebastian, ☎ 407/589–3275); $25 ($21.50 senior citizens) for a half day covers rod, reel, and bait. For charter boats and fishing guides try the **Fort Pierce Yachting Center** (1 Ave. A, Fort Pierce, ☎ 407/264–1245), the **Sailfish Marina** (3565 S.E. St. Lucie Blvd., Stuart, ☎ 407/283–1122), the **Sailfish Marina Resort** (98 Lake Dr., Palm Beach Shores, ☎ 407/844–1724), and **Sebastian Inlet Marina at Capt. Hiram's** (1606 Indian River Dr., Sebastian, ☎ 407/589–4345).

For marsh fishing, two sites west of Vero Beach are tops for bluegills, catfish, largemouth bass, shellcrackers, and speckled perch. Cypress-lined 3-by-7-mile Blue Cypress Lake is 5 miles north of Route 60 on Blue Cypress Lake Road. Stick Marsh, farther up Blue Cypress Lake Road, produces even greater catches, but it's strictly catch-and-release. The best contact for either site is **Middleton Fish Camp** (Blue Cypress Lake, ☎ 407/778–0150).

Golf

There are 150 public, private, and semiprivate golf courses in the Palm Beach County area. A **Golf-A-Round** program lets guests at more than 100 hotels play at one of 10 courses each day, without greens fees, between April and December. For details, contact the Palm Beach County Convention & Visitors Bureau (*see* Important Addresses and Numbers *in* Palm Beach and the Treasure Coast Essentials, *below*). The Treasure Coast offers an additional dozen or so public courses.

Top-flight courses that you can arrange to play on include:

BOCA RATON
Boca Raton Resort & Club (501 E. Camino Real, 33432, ☎ 407/395–3000 or 800/327–0101), 72 holes.

BOYNTON BEACH
Boynton Beach Municipal Golf Course (8020 Jog Rd., 33437, ☎ 407/969–2200), 27 holes.

HUTCHINSON ISLAND
Indian River Plantation Beach Resort (555 N.E. Ocean Blvd., Hutchinson Island, Stuart 34996, ☎ 407/225–3700 or 800/444–3389), 18 holes.

PALM BEACH AREA
Breakers Hotel Golf Club (1 S. County Rd., Palm Beach 33480, ☎ 407/655–6611 or 800/833–3141), 36 holes; **Emerald Dunes Golf Club** (2100 Emerald Dunes Dr., West Palm Beach 33411, ☎ 407/684–4653), 18 holes; **Palm Beach Polo and Country Club** (13198 Forest Hill Blvd., West Palm Beach 33414, ☎ 407/798–7000 or 800/327–4204), 45 holes; **PGA National Resort & Spa** (1000 Ave. of the Champions, Palm Beach Gardens 33418, ☎ 407/627–1800), 90 holes; and **Royal Palm Beach Country Club** (900 Royal Palm Beach Blvd., Royal Palm Beach 33411, ☎ 407/798–6430), 18 holes.

VERO BEACH
Dodgertown (4600 26th St., 32966, ☎ 407/569–4400), 27 holes.

Kayaking
Southern Exposure Sea Kayaks (18487 S.E. Federal Hwy., at Blowing Rocks Marina, Tequesta, ☎ 407/575–4530) sells and rents sea kayaks, provides instruction, and operates tours.

Spas
Hippocrates Health Institute (1443 Palmdale Ct., West Palm Beach 33411, ☎ 407/471–8876 or 800/842–2125 for reservations, FAX 407/471–9464) is adding a 3,800-square-foot therapy building, followed by additional living units and dining and recreation areas. Guests receive complete examinations by traditional and alternative health-care professionals. Personalized programs include juice fasts and the eating of strictly vegetarian raw foods.

The Spa at PGA National Resort (400 Ave. of the Champions, Palm Beach Gardens 33418-3698, ☎ 407/627–3111 or 800/843–7725, FAX 407/622–0261), in an 11,564-square-foot building styled after a Mediterranean fishing village, has six outdoor therapy pools that make up the

"Waters of the World," a collection of imported mineral salt pools, as well as men's and women's Jacuzzis and saunas. There are 22 rooms for private treatments, too, including Swedish and shiatsu massage, hydrotherapy, and mud treatments. A 28,500-square-foot Health & Racquet Center, staffed for one-on-one training, contains five racquetball courts, a complete Nautilus center, aerobics and dance studios, men's and women's locker rooms, and a fitness-oriented Health Bar. All four restaurants at the resort offer spa cuisine as an option.

Tennis

Palm Beach County has more than 1,100 tennis courts. Big tournaments and big names, including Carling Bassett, Chris Evert, Steffi Graf, Robbie Seguso, and Wendy Turnbull, keep the game in the spotlight. Accordingly, tennis is a favorite sport with locals, and, in addition to the courts at large hotels, many of which are lighted for night play, municipal and club courts open to the public are plentiful from Boca Raton to Vero Beach. Contact chambers of commerce and convention and visitors bureaus (*see* Important Addresses and Numbers *in* Palm Beach and the Treasure Coast Essentials, *below*) for lists.

Water Sports

Florida Boat Club (626 Beverly Dr., Lake Wales, ☎ 813/676–1176) sets people afloat in houseboats through much of southern Florida, including the Intracoastal Waterway. The boats have two master staterooms and twin-bunk cabins, all-electric galleys, and considerable amenities, including AM/FM stereo cassette player and full shower. Rates average about $250 a day—closer to $200 for three days and longer—for up to six people.

The **Sailboard School** (9125 U.S. 1, Sebastian, ☎ 407/589–2671 or 800/253–6573, ℻ 407/589–7963) provides year-round one-day, weekend, and five-day programs of sailboarding instruction, including boards, for $120 a day, $575 for five days.

SPECTATOR SPORTS

The *Palm Beach Post*'s weekly "TGIF" section on Friday carries information on sports activities. For tickets to events call **Ticketmaster** (☎ 407/839–3900).

Auto Racing

Weekly ¼-mile drag racing; monthly 2¼-mile, 10-turn road racing; and monthly AMA motorcycle road racing take place year-round at the **Moroso Motorsports Park** (17047 Beeline Hwy., Box 31907, Palm Beach Gardens 33420, ☎407/622–1400).

Baseball

The **Atlanta Braves** and the **Montreal Expos** both conduct spring training in West Palm Beach's Municipal Stadium (1610 Palm Beach Lakes Blvd., Box 3087, West Palm Beach 33402, ☎ 407/683–6012), which is also home to the **Palm Beach Expos,** a Class-A team in the Florida State League. For tickets, contact the Expos (Box 3566, West Palm Beach 33402, ☎ 407/684–6801) or the Braves (Box 2619, West Palm Beach 33402, ☎ 407/683–6100).

The **Los Angeles Dodgers** train each March in the 6,500-seat Holman Stadium at Dodgertown (4101 26th St., Box 2887, Vero Beach 32961, ☎ 407/569–4900).

The **New York Mets** hold spring training in the 7,300-seat St. Lucie County Sport Complex (525 N.W. Peacock Blvd., Port St. Lucie 34986,

☎ 407/871–2115), home stadium for the Florida League's **St. Lucie Mets.** Take Exit 63C off I–95 and follow St. Lucie West Boulevard east to Peacock Boulevard.

Dog Racing

Palm Beach Kennel Club opened in 1932 and has 4,300 seats. *1111 N. Congress Ave., Palm Beach 33409,* ☎ *407/683–2222.* ☛ *50¢ general admission, $1 terrace level; free parking. Racing Mon. at 12:30; Wed., Thurs., Sat. at 12:30, 7:30; Fri. at 7:30; Sun. at 1. Simulcasts Mon., Fri. at noon; Tues. at 12:30.*

Equestrian Sports and Polo

Palm Beach County and the Treasure Coast are home to four major polo organizations. Although only the rich can support a four-member polo team, you don't have to be rich to watch—admission is free for some games and priced reasonably for others.

Polo teams play under a handicap system in which the U.S. Polo Association ranks each player's skills; a team's total handicap reflects its members' individual handicaps. The best players have a 10-goal handicap. The average polo game lasts about 90 minutes; each consists of six periods, or chukkers, of 7½ minutes each.

Gulfstream Polo Club, the oldest club in Palm Beach, began in the 1920s and plays medium-goal polo (for teams with handicaps of 8–16 goals). There are six polo fields. *4550 Polo Rd., Lake Worth 33467,* ☎ *407/ 965–2057.* ☛ *Free. Games Dec.–Apr., Fri. at 3, Sun. at 1.*

Palm Beach Polo and Country Club, founded in 1979, has the longest season in Florida and the top players. It's the Wimbledon of polo in North America and site each spring of the $100,000 World Cup competition. *13420 South Shore Blvd., West Palm Beach 33414,* ☎ *407/793–1440.* ☛ *$8 general admission, $15–$25 ($27–$35 for World Cup) box seats and chalet. Games Dec.–Apr., Sun. at 3.*

Royal Palm Polo, founded in 1959 by Oklahoma oilman John T. Oxley, has seven polo fields with two stadiums. The complex is home to the $100,000 International Gold Cup Tournament. *6300 Old Clint Moore Rd., Boca Raton 33496,* ☎ *407/994–1876.* ☛ *$6 general admission, $10–$25 box seats. Games Jan.–Apr., Sun. at 1, 3.*

Windsor is the home of the annual Prince of Wales Cup in late February or early March. (Prince Charles helped inaugurate Windsor polo in February 1989 with a special charity game.) The cup benefits the international Friends of Conservation, of which the prince is a patron. *3125 Windsor Blvd., Vero Beach 32963,* ☎ *407/589–9800.* ☛ *$10 general admission, $50 fieldside; Prince of Wales Cup $20, $125. High-goal season games Jan.–Mar., Sun. at 2.*

Jai Alai

Fort Pierce Jai Alai operates seasonally for live jai alai and year-round for off-track betting on horse-racing simulcasts. *1750 S. Kings Hwy., off Okeechobee Rd., Fort Pierce,* ☎ *407/464–7500 or 800/524–2524.* ☛ *$1. Games Jan.–Apr., Wed., Sat. at 12:30, 7; Thurs.–Fri. at 7; Sun. at 1 (call to double-check schedule). Simulcasts year-round, Wed.–Mon. at noon, 7.*

Palm Beach Jai Alai reopened under new owners in late 1994 after being closed a year. A five-week reinaugural season may be lengthened in future years if more players can be contracted, so double-check dates and prices. *1415 W. 45th St., West Palm Beach,* ☎ *407/844–2444.* ☛ *50¢.*

Games late Nov.–Dec., Fri., Sat. at 12:15, 7:15; Sun., Mon., Wed., Thurs. at 12:15.

BEACHES

Every town has at least one public beach, though Palm Beach County, where beaches are typically tucked among the high-rises, has fewer than its neighbors to the north. The widest beaches in Palm Beach County are in the Jupiter area, on Singer Island, and in Boca Raton. Palm Beach's are the most eroded, often to the seawall. Parking charges are rising, now up to $1 an hour in many places. Treasure Coast beaches are wider, less busy, and less expensive to park at. Hobe Sound National Wildlife Refuge and Fort Pierce Inlet State Park have some of the least-crowded shores around, while North Hutchinson Island, north of the condos, offers more quiet and wide beaches than anywhere in the region.

Boca Raton

Three of the most popular beaches in Boca Raton are **South Beach Park** (400 N. Rte. A1A), which has no picnic facilities, and **Red Reef Park** (1400 N. Rte. A1A) and **Spanish River Park** (3001 N. Rte. A1A), both with picnic tables, barbecue grills, and playgrounds. All are open 8–sunset.

Boynton Beach

Oceanfront Park (Ocean Ave. at Rte. A1A) offers a boardwalk, concessions, grills, a jogging trail, and playground, but parking is expensive for non-Boynton residents ($10 in winter, $5 the rest of the year).

Delray Beach

Municipal Beach (Atlantic Ave. and Rte. A1A) has a boat ramp and volleyball court and is open 8–sunset.

Hutchinson Island

Bathtub Beach (MacArthur Blvd., off Rte. A1A), at the north end of the Indian River Plantation Beach Resort, is ideal for children because the waters are shallow for about 300 feet offshore and usually calm. At low tide, bathers can walk to the reef. Facilities include rest rooms and showers.

Jupiter

Carlin Park (400 Rte. A1A) provides beachfront picnic pavilions, hiking trails, a baseball diamond, playground, six tennis courts, and fishing sites. The Park Galley, serving snacks and burgers, is usually open daily 9–5.

Lake Worth

Lake Worth Municipal Beach (Rte. A1A at end of Lake Worth Bridge) has an Olympic-size swimming pool and a free fishing pier, picnic areas, shuffleboard, restaurants, and shops on the upland side of the street. Admission to the beach is free; admission to the pool is $2 adults, $1 senior citizens and children 15 and under. Metered parking costs 25¢ per quarter hour.

Lantana

Lantana Public Beach (100 N. Ocean Ave.), next to the Ritz-Carlton, has one of the best food concessions around, open 365 days a year 8–5 (service to 4:30). Food is eaten outdoors under beach umbrellas, and there are breakfast and lunch specials, including fresh fish on weekends. Parking is 25¢ for 20 minutes.

Palm Beach

Phipps Ocean Park (Rte. A1A) offers picnic tables. Meters are 25¢ per quarter hour.

Sebastian Inlet

South and north of the inlet and inland of the bridge are fine sandy beaches. A concession stand on the north side of the inlet, open 8–5 (bait and tackle available 7:30–6), sells short-order food; rents canoes, kayaks, and paddleboats; and has an apparel and surf shop.

Singer Island

John D. MacArthur State Park (10900 Rte. A1A, North Palm Beach) has almost 2 miles of beach as well as interpretive walks to a mangrove estuary along the upper reaches of Lake Worth. Admission is $3.25 per vehicle with up to eight people, and it's open 8–sunset.

Vero Beach

All through town there are beach-access parks (☛ Free; ☉ Daily 7 AM–10 PM) with boardwalks and steps bridging the foredune. **Humiston Park** (Ocean Dr., just below Beachland Blvd.) has a large children's play area and picnic tables and is across the street from shops.

DINING AND LODGING

Dining

The wealth and sophistication of Palm Beach County's seasonal residents ensure a good supply of top-end restaurants; quick, casual, cheap restaurants along the beach are harder to find. Especially along the Treasure Coast, restaurants woo business with dollar-saving early-bird menus.

Lodging

Palm Beach County deserves its nickname "the Gold Coast"—hotel prices hover at the high end of the scale, and it's tough to find a bargain. However, many lodgings in Palm Beach County dropped their rates in 1994–95 after a downturn in business in 1993–94, and some establishments are likely to keep 1996 rates the same. Accommodations in Lake Worth, Palm Beach Shores, and Fort Pierce are often more affordable, but to get the best for the least you should book far in advance.

Boca Raton

DINING

$$$–$$$$ **La Vieille Maison.** This French restaurant remains the temple of haute
★   cuisine along the Gold Coast. It occupies a 1920s-era, two-story dwelling (hence the name, meaning "old house") believed to be an Addison Mizner design. Closets and cubbyholes have been transformed into intimate and elegant private dining rooms, where guests order from a fixed-price, à la carte, Temptations, or Grand menu (the last, with more traditional French cuisine, is the highest priced). In summer, a separate fixed-price menu available Sunday through Thursday offers a sampling of the other three at a more modest price. Menus currently feature many Provençal dishes, such as *soupe au pistou* (vegetable soup with basil and Parmesan cheese), roasted rabbit with artichokes and green olives and walnut gnocchi, and herb-crusted roast rack of midwestern lamb with potatoes au gratin. New dessert choices include a flourless chocolate cake with milk chocolate macadamia praline mousse and raspberry sauce, and a napoleon with candied walnuts, cinnamon-poached pears, dried-fruit compote, and pear ice cream. ✕ 770 E. Palmetto Park Rd., ☎ 407/391–6701 in Boca Raton or 407/737–5677 in Delray Beach and Palm Beach. AE, D, DC, MC, V. Closed Labor Day, sometimes July 4.

$$$ **Gazebo Cafe.** The locals who patronize this popular restaurant know where it is, even though there is no sign and it's difficult to find: Look for the Barnett Bank Hyde Park Plaza, a block north of Spanish River Boulevard. Once you find the place, await your table in the open kitchen, where chef Paul Sellas (co-owner with his mother, Kathleen) and his staff perform a gastronomic ballet. The high noise level of the main dining room has been reduced with an acoustical ceiling, but you may still be happier in the smaller back dining room. Specialties include fresh lump crabmeat with an excellent glaze of Mornay sauce on a marinated artichoke bottom; spinach salad with heart of palm, egg white, bacon, croutons, mushrooms, fruit garnish, and a dressing of olive oil and Dijon mustard; Sellas's "classic" bouillabaisse with Maine lobster, shrimp, scallops, clams, and mussels topped with julienne vegetables in a robust broth; and raspberries with a Grand Marnier–sabayon sauce. ✗ *4199 N. Federal Hwy.,* ☎ *407/395–6033; 287 E. Indiantown Rd., Jupiter,* ☎ *407/744–0605. AE, D, DC, MC, V. Closed Sun. mid-May–Dec.*

$$$ **Maxaluna Tuscan Grill.** Virtually *the* neighborhood restaurant of choice
★ for affluent Bocans, this 150-seat shrine to *nuovo* Italian gastronomy is also hard to find. It's set in the beautifully landscaped courtyard of the Crocker Center, a mixed-use office park and shopping mall. If you have friends in Boca, let them take you. The setting is as artful as the modern art hanging from the walls. Orchids rise from slender bud vases, and halogen lights drop from colorful ceiling panels, above which the black roof interior looms. Tables set with white covers are laid out zigzag on natural wood floors that lead back to even more quiet spaces. At the rear, past the polished aluminum bar and brick walls, chefs in the open kitchen work in Italian bicycle caps. Lighthearted in style, Maxaluna's is serious about food. Founder Dennis Max introduced *new* (nouvelle, nuovo, California, Floribbean—call it what you will) cuisine to the Gold Coast in the mid-'80s. Diners exult in chef Pierre Viau's informed pastas, risottos, and Italian-American entrées. A menu that changes daily contains such notable dishes as lemon-thyme tagliatelle with shrimp, scallops, calamari, garlic, tomato, and herbs; a risotto of Maine lobster, Vidalia onions, white corn, escarole, garlic butter, and Parmesan; and an oak-grilled veal chop filled with a prosciutto wrap of mozzarella, plum tomato, and basil. There's also a large selection of wines by the glass. ✗ *Crocker Center, 5050 Town Center Circle,* ☎ *407/391–7177. AE, D, DC, MC, V. Closed Thanksgiving, Super Bowl Sun. No lunch weekends.*

$ **Tom's Place.** "This place is a blessing from God," says the sign over the fireplace, to which, when you're finally in and seated (this place draws long lines) you'll add, "Amen!" That's in between mouthfuls of Tom Wright's soul food—sauce-slathered ribs, pork-chop sandwiches, chicken cooked in a peppery mustard sauce over hickory and oak, sweet-potato pie. You'll want to leave with a bottle or two of Tom's barbecue sauce ($2.25/pint) and to return, just as Lou Rawls, Ben Vereen, Sugar Ray Leonard, and a rush of NFL players do. You can bet the place is family run. ✗ *7251 N. Federal Hwy.,* ☎ *407/997–0920. MC, V. Closed Sun., Mon. May–mid-Nov., holidays, and sometimes a month around Sept.*

LODGING

$$$$ **Boca Raton Resort & Club.** Architect-socialite Addison Mizner de-
★ signed and built the original Mediterranean-style Cloister Inn in 1926; the 27-story tower was added in 1961 and the ultramodern Boca Beach Club in 1980. In 1991 an eight-year, $55 million renovation was completed, upgrading the tower accommodations, adding a new fit-

ness center, redesigning the Cloister lobby and adjacent golf course, and creating a new restaurant, Nick's Fishmarket, at the Beach Club. In 1992 the 27-story-high Top of the Tower Italian Restaurant opened. Room rates during the winter season are European Plan (no meals included), but a daily MAP supplement (breakfast and dinner) can be had for $50 per person. Rooms in the Cloister tend to be small and warmly traditional; those in the tower are in like style but larger, while rooms in the Beach Club are light, airy, and contemporary in color schemes and furnishings. In-room safes are available. An international concierge staff speaks at least 12 languages. ☎ *501 E. Camino Real, 33431-0825, ☎ 407/395–3000 or 800/327–0101. 963 rooms, suites, studio rooms, and golf villas. 7 restaurants, 3 lounges, 5 pools, 2 championship golf courses, 34 tennis courts (9 lighted), basketball, 3 fitness centers, beach, boating, fishing. AE, DC, MC, V.*

Delray Beach

DINING

$–$$
★ **Arcade Pasta Grill.** After 45 years in the restaurant business in Queens, New York, and New Jersey, William Kontos came here for dinner, got to talking, learned the restaurant was for sale, and bought it. Exceptional cooking, affordable prices without pretense, and an unusual setting make this Delray landmark worth putting at the top of any south Palm Beach County itinerary. The hexagonal room with a peaked ceiling framed in pecky cypress is a cross between tacky and smart, filled with real carnations in bud vases, blue-green Tanqueray umbrellas, butcher paper over green covers, and fan-back chairs. The menu may be standard Italian fare—pastas, chicken, veal, seafood, and a few lamb and beef choices—but it's the preparations that stand out. In one superb choice prepared to special order, penne comes with pressed fresh garlic flecked across steamed broccoli, the dish glistening with, but not pooled in, olive oil. More than 20 different pastas can be ordered with a half dozen "extras" (e.g., meatballs, mushrooms, sausage, eggplant, chicken) for $11. ✕ *411 E. Atlantic Ave., ☎ 407/274–0099. AE, D, DC, MC, V.*

LODGING

$$$–$$$$
Seagate Hotel & Beach Club. The best garden hotel in Palm Beach County, it offers value, comfort, style, and personal attention. You can dress up and dine in a smart little mahogany- and lattice-trimmed beachfront salon or have the same Continental fare in casual attire in the equally stylish bar. Lodgings are on the west side of the two-lane road, and it still feels like the country here. The deluxe one-bedroom suite features chintz and rattan, with many upholstered pieces. All suites have at least kitchenettes; even those in the least expensive studio suites are complete, though compact, behind foldaway doors. The standard one-bedroom suite has its own touches: makeup lights, double doors between bedroom and living room, and access to the bathroom from both. Guests receive membership in the private beach club. Rates are high in winter but drop substantially May–mid-November. ☎ *400 S. Ocean Blvd., 33483, ☎ 407/276–2421 or 800/233–3581. 70 1- and 2-bedroom suites. Restaurant, lounge, heated freshwater and heated saltwater pools, beach. AE, DC, MC, V.*

$$–$$$$
Harbor House. The exceptional feature of these white, two-story, tropically planted, 1950s-era buildings are their privileged location in a quiet residential enclave three blocks east of U.S. 1 and across from the Delray Marina. In addition to two tiny motel rooms, there are 23 efficiencies and one- and two-bedroom apartments with electric kitchens and a mix of seating generally done in white, beige, tan, and blue. Everything retains a '50s look, but carpets and upholstery are replaced before they

get tired. In a nice touch, the matching bedroom fabrics are changed by the season: solid blue in summer, blue florals in winter. ⌂ *124 Marine Way, 33483,* ☎ *407/276–4221. 25 units. Pool, shuffleboard, coin laundry. MC, V.*

$$–$$$$ **Sea Breeze of Delray Beach.** Considering its top location—opposite the Gulfstream Bath & Tennis Club, across from the beach (though a three- to five-minute walk to access it), in very resorty but quiet Delray—this is an exceptional buy. The look is garden-apartment white with aqua trim; the one- and two-story buildings are set around beautiful lawns. Each of the studios and one- or two-bedroom apartments has a full kitchen; the updated ones have microwaves. Some floors are being redone with cool resort tiles, while others still have carpets. Furnishings include lots of floral prints, brocaded pieces, and French provincial reproductions, which create a beachy yet homey look. Though dating from the 1950s, the place remains beautifully maintained and clean, though guests may find kitchenware mismatched. There is twice-weekly maid service May to October. ⌂ *820 N. Ocean Blvd., 33483,* ☎ *407/276–7496. 23 units. Pool, shuffleboard, coin laundry. MC, V.*

Fort Pierce

DINING

$$ **Mangrove Mattie's.** Since its opening eight years ago, this upscale rustic spot on Fort Pierce Inlet has provided dazzling views and imaginative decor with seafood to match. Try the coconut-fried shrimp or the chicken and scampi, or come by for the happy hour with free buffet (Monday through Friday 5–8). The dinner-at-dusk early-bird special (4:30–6 except Sunday) offers a choice of a half dozen entrées with a glass of wine for under $10. ✕ *1640 Seaway Dr.,* ☎ *407/466–1044. AE, D, DC, MC, V. Closed Dec. 25.*

$ **Theo Thudpucker's Raw Bar.** Businesspeople dressed for work mingle here with people who come in off the beach wearing shorts. On squally days everyone piles in off the jetty. Specialties include oyster stew, smoked fish spread, conch salad and fritters, fresh catfish, and alligator tail. New early-bird menus (Monday through Friday 3–5:30) feature $6–$7 entrées with potatoes. ✕ *2025 Seaway Dr. (South Jetty),* ☎ *407/465–1078. No credit cards. Closed Thanksgiving, Dec. 25.*

LODGING

$$–$$$ **Harbor Light Inn.** The pick of the pack of lodgings lining the Fort Pierce Inlet along Seaway Drive is this modern, nautical, blue-trimmed gray motel. Spacious units on two floors feature kitchen or wet bar, carpeting, tub-shower, and routine but well-cared-for furnishings. Most rooms have a waterfront porch or balcony. Augmenting the motel units are a set of four apartments across the street (off the water), where, if you can get one, in-season weekly rates are $350. Book everything at least a year in advance. ⌂ *1156–1160 Seaway Dr., 34949,* ☎ *407/468–3555 or 800/433–0004. 25 units. Pool, fishing, coin laundry. AE, D, DC, MC, V.*

$$ **Mellon Patch Inn.** This new bed-and-breakfast has an excellent location—across the shore road from a beach park, at the end of a canal leading to the Indian River Lagoon. One side of the canal has a bank of attractive new homes; the other, the Jack Island Wildlife Refuge (*see* Tour 4, *above*). Andrea and Arthur Mellon opened their two-story B&B in 1994. The delightful decor features half melons everywhere—in pillows, in crafts, in candies on night tables. The four guest rooms (two upstairs, two down) are named Seaside Serenity, Santa Fe Sunset, Patchwork Quilt, and Tropical Paradise. Each has imaginative accessories, art, and upholstery appropriate to its theme. The cathedral-ceil-

ing living room features a wood-burning fireplace and "Howie," a Native American in effigy who will surprise you every time you enter. Full breakfast is included. ☎ *3601 N. Rte. A1A, North Hutchinson Island 34949,* ☎ *407/461–5231. 4 rooms. MC, V.*

Gulf Stream

LODGING

$$ **Riviera Palms Motel.** This small 1950s-era motel has two chief virtues: It's clean and it's well located, across Route A1A from mid-rise apartment houses on the water, with beach access between them. Hans and Herter Grannemann have owned this two-story property, three wings surrounding a grassy front yard and heated pool, since 1978, and they have lots of repeat guests—you'll have to book early in winter. The decor features Danish modern furniture and colors of blue, brown, and tan. Rooms have at least a fridge but no phone. ☎ *3960 N. Ocean Blvd., 33483,* ☎ *407/276–3032. 17 rooms, efficiencies, and suites. Pool. No credit cards.*

Jensen Beach

DINING

$$$ **11 Maple Street.** This 16-table cracker-quaint restaurant run by Margee
★ and Mike Perrin offers Continental gourmet specialties on a nightly changing menu. For food and setting, this is as good as the Treasure Coast gets. An old house alive with waxed floors, plank walls hung with local art and flower baskets, soft recorded jazz, and earnest, friendly staff satisfy as fully as the brilliant presentations served in ample portions. Appetizers might include walnut bread with melted fontina cheese; pan-fried conch with balsamic vinegar; or pear, Gorgonzola, and pine-nut salad with balsamic vinegar and grilled polenta. Among the entrées might be rosemary-spiced salmon with leeks, lobster and blue-crab cake, or dried porcini mushroom risotto. Desserts might include a cherry *clafouti* (like a bread pudding), a white-chocolate custard with blackberry sauce, or an old-fashioned chocolate cream pie with poached pear. ✕ *3224 Maple Ave.,* ☎ *407/334–7714. Reservations required. MC, V. Closed Mon., Tues., Dec. 25. No lunch.*

$$ **Conchy Joe's.** This classic Florida stilt house full of antique fish mounts, gator hides, and snakeskins dates from the late 1920s, but Conchy Joe's, like a hermit crab sidling into a new shell, only sidled up from West Palm Beach in '83 for the relaxed atmosphere of Jensen Beach. Under a huge Seminole-built chickee (raised wood platform) with a palm through the roof, you get the freshest Florida seafoods from a menu that changes daily— though some things never change: grouper Marsala, the house specialty; broiled sea scallops; fried cracked conch. Try the rum drinks with names like Goombay Smash, Bahama Mama, and Jamaica Wind, while you listen to steel-band calypsos Thursday through Sunday nights. Happy hour is 3–6 daily and during all NFL games. ✕ *3945 N. Indian River Dr.,* ☎ *407/334–1131. AE, D, MC, V. Closed Super Bowl Sun., Thanksgiving, Dec. 25. No dinner Dec. 24.*

LODGING

$$–$$$ **Hutchinson Inn.** Sandwiched among the high-rises, this modest and affordable two-story motel from the mid-1970s has the feel of a bed-and-breakfast, thanks to its pretty canopies, bracketing, and the fresh produce stand across the street. You do in fact get an expanded Continental breakfast in the well-detailed, homey lobby, and you can also borrow a book or a stack of magazines to take to your room, where homemade cookies are served in the evenings. On Saturday there's a barbecue at noon. Rooms range from small but comfy, with chintz bedcovers, wicker chair, and contract dresser, to fully equipped efficiencies and seafront suites with private balconies. You have to book a year ahead to get a room in winter. ☎ *9750 S. Ocean Dr., 34957,* ☎ *407/ 229–2000,* FAX *407/229–8875. 21 units. Pool, tennis court, beach. MC, V.*

Jupiter

DINING

$$–$$$ **Charley's Crab.** The grand view across the Jupiter River complements
★ the soaring ceiling and striking interior architecture of this 350-seat marina-side restaurant, much preferred by the affluent retirees of Jupiter. Between about November and Easter, weather accommodates outdoor seating. Otherwise, tiered seating and a second level of window seats on an indoor balcony provide good water views. Early diners save about 25%, but a better argument can be made for coming late and watching the searching beam of historic Jupiter Light (just downriver), a reminder of the region's long seafaring history. Ultimately the best reason to eat here is the expertly prepared seafood, including outstanding pasta choices: *pagliara* with scallops, fish, shrimp, mussels, spinach, garlic, and olive oil; fettuccine *verde* with lobster, sun-dried tomatoes, fresh basil, and goat cheese; and shrimp and tortellini boursin with cream sauce and tomatoes. Consider also such fresh fish as citrus-marinated halibut with black-bean basmati rice and pineapple relish or the tender, flaky swordfish. A big Sunday brunch features 75 items and a glass of champagne. Other Charley's are in Boca Raton, Deerfield, Fort Lauderdale, Palm Beach, and Stuart. ✕ *1000 N. U.S. 1,* ☎ *407/744–4710. AE, D, DC, MC, V.*

$–$$ **Log Cabin Restaurant.** "Too much!" exclaim first-timers, responding
★ to the decor and whopping portions of American food at this rustic roadhouse (very easy to miss driving past). Everybody takes home a doggie bag, unless you've ordered the nightly all-you-can-eat special, for which the policy is suspended. Many also tote an antique home, because everything hung on the walls and from the rafters is for sale: old bikes, sleds, clocks, and quilts. The surprising menu variety starts with the big early-bird breakfast (7–8) for $1.99 and continues with old-fashioned pit barbecue, steaks, country dinners (e.g., roasted half chicken, liver and onions, pot roast, meat loaf), and fresh seafood— all with many side dishes—plus salad bar and hot sandwiches. Dine indoors or on the newly enclosed and air-conditioned front porch. There's a full bar and happy hour. ✕ *631 N. Rte. A1A,* ☎ *407/746–6877. AE, D, DC, MC, V.*

$ **Lighthouse Restaurant.** Amsterdam-born brothers John and Bill Verehoeven bought this long-established place late in 1991 and have since toned the place up by bringing in the former chef of the Jupiter Island Club and Old Port Cove Yacht Club. Though the prices are still low, you can get items like chicken breast stuffed with sausage and fresh vegetables, burgundy beef stew, fresh fish, and king crab cakes. A fulltime pastry chef's at work, too. In addition the restaurant still has the same people-pleasing formula of more than 60 years: round-the-clock service (except 10 PM Sunday–6 AM Monday) and daily menu changes that take advantage of the best market buys. Typical specials are veal parmigiana with spaghetti, hearty beef stew, and grilled center-cut pork chops with apple sauce. Also served nightly are affordable "lite dinners." You can get breakfast 24 hours a day and Sunday dinner starting at 1. ✕ *1510 U.S. 1,* ☎ *407/746–4811. D, DC, MC, V. Closed Dec. 24.*

Lake Worth
LODGING

$–$$ **Holiday House.** Ah, Lake Worth—the budget traveler's destination.
★   Standing out amid a strip of wall-to-wall motels, a five-minute walk from
the heart of town, is this uncommercial-looking, shipshape lodging of
bright white plaster trimmed in blue, with bougainvilleas twined around
crosshatched balconies and rich tropical gardens. Units—motel rooms,
efficiencies, and one-bedroom apartments—live up to expectations. Located in two adjacent two-story buildings dating from the late 1940s,
but kept up nicely, each is warmly furnished with carpet, upholstered
chairs, table, desk, and miscellaneous art. Though the units are different, they are all clean and contain fridge, phone, and reverse-cycle air-
conditioning. Those rooms that don't already have a microwave are getting
one. The owners are thoughtful enough to keep windows open when
rooms are vacant. Maid service is provided daily for motel rooms,
weekly for efficiencies and apartments. ⌂ *320 N. Federal Hwy., 33460,*
☎ *407/582–3561,* ℻ *407/582–3561, ext. 314. 30 units. Pool, coin
laundry. MC, V.*

Lantana
DINING

$$ **Old House.** Partners Wayne Cordero and Captain Bob Hoddinott have
turned the old Lyman House, dating from 1889, into an informal, Old-
Florida seafood house. Located on the water, the house has been ex-
panded many times into a patchwork of shedlike spaces. All were
air-conditioned in 1994, but in cool weather and most evenings guests
still enjoy open-air dining. Though most of the seafood is from Florida,
Baltimore steamed crab is a specialty. All dinners come with unlimited
salad, fresh baked bread, fries, and parsley potatoes or rice. ✗ *300 E.
Ocean Ave.,* ☎ *407/533–5220. AE, MC, V.*

Palm Beach
DINING

$$$–$$$$ **Cafe L'Europe.** Sumptuous oak paneling, shirred curtains over fanlight
★   windows, elaborate dried-flower bouquets, and vintage Sinatra in the
background set the mood here. Even the bar habitués are elegantly
coiffed, surrounded by details of brass, etched and leaded glass, and
tapestry fabrics. Under chef Joseph Eisenbuchner the Mandarin way
cuisine has been replaced, and spa cuisine has been folded into the lun-
cheon menu. Guests at dinner dine expensively on specialty pastas, such
as spinach, shiitake mushroom, and mascarpone ravioli with pine-nut
hazelnut butter; seafoods that may include a sautéed potato-crusted
fresh Florida snapper, shaved baby fennel, and garlic-scallion beurre
blanc; or the likes of roast Cornish hen, double lamb chops, and black
Angus steak. Desserts include numerous fruit tarts and chocolate cakes
prepared daily in the café bakery, as well as the signature apple pan-
cake with lingonberries. ✗ *150 Worth Ave., in the Esplanade,* ☎ *407/
655–4020. Reservations required in winter. Jacket required in main din-
ing room. AE, DC, MC, V. No lunch Sun.*

$$$ **Bice Ristorante.** This classically Milanese restaurant (the original dates
from 1926) is so thoroughly Italian that it's easy to be disappointed
when, upon leaving, the parking attendant speaks to you in English.
"Bice" is short for Beatrice, mother of Roberto Ruggeri, who founded
the original in Milan and since has opened branches here in Palm
Beach and other smart places—Paris, London, Tokyo, New York,
Washington, Chicago, and Cancún. Brilliant flower arrangements and
Italian stylings—brass, greens, and a dark beige-and-yellow color
scheme—are matched by exquisite aromas of *antipasti* and *piatti del
giorno* laced with basil, chive, and oregano. Divine home-baked fo-

caccia—a Tuscan-style bread—accompanies such house favorites as *robespierre alla moda della bice* (sliced steak topped with arugula salad), *costoletta di vitello impanata alla milanese* (breaded veal cutlet with a tomato salad), and *trancio di spada alla mediterranea* (grilled swordfish with black olives, capers, and plum tomatoes). Leave room for the *gelati* and other desserts. ✕ *313½ Worth Ave.,* ☎ *407/835–1600. Jacket required in season. AE, DC, MC, V. Closed Dec. 25, Jan. 1.*

$$$ **The Breakers.** The main hotel dining area at The Breakers consists of the elegant Florentine Dining Room, decorated with fine 15th-century Flemish tapestries; the adjoining Celebrity Aisle, where the maître d' seats his most honored guests; and the Circle Dining Room, with a huge circular skylight framing a bronze-and-crystal Venetian chandelier. A lighter, so-called Palm Beach cuisine has been introduced: poached chicken breast and grilled papaya-marinated swordfish, for example. Devotees of the Continental specialties can still find items such as herb-crusted rack of lamb, polenta-seared veal loin, and sautéed tournedos of beef, along with the usual rich desserts, including *vacherin glacé* (praline-flavored ice cream encased in fresh whipped cream and frozen in a baked meringue base) and Key lime pie. ✕ *1 S. County Rd.,* ☎ *407/655–6611 or 800/833–3141. Reservations required. AE, D, DC, MC, V.*

$$$ **Jo's.** After 11 years tucked behind the Church Mouse Thrift Shop, this pastel, lattice, and mirrored exemplar of French cuisine expanded to 150 seats as it moved across South County Road to a prominent new corner. Chef Richard Kline, son of the owner, Jo, holds sway in the kitchen, and the restaurant, now with full bar, has become one of the few open for lunch and dinner seven days a week. The well-rehearsed French menu features a three-soup sampler: buttery lobster bisque, potage St. Germain (green pea soup), and beef consommé; osso buco served with rice and vegetables; and a moist (but never rare) half roast duckling (boned) with orange demiglaze. For dessert try the fresh apple *tarte tatin* or fresh raspberries Josephine. ✕ *375 S. County Rd.,* ☎ *407/ 659–6776. AE, MC, V. Closed Dec. 25.*

$$ **Chuck & Harold's.** Ivana Trump, Larry Holmes, Brooke Shields, and Michael Bolton are among the celebrities who frequent this combination power-lunch bar, celebrity sidewalk café, and nocturnal big-band/jazz garden restaurant. Locals who want to be part of the scenery linger in the front-porch area, next to pots of red and white begonias mounted along the sidewalk rail. Specialties include a mildly spiced conch chowder with a liberal supply of conch; an onion-crunchy gazpacho with croutons, a cucumber spear, and sour cream; a frittata (an omelet of bacon, spinach, the hot salami-like pepperoncini, potatoes, smoked mozzarella, and fresh tomato salsa); and a tangy Key lime pie with a graham-cracker crust and a squeezeable lime slice for even more tartness. A big blackboard lists daily specials and celebrity birthdays. ✕ *207 Royal Poinciana Way,* ☎ *407/659–1440. AE, DC, MC, V.*

$$ **Dempsey's.** A New York–style Irish pub under the palms: paisley table covers, plaid café curtains, burgundy banquettes, horse prints, and antique coach lanterns. George Dempsey was a Florida cattle rancher until he entered the restaurant business 17 years ago. This place is packed, noisy, and as electric as a frenzied Friday at the stock exchange when major sports events are on the big TV. Along with much socializing, people put away fresh Maine lobster, fresh Florida seafood, plates of chicken hash Dempsey (with a dash of Scotch), shad roe, prime rib, and hot apple pie. There's live piano Thursday to Sunday evenings, Sunday brunch 10–2:30, and round-the-clock valet parking. ✕ *50 Cocoanut Row,* ☎ *407/835–0400. AE, MC, V. Closed Thanksgiving, Dec. 25.*

$$ **Ta-boo.** Real estate investor Franklyn P. deMarco, Jr., has teamed up with Maryland restaurateur Nancy Sharigan to successfully re-create the legendary Worth Avenue bistro that debuted in 1941. Decorated in gorgeous pinks, greens, and florals, the space is divided into discrete salons: One resembles a courtyard; another, an elegant living room with a fireplace; a third, a gazebo under a skylight. The Tiki Tiki bar serves as an elegant saloon for the neighborhood crowd. Nightly dinners include chicken and arugula from the grill, prime ribs and steaks, gourmet pizzas, and main course salads (a tangy warm steak salad, for instance, comes with grilled strips of marinated filet mignon tossed with greens, mushrooms, tomato, and red onion). A dish of portobello mushrooms, arugula, and asparagus with tomatoes and pine nuts has been added for lighter dining. ✕ *221 Worth Ave.,* ☎ *407/835–3500. AE, MC, V.*

$ **TooJay's.** New York deli food served in a California-style setting—what could be more Florida? Menu includes matzoh-ball soup, corned beef on homemade rye, killer cake with five chocolates, and homemade whipped cream. A sandwich of Hebrew National kosher salami layered with onions, Muenster cheese, coleslaw, and Russian dressing on rye is a house favorite. There's also dill chicken; seafood with crabmeat, shrimp, and sour cream; and for the vegetarians, hummus, tabouli, and a wheatberry salad. On the High Holidays look for carrot *tzimmes* (a sweet compote), beef brisket with gravy, potato pancakes, and roast chicken. Wisecracking waitresses set the fast pace of this bright restaurant with a high, open packing-crate board ceiling and windows overlooking the gardens. In addition to this location, there are nine other TooJay's restaurants along the Gold and Gulf coasts and in mid-Florida. ✕ *313 Royal Poinciana Plaza,* ☎ *407/659–7232. AE, DC, MC, V. Beer and wine only. Closed Thanksgiving, Dec. 25.*

LODGING

$$$$ **Brazilian Court.** Close to the beach but making no waves, the BC re-
★ furbished its marble baths, stripped and refinished its wood floors, and replaced bedcovers and drapes in 1993 and 1994, but the color palette continues to capture the magic of the bright Florida sun indoors and out. With its courtyard rooms and suites, the hotel remains the pick of Palm Beach without snoot. Spread out over half a block, the yellow-stucco facade with gardens and a red tile roof helps you imagine what the place must have been like 69 years ago, at its birth. Rooms are brilliantly floral—yellows, blues, greens—with theatrical bed canopies, signature white-lattice patterns on carpets, and sunshiny pane windows. Shelf space is small in the bathrooms, but closets will remind you that people once came with trunks enough for the entire season. (Some still do.) French doors, bay windows, rattan loggias, cherub fountains, and chintz garden umbrellas beneath royal palms are just some of the elements that compose the lyrical style. Rooms are stocked with Evian water, and classical music plays as guests enter. ▥ *301 Australian Ave., 33480,* ☎ *407/655–7740 or 800/552–0335; in Canada, 800/228–6852;* FAX *407/655–0801. 128 rooms, 6 suites. 2 restaurants, bar, pool. AE, D, DC, MC, V.*

$$$$ **The Breakers.** To build from the ground up, other hotels would spend
★ less than half of the $75 million the Breakers recently laid out just to renovate, keeping this oceanfront hotel the standard of Florida resort excellence. Seven stories and palatial, it is built in Italian Renaissance style, dating from 1926 and enlarged in 1969. It sprawls over 140 acres of splendor in the heart of some of the most expensive real estate in the world. Cupids wrestle alligators in the Florentine fountain in front of the main entrance. Inside the lofty lobby, your eyes lift to majestic

ceiling vaults and frescoes. The hotel still blends formality with tropical resort ambience, even if, conceding to the times, men and boys are no longer *required* (only requested) to wear jackets and ties after 7 PM. Room decor follows two color schemes: cool greens and soft pinks in an orchid-pattern English cotton chintz fabric, and shades of blue with a floral and ribbon chintz. Both designs include white plantation shutters and wall coverings, Chinese porcelain table lamps, and 1920s furniture restored to its period appearance. The original building has 15 different room sizes and shapes. If you prefer more space, ask to be placed in the newer addition. ☎ *1 S. County Rd., 33480, ☎ 407/655–6611 or 800/833–3141, FAX 407/659–8403. 567 rooms, 48 suites. 4 restaurants, lounge, pool, saunas, 2 golf courses, 20 tennis courts, croquet, fitness center, jogging, shuffleboard, beach, boating, children's programs. AE, D, DC, MC, V.*

$$$$ **The Colony.** An attentive, youthful, yet experienced new staff sets this
★ legendary 50-year-old hotel apart. The Colony always was "the scene" for the glitterati after charity balls at The Breakers. It's where Roxanne Pulitzer retreated after her infamous seven-week marriage in 1992. Now there's a recharged buzz of competence, of guest-pleasing service behind the distinctive yellow, Georgian-style exterior. The change shows in policy shifts as simple as relaxing the dress code in summer; in whimsical detail, such as in the dining room, where new palm stanchions blend into the ceiling; and in the cool yet classical guest rooms, refurbished in a style suggestive of Greece, with fluted, brushed blond-wood cabinetry and matching draperies and bedcovers in custom pink-red, beige, and blue stripes. Only steps from Worth Avenue, The Colony retains its Palm Beach connections; it is in touch with both the times and its heritage in a very satisfying balance. The only complaint is that the bathrooms are looking tired; at least the lack of shelf space has been partly alleviated by cabinets above the sink. ☎ *155 Hammon Ave., 33480, ☎ 407/655–5430 or 800/521–5525, FAX 407/832–7318. 63 rooms, 36 suites and apartments, 7 villas, 3 penthouses. Restaurant, pool, spa. AE, D, DC, MC, V.*

$$$$ **Four Seasons Ocean Grand.** This 6-acre property at the south end of Palm
★ Beach is coolly elegant but warm in detail and generous in amenities. Marble, art, fanlight windows, swagged drapes, chintz, and palms create an ambience of Grecian serenity. Piano music accompanies cocktails daily in the Living Room, with jazz on weekend evenings and classical recitals on Sunday afternoon. Although the hotel's name suggests grandeur, it's more like a small jewel, with only four stories and a long beach. All rooms are spacious—equivalent to suites in other hotels—and all were upgraded during 1993–94 in a $1 million renovation. Each has a private balcony and is furnished in finery typical of Palm Beach. Muted natural tones prevail in guest rooms, with teal, mauve, and salmon accents. Every room has a love seat, upholstered chairs, desk, TV, armoire, and large closet. A thoughtful touch: all lamps have three-way bulbs. ☎ *2800 S. Ocean Blvd., 33480, ☎ 407/582–2800 or 800/432–2335, FAX 407/547–1557. 210 rooms and suites. 2 restaurants, lounge, pool, saunas, 3 tennis courts, health club, beach. AE, D, DC, MC, V.*

$$$–$$$$ **Plaza Inn.** This three-story hotel operates bed-and-breakfast style, including
★ a full cooked breakfast with the room rate. The hotel is deco-designed from the 1930s, with pool and gardens and a bar with the intimate charm of a trysting place for the likes of Cary Grant and Katharine Hepburn. Inn owner Ajit Asrani is a retired Indian Army officer who raises show horses and polo ponies. Uncluttered rooms, all with phone and fridge, provide a welcome change of pace from other B&Bs, while the courteous staff and location in the heart of Palm Beach further make this a good choice. ☎ *215 Brazilian Ave., 33480, ☎ 407/832–8666 or 800/233–2632, FAX 407/835–8776. 50 rooms and suites. Pool. AE, MC, V.*

$$$ **Palm Beach Historic Inn.** Longtime hoteliers Harry and Barbara Kehr manage this delightfully unexpected inn in the heart of downtown Palm Beach. The setting nicely combines town and vacationland; it's across the street from the Town Hall in a classically arcaded, barrel tile–roofed, Mediterranean-style structure that stands between County Road shops and a residential area extending a block to the sea. B&B touches include fresh flowers, wine and fruit, snacks, seasonal turndown, tea and cookies in rooms, and an expanded Continental breakfast. Guest rooms tend to the frilly with lots of lace, ribbons, and scalloped edges. Most are furnished with Victorian antiques and reproductions (some out of old Palm Beach mansions, others looking more secondhand than authentic) and chiffon wall drapings above the bed. With typical B&B whimsy, a 1944 Coke machine on the second floor still supplies an 8-ounce bottle for a dime. Bath towels are as thick as parkas. ☎ *365 S. County Rd., 33480,* ☎ *407/832–4009,* FAX *407/832–6255. 13 rooms and suites. Library. AE, D, DC, MC, V.*

$$–$$$ **Sea Lord Hotel.** If you don't need glamour or brand names, and you're not the bed-and-breakfast type, this garden-style hideaway is for you. Choose from accommodations that overlook Lake Worth, the pool, or the ocean; all were given a face-lift in 1993–94—new paint, new furniture, and new bedspreads and drapes as needed. The reasonably priced 20-seat café, now with tablecloths and cloth napkins in the evening, adds to the at-home, comfy feeling and attracts repeat customers. Rooms are plain but not cheap and come with carpet, at least one comfortable chair, small or large fridge, and tropical print fabrics. ☎ *2315 S. Ocean Blvd., 33480,* ☎ *and* FAX *407/582–1461. 19 rooms, 11 apartments, 6 efficiencies. Restaurant, pool, beach. D, MC, V.*

Palm Beach Gardens
DINING

$$ **Arezzo.** The pungent smell of fresh garlic and olive oil tips you off that
★   the food's the thing at this outstanding Tuscan grill at the PGA National Resort, but art and service equally rate. The whole scene draws locals as well as an international clientele—and lots of them. In this unusually relaxed, upscale resort setting, you can dine in shorts or in jacket and tie. An early-bird menu (5:30–6:30) has three-course dinners for $12.95. Families are attracted by the affordable prices (as well as the food), so romantics might be tempted to pass Arezzo up. Their loss. Dishes include the usual variety of chicken, veal, fish, and steaks, but there are a dozen different pastas (half orders for $3 off regular price) and an almost equal number of pizzas. Examples are rigatoni *alla Bolognese* (with ground veal, marinara sauce, and Parmesan), linguine *alla Catalana* (with eggplant, garlic, onions, marinara sauce, and Parmesan), and pizza *Stromboli* (with prosciutto, capicola, salami, mozzarella, and marinara sauce). The decor, too, has the right idea: an herb garden in the center of the room, slate floors, upholstered banquettes to satisfy the upscale mood, and butcher paper over yellow table covers to establish the light side. Pennants from Siena, posters, tapestries, and an open kitchen make it all festive. ✕ *400 Ave. of the Champions,* ☎ *407/627–2000. AE, MC, V. No lunch.*

$$ **River House.** Much of what south Florida dining is all about can be found at this dinner-only, waterfront restaurant. People keep returning for the large portions of straightforward American fare; the big salad bar and fresh, slice-it-yourself breads; the competent service; the smart setting; and, thanks to the animated buzz of a rewarded local clientele, the feeling that you've come to the right place. Choices include seafoods (always with a daily catch), steaks, chops, and seafood/steak combo platters. Booths and freestanding tables are surrounded by lots of blond wood, high ceilings, and nautical art under glass. The wait on Saturday nights in season can be up to 45 minutes. A better bet is to reserve one of the 20 upstairs tables, available weekends only; the upstairs is a little more formal and doesn't have a salad bar (bread comes from below), but it does possess a cathedral ceiling. ✕ *2373 PGA Blvd., ☎ 407/694–1198. AE, MC, V. Closed Thanksgiving, Dec. 25. No lunch.*

LODGING

$$$$ PGA National Resort & Spa. Outstanding mission-style rooms are decorated in deep, dark, conservative, almost somber florals that lend a thoughtful and settled-in feeling. Facilities throughout the resort are equally richly detailed, from the $10 million spa, opened in 1992, to the limitless sports facilities and excellent dining (*see Arezzo, above*). The sprawling resort is the focus of the 2,340-acre PGA National community, which contains 39 neighborhoods and 4,250 residences. Championship golf courses and croquet courts are adorned with 25,000 flowering plants amid a 240-acre nature preserve. Rooms for nonsmokers and guests with disabilities and two-bedroom, two-bath cottages with fully equipped kitchens are available, too. ⌂ *400 Ave. of the Champions, 33418, ☎ 407/627–2000 or 800/633–9150. 275 rooms, 60 suites, 85 cottages. 6 restaurants, lake, pool, sauna, spa, 5 golf courses, 19 tennis courts (12 lighted), croquet, racquetball, boating. AE, D, DC, MC, V.*

Palm Beach Shores

LODGING

$$-$$$ Sailfish Marina. Palm Beach Shores, a residential town rimmed mostly
★ by mom-and-pop motels, sits at the southern tip of Singer Island, across Lake Worth Inlet from Palm Beach. By staying here, you get Palm Beach weather and a Palm Beach view without the pretense and for half the price of anything comparable in Palm Beach. This long-established, one-story motel has a marina with 94 deep-water slips and 15 rooms and efficiencies that open to landscaped grounds. None is directly on the waterfront, but units 9–11 have water views across the blacktop drive. Rooms have peaked ceilings, carpeting, king or twin beds, stall showers, the usual variety of dressers and cushioned chairs; many have ceiling fans. Much of the art is original, traded with artists who display in an informal show on the dock every Thursday night. Lately this has attracted some 35 artists and as many as 4,000 browsers and buyers each week. From the seawall, there's a good view of fish through the clear inlet water. The staff is informed and helpful, the proprietors as promotional as they are friendly. Inquire about May–September, Sunday–Thursday two-for-one packages (holidays and tournament days excluded) and other slow-season specials. There are neither nosmoking rooms nor in-room phones, but there are several pay phones on the property and messages are taken. ⌂ *98 Lake Dr., 33404, ☎ 407/844–1724 or 800/446–4577, ℻ 407/848–9684. 15 units. Restaurant, bar, grocery, pool. AE, MC, V.*

Sebastian

DINING

$-$$ Capt. Hiram's. This 250-seat restaurant on the Indian River Lagoon is family-friendly and easygoing, fanciful and fun, not purposefully hip. "Neckties," as the sign says, "are prohibited." Other than molded-plastic tables, the place is "real"—full of wood booths, stained glass, umbrellas on the open deck, and ceiling fans. Don't miss Capt. Hiram's Sandbar, a bar in the sand where kids can play while parents enjoy a beer at stools set around an outdoor shower or in a beached boat. Dinner entrées are served with a tossed salad, fresh vegetables, and choice of rice, fries, or slaw, along with roll and butter. Choose from among grilled chicken breast, seafood brochette, New York strip steak, fresh catch, and lots of other seafood dishes as well as raw-bar items. The full bar has a weekday happy hour and free hot hors d'oeuvres Friday 5–6. There's nightly entertainment in season. ✗ *1606 N. Indian River Dr.,* ☏ *407/589–1345. Closed Thanksgiving, Dec. 25. AE, D, MC, V.*

$–$$ Hurricane Harbor. A year-round crowd of retirees and locals frequent this down-home, open-beam, Old Florida–style waterfront restaurant (though note, it's all indoors), built in 1927 as a garage and during Prohibition used as a smugglers' den. Guests love the window seats on stormy nights, when sizeable waves break outside in the Indian River Lagoon. The menu features seafood, steaks, and grills, along with sandwiches, soups, and salads. Friday and Saturday nights they open the Antique Dining Room, with its linen, stained glass, and a huge antique breakfront. There's live music nightly—jazz, pop, Dixieland, German, country and western, or oldies. ✗ *1540 Indian River Dr.,* ☏ *407/589–1773. AE, D, MC, V. Closed Mon., Dec. 25.*

LODGING

$–$$ Captain's Quarters. Four Key West–style units—three overlooking the Indian River Lagoon and the marina at Capt. Hiram's and one two-room suite—are all cute. They are painted in bright colors with matching fabrics and contain pine and white wicker furniture, pine plank floors with grass rugs, a ceiling fan, a little fridge, air-conditioning and heat, and nautical and miscellaneous art. The adequate bathrooms have large stall showers. Glass doors open to a plank porch with two molded chairs, but the porches are all within sight of each other. ▯ *1606 Indian River Dr., 32958,* ☏ *407/589–4345. 3 rooms, 1 suite. Restaurant. AE, D, MC, V.*

$–$$ Davis House Inn. Vero native Steve Wild modeled his two-story inn after the clubhouse at Augusta National. Wide overhung roofs shade wraparound porches. In a companion house that Steve calls the Gathering Room, he serves a complimentary expanded Continental breakfast. Though the inn only opened in 1992, it looks established, fitting right in with the fishing-town look of Sebastian, on the Indian River Lagoon. Rooms are huge—virtual suites, with a large sofa sitting area—though somewhat underfurnished. Each has a hand-painted, pine, king-size bed and microwave kitchenette. It's a terrific value. ▯ *607 Davis St., 32958,* ☏ *407/589–4114. 12 efficiencies. Bicycles. MC, V.*

Stuart

DINING

$$ The Ashley. Since expanding in late 1993, this restaurant, the first of a number of immensely popular eateries in revived downtown Stuart, has more tables, more art, and more plants. Now with seating for 100 and a full bar, it still has elements of the old bank that was robbed here three times early in the century by the Ashley Gang (hence the name). The big outdoor mural in the French Impressionist style was paid for by good sports helping to revive the downtown, their names duly inscribed on wall plaques inside. The Continental menu appeals with the freshest foods and features lots of salads, fresh fish, and pastas. Breakfast is served on Sunday. ✗ *61 S.W. Osceola St.,* ☏ *407/221–9476. AE, MC, V. Closed Mon. in off-season. No lunch or dinner Sun.*

$$ Scalawags. The look is plantation tropical—coach lanterns, gingerbread, wicker, slow-motion paddle fans—but the top-notch buffets are aimed at today's resort guests. Standouts are the all-you-can-eat Wednesday evening seafood buffet, which features jumbo shrimp, Alaskan crab legs, clams on the half shell, marinated salmon, and fresh catch, and the Friday prime rib buffet with traditional Yorkshire pudding and baked potato station. Each features a 10-foot dessert table. A regular menu with a big selection of fish, shellfish, and grills, plus a big salad bar, is also offered. Seating is in the main dining room, overlooking the Indian River; in the private 20-seat wine room; or on the terrace, looking out on the marina. ✕ *555 N.E. Ocean Blvd., Hutchinson Island,* ☎ *407/225–3700. AE, DC, MC, V.*

$ **The Emporium.** Indian River Plantation's coffee shop is an old-fashioned soda fountain and grill that also serves hearty breakfasts. Specialties include eggs Benedict, omelets, deli sandwiches, and salads. ✕ *555 N.E. Ocean Blvd., Hutchinson Island,* ☎ *407/225–3700. AE, DC, MC, V.*

LODGING

$$$$ **Indian River Plantation Beach Resort.** Longtime Florida visitors recognize
★ this 192-acre residential-sports complex as one of a kind among full-service resorts because of its oceanfront setting in the assuredly warm subtropics. Its unpretentious style fits well on Hutchinson Island, where unusual care limits development, shunning the commercial crowding found north and south. Guests lodge luxuriously in rooms and suites in three three-story buildings and in rentals available in new condominiums, mostly designed with bright island themes that feature abundant latticework and balconies. The condominium lodgings contain kitchens with microwaves and range tops. Rooms for people with disabilities are available. ⊞ *555 N.E. Ocean Blvd., Hutchinson Island 34996,* ☎ *407/225–6990 or 800/947–2148. 326 rooms and suites, 150 condominiums. 5 restaurants, bar, 4 pools, spa, 2 golf courses, 13 tennis courts (5 lighted), boating. AE, DC, MC, V.*

$$–$$$ **HarborFront.** On a quiet site that slopes to the St. Lucie River in a historic enclave west of U.S. 1, this B&B combines an unusual mix of accommodations and imaginative extras—a Friday fresh-fish grill, picnic baskets, and concierge-like custom planning. Rooms and cottages are cozy and eclectic. Choose from a spacious chintz-covered suite or apartment or maybe the 33-foot moored sailboat (small rowing dinghy provided). Rooms include wicker and antiques, some airy and bright with private deck, others more tweedy and dark. From hammocks in the yard you can watch pelicans and herons. ⊞ *310 Atlanta Ave., 34994,* ☎ *407/288–7289. 8 apartments, cottages, suites, rooms, boat. Lounge. MC, V.*

$$ **The Homeplace.** The house was built in 1913 by pioneer Sam Matthews, who contracted much of the early town construction for railroad developer Henry Flagler. Jean Bell has restored the house to its early look, from hardwood floors to fluffy pillows. Fern-filled dining and sunrooms, full of chintz-covered cushioned wicker, overlook a pool and patio. Three guest rooms are Captain's Quarters, Opal's Room, and Prissy's Porch. A full breakfast is included. ⊞ *501 Akron Ave., 34994,* ☎ *407/220–9148. 3 rooms. Pool, hot tub. MC, V.*

Vero Beach

DINING

$$ **Black Pearl.** This intimate restaurant (19 tables) with pink and green art deco furnishings offers entrées that combine fresh local ingredients with the best of the Continental tradition. Specialties include chilled leek-and-watercress soup, local fish in parchment paper, feta cheese and spinach fritters, mesquite-grilled swordfish, and pan-fried veal with local shrimp and vermouth. Pearl's Bistro (54 Royal Palm Blvd., ☎ 407/778–2950), a more casual and less expensive sister restaurant, serves Caribbean-style food for lunch and dinner. ✕ *1409 Rte. A1A,* ☎ *407/234–4426. AE, MC, V. Closed Super Bowl Sun., holidays. No lunch.*

$$ **Ocean Grill.** Opened by Waldo Sexton as a hamburger shack in 1938, the Ocean Grill is nowadays furnished with Tiffany lamps, wrought-iron chandeliers, and Beanie Backus paintings of pirates and Seminole

Indians. The menu includes black-bean soup, crisp onion rings, jumbo lump crabmeat salad, at least three kinds of fish every day, prime rib, and a tart Key lime pie. The bar looks out on the remains of the *Breconshire,* an 1894 near-shore wreck, from which 34 British sailors escaped. The event is commemorated by the Leaping Limey, a curious blend of vodka, blue curaçao, and lemon. ✕ *1050 Sexton Plaza (Beachland Blvd. east of Ocean Dr.),* ☎ *407/231–5409. AE, D, DC, MC, V. Closed Super Bowl Sun., 2 wks following Labor Day, Thanksgiving. No lunch weekends.*

LODGING

$$$$ **Guest Quarters Suite Hotel.** Built in 1986 and completely refurbished in 1993, this five-story rose-color stucco hotel on Ocean Drive provides easy access to Vero Beach's specialty shops and boutiques. One- and two-bedroom suites have patios opening onto the pool or balconies and ocean views; coffeemakers, VCRs, and movie rentals are provided. ⌧ *3500 Ocean Dr., 32963,* ☎ *407/231–5666 or 800/841–5666. 55 suites. Bar, pool, wading pool, hot tub. AE, D, DC, MC, V.*

$$–$$$ **Islander Resort.** The aqua-and-white-trim Islander has a snoozy Key West style that contrasts stylishly with the smart shops across from the beach along Ocean Drive. Jigsaw-cut brackets and balusters and beach umbrellas dress up the pool. All rooms feature white wicker, pickled paneled walls, Caribbean art, colorful carpets, floral bedcovers, paddle fans hung from vaulted ceilings, and fresh flowers. It's just right for beachside Vero. ⌧ *3101 Ocean Dr., 32963,* ☎ *407/231–4431 or 800/952–5886. 16 rooms, 1 efficiency. Pool. AE, DC, MC, V.*

West Palm Beach

DINING

$–$$ **Comeau Bar & Grill.** Everybody still calls it Roxy's, its name from 1934 until it moved into an art deco downtown high-rise's lobby in 1989. Outside there are tables under the canopy; inside, behind the authentic old saloon, is a clubby, pecky cypress–paneled room that serves no-surprise, all-American food: steaks, shrimp, chicken, duck, some pastas, and Caesar and Greek salads. Try the Roxy Burger—a combination of veal and beef herbed and spiced. ✕ *319–323 Clematis St.,* ☎ *407/833–2402 or 407/833–1003. AE, MC, V. Closed Dec. 25. No dinner Sun.*

$–$$ **Narcissus.** Get acquainted with the vitality of downtown West Palm Beach at this lively two-level jazz café across the park from the public library. The grazing menu features salads, pastas, crab cake, tuna pizza melt, burgers, and specialty sandwiches like falafel. Top-value twilight dinner specials are $8.95 for a selection of entrées, soup or salad, plus beverage and dessert. During the daily happy hour, 4:30–7, drinks and hors d'oeuvres are half price. There's a live jazz brunch Sunday noon–4 and jazz jamming 5–10. ✕ *200 Clematis St.,* ☎ *407/ 659–1888. AE, MC, V.*

LODGING

$$$$ **Palm Beach Polo and Country Club.** Privately owned and spacious studios, one- and two-bedroom villas, and condominiums are available for daily, weekly, or monthly rental in this exclusive 2,200-acre resort, where World Cup and USPA Gold Cup tournaments are hosted. Each residence is furnished by its owner according to quality standards set by the resort. Still, units can range from stagily backlit and modern to Ozzie and Harriet plaids and bulky rattan styles. Be specific about your preferences when reserving. You might also want to request a dwelling closest to the sports activity that interests you: polo, tennis, or golf. All units have kitchens and a wide range of amenities. ⌧ *11809 Polo Club Rd., 33414,* ☎ *407/798–7000 or 800/327–4204. 100 villas and*

condominiums. 5 dining rooms, 10 pools, saunas, 2 18-hole and 1 9-hole golf courses, 24 tennis courts (10 lighted), croquet, horseback riding, racquetball, squash. AE, DC, MC, V.

$$–$$$ **Royal Palm House Bed & Breakfast.** The third of the Old Northwood neighborhood's B&Bs (licensed early in 1995), this Dutch colonial–revival house was built in 1925 with a gambrel roof and shed dormers. Of the three second-floor units with wickery interiors, one is a two-room suite and two share a bath. Even better are innkeeper Anne Walker's wealth of stories about behind-the-scenes Washington, where in 1994 she retired as director of food for the U.S. House of Representatives. Guests get a big Southern breakfast with helpings of tales and can sometimes talk Anne into a North Carolina barbecue in the evening. ⌂ 3215 Spruce Ave., 33407, ☎ 407/863–9836. 3 units. Pool. No credit cards.

$$ **Hibiscus House.** Few B&B hosts in Florida work harder at hospitality
★ and at looking after their neighborhood than Raleigh Hill and Colin Rayner. As proof, since the inn opened in the late 1980s, 11 sets of guests have bought houses in Old Northwood, which is listed on the National Register of Historic Places thanks to Hill and Rayner's efforts. Their Cape Cod–style bed-and-breakfast is full of the antiques Hill has collected during decades of in-demand interior designing: a 150-year-old four-square piano in the Florida room, a gorgeous green and cane planter chair beside an Oriental fan and bamboo poles, and Louis XV pieces in the living room. Outstanding, too, is the landscaped, tropical pool-patio area behind a high privacy fence. Both Hill and Rayner are informed about the best—as well as the most affordable—dining in the area. This is an excellent value. ⌂ 501 30th St., 33407, ☎ 407/863–5633 or 800/203–4927. 8 rooms. Pool. AE, DC, MC, V.

$$ **West Palm Beach Bed & Breakfast.** Also in Old Northwood, but more informal and Key West–like, this cottage-style B&B has a clump of rare paroutis palms out front. All rooms are vividly colored. (The aqua room is AQUA; the formerly pink room is now AMETHYST.) However, the splashy poolside carriage house and the new, brightly striped cottage with the fruity fabrics and Peter Max–style posters are where you want to be. The parlor has a delightful montage of work by Florida's favorite painter of hotel art, Eileen Seitz. Owners are Dennis Keimel and Ron Seitz (unrelated to the artist). ⌂ 419 32nd St., 33407, ☎ 407/848–4064 or 800/736–4064, ℻ 407/842–1688. 2 rooms, carriage house, cottage. Pool. AE, MC, V.

THE ARTS AND NIGHTLIFE

The Arts

The *Palm Beach Post*, in its "TGIF" entertainment insert on Friday, lists all events for the weekend, including concerts. Admission to some cultural events is free or by donation. Call **Ticketmaster** (☎ 407/839–3900) for tickets for performing arts events.

For additional arts venues, including museums and performance halls, *see* Exploring *and* What to See and Do with Children, *above*.

The **Raymond F. Kravis Center for the Performing Arts** (701 Okeechobee Blvd., West Palm Beach, ☎ 407/832–7469) is the three-year-old, $55 million, 2,200-seat, glass-copper-and-marble showcase that occupies the highest ground in West Palm Beach. Its newest stage is the 250-seat Rinker Playhouse, which in late 1994 added a "black box" space for children's programming, family productions, and other special events. Some 300 performances of drama, dance, and music—everything from gospel and bluegrass to jazz and classical—are scheduled each year.

Theater

Caldwell Theatre Company (7873 N. Federal Hwy., Boca Raton 33429, ☎ 407/241–7432 in Boca Raton, 407/832–2989 in Palm Beach, 305/462–5433 in Broward County), a professional Equity regional theater, hosts the annual multimedia Mizner Festival each April–May and stages four productions each winter.

Jan McArt's Royal Palm Dinner Theatre (303 S.E. Mizner Blvd., Royal Palm Plaza, Boca Raton 33432, ☎ 407/392–3755 or 800/841–6765), an Equity theater in its 18th year, presents five or six musicals on a year-round schedule.

Jupiter Dinner Theatre (1001 E. Indiantown Rd., Jupiter 33477, ☎ 407/746–5566) features Broadway and Hollywood stars in professionally staged productions.

Pope Theatre Company (262 S. Ocean Blvd., Manalapan 33462, ☎ 407/585–3433) is the newest Equity stage in Palm Beach County. The intimate 250-seat, state-of-the-art theater presents five five-week productions during its winter season (October–May), concentrating on new works by American playwrights. A summer schedule is also offered.

Quest Theatre (444 24th St., West Palm Beach 33407, ☎ 407/832–9328) enters its sixth season showcasing African-American productions in its own performance hall and on tour throughout the county.

Riverside Theatre (3250 Riverside Park Dr., Vero Beach 32963, ☎ 407/231–6990) stages six productions each season in its 633-seat performance hall. Children's productions are mounted in the compound at the **Agnes Wahlstrom Youth Playhouse** (☎ 407/234–8052).

Royal Poinciana Playhouse (70 Royal Poinciana Plaza, Palm Beach 33480, ☎ 407/659–3310) presents seven productions each year between December and April.

Music

The **Harid Conservatory** (2285 Potomac Rd., Boca Raton 33431, ☎ 407/997–2677) offers student and faculty performances at its 5-acre campus west of Boca Raton and frequently at the Morikami Museum.

Opera

Palm Beach Opera (415 S. Olive Ave., West Palm Beach 33401, ☎ 407/833–7888) stages three productions each winter at the Kravis Center.

Dance

Ballet Florida (500 Fern St., West Palm Beach 33401, ☎ 407/659–2000 or 800/540–0172), one of Florida's chief artistic companies, has a winter season at the Kravis Center and also goes on tour.

Demetrius Klein Dance Company (3208 2nd Ave. N, #10, Lake Worth 33461, ☎ 407/964–9779) is a nationally acclaimed, world-touring, professional troupe with a commitment to drawing local youth into dance. It's not to be missed.

Film

Carefree Theatre (2000 S. Dixie Hwy., West Palm Beach 33401, ☎ 407/833–7305) is Palm Beach County's premier showcase of foreign and art films. **Narcissus** (*see* Dining and Lodging, *above*) gives free movie passes with dinner.

Nightlife

Thursday evening after work, West Palm Beach closes Clematis Street to traffic. Local country, folk, and rock bands come out. Tables come out. People eat. People drink. People dance and carry on. Friday and Saturday nights after the three-piece-suiters drive home, the street unmasks. Clematis becomes the hub of West Palm's California-style indoor-outdoor nightclubs—lighter, less smoky and boozy, and more given to jazz brunches and reggae. Hip young professionals living in new downtown apartments supply the sense that something real is happening, and for the first time in 100 years West Palm is rivaling Palm Beach for night action.

Boca Raton

Pete Rose's Ballpark Cafe (8144 Glades Rd., ☎ 407/488–7383), next to the Holiday Inn at Florida's Turnpike, is, not too surprisingly, a sports bar. You can shoot pool at three tables, watch TV at your own table, or listen to recorded rock and roll. **Wildflower Waterway Cafe** (551 E. Palmetto Park Rd., ☎ 407/391–0000) has nightly DJs spinning the top of the pop charts for a mostly young crowd.

Delray Beach

Back Room Blues Lounge (303 W. Atlantic Blvd., ☎ 407/276–6492), behind Westside Liquors, has live blues bands Wednesday through Friday. **Boston's on the Beach** (40 S. Ocean Blvd., ☎ 407/278–3364) is full of Boston Red Sox, Boston Bruins, and New England Patriots paraphernalia—including a veritable shrine to Ted Williams. There's live reggae music Monday and rock and roll Tuesday through Sunday. **Cafe Mocha** (44 E. Atlantic Ave., ☎ 407/274–0084) combines a coffee bar, coffee shop, and art gallery with live music most nights.

Jupiter

Barbados (4300 U.S. 1, Bluff Square Shops, ☎ 407/627–2260) features bands that scan the rock-and-roll era.

Palm Beach

Au Bar (336 Royal Poinciana Way, ☎ 407/832–4800), still popular even though the Kennedy-Smith scandal has faded, has a packed dance floor on weekends.

Palm Beach Gardens

Irish Times (9920 Alternate A1A, Promenade Shopping Plaza, ☎ 407/624–1504) is a four-leaf-clover find, featuring a microbrewery and live Irish acts.

West Palm Beach

The pick of the downtown nightspots is **Narcissus** (200 Clematis St., ☎ 407/659–1888), which, in addition to food (*see* Dining and Lodging, *above*), features daily live jazz and a Sunday jazz brunch and jazz jam. Downstairs from Narcissus is the **Underground Coffeeworks** (105 Narcissus Ave., ☎ 407/835–4792), a sort of '60s spot. **Respectable Street Cafe** (518 Clematis St., ☎ 407/832–9999) explodes in high energy like an indoor Woodstock.

PALM BEACH AND THE TREASURE COAST ESSENTIALS

Arriving and Departing

By Plane

Palm Beach International Airport (PBIA) (Congress Ave. and Belvedere Rd., West Palm Beach, ☎ 407/471–7400) is served by Air Canada (☎ 800/776–3000), American/American Eagle (☎ 800/433–7300), American Trans-Air (☎ 800/225–2995), Canadian Holidays (☎ 800/661–8881), Carnival Airlines (☎ 800/824–7386), Comair (☎ 800/354–9822), Continental (☎ 800/525–0280), Delta (☎ 800/221–1212), KIWI Intl. Airlines (☎ 800/538–5494), Laker Airways Ltd. (☎ 800/331–6471), Northwest (☎ 800/225–2525), Paradise Island (☎ 800/432–8807), Republic Air Travel (☎ 800/233–0225), TWA (☎ 800/221–2000), United (☎ 800/241–6522), and USAir/USAir Express (☎ 800/428–4322).

Route 10 of Tri-Rail Commuter Bus Service (☎ 800/874–7245) runs from the airport to Tri-Rail's nearby Palm Beach Airport station daily. **Co-Tran** (*see* Getting Around by Bus, *below*) Route 4-S operates from the airport to downtown West Palm Beach every two hours at 35 minutes after the hour from 7:35 AM until 5:35 PM. The fare is $1.

Palm Beach Transportation (☎ 407/689–4222) provides taxi and limousine service from PBIA. Reserve at least a day in advance for a limousine. The lowest fares are $1.50 per mile, with the meter starting at $1.25. Depending on your destination, a flat rate (from PBIA only) may save money. Wheelchair-accessible vehicles are available.

By Car

I–95 runs north–south, linking West Palm Beach with Miami and Fort Lauderdale to the south and with Daytona, Jacksonville, and the rest of the Atlantic Coast to the north. To get to central Palm Beach, exit at Belvedere Road or Okeechobee Boulevard. Florida's Turnpike runs up from Miami through West Palm Beach before angling northwest to reach Orlando.

By Train

Amtrak (☎ 800/872–7245) connects West Palm Beach (201 S. Tamarind Ave., ☎ 407/832–6169) with cities along Florida's east coast and the Northeast daily and via the *Sunset Limited* to New Orleans and Los Angeles three times weekly.

By Bus

Greyhound Lines (☎ 800/231–2222) buses arrive at the station in West Palm Beach (100 Banyan Blvd., ☎ 407/833–8534).

Getting Around

A new Downtown Transfer Facility is to open in 1996 at Banyan Boulevard and Clearlake Drive, off Australian Avenue at the western entrance to downtown. It links the downtown shuttle, Amtrak, Tri-Rail (the commuter line of Dade, Broward, and Palm Beach counties), CoTran (the county bus system), and taxis. Greyhound is also expected to tie in.

By Car

U.S. 1 threads north–south along the coast, connecting most coastal communities, while the more scenic Route A1A ventures out onto the barrier islands. The interstate, I–95, runs parallel to U.S. 1 a bit farther inland. Southern Boulevard (U.S. 98) runs east–west from West Palm Beach to Lake Okeechobee.

In 1995 a new nonstop four-lane route, Okeechobee Boulevard, began carrying traffic from west of downtown West Palm Beach, near the Amtrak station in the airport district, directly to the Flagler Memorial Bridge and into Palm Beach. Flagler Drive will be turned over for pedestrian use only before the end of the decade.

By Train
Tri-Rail (☎ 305/728–8445 or 800/874–7245), the commuter rail system, has six stations in Palm Beach County (13 stops altogether between West Palm Beach and Miami). The round-trip fare is $5, $2.50 for students and senior citizens.

By Bus
CoTran (Palm Beach County Transportation Authority) buses require exact change. The cost is $1, 50¢ for students, senior citizens, and people with disabilities (with $1 reduced-fare ID); transfers are 20¢, 10¢ for students, senior citizens, and people with disabilities. Service operates between 5 AM and 8:30 PM, though pickups on most routes are 5:30 to 7. For details, call 407/233–1111 (Palm Beach) or 407/930–5123 (Boca Raton–Delray Beach).

Palmtran (☎ 407/833–8873) is a shuttle system that provides free transportation around downtown West Palm Beach from 6:30 AM to 7:30 PM weekdays.

By Taxi
Palm Beach Transportation (☎ 407/689–4222) has a single number serving several cab companies. Meters start at $1.25, and the charge is $1.25 per mile within West Palm Beach city limits; if the trip at any point leaves the city limits, the fare is $1.50 per mile. Some cabs may charge more. Waiting time is 25¢ per 75 seconds.

Guided Tours

Special-Interest Tours
AIRBOAT TOURS
Loxahatchee Everglades Tours (☎ 407/482–6107) operates year-round airboat tours from west of Boca Raton through the marshes between the built-up coast and Lake Okeechobee.

BOAT TOURS
Capt. Doug's (☎ 407/589–2329) offers three-hour lunch or dinner cruises from Sebastian along the Indian River on board the 35-foot sloop *Bobo*. Accommodating up to four couples, the sailboat tour costs $100 per couple, the same price as in 1984, including the meal, tips, beer, and wine.

Jonathan Dickinson's River Tours (☎ 407/746–1466) runs two-hour narrated river cruises from Jonathan Dickinson State Park in Hobe Sound daily at 9, 11, 1, and 3 and one night trip a month (at the full moon) at 7. The cost is $10 adults, $5 children under 12.

Louie's Lady (☎ 407/744–5550) gives steamboat-style sightseeing and luncheon tours of Jupiter Island and the Intracoastal Waterway. The boat leaves from docks behind Harpoon Louie's Restaurant on the Jupiter River.

Manatee Queen (☎ 407/744–2191), a 49-passenger catamaran, offers day and evening cruises on the Intracoastal Waterway and into the cypress swamps of Jonathan Dickinson State Park, November to May.

Ramblin' Rose Riverboat (☎ 407/243–0686) operates luncheon, dinner-dance, and Sunday brunch cruises from Delray Beach along the Intracoastal Waterway.

The Spirit of St. Joseph (☎ 407/467–2628) offers seven lunch and dinner cruises weekly on the Indian River, leaving from alongside the St. Lucie County Historical Museum, November through April.

Star of Palm Beach (☎ 407/842–0882) runs year-round from Singer Island, each day offering one dinner-dance and three sightseeing cruises on the Intracoastal Waterway.

ENVIRONMENTAL TOURS

Audubon Society of the Everglades (☎ 407/588–6908) leads field trips through Palm Beach County, the Treasure Coast, and the Space Coast (the region centered on the Kennedy Space Center), except during midsummer. Shorter nature walks take place on Saturday, January through March.

HISTORICAL TOURS

Boca Raton Historical Society (☎ 407/395–6766) offers afternoon tours of the Boca Raton Resort & Club on Tuesday year-round, as well as group tours to other south Florida sites. (Call for departure points.)

Indian River County Historical Society (2336 14th Ave., Vero Beach, ☎ 407/778–3435) maintains an exhibit center at and leads tours from the old Florida East Coast Railroad Station. Walking tours of downtown Vero are given on Wednesday at 11 and 1 (by reservation), and there are occasional driving tours of the historic 7-mile Jungle Trail along the Indian River.

Old Northwood Historic District Tours (☎ 407/863–5633) offers two-hour group walking tours on Sunday year-round through the 1920s-era historic district of West Palm Beach, including historic home interiors. The district is listed on the National Register of Historic Places and hosts special events much of the year. A $5 donation is requested.

Important Addresses and Numbers

Emergencies
Dial 911 for **police** or **ambulance**.

HOSPITALS
The following hospitals have a 24-hour emergency room: **Good Samaritan Hospital** (Flagler Dr. and Palm Beach Lakes Blvd., West Palm Beach, ☎ 407/655–5511; physician referral, ☎ 407/650–6240), **JFK Medical Center** (5301 S. Congress Ave., Atlantis, ☎ 407/965–7300; physician referral, ☎ 407/642–3628), **Palm Beaches Medical Center** (2201 45th St., West Palm Beach, ☎ 407/881–2670; physician referral, ☎ 407/881–2661), **Palm Beach Regional Hospital** (2829 10th Ave. N, Lake Worth, ☎ 407/967–7800; physician referral, ☎ 800/237–6644), and **St. Mary's Hospital** (901 45th St., West Palm Beach, ☎ 407/844–6300; physician referral, ☎ 407/881–2929).

LATE-NIGHT PHARMACIES
Eckerd Drug (3343 S. Congress Ave., Palm Springs, ☎ 407/965–3367). **Walgreen Drugs** (1688 S. Congress Ave., Palm Springs, ☎ 407/968–8211; 7561 N. Federal Hwy., Boca Raton, ☎ 407/241–9802; 1634 S. Federal Hwy., Boynton Beach, ☎ 407/737–1260; 1208 Royal Palm Beach Blvd., Royal Palm Beach, ☎ 407/798–9048; 6370 Indiantown Rd., Jupiter, ☎ 407/744–6822; 20 E. 30th St., Riviera Beach, ☎ 407/848–6464).

Tourist Information

Palm Beach County Convention & Visitors Bureau (1555 Palm Beach Lakes Blvd., Suite 204, West Palm Beach 33401, ☎ 407/471–3995) is open weekdays 8:30–5. **Chamber of Commerce of the Palm Beaches** (401 N. Flagler Dr., West Palm Beach 33401, ☎ 407/833–3711) is open weekdays 8:30–5. **Indian River County Tourist Council** (1216 21st St., Box 2947, Vero Beach 32961, ☎ 407/567–3491) is open weekdays 9–5. **Palm Beach Chamber of Commerce** (45 Cocoanut Row, Palm Beach 33480, ☎ 407/655–3282) is open weekdays 9–5. **St. Lucie County Tourist Development Council** (2300 Virginia Ave., Fort Pierce 34982, ☎ 407/462–1535 or 800/344–8443) is open weekdays 8–5. **Stuart/Martin County Chamber of Commerce** (1650 S. Kanner Hwy., Stuart 34994, ☎ 407/287–1088) is open weekdays 9–5.

6 The Florida Keys

This slender necklace of landfalls off the southern tip of Florida is strung together by a 110-mile-long highway. The Keys have two faces: one a wilderness of flowering jungles and shimmering seas amid mangrove-fringed islands dangling toward the tropics, the other a traffic jam with a view of billboards, shopping centers, and trailer courts. You don't come here for the beaches, but for the deep-sea fishing and the snorkeling and diving.

Updated by
Herb Hiller

THE FLORIDA KEYS are a wilderness of flowering jungles and shimmering seas, a jade necklace of mangrove-fringed islands dangling toward the tropics. The Florida Keys are also a 110-mile traffic jam lined with garish billboards, hamburger stands, shopping centers, motels, and trailer courts. Unfortunately, in the Keys you can't have one without the other. A river of tourist traffic gushes along U.S. 1 (also called the Overseas Highway), the only road to Key West. Residents of Monroe County live by diverting that river's green dollar flow to their own pockets. In the process, however, the fragile beauty of the Keys—or at least the 45 that are inhabited, linked to the mainland by 43 bridges—has paid the price.

Despite a state-mandated county-development slowdown, the Keys' natural resources are still imperiled. Since 1992, new building has been severely restricted, with an eye to protecting the environment as well as to improving hurricane evacuation procedures. Nevertheless, increased salinity in Florida Bay has caused large areas of sea grass to die off, drift in mats out of the bay onto the coral reefs, and prevent sunlight from reaching the corals, thereby stifling their growth and threatening the Keys' significant recreational diving economy and tourism in general. In 1995 the National Oceanic and Atmospheric Administration (NOAA) was expected to implement a controversial management plan for the 200-mile-long Florida Keys National Marine Sanctuary (the largest in the nation). The sanctuary plan is intended to help protect the coral reefs and restore badly depleted fish reserves, but it has been challenged by shortsighted fishing interests, even while many of these same interests agree on the need to renourish Florida Bay. The plan was expected to include a new maritime zoning concept that would restrict commercial and recreational activities in designated areas. Dive shops and places where visitors stay would alert people to these restrictions.

For now, however, take pleasure as you drive down U.S. 1 along the islands. Most days show only the silvery blue and green Atlantic and its still-living reef on your left; Florida Bay, the Gulf of Mexico, and the backcountry on your right. (The Keys extend east–west from the mainland.) At some points, the ocean and the Gulf are 10 miles apart; on the narrowest landfill islands, they are separated only by the road.

The Overseas Highway varies from a frustrating traffic-clogged trap to a mystical pathway skimming the sea. More islands than you can remember appear. Follow the green mile markers by the side of the road, and even if you lose track of the names of the islands, you won't get lost.

Things to do and see are everywhere, but first you have to remind yourself to get off the highway. Once you do, you can rent a boat and find a secluded anchorage at which to fish, swim, and marvel at the sun, sea, and sky. In the Atlantic, you can dive to spectacular coral reefs or pursue dolphin, blue marlin, and other deep-water game fish. Along the Florida Bay coastline you can seek out the bonefish, snapper, snook, and tarpon that lurk in the grass flats and in the shallow, winding channels of the backcountry.

Along the reefs and among the islands are more than 600 kinds of fish. Diminutive deer and pale raccoons, related to but distinct from their mainland cousins, inhabit the Lower Keys. And throughout the islands you'll find such exotic West Indian plants as Jamaica dogwood, pigeon plum, poisonwood, satinwood, and silver and thatch palms, as well as tropical birds, including the great white heron, mangrove cuckoo, roseate spoonbill, and white-crowned pigeon.

Another Keys attraction is the weather: In the winter it's typically 10° warmer than on the mainland; in the summer it's usually 10° cooler. The Keys also get substantially less rain, around 30 inches annually compared to 55–60 inches in Miami and the Everglades. Most of the rain falls in quick downpours on summer afternoons. In winter, continental cold fronts occasionally stall over the Keys, dragging overnight temperatures down to the 40s.

The Keys were only sparsely populated until the early 20th century. In 1905, however, railroad magnate Henry Flagler began building the extension of his Florida railroad south from Homestead to Key West. His goal was to establish a rail link to the steamships that sailed between Key West and Havana, just 90 miles away across the Straits of Florida. The railroad arrived at Key West in 1912 and remained a lifeline of commerce until the Labor Day hurricane of 1935 washed out much of its roadbed. For three years thereafter, the only way in and out of Key West was by boat. The Overseas Highway, built over the railroad's old roadbeds and bridges, was completed in 1938, and many sections and bridges have recently been widened or replaced.

Although most mainlanders tend to see the Keys as much alike, they are actually quite different from each other. Key Largo, the largest and closest to the mainland, has become a bedroom community for Homestead, South Dade, and even the southern reaches of Miami. Most of the residents of the Upper Keys moved to Florida from the Northeast and Midwest; many are retirees. In the Middle Keys, fishing dominates the economy, and many residents descend from people who moved here from elsewhere in the South. The Lower Keys reflect a diverse population: native "Conchs" (white Key Westers, many of whom trace their ancestry to the Bahamas), freshwater Conchs (longtime residents who migrated from somewhere else years ago), gays (who now make up at least 20% of Key West's citizenry), Bahamians, Hispanics (primarily Cubans), recent refugees from the urban sprawl of Miami and Fort Lauderdale, transient Navy and Air Force personnel, students waiting tables, and a miscellaneous assortment of vagabonds, drifters, and dropouts in search of refuge at the end of the road.

EXPLORING

For the purposes of exploration, the Keys are divided into three tours: the Upper Keys, from Key Largo to Long Key Channel; the Middle Keys, from Long Key Channel through Marathon to Seven Mile Bridge; and the Lower Keys, from Seven Mile Bridge down to Key West. The fourth tour is a walking tour around Key West.

Finding your way around the Keys isn't hard once you understand the unique address system. The only address many people have is a mile marker (MM) number. The markers themselves are small green rectangular signs along the side of the Overseas Highway (U.S. 1). They begin with MM 126 a mile south of Florida City and end with MM 0 on the corner of Fleming and Whitehead streets in Key West. Keys residents use the abbreviation BS for the bay side of U.S. 1 and OS for the ocean side.

Tour 1: The Upper Keys

Numbers in the margin correspond to points of interest on the Florida Keys map.

This tour begins on Key Largo, the northeasternmost of the Florida Keys accessible by road. The tour assumes that you have come south from Florida City on Card Sound Road (Route 905A). If you take the Overseas Highway (U.S. 1) south from Florida City, you can begin the tour with Key Largo Undersea Park.

❶ Cross the Card Sound Bridge (toll: $1.25) onto **North Key Largo,** where a new fence along Card Sound Road forms the eastern boundary of **Crocodile Lakes National Wildlife Refuge.** In the refuge dwell some 300 to 500 crocodiles, the largest single concentration of these shy, elusive reptiles in North America. There's no visitor center here—just 6,800 acres of mangrove swamp and adjoining upland jungle. For your best chance to see a crocodile, park on the shoulder of Card Sound Road and scan the ponds along the road with binoculars. In winter, crocodiles often haul themselves out to sun on the banks farthest from the road. Don't leave the road shoulder; you could disturb tern nests on the nearby spoil banks or aggravate the rattlesnakes.

Take Card Sound Road to Route 905, turn right, and drive for 10 miles through **Key Largo Hammock,** the largest remaining stand of the vast West Indian tropical hardwood forest that once covered most of the upland areas in the Florida Keys. The state and federal governments are busy acquiring as much of the hammock as they can to protect it from further development, and they hope to establish visitor centers and nature trails. For now, it's best to admire this wilderness from the road. According to law-enforcement officials, this may be the most dangerous place in the United States, a haven for modern-day pirates and witches. The "pirates" are drug smugglers who land their cargo along the ocean shore or drop it into the forest from low-flying planes. The "witches" are practitioners of voodoo, Santeria, and other occult rituals. What's more, this jungle is full of poisonous plants. The most dangerous, the manchineel or "devil tree," has a toxin so potent that rainwater falling on its leaves and then onto a person's skin can cause sores that resist healing. Florida's first tourist, explorer Juan Ponce de León, died in 1521 from a superficial wound inflicted by an Indian arrowhead dipped in manchineel sap.

Just after joining U.S. 1, you'll see the **St. Justin Martyr Catholic Church** (MM 105.5, BS, ☎ 305/451–1316), notable for its architecture, which evokes the colors and materials of the Keys. Among its art are a beautiful fresco of the Last Supper and an altar table formed of a 5,000-pound mass of Carrara marble quarried in Tuscany.

❷ Continue on U.S. 1 toward **Key Largo.** At Transylvania Avenue (MM 103.2), turn left to visit the **Key Largo Undersea Park.** Family attractions include an underwater archaeology exhibit that you have to snorkel or dive to reach, underwater music, and an air-conditioned grotto theater with a 13-minute multimedia slide show devoted to the history of people and the sea. Also at the site are a pilot submarine, which gives three-hour tours for up to six people, and **Jules' Undersea Lodge** (*see* Dining and Lodging, *below*). *51 Shoreland Dr., ☎ 305/451–2353.* ☛ *Aquarium theater free; scuba fee, including tanks and gear: $20–$30; snorkel fee, including gear: $10, $35 for family of 4; submarine tour: $199.* ☉ *Daily 9–3.*

The Florida Keys

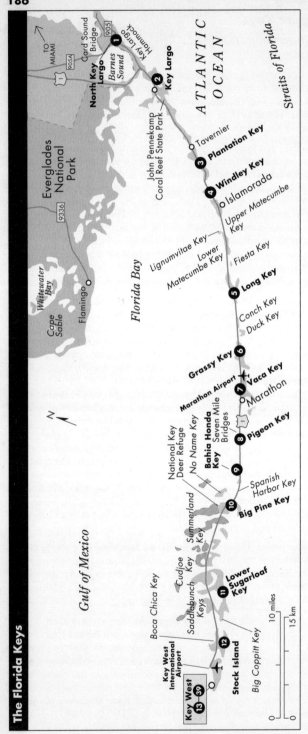

TIME OUT The first real hangout you come to in the Keys is the **Caribbean Club** (MM 104, BS, ☎ 305/451–9970), a local bar where scenes from the classic 1948 Bogart-Bacall flick *Key Largo* were shot. The place is plastered with memorabilia of Bogart films. Stop here for postcard sunsets.

Less than 1 mile south on the Overseas Highway is the **Maritime Museum of the Florida Keys.** This small but earnest museum offers exhibits depicting the history of shipwrecks and salvage efforts along the Keys: retrieved treasures, reconstructed wreck sites, and artifacts in various stages of preservation. Artifacts newly added in 1994 and 1995 have come from a fleet of treasure ships wrecked in 1715 by a hurricane 250 miles farther north along the Gulf Stream. *MM 102.5, BS,* ☎ *305/451–6444.* ☛ *$5 adults, $3 children 6–12.* ☺ *Fri.–Wed. 10–5.*

★ Across the road is the entrance to **John Pennekamp Coral Reef State Park.** The primary attraction here is diving on the offshore coral reefs (*see* Diving and Snorkeling *in* Sports and the Outdoors, *below*), but even a landlubber can appreciate the superb interpretive aquarium in the park's visitor center. A concessioner rents canoes and sailboats and offers boat trips to the reef. The park also includes a nature trail through a mangrove forest, a swimming beach, picnic shelters, a snack bar, a gift shop, and a campground. *MM 102.5, OS,* ☎ *305/451–1202.* ☛ *$3.25 per vehicle with up to 8 people, plus 50¢ per person county surcharge.* ☺ *Daily 8–sunset.*

Return to U.S. 1 and turn left. At MM 100, turn left again into the parking lot of the Holiday Inn Key Largo Resort. In the adjoining Key Largo Harbor Marina you'll find the **African Queen,** the steam-powered workboat on which Katharine Hepburn and Humphrey Bogart rode in their movie of the same name. Also displayed at the resort is the **Thayer IV,** a 22-foot mahogany Chris Craft built in 1951 and used by Ms. Hepburn and Henry Fonda in Fonda's last film, *On Golden Pond.*

❸ Continuing south on U.S. 1 you'll cross **Plantation Key** (MM 93–86), named for the plantings of limes, pineapples, and tomatoes cultivated here at the turn of the century. In 1991 woodcarver and teacher Laura Quinn moved her **Florida Keys Wild Bird Rehabilitation Center** here. Enter at the sign that says, "Tern Here." Nowhere else in the Keys can you see bird life so close up. Many are kept for life because of injuries that can't be healed. Others are brought for rehabilitation, and then set free. At any time the resident population can include ospreys, hawks, pelicans, cormorants, terns, and herons of various types. A short nature trail has been built into the mangrove forest (bring mosquito repellent), and a new office with a few items for sale has been added. A helpful notice explains that wild animals *do* feel pain when injured but don't scream because screaming would attract predators. *MM 93.6, BS, 93600 Overseas Hwy., Tavernier,* ☎ *305/852–4486.* ☛ *Donations welcome.* ☺ *Daily sunrise–sunset.*

❹ Next comes **Windley Key,** notable for **Theater of the Sea,** where 12 dolphins, two sea lions, and an extensive collection of tropical fish swim in the pits of a 1907 railroad quarry. Allow at least two hours to attend the dolphin and sea-lion shows and visit all the exhibits, which include an injured birds of prey display, a "bottomless" boat ride, touch tank, a pool where sharks are fed by a trainer, and a 300-gallon "living reef" aquarium with invertebrates and small reef fishes. For an additional fee, you can even swim with dolphins for 30 minutes, after a 30-minute orientation. *MM 84.5, OS, Box 407, Islamorada 33036,*

☎ *305/664–2431.* ☛ *$13.25 adults, $7.75 children 3–12. Swim with dolphins: $75, reservations required with 50% deposit; video or still photos: $70 (inquire at concession).* ⊙ *Daily 9:30–4.*

Watch for the **Hurricane Memorial** (MM 82) beside the highway. It marks the mass grave of 423 victims of the 1935 Labor Day hurricane. Many of those who perished were veterans who had been working on the Overseas Highway; they died when a tidal surge overturned a train sent to evacuate them. The art deco–style monument depicts wind-driven waves and palms bowing before the storm's fury.

Near here are three unusual state parks accessible only by water—and not easily at that; you'll need your own boat or a rental for each. The nearest boat source is **Robbie's Boat Rentals & Charters** (*see* Fishing and Water Sports *in* Sports and the Outdoors, *below*). The **San Pedro Underwater Archaeological Preserve** (*see* Diving and Snorkeling *in* Sports and the Outdoors, *below*) features an underwater, wrecked, 18th-century Spanish treasure fleet. You have to dive to see the remains.

Small as it is—only 11½ acres—**Indian Key State Historic Site** (OS) was a county-seat town and base for wreckers (early 19th-century shipwreck salvagers) until an Indian attack wiped out the settlement in 1840. Dr. Henry Perrine, a noted botanist, was killed in the raid. Today you can see his plants overgrowing the town's ruins. Though no guide is available, trails are marked and sites labeled.

A virgin hardwood forest still cloaks **Lignumvitae Key State Botanical Site** (BS), punctuated only by the home and gardens that chemical magnate William Matheson built as a private retreat in 1919. Even with your own boat, you need to reserve a guided ranger tour, given Thursday–Monday at 10:30, 1, and 2:30 and costing $1 for ages over six. Request a list of native and well-naturalized plants from the ranger. Contact **Long Key State Recreation Area** (MM 67.5, Box 776, Long Key 33001, ☎ 305/664–4815).

❺ Continue on the Overseas Highway down to **Long Key** (MM 72–67), where you'll pass a tract of undisturbed forest on the right (BS) just below MM 67. Watch for a historical marker partially obscured by foliage. Pull off the road here and explore **Layton Trail,** named after Del Layton, who incorporated the city of Layton in 1963 and served as its mayor until his death in 1987. The marker relates the history of the Long Key Viaduct, the first major bridge on the rail line, and the Long Key Fishing Club, which Henry Flagler established nearby in 1906. Zane Grey, the noted western novelist, was president of the club. It consisted of a lodge, guest cottages, and storehouses—all obliterated by the 1935 hurricane. The clearly marked trail, which should take 20–30 minutes to walk, leads through tropical hardwood forest to a rocky Florida Bay shoreline overlooking shallow grass flats offshore.

Less than 1 mile below Layton Trail, turn left into **Long Key State Recreation Area,** then left again to the parking area for the **Golden Orb Trail.** This trail leads onto a boardwalk through a mangrove swamp alongside a lagoon where many herons and other waterbirds congregate in winter. The park also has a campground, a picnic area, a canoe trail through a tidal lagoon, and a not-very-sandy beach fronting on a broad expanse of shallow grass flats. Bring a mask and snorkel to observe the marine life in this rich nursery area. *MM 67.5, OS, Box 776, Long Key 33001,* ☎ *305/664–4815.* ☛ *$3.25 per vehicle with up to 8 people, plus 50¢ per person county surcharge. Bike or canoe rental: $10 deposit and $2.14 per hr (includes tax).* ⊙ *Daily 8–sunset.*

Tour 2: The Middle Keys

Below Long Key, the Overseas Highway crosses Long Key Channel on a new highway bridge beside the railroad's **Long Key Viaduct.** The second-longest bridge on the former rail line, this 2-mile-long structure has 222 reinforced-concrete arches. It ends at **Conch Key** (MM 63), a tiny fishing and retirement community. Below Conch Key, the causeway on your left at MM 61 leads to **Duck Key,** site of an upscale residential community and the **Hawk's Cay Resort** (*see* Dining and Lodging, *below*).

⑥ Next comes **Grassy Key** (MM 60–57). Watch on the right for the **Dolphin Research Center** and the 35-foot-long concrete sculpture of the dolphin Theresa and her offspring Nat outside the former home of Milton Santini, creator of the original *Flipper* movie. The 14 dolphins here today frequently leave the fenced area that protects them from boaters and predators and return later. A half-day program called Dolph*Insight* teaches about dolphin biology and human-dolphin communications and allows you to touch the dolphins out of the water. A 2½-hour instruction-education program aptly called Swim with Dolphins enables you to do just that for 20 minutes. *MM 59, BS, Box 522875, Marathon Shores 33052, ☎ 305/289–1121. ☞ $9.50 adults, $7.50 senior citizens, $6 children 4–12; Dolph*Insight: $75; Swim with Dolphins: $90. Children 5–12 must swim with an accompanying, paying adult. Reserve for dolphin swim after 1st day of any month for the next month (e.g., Mar. 1 for Apr.). ☉ Wed.–Sun. 9–4; Dolph*Insight Wed., Sat., Sun. at 9:15; walking tours Wed.–Sun. at 10, 11, 12:30, 2, 3:30. Closed Thanksgiving, Dec. 25, Jan. 1.*

Continuing down U.S. 1, you will pass the road to **Key Colony Beach** (MM 54, OS), an incorporated city developed in the 1950s as a retirement community. It has a golf course and boating facilities. Soon
⑦ after, you'll cross a bridge onto **Vaca Key** and enter **Marathon** (MM 53–47), the commercial hub of the Middle Keys.

★ On your right, across from the Kmart, are the **Museums of Crane Point Hammock.** This group of museums, part of a 63-acre tract that includes the last known undisturbed thatch-palm hammock, is owned by the Florida Keys Land Trust, a private, nonprofit conservation group. In the **Museum of Natural History of the Florida Keys,** behind a stunning bronze-and-copper door crafted by Roy Butler of Plantation, Florida, are dioramas and displays on the Keys' geology, wildlife, and cultural history. Also here is the **Florida Keys Children's Museum.** Outside, on the 1-mile indigenous loop trail, you can visit the remnants of a **Bahamian village,** site of the restored **George Adderly House,** the oldest surviving example of Conch-style architecture outside Key West. From November to Easter, weekly docent-led hammock tours may be available; bring good walking shoes and bug repellent. During **Pirates in Paradise,** an annual four-day festival held the first weekend in May, the museums sponsor a celebration of the region's history throughout the Middle Keys. *MM 50, BS, 5550 Overseas Hwy., Box 536, Marathon 33050, ☎ 305/743–9100. ☞ $5 adults, $4 senior citizens, $2 students 13 and over (including tour). ☉ Mon.–Sat. 9–5, Sun. noon–5.*

Look to your left as you approach the new **Seven Mile Bridge;** there on **Knight's Key** (MM 47), the Pigeon Key Visitor's Center and gift shop have been set up in an old Florida East Coast Railway car. The key was an assembly site during construction of the bridge and today serves as
★ ⑧ the depot for shuttle access to **Pigeon Key** (MM 45). If you don't want to take the shuttle, you can walk across a 2-mile stretch of the **Old Seven**

Mile Bridge (the entrance is across the highway from the shuttle depot); no private cars are allowed. Listed on the National Register of Historic Places, the old bridge is maintained by the Florida Department of Transportation to provide access to the key. An engineering marvel in its day, the bridge rested on 546 concrete piers spanning the broad expanse of water that separates the Middle and Lower keys. Pigeon Key itself was once a railroad work camp and later site of a bar and restaurant, a park, and government administration building. Should you decide to tour the key, where portions of the Arnold Schwarzenegger movie *True Lies* were filmed, you can watch a 1930 "home movie" of a trip on the Florida East Coast Railway from Key West to Miami. In 1993 the nonprofit Pigeon Key Foundation leased the site, a National Historic District, from Monroe County and started developing it as a center focusing on the encompassing culture of the Florida Keys. Its first project is the restoration of the old railroad work-camp buildings, the earliest of which date from 1908, and a museum recalling the history of the railroad and the Keys is taking shape, too. Among its first exhibits are two old Cuban fishing boats. The site is also being used for research on the Florida Bay system and for cancer studies involving sharks, conducted by Mote Marine Laboratories of Sarasota. For information, contact the Pigeon Key Foundation. *Box 500130, Pigeon Key 33050, ☎ 305/289–0025, FAX 305/289–1065. Shuttle: $1 each way; key admission and tour: $2. Shuttle: Tues.–Sun. 9–5.*

Return to U.S. 1 and proceed across the new Seven Mile Bridge (actually 6.79 miles long). Built between 1980 and 1982 at a cost of $45 million, it is believed to be the world's longest segmental bridge, with 39 expansion joints separating its cement sections. Each April runners gather in Marathon for the annual Seven Mile Bridge Run.

Tour 3: The Lower Keys

9 ★ On **Bahia Honda Key,** you'll find **Bahia Honda State Park** and its sandy (most of the time) beach. Lateral drift builds up the beach in summer; storms whisk away much of the sand in winter. The park's Silver Palm Trail leads through a dense tropical forest where you can see rare West Indian plants, including the Geiger tree, sea lavender, Key spider lily, bay cedar, thatch and silver palms, and several species found nowhere else in the Florida Keys: the West Indies yellow satinwood, Catesbaea, Jamaica morning glory, and wild dilly. The park also includes a campground (call for reservations up to 60 days in advance), cabins, gift shop, snack bar, marina, and dive shop offering offshore-reef snorkel trips and, new since 1993, scuba trips and boat rentals. *MM 37, OS, Box 782, Big Pine Key 33043, ☎ 305/872–2353. ☛ $3.25 per vehicle with up to 8 people, plus 50¢ per person county surcharge. ⊙ Daily 8–sunset; concession open 8–5 (food to 6:30).*

10 Cross the Bahia Honda Bridge and continue past Spanish Harbor Key and Spanish Harbor Channel onto **Big Pine Key** (MM 32–30), where signs alert drivers to be on the lookout for Key deer. Every year cars kill 50 to 60 of the delicate creatures. A subspecies of the Virginia white-tailed deer, Key deer once ranged throughout the Lower and Middle keys, but hunting and habitat destruction reduced the population to fewer than 50 in 1947. In 1954 the **National Key Deer Refuge** was established to protect them, and the deer herd grew to about 750 by the early 1970s. But the government owns only about a third of Big Pine Key, and as the human population on the remaining land grew during the 1980s, the deer herd declined again until today only 250 to 300 remain. To visit refuge headquarters, turn right at the stoplight, bear left at the fork onto Key Deer Boulevard (Route 940), and follow the signs. A new, more accessible refuge office has opened in the Big Pine Shopping Plaza (off Wilder Rd., ☎ 305/872–2239).

The best place in the refuge to see Key deer is on **No Name Key,** a sparsely populated island just east of Big Pine Key. To get there from refuge headquarters, return east on Watson Boulevard to Wilder Road, and turn left. Go 3½ miles from Key Deer Boulevard across the Bogie Channel Bridge and onto No Name Key. At the end of the road you can get out of your car to walk around, but close all doors and windows to keep raccoons from wandering in. Deer may turn up along this road at any time of day—especially in early morning and late afternoon. Admire their beauty, but don't try to feed them—it's against the law.

Continue on across **Big Torch, Middle Torch,** and **Little Torch keys** (named for the torchwood tree, which settlers used for kindling because it burns easily even when green). Next comes **Ramrod Key** (MM 27.5), a base for divers headed for **Looe Key National Marine Sanctuary** (*see* Diving and Snorkeling *in* Sports and the Outdoors, *below*), 5 miles offshore.

TIME OUT   Enjoy outstanding Keys cooking at **Mangrove Mama's** (MM 20, BS, Sugarloaf Key, ☎ 305/745–3030), a lattice-front Conch house, a remnant from around 1919, when trains outnumbered cars in the Keys. Fresh fish, seafood, some decent beers, and rave-worthy Key lime pie are served. Concrete floors, Keys art, a Tennessee oak bar, and lights twinkling at night in the banana trees all contribute to the romantic ambience here.

⓫ On **Lower Sugarloaf Key,** a performing dolphin named Sugar lives in a lagoon behind the very visible **Sugar Loaf Lodge** (*see* Dining and Lodging, *below*). From the motel, follow the paved road northwest ⁴⁄₁₀ mile, past an airstrip, and bear right down a newly paved road. One-tenth of a mile later, in bleak, gravel-strewn surroundings, you'll find a reconstruction of R. C. Perky's **bat tower.** Perky, an early real-estate promoter, built the tower in 1929 to attract mosquito-eating bats, but no bats ever roosted in it.

Continue on through the **Saddlebunch Keys** and **Big Coppitt Key** to **Boca Chica Key** (MM 10), site of the Key West Naval Air Station. You may
⓬ hear the roar of jet-fighter planes in this vicinity. At last you reach **Stock Island** (MM 5), the gateway to Key West. Pass the Key West Resort Golf Course, turn right onto Junior College Road, and pause at the **Key West Botanical Garden,** where the Key West Garden Club has labeled an extensive assortment of native and exotic tropical trees. You can continue less than ½ mile farther on this road to reach Florida Keys Community College and its Tennessee Williams Fine Arts Center (*see* The Arts and Nightlife, *below*) or backtrack and turn right on the Overseas Highway to enter Key West.

Tour 4: Key West

In April 1982 the U.S. Border Patrol threw a roadblock across the Overseas Highway just south of Florida City to catch drug runners and illegal aliens. Traffic backed up for miles as Border Patrol agents searched vehicles and demanded that the occupants prove U.S. citizenship. City officials in Key West, outraged at being treated like foreigners by the federal government, staged a mock secession and formed their own "nation," the so-called Conch Republic. They hoisted a flag and distributed mock border passes, visas, and Conch currency. The embarrassed

Border Patrol dismantled its roadblock, and now an annual festival recalls the secessionists' victory.

The episode exemplifies Key West's odd station in Florida affairs. Situated 150 miles from Miami and just 90 miles from Havana, this tropical island city has always maintained its strong sense of detachment, even after it was connected to the rest of the United States—by the railroad in 1912 and by the Overseas Highway in 1938.

⑬ The U.S. government acquired **Key West** from Spain in 1821 along with the rest of Florida. The Spanish had named the island Cayo Hueso (Bone Key) after the Native American skeletons they found on its shores. In 1822 Uncle Sam sent Commodore David S. Porter to the Keys to chase pirates away.

For three decades, the primary industry in Key West was "wrecking"—rescuing people and salvaging cargo from ships that foundered on the nearby reefs. According to some reports, when pickings were lean, the wreckers hung out lights to lure ships aground. Their business declined after 1852, when the federal government began building lighthouses along the reefs.

In 1845 the Army started construction of Ft. Taylor, which held Key West for the Union during the Civil War. After the war, an influx of Cuban dissidents unhappy with Spain's rule brought the cigar industry to Key West. Fishing, shrimping, and sponge gathering became important industries, and a pineapple-canning factory opened. Major military installations were established during the Spanish-American War and World War I. Through much of the 19th century and into the second decade of the 20th, Key West was Florida's wealthiest city in per-capita terms.

In the 1920s the local economy began to unravel. Modern ships no longer needed to provision in Key West, cigar making moved to Tampa, Hawaii dominated the pineapple industry, and the sponges succumbed to a blight. Then the Depression hit, and even the military moved out. By 1934 half the population was on relief. The city defaulted on its bond payments, and the Federal Emergency Relief Administration took over the city and county governments.

Federal officials began promoting Key West as a tourist destination. They attracted 40,000 visitors during the 1934–35 winter season. Then the 1935 Labor Day hurricane struck the Middle Keys, sparing Key West but wiping out the railroad and the tourist trade. For three years, until the Overseas Highway opened, the only way in and out of town was by boat.

Ever since, Key West's fortunes have waxed and waned with the vagaries of world affairs. An important naval center during World War II and the Korean conflict, the island remains a strategic listening post on the doorstep of Fidel Castro's Cuba.

As a tourist destination, Key West has a lot to sell—superb frost-free weather with an average temperature of 79°F, quaint 19th-century architecture, and a laid-back lifestyle. Promoters have fostered fine restaurants, galleries and shops, and new museums to interpret the city's intriguing past. There's also a growing calendar of artistic and cultural events and a lengthening list of annual festivals—including the Conch Republic celebration in April, Hemingway Days in July, and a Halloween Fantasy Fest rivaling the New Orleans Mardi Gras. No other city of its size—a mere 2 miles by 4 miles—offers the joie de vivre of this one.

Yet as elsewhere that preservation has successfully revived once tired towns, next have come those unmindful of style, eager for a buck. Duval Street is becoming show biz—an open-air mall of T-shirt shops and tour shills. Mass marketers directing the town's tourism have attracted cruise ships, which dwarf the town's skyline and flood Duval Street with day-trippers who gawk at the earringed hippies with dogs in their bike baskets and the otherwise oddball lot of locals. You can still find fun, but the best advice is to come sooner rather than later.

Numbers in the margin correspond to points of interest on the Key West map.

★ ⑭ Start your tour at **Mallory Square,** named for Stephen Mallory, secretary of the Confederate Navy, who later owned the Mallory Steamship Line. On the nearby **Mallory Dock,** a nightly sunset celebration draws street performers, food vendors, and thousands of onlookers. (Parking is $1.50 an hour.)

⑮ Facing Mallory Square is the **Key West Aquarium,** which features hundreds of brightly colored tropical fish and other fascinating sea creatures from the waters around Key West. A touch tank enables you to handle starfish, sea cucumbers, horseshoe and hermit crabs, even horse and queen conchs—living totems of the Conch Republic. Built in 1934 by the Works Progress Administration as the world's first open-air aquarium, the building has been enclosed for all-weather viewing, though an outdoor area with a small Atlantic shores exhibit, including red mangroves, remains. *1 Whitehead St., ☎ 305/296–2051. ☞ $6.50 adults, $5.50 senior citizens, $3.50 children 8–15. ⊙ Daily 10–6; guided tours (with shark feeding) at 11, 1, 3, 4:30.*

TIME OUT For $4 you can get six (a dozen for $7.50) of what may be the Keys' most authentic conch fritters at the strictly stand-up **Original Conch Fritters** (1 Whitehead St., ☎ 305/294–4849), previously a Cuban snack stand from the '30s. Current owners flaunt their buttermilk and peanut oil recipe. Aficionados say it's the conch that counts.

Turn east on Front Street and turn right to **Clinton Place,** where a Civil War memorial to Union soldiers stands in a triangle formed by the intersection of Front, Greene, and Whitehead streets. On your right is the **U.S. Post Office and Customs House,** a Romanesque revival structure designed by prominent local architect William Kerr and completed in 1891. Tour guides claim that federal bureaucrats required the roof to have a steep pitch so it wouldn't collect snow.

⑯ On your left is the **Mel Fisher Maritime Heritage Society Museum,** which displays gold and silver bars, coins, jewelry, and other artifacts recovered in 1985 from the Spanish treasure ships *Nuestra Señora de Atocha* and *Santa Margarita.* The two galleons foundered in a hurricane in 1622 near the Marquesas Keys, 40 miles west of Key West. In the museum you can lift a gold bar weighing 6.3 Troy pounds and see a 77.76-carat natural emerald crystal worth almost $250,000. *200 Greene St., ☎ 305/294–2633. ☞ $6 adults; $5 AAA and AARP members, military personnel; $2.50 children 6–12. ⊙ Daily 9:30–5 (last video showing 4:30).*

Mel Fisher's museum occupies a former Navy storehouse that he bought from Pritam Singh, a Key West hippie-turned-millionaire. Singh has been
⑰ the developer (lately along with banks) behind **Truman Annex,** a 103-acre former military parade grounds and barracks. During World War II, Truman Annex housed some 18,000 military and civilian employees. Singh is successfully transforming it into a suburban community

Key West

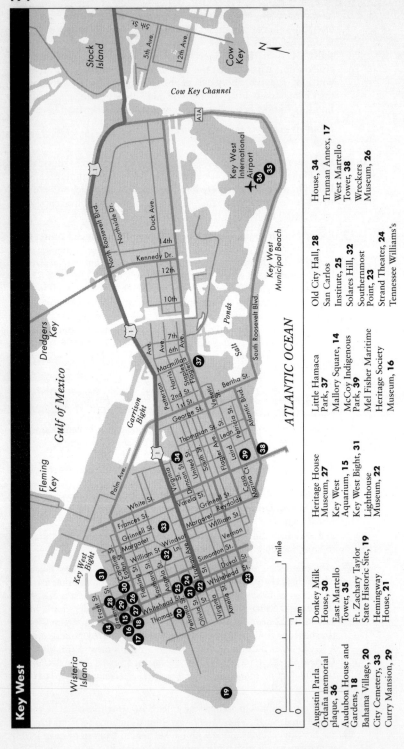

Augustin Parla
Ordaña memorial
plaque, **36**
Audubon House and
Gardens, **18**
Bahama Village, **20**
City Cemetery, **33**
Curry Mansion, **29**

Donkey Milk
House, **30**
East Martello
Tower, **35**
Ft. Zachary Taylor
State Historic Site, **19**
Hemingway
House, **21**

Heritage House
Museum, **27**
Key West
Aquarium, **15**
Key West Bight, **31**
Lighthouse
Museum, **22**

Little Hamaca
Park, **37**
Mallory Square, **14**
McCoy Indigenous
Park, **39**
Mel Fisher Maritime
Heritage Society
Museum, **16**

Old City Hall, **28**
San Carlos
Institute, **25**
Solares Hill, **32**
Southernmost
Point, **23**
Strand Theater, **24**
Tennessee Williams's

House, **34**
Truman Annex, **17**
West Martello
Tower, **38**
Wreckers
Museum, **26**

of pastel, picket, and lattice charm, a mix of affordable condominiums and grassy-yard family homes surrounded by colorful bougainvillea and allamanda vines. Recent additions have included three-story town houses in the old brick machine shop. The whole community, set behind high black wrought-iron gates, is designed in the Victorian style that knits Old Town together. Pedestrians and cyclists are welcome on the grounds daily between 8 AM and sunset. Also on the grounds is the **Harry S. Truman Little White House Museum,** the president's former vacation home, with Truman family memorabilia on display. *111 Front St., ☎ 305/294–9911. ☛ $6 adults, $3 children under 13. ☉ Daily 9–5.*

⑱ From Mel Fisher's museum, cross Whitehead Street to visit the **Audubon House and Gardens.** A museum in this three-story dwelling built in the mid-1840s commemorates ornithologist John James Audubon's 1832 visit to Key West. On display are several rooms of period antiques, a children's room, and a large collection of Audubon engravings. A docent guides you through the first floor; then proceed on your own through the upper stories. A self-guided walking tour of the tropical gardens is keyed to an updated 12-page brochure. *205 Whitehead St., ☎ 305/294–2116. ☛ $6 adults; $5 senior citizens, AAA members, military personnel; $4 children 6–12; $2 children under 6. ☉ Daily 9:30–5.*

Continue on to **301 Whitehead Street,** which was the original headquarters of Pan American Airways, one of the first U.S. airlines to operate scheduled international air service. Its inaugural flight took off from Key West International Airport on October 28, 1927, and passengers paid $9.95 for the 90-mile, 80-minute flight from Key West to Havana aboard *The General Machado,* a Fokker F–7 trimotor. The building is now occupied by **Kelly's,** a popular local bar, grill, and the continental United States' southernmost brewery.

TIME OUT Pause for a libation at the open-air **Green Parrot Bar** (601 Whitehead St., corner of Southard St., ☎ 305/294–6133). Built in 1890, the bar is said to be Key West's oldest, a sometimes-rowdy saloon where locals outnumber the tourists, especially on weekends when bands play.

⑲ Turn right onto Southard Street and follow the signs to the **Ft. Zachary Taylor State Historic Site.** Built between 1845 and 1866, the fort served as a base for the Union blockade of Confederate shipping during the Civil War. More than 1,500 Confederate vessels captured while trying to run the blockade were brought to Key West's harbor and detained under the fort's guns. What you will see at Ft. Taylor today is a fort within a fort; a new moat suggests how the fort originally looked when it was surrounded by water. Because of an artificial reef, snorkeling is excellent here, except when the wind blows south–southwest and muddies the water. *☎ 305/292–6713. ☛ $3.25 per vehicle with up to 8 people, $1 per pedestrian or bicyclist, plus 50¢ per person county surcharge. ☉ Park: daily 8–sunset; fort: 9–5; free 50-min tour daily at noon and 2.*

⑳ Return to Thomas Street, and go right two blocks to the corner of Petronia Street and the heart of **Bahama Village,** where Bahamians settled Key West a century and a half ago.

★ **㉑** Take Petronia Street east back to Whitehead Street, turn right, and go one block to the **Hemingway House,** now a museum dedicated to the novelist's life and work. Built in 1851, this two-story Spanish colonial dwelling was the first house in Key West to have running water and a fireplace. Hemingway bought the house in 1931 and wrote about 70% of his life's work here, including *For Whom the Bell Tolls* and

The Old Man and the Sea. Three months after Hemingway died in 1961, local jeweler Bernice Dickson bought the house and its contents from Hemingway's estate and two years later opened it as a museum. Of special interest are the huge bed with a headboard made from a 17th-century Spanish monastery gate, a ceramic cat by Pablo Picasso (a gift to Hemingway from the artist), the hand-blown Venetian glass chandelier in the dining room, and the swimming pool. The museum staff gives guided tours rich with anecdotes about Hemingway and his family and feeds the more than 50 feline habitants, descendants of Hemingway's own 50 cats. Tours begin every 10 minutes and take 25–30 minutes; then you're free to explore on your own. *907 Whitehead St.,* ☎ *305/294–1575.* ☛ *$6.50 adults, $2.50 children 6–12.* ☉ *Daily 9–5.*

Down the block and across the street from Hemingway House (behind a spic-and-span white picket fence) is the **Lighthouse Museum,** a 92-foot lighthouse built in 1847 and an adjacent 1887 clapboard house, where the keeper lived. You can climb 98 steps to the top of the lighthouse for a spectacular view of the island town, as well as of the first order (biggest) Fresnel lens, installed at a cost of $1 million in the 1860s. On display in the keeper's quarters are vintage photographs, ship models, nautical charts, and lighthouse artifacts from all along the Key reefs. *938 Whitehead St.,* ☎ *305/294–0012.* ☛ *$5 adults, $1 children 7–12.* ☉ *Daily 9:30–5 (last admission 4:30).*

Continue to the foot of Whitehead Street, where a huge concrete marker wrongly proclaims this spot to be the **Southernmost Point** in the United States. Most tourists snapping pictures of each other in front of the marker are oblivious to Key West's real southernmost point, on a nearby Navy base off limits to civilians but visible through the fence to your right. Bahamian vendors of shells and straw hats line the sidewalk and blow a conch horn at passing Conch Tour Trains and Old Town Trolleys.

Turn left on South Street. To your right are two dwellings both claimed to be the **Southernmost House:** the cream-brick Queen Anne mansion at 1400 Duval Street and the Spanish-style home at 400 South Street, built in the 1940s by Thelma Strabel, author of *Reap the Wild Wind,* a novel about the wreckers who salvaged ships aground on the reef in Key West's early days. Neither is open to the public. Turn right onto Duval Street, which ends at the Atlantic Ocean and the **Southernmost Beach** (*see* Beaches, *below*).

TIME OUT They don't call it the southernmost eatery (which it is), but it's worth stopping for breakfast, lunch, or dinner at the **South Beach Seafood & Raw Bar** (1405 Duval St., ☎ 305/294–2727) alongside the Southernmost Beach.

Now go north on Duval Street toward downtown Key West. Pause at the **Cuban Club** (1108 Duval St.). The original building—a social club for the Cuban community—burned in 1983 and has been replaced by shops and luxury condominiums; some of the original facade was retained. Continuing on, you'll pass several art galleries between the 1100 and 800 blocks.

Pause to admire the colorful marquee and ornamental facade of the **Strand Theater,** built in 1918 by Cuban craftsmen. After a period as a movie theater and a music hall, the Strand is now the **Odditorium,** one of a chain of **Ripley's Believe It or Not** museums, displaying weird and eccentric artifacts. *527 Duval St.,* ☎ *305/293–9686.* ☛ *$8.95 adults, $5.95 children 4–11.* ☉ *Sun.–Thurs. 10–11, Fri.–Sat. 10–midnight.*

★ ㉕ Continue on to the **San Carlos Institute,** a Cuban-American heritage center, which houses a museum and research library focusing on the history of Key West and of 19th- and 20th-century Cuban exiles. The San Carlos Institute was founded in 1871 by Cuban immigrants who wanted to preserve their language, customs, and heritage while organizing the struggle for Cuba's independence from Spain. Cuban patriot Jose Martí delivered many famous speeches from the balcony of the auditorium. Opera star Enrico Caruso sang in the 400-seat hall of the Opera House, which reportedly has the best acoustics of any concert hall in the South. The original building (built in 1871) burned in the Key West fire of 1886, in which two-thirds of the city was destroyed, and a second version succumbed to the hurricane of 1919. The current building was completed in 1924, but after Cuba and the United States broke off diplomatic relations in 1961, it deteriorated. It was saved from demolition when Miami attorney Rafael A. Peñalver, Jr., secured a $3 million state grant for its restoration. The building re-opened January 3, 1992, exactly 100 years after Martí founded the Cuban Revolutionary Party here. A self-guided tour takes close to an hour; on weekends you can top it off by watching the almost hour–long documentary *Nostalgia Cubano,* about Cuba in the 1930s to 1950s. *516 Duval St.,* ☎ *305/294–3887.* 🖝 *$3 adults, $1 children.* ☉ *Tues.–Fri. 11–5, Sat. 11–9, Sun. 11–6.*

㉖ Continue north on Duval Street to the **Wreckers Museum,** alleged to be the oldest house in Key West. It was built in 1829 as the home of Francis Watlington, a sea captain and wrecker. He was also a Florida state senator but resigned to serve in the Confederate Navy during the Civil War. Six of the home's eight rooms are now a museum furnished with 18th- and 19th-century antiques. In an upstairs bedroom is an eight-room dollhouse of Conch design, outfitted with tiny Victorian furniture. *322 Duval St.,* ☎ *305/294–9502.* 🖝 *$3 adults, 50¢ children 3–12.* ☉ *Daily 10–4.*

At Caroline Street, turn left and go half a block to the house known ㉗ as **Heritage House Museum.** This was until recently the home of Jessie Porter Newton, grand dame of Old Town restoration. The Caribbean-colonial house dates from the 1830s, when it was home to ship's captain George Carey, and it includes among its original furnishings antiques and seafaring artifacts from 19th-century China. Out back in beautiful gardens is a cottage that was often occupied by the late poet Robert Frost, and where recordings of his poetry can be heard. *410 Caroline St.,* ☎ *305/296–3573.* 🖝 *$6 ages over 12, $5 senior citizens.* ☉ *Mon.–Sat. 10–5, Sun. 1–5.*

Return to Duval Street, turn left, continue to Greene Street, and turn ㉘ right to see the restored **Old City Hall** (510 Greene St.), where the City Commission has its meetings. Designed by William Kerr, the architect responsible for the customhouse, the hall opened in 1891. It has a rectangular tower with four clock faces and a fire bell. The ground floor was used as a city market for many years. Inside Old City Hall is a permanent exhibition of old Key West photographs, including an 1845 daguerreotype, the oldest known photographic image of Key West. Next door, on the second-story landing are the offices of the **Historic Florida Keys Preservation Board** (☎ 305/292–6718), the principal information source about preservation throughout the Keys.

TIME OUT Stop in at the **Cuban Coffee Queen Cafe** (512 Greene St., ☎ 305/296–2711), run by a mother-daughter team from Central Chaparra, in Cuba's

Oriente Province. Locals love the hot *bollos* (baked buns with butter), conch fritters, pigs' feet, ham and eggs, sangria, and Cuban coffee.

㉙ At Simonton Street, turn right, go one block to Caroline Street, and turn right again. The 22-room Victorian **Curry Mansion,** built in 1899 for Milton Curry, the son of Florida's first millionaire, is an adaptation of a Parisian town house. It has Key West's only widow's walk open to the public. Owners Edith and Al Amsterdam have restored and redecorated most of the house and turned it into a winning bed-and-breakfast (*see* Dining and Lodging, *below*). Take an unhurried self-guided tour with a comprehensive brochure, which includes floor plans and is full of detailed information about the history and contents of the house. *511 Caroline St.,* ☎ *305/294–5349.* ☞ *$5 adults, $1 children under 12.* ⊙ *Daily 10–5.*

㉚ Return to Simonton Street; turn right and then left on Eaton Street to get to the **Donkey Milk House.** This Key West classical revival house was built around 1866 by prominent businessman and U.S. marshal Peter "Dynamite" Williams, a hero of the great fire of 1886. Antiques and artifacts fill its two balconied floors. The house won a 1992 restoration award. *613 Eaton St.,* ☎ *305/296–1866.* ☞ *$5.* ⊙ *Daily 10–5.*

㉛ Return to Simonton Street, turn right and then right again on Greene Street. A three-block walk with a jog at Elizabeth Street onto Lazy Way brings you to the **Key West Bight** (also known as Harbor Walk). Formerly site of the Singleton Shrimp Fleet and Ice & Fish House, this is the last funky area of Old Key West. The nearby Turtle Kraals is a historic site, and a restaurant adjoins. Also in the area are numerous charter boats, classic old yachts, and the **Reef Relief Environmental Center** (201 William St., ☎ 305/394–3100), a public facility with videos, displays, and free information about the coral reef, open 9–5 weekdays and most weekends in season. Next door is the **Waterfront Market** (*see* Shopping, *below*), the only natural-foods market and juice bar in town.

TIME OUT Across the street is **Schooner Wharf Bar** (202 William St., ☎ 305/ 292–9520), a laid-back tiki hut called "the last little piece of Old Key West." It's where the town's waiters and waitresses hang out. You can hear live music weekends (and sometimes at other times) in the warehouse space next door.

㉜ Go south on Margaret Street to Angela Street. To the west rises **Solares Hill,** the "steepest" natural grade in Key West. Its summit, the island's loftiest elevation, is 18 feet above sea level.

★ ㉝ Go down Windsor Lane to Passover Lane, turn left, and go to Margaret Street and the entrance of the **City Cemetery.** Clustered near a flagpole resembling a ship's mast are the graves of 22 sailors killed in the sinking of the battleship U.S.S. *Maine.* Historian Sharon Wells leads six guided tours a week from the sexton's office at Margaret and Angela streets. No reservations are necessary. ☎ *305/296–3913 for tour information.* ☞ *Free; tour donation: $5.* ⊙ *Sunrise–sunset; tours Tues., Wed. at 9, 10, 11.*

㉞ Walk east to White Street, turn right and go south to Duncan Street, and then go four blocks east to Leon Street. Here you find **Tennessee Williams's House** (1431 Duncan St.), a modest two-story, red-shutter Bahamian-style cottage behind a white picket fence, where the playwright lived from 1949 until his death in 1983. After years of neglect, the house was purchased in 1992 and fixed up by a couple named Paradise. The house is not open to the public, nor is there any historical marker.

The last few Key West sights are better visited on wheels, either car or bicycle. Take Truman Avenue (U.S. 1) east from downtown, past **Garrison Bight Yacht Basin,** where many charter fishing boats dock. Continue east, as U.S. 1 becomes North Roosevelt Boulevard. Past the turnoff to Stock Island at the east end of Key West, North Roosevelt Boulevard (now Route A1A) swings south and then, at the bottom of the island, turns west, becoming South Roosevelt Boulevard. On your left is a small community of houseboats. On your right, just past the entrance to Key West International Airport, stands **East Martello Tower,** one of two Civil War forts of similar design overlooking the Atlantic Ocean. Housed in a portion of this tower (restored in 1993) are military uniforms and relics of the battleship U.S.S. *Maine,* which was blown up in Havana Harbor in 1898. The Key West Art and Historical Society operates a museum in East Martello's vaulted casemates. The collection includes Stanley Papio's "junk art" sculptures, Cuban primitive artist Mario Sanchez's chiseled and painted wood carvings of historic Key West street scenes, memorabilia from movies shot on location in the Keys, and a display of books by many of the 60-some famous writers (including seven Pulitzer Prize winners) who have lived in Key West. Historical exhibits present a chronological history of the Florida Keys. A circular 48-step staircase in the central tower leads to a platform overlooking the airport and surrounding waters. *3501 S. Roosevelt Blvd.,* ☎ *305/296–6206 or 305/296–3913.* ☛ *$5 adults, $1 children.* ☺ *Daily 9:30–5.*

Walk east to the terminal of Key West International Airport. In the front of the parking lot, facing the terminal, is the **Agustin Parla Ordaña memorial plaque.** Born in Key West in 1887 to Cuban exile parents, Ordana was the first to fly the 119 miles from Key West to El Mariel, Cuba, in 1913.

Continue west on South Roosevelt Boulevard past **Smathers Beach** (*see* Beaches, *below*) on your left. To your right are the **salt ponds** where early residents evaporated seawater to collect salt. This area, a vestige of the old Key West and for years a wildlife sanctuary, was saved from condo development in 1991 and turned into **Little Hamaca Park.** To enter, take Bertha Street to Flagler Avenue (Route 5-A), turning right and right again onto Government Road. The entrance is just ahead, and a boardwalk leads into the natural area. (Although the sign says that the park is open 7 AM to dusk, the gates are not necessarily open. Cyclists lift their bikes over.)

Return to Flagler Avenue, turn left on First Street, and turn right onto Atlantic Boulevard. Near White Street, where Atlantic Boulevard ends, are **Higgs Memorial Beach** (*see* Beaches, *below*) and **West Martello Tower,** a fort built in 1861 and used as a lookout post during the Spanish-American War. Within its walls the Key West Garden Club maintains an art gallery and tropical garden. *Atlantic Blvd. and White St.,* ☎ *305/294–3210.* ☛ *Donations welcome.* ☺ *Wed.–Sun. 9:30–3:30. Closed holidays.*

Turn right onto White Street; on your right is the city-operated **McCoy Indigenous Park.** The park contains more than 100 species of trees and shrubs; the largest collection of native tropical plants in the Florida Keys, including many fruit-bearing trees; migrating songbirds spring and fall; and many species of colorful butterflies. *Atlantic Blvd. and White St.,* ☎ *305/292–8155.* ☛ *Free.* ☺ *Weekdays 7–4.*

SHOPPING

In season, supermarkets and roadside stands sell tropical fruits. Look for Key limes (April to January), guavas (August to October), litchi nuts (June), and sapodillas (February to March).

Islamorada

Rain Barrel (MM 86.7, BS, 86700 Overseas Hwy.), a 3-acre crafts village attended by free-running cats, represents 450 local and national artists and has eight resident artists. During the third weekend of March each year, the largest arts show of the Keys takes place here, when some 20,000 visitors view the work of 100 artists. A tearoom and bakery are to be added by 1996.

Where salvage master Art McKee ran McKee's Treasure Museum in the 1950s and an enormous fabricated crustacean now stands, a dozen crafts and specialty shops plus the excellent little Made to Order eat-in and carryout restaurant operate as **Treasure Village** (MM 86.7, OS).

Key West

Like a parody of Duval Street T-shirt shops, the hole-in-the-wall **Art Attack** (606 Duval St., ☎ 305/294–7131) throws in every icon and trinket anyone nostalgic for the days of peace and love might fancy: beads, necklaces, medallions, yin-yang banners, harmony bells, and of course Dead and psychedelic T-shirts.

Take time, even if you're not buying, to enjoy the smells at **Bailey's Place Espresso Bar** (1111 Duval St., ☎ 305/292–3739), the "southernmost coffee roasters." Dozens of varieties of beans plus fresh-baked pastries are for sale.

Fast Buck Freddie's (500 Duval St., ☎ 305/294–2007) sells imaginative items you'd never dream of, including battery-operated alligators that eat Muenster cheese, banana leaf–shape furniture, fish-shape flatwear, and every flamingo item anyone's ever come up with.

Fausto's Food Palace (522 Fleming St., ☎ 305/296–5663; 1105 White St., ☎ 305/294–5221) may be under a roof, but it's a market in the traditional town-square style. Since 1926, Fausto's has been where everyone meets to catch up on the week's gossip, and it's also where you chill out in summer, because it's got the heaviest air-conditioning in town.

The oldest gallery in Key West, **Gingerbread Square Gallery** (1207 Duval St., ☎ 305/296–8900) mainly represents Keys artists who have attained national prominence.

Haitian Art Co. (600 Frances St., ☎ 305/296–8932) sells the works of 200 or more Haitian artists.

H. T. Chittum & Co. (725 Duval St., ☎ 305/292–9002) sells the kind of informal clothing beloved by Key Westers (and Key West visitors)—aviator hats and fish-cleaning knives as well as smart ready-to-wear. There's also a branch in Islamorada (MM 82.7, OS, ☎ 305/664–4421).

Inter Arts (506 Southard St., ☎ 305/296–4081) features textiles to wear, display, walk on, and keep you warm in bed.

Key West Aloe (524 Front St., ☎ 305/294–5592 or 800/445–2563) was founded in a garage in 1971; today it produces some 300 perfume, sunscreen, and skin-care products for men and women. You can also visit the factory store (Greene and Simonton Sts.), open seven days a week, where you can watch the staff measure and blend ingredients, then fill and seal the containers.

Key West Hand Print Fabrics (201 Simonton St., ☏ 305/294–9535) was made famous in the 1960s by Lilly Pulitzer's designs. Weekday shoppers can watch workers making hand-printed fabric on five 50-yard-long tables in the Curry Warehouse, a brick building erected in 1878 to store tobacco. The shop is open seven days.

Key West Island Bookstore (513 Fleming St., ☏ 305/294–2904) is the literary bookstore of the large Key West writers' community.

In a town with a gazillion T-shirt shops, **Last Flight Out** (710 Duval St., ☏ 305/294–8008) offers classic namesake T's that recall the pre–World War II heyday of tourist flights between Key West and Havana.

Lazy Way Shops (Elizabeth and Greene Sts., ☏ 305/294–3003) sells a constantly changing sampling of local arts and crafts in an old shrimpers' net shop.

Lucky Street Gallery (919 Duval St., ☏ 305/294–3973) shows the best tropical work for hanging and mounting.

L. Valladares & Son (1200 Duval St., ☏ 305/296–5032) is a fourth-generation newsstand selling more than 2,000 periodicals and 3,000 paperback books along with Florida, national, and international newspapers.

Pelican Poop (314 Simonton St., ☏ 305/296–3887) sells Haitian and Ecuadorean art. It's worth buying something just to gain admittance to the lush, tropical courtyard garden with its gorgeous aqua pool—the kind of place you could imagine Tennessee Williams coming for inspiration. (Hemingway actually once lived here, in the apartments out back called Casa Antigua.)

A welcome survivor of Key West's seafaring days, **Perkins & Son Chandlery** (901 Fleming St., ☏ 305/294–7635) offers the largest selection of used marine gear in the Keys among a pine tar– and kerosene–redolent trove of nautical antiques, books, outdoor clothing, and collectibles.

Plantation Pottery (521 Fleming St., ☏ 305/294–3143) is not to be missed for local and brought-in-from-elsewhere pottery that's original, not commercial.

Tikal Trading Co. (129 Duval St., ☏ 305/296–4463) sells its own well-known line of double-stitched women's clothing of hand-woven Guatemalan cotton and tropical prints.

Waterfront Market (201 William St., ☏ 305/294–8418 or 305/296–0778) sells health and gourmet foods, deli items, fresh produce, salads, an outstanding selection of cold beer, and wine. If you're there, be sure to check out the baaadest bulletin board in Key West. Absorbed into the same building are Waterfront Fish Market, Inc. (☏ 305/294–0778) for fresh seafood and Waterfront Baits & Tackle (☏ 305/292–1961) for bait and fishing gear.

Potters Charles Pearson and Timothy Roeder are **Whitehead St. Pottery** (1011 Whitehead St., ☏ 305/294–5067), which has displayed their raku-fired pieces since 1986.

Marathon

In the Gulfside Village, **Food For Thought** (MM 51, BS, 5800 Overseas Hwy., ☏ 305/743–3297) is a bookstore and a natural-foods store with a good selection of Florida titles—including *The Monroe County*

Environmental Story, "must" reading for anyone who wants the big picture on the Keys ($35—not cheap but worth it).

T.L.C. Nursery & Botanical Garden (7455 Overseas Hwy., ☏ 305/743–6428) lets you browse through a fairyland of brilliant plantings, indoors and out, all for sale. The displays make up one of the Keys' best attractions.

SPORTS AND THE OUTDOORS

Biking

Touring opportunities steadily improve in the Keys, although riding along the 17 miles of the Card Sound Road from the mainland to the easier-to-navigate section on North Key Largo will remain difficult until the year 2000, when paved shoulders are expected to lessen the risks at least from the toll bridge to the south turn. By 1996, cyclists will be able to ride all but 2 of the next 20 miles south from MM 106 on Key Largo on a combination of bike paths and old roads separate from the Overseas Highway. A new 4-mile section south of Islamorada along Old Highway extends most of the length of Lower Matecumbe Key. An additional 1.8 miles along Indian Key Fill will be complete before the end of 1996. **Key Largo Bikes** (MM 99, BS, 105 Laguna Ave., ☏ 305/451–1910), just east of the Overseas Highway behind Blockbuster Video, stocks adult, children's, and tandem bikes—single-speed bicycles with coaster brakes and multispeed mountain bikes—for sale or rent.

The Marathon area is popular with cyclists. Some of the best paths include those along Aviation Boulevard on the bay side of Marathon Airport, the four-lane section of the Overseas Highway through Marathon, Sadowski Causeway to Key Colony Beach, Sombrero Beach Road from the Overseas Highway to the Marathon public beach, and the roads on Boot Key (across a bridge from Vaca Key on 20th Street, OS). There's easy cycling at the south end of Marathon, where a 1-mile off-road path connects to the 2 remaining miles of the Old Seven Mile Bridge to Pigeon Key, where locals like to ride to watch the sunset. **Equipment Locker Sport & Cycle** (MM 53, BS, 11518 Overseas Hwy., ☏ 305/289–1670) rents mountain bikes, multispeed road bikes, and single-speed adult and children's bikes.

Opportunities in the Lower Keys are mostly for off-road bikes. On Big Pine Key, a good 10 miles of paved and unpaved roads run from MM 30.3, BS, along Wilder Road across the bridge to No Name Key and along Key Deer Boulevard into the National Key Deer Refuge. You might see some Key deer. Stay off the trails that lead into wetlands, where fat tires can do damage. A mile of Big Coppitt Key will get a separated path along the highway before the end of 1996. Farther south, on Sugarloaf Key, there's another 10 miles of roads with little traffic; Routes 939 and 939-A leave the Overseas Highway on the ocean side at MM 20 (Mangrove Mama's) and loop back at MM 17 (Sugar Loaf Lodge).

Key West is a cycling town, but many tourists aren't accustomed to driving with so many bikes around, so ride carefully. Paved road surfaces are poor, so it's best to ride a "Conch cruiser" (fat-tired bike). Some hotels rent bikes to guests; others will refer you to a nearby shop and reserve a bike for you. **Keys Moped & Scooter** (523 Truman Ave., ☏ 305/294–0399) rents beach cruisers with large baskets as well as mopeds and scooters. **Moped Hospital** (601 Truman Ave., ☏ 305/296–3344) supplies balloon-tire bikes with yellow safety baskets, as well as mopeds.

Camping

The State of Florida operates recreational-vehicle and tent campgrounds in **John Pennekamp Coral Reef State Park** (MM 102.5, Box 1560, Key Largo 33037, ☎ 305/451–1202), **Long Key State Recreation Area** (MM 67.5, Box 776, Long Key 33001, ☎ 305/664–4815), and **Bahia Honda State Park** (MM 37, Box 782, Big Pine Key 33043, ☎ 305/872–2353). Bahia Honda also has duplex rental cabins. The best bet to reserve one is to call at 8 AM 60 calendar days before your planned visit.

Overnight camping is also permitted at **Dry Tortugas National Monument,** 70 miles off the shores of Key West. It consists of seven small islands, whose main facility is the long-deactivated Ft. Jefferson, where Dr. Samuel Mudd was imprisoned for his alleged role in Lincoln's assassination. For information, contact Everglades National Park (40001 Rte. 9336, Homestead 33034-6733, ☎ 305/242–7700).

Diving and Snorkeling

Although there are reefs and wrecks all along the east coast of Florida, the state's most extensive diving grounds are in the Keys. Divers come for the quantity and quality of living coral reefs within 6 or 7 miles of shore, the kaleidoscopic beauty of 650 species of tropical fish, and the adventure of probing wrecked ships that foundered in these seemingly tranquil seas during almost four centuries of exploration and commerce. South Florida residents fill dive boats on weekends, so plan to dive Monday through Thursday, when the boats and reefs are less crowded.

From shore or from a boat, snorkelers can easily explore grass flats, mangrove roots, and rocks in shallow water almost anywhere in the Keys. You may see occasional small clusters of coral and fish, mollusks, and other sea creatures. Ask dive shops for snorkeling information and directions. Diving and snorkeling are prohibited around bridges and near certain keys.

A new administrative attempt to manage the natural resources of the Keys for private use (mainly fisheries and tourism), research, and preservation, the **Florida Keys National Marine Sanctuary** (Planning Office, 9499 Overseas Hwy., Marathon 33050, ☎ 305/743–2437) plan should be implemented sometime in 1996. In addition to widespread changes affecting fishing and water quality, the new plan will call for the administration of Key Largo and Looe Key national marine sanctuaries (*see below* for both) to be centralized in Marathon, with satellite offices in Key Largo and Key West.

UNDERWATER PARKS AND SANCTUARIES

John Pennekamp Coral Reef State Park encompasses 78 square miles of coral reefs, sea-grass beds, and mangrove swamps on the ocean side of Key Largo. The park is 21 miles long and extends to the seaward limit of state jurisdiction 3 miles offshore. Its reefs contain 40 of the 52 species of coral in the Atlantic Reef System. **Coral Reef Park Co.** (*see* Fishing and Water Sports, *below*), a concessioner, offers glass-bottom boat, scuba, sailing, and snorkeling tours. MM 102.5, OS, ☎ 305/451–1202. ☛ *$3.25 per vehicle with up to 8 people, plus 50¢ per person county surcharge.* ☉ *Daily 8–sunset.*

The **Key Largo National Marine Sanctuary** (Box 1083, Key Largo 33037, ☎ 305/451–1644) protects 103 square miles of coral reefs from the eastern boundary of John Pennekamp Coral Reef State Park, 3 miles off Key Largo, to a depth of 300 feet some 8 miles offshore. Managed by NOAA, the sanctuary includes Elbow, French, and Molasses reefs; the 1852 Carysfort Lighthouse and its surrounding reefs; Grecian Rocks; Key Largo Rocks; the torpedoed World War II freighter *Ben-*

wood; and the 9-foot **Christ of the Deep** statue. A popular dive destination, the statue, a gift to the Underwater Society of America from an Italian dive equipment manufacturer, is a smaller copy of the 50-foot Christ of the Abysses off Genoa, Italy. It is about 6 miles east–northeast of Key Largo's South Cut in about 25 feet of water.

San Pedro Underwater Archaeological Preserve is an underwater park in 18 feet of water about 1 mile off the western tip of Indian Key. The *San Pedro* was part of a Spanish treasure fleet wrecked by a hurricane in 1733. You can get there only with your own boat or by renting one from **Robbie's Boat Rentals & Charters** (*see* Fishing and Water Sports, *below*).

Marathon Marine Sanctuary, in Hawk Channel opposite MM 50, OS, runs from Washerwoman Shoal on the west to navigation marker 48 on the east. The 2-square-mile underwater park contains a dozen patch reefs ranging from the size of a house to about an acre. Contact the **Marathon Chamber of Commerce** (*see* Important Addresses and Numbers *in* Florida Keys Essentials, *below*).

National Key Deer Refuge and the adjacent **Great White Heron National Wildlife Refuge** (Box 430510, Big Pine Key 33043-0510, ☎ 305/872–2239 for both) contain reefs where the Keys' northern margin drops off into the Gulf. These parks attract fewer divers than the better-known Atlantic reefs. A favorite Gulf spot for local divers is the **Content Key** (MM 30), 5 miles off Big Pine Key.

Looe Key National Marine Sanctuary (216 Ann St., Key West 33040, ☎ 305/292–0311) contains a reef 5 miles off Ramrod Key (MM 27.5), perhaps the most beautiful and diverse coral community in the entire region. It has large stands of elkhorn coral on its eastern margin, large purple sea fans, and abundant populations of sponges and sea urchins. On its seaward side, it has an almost-vertical drop-off to a depth of 50–90 feet. The reef is named for H.M.S. *Looe,* a British warship wrecked there in 1744.

DIVE SHOPS

All of the dive shops listed below organize dives, fill air tanks, and sell or rent diving equipment. All have NAUI and/or PADI affiliation. Listings are arranged from the Upper Keys to Key West. For charter boats that take snorkelers and scuba divers, *see* Fishing and Water Sports, *below.*

Captain Slate's Atlantis Dive Center (MM 106.5, OS, 51 Garden Cove Dr., Key Largo 33037, ☎ 305/451–3020 or 800/331–3483) is a full-service dive shop (NAUI, PADI, and YMCA certified) that also offers underwater weddings.

American Diving Headquarters (MM 105.5, BS, Key Largo 33037, ☎ 305/451–0037 or 800/634–8464) is the oldest dive shop in the Keys (since 1962) and operates a complete photographic department.

Quiescence Diving Service, Inc. (MM 103.5, BS, 103680 Overseas Hwy., Key Largo 33037, ☎ 305/451–2440) takes groups of up to six people per boat.

Capt. Corky's Diver's World of Key Largo (MM 92.5, OS, Box 1663, Key Largo 33037, ☎ 305/451–3200 or 305/852–5176) offers reef and wreck-diving packages, exploring the *Benwood,* Coast Guard cutters *Bibb* and *Duane,* and French and Molasses reefs.

Florida Keys Dive Center (MM 90.5, OS, 90500 Overseas Hwy., Box 391, Tavernier 33070, ☎ 305/852–4599 or 800/433–8946) organizes dives from John Pennekamp Coral Reef State Park to Alligator Light. This center has two Coast Guard–approved dive boats and offers training from introductory scuba through instructor course.

Lady Cyana Divers (MM 85.9, BS, Box 1157, Islamorada 33036, ☎ 305/664–8717 or 800/221–8717), a PADI five star–rated training center, operates 40-, 45-, and 50-foot dive boats.

Hall's Diving Center and Career Institute (MM 48.5, BS, 1994 Overseas Hwy., Marathon 33050, ☎ 305/743–5929 or 800/331–4255) offers trips to Looe Key, Sombrero Reef, Delta Shoal, Content Key, Coffins Patch, and the 110-foot wreck *Thunderbolt*.

Bahia Honda Dive Shop (MM 37, OS, Bahia Honda Key 33043, ☎ 305/872–1127), the concessioner at Bahia Honda State Park, operates snorkel trips daily at 10 and 2. Included in the cost ($22 adults, $18 children under 16) are instruction, a safety vest, and 90 to 120 minutes in the water. For nonsnorkelers, 90-minute sunset eco tours are offered Wednesday, Friday, and Saturday for $12.50 per person.

Looe Key Dive Center (MM 27.5, OS, Box 509, Ramrod Key 33042, ☎ 305/872–2215 or 800/942–5397), the dive shop closest to Looe Key National Marine Sanctuary, offers overnight dive packages.

Captain's Corner (511-A Greene St., Key West 30040, ☎ 305/296–8865), a PADI five star–rated shop, provides dive classes in English, French, German, Italian, Swedish, and Japanese. All captains are licensed dive masters. Reservations are accepted for regular reef and wreck diving, spear and lobster fishing, and archaeological and treasure hunting. The shop also runs fishing charters and a 60-foot dive boat—*Sea Eagle*—which departs twice daily.

Fishing and Water Sports

Fishing is popular throughout the Keys. You have a choice of deep-sea fishing on the ocean or the Gulf or flat-water fishing in the mangrove-fringed shallows of the backcountry. Each of the areas protected by the state or federal government has its own set of rigorously enforced regulations; check with your hotel or a local chamber of commerce. The same sources can refer you to a reliable charter-boat or party-boat captain who will take you where the right kind of fish are biting.

Motor yachts, sailboats, Hobie Cats, Windsurfers, canoes, and other water-sports equipment are all available for rent by the day or on a long-term basis. Some hotels have their own rental services; others will refer you to a separate vendor.

The following well-established suppliers are listed geographically, from the Upper Keys to Key West:

Florida Bay Outfitters (MM 104, BS, Key Largo, ☎ 305/451–3018) arranges camping, canoeing, kayaking, and sailing adventures in the Upper Keys and beyond, from one to 14 days. It also rents equipment, such as one- and two-person sea kayaks, by the hour, half day, or day.

Coral Reef Park Co. (John Pennekamp Coral Reef State Park, MM 102.5, OS, Key Largo, ☎ 305/451–1621) runs scuba, snorkeling, and sailing trips on a 38-foot catamaran as well as glass-bottom boat tours. It also rents boats and equipment for sailing, canoeing, and windsurfing.

Key Largo Princess (MM 100, OS, Key Largo, ☎ 305/451–4655) offers glass-bottom boat trips and sunset cruises on a luxury 70-foot motor yacht with a 280-square-foot glass viewing area, departing from the Holiday Inn docks.

Sailors Choice (MM 100, OS, Key Largo, ☎ 305/451–1802 or 305/451–0041) operates daily charters, including a nighttime trip, on a 50-foot, 49-passenger boat, from the Holiday Inn docks.

Treasure Harbor Marine (MM 86.5, OS, 200 Treasure Harbor Dr., Islamorada, ☎ 305/852–2458 or 800/352–2628, FAX 305/852–5743) rents bareboat and crewed sailboats, from a 19-foot Cape Dory to a 41-foot custom-built ketch, plus a 43-foot Carver luxury cruising yacht. Reservations and advance deposit are required; there's a $100-per-day captain fee. Also on site are a library of Keys videos for free use, a ship's store, and barbecue area.

Caloosa (MM 83.5, OS, Whale Harbor Marina, ☎ 305/852–3200) is a 65-foot party fishing boat captained by Ray and David Jensen.

Gulf Lady (MM 79.8, OS, Islamorada, ☎ 305/664–2628 or 305/664–2451) is a 65-foot deluxe party boat operating full day and night fishing trips from Bud 'n' Mary's Marina.

Robbie's Boat Rentals & Charters (MM 77.5, Islamorada, ☎ 305/664–9814) rents a 14-foot skiff with a 25-horsepower outboard (the smallest you can charter) for $25 an hour, $60 for four hours, and $80 for the day. Boats up to 27 feet are also available. At a second location (MM 84.5, OS, Holiday Isle, ☎ 305/664–8070), Robbie's operates deep-sea– and reef–fishing boats.

Captain Kevin (MM 68.5, BS, Long Key, ☎ 305/664–0750) arranges for backcountry fishing guides and operates recreational watercraft from Lime Tree Bay Resort.

Marathon Lady and **Marathon Lady III** (MM 53, OS, Marathon, ☎ 305/743–5580), a pair of 65-footers, offer half- and full-day fishing charters from the Vaca Cut Bridge, north of Marathon.

Captain Pip's (MM 47.5, BS, ¼ mi east of Seven Mile Bridge, Marathon, ☎ 305/743–4403) lets you rent your own 20-foot or larger motor-equipped boat.

Strike Zone Charters (MM 29.5, BS, Big Pine Key, ☎ 305/872–9863 or 800/654–9560), run by Lower Keys native Capt. Larry Threlkeld, offers fishing and sightseeing excursions into the backcountry; Looe Key and offshore snorkeling, diving, and deep-sea-fishing outings; and three- and five-day trips into the Dry Tortugas.

Scandia-Tomi (MM 25, BS, Summerland Chevron Station, Summerland Key, ☎ 305/745–8633 or 800/257–0978), under Capt. Bill Hjorth, takes up to six passengers on reef–, deep-drop–, and offshore–fishing trips; he also takes divers and snorkelers to Looe Key.

Linda D III & IV (Dock 19, Amberjack Pier, City Marina, Garrison Bight, Key West, ☎ 305/296–9798), captained by third-generation Key Wester Bill Wickers, Jr., offers half-day, full-day, and night sportfishing.

Golf

Key Colony Beach Par 3 (MM 53.5, OS, 8th St., Key Colony Beach, ☎ 305/289–1533), a nine-hole course near Marathon, charges $6 for nine holes, $4 for each additional nine.

Key West Resort Golf Course (6450 E. Junior College Rd., Key West, ☎ 305/294–5232) is an 18-hole course on the bay side of Stock Island. Visitor fees are $49 for 18 holes (cart included) in season.

BEACHES

Keys shorelines are either mangrove-fringed marshes or rock outcrops that fall away to mucky grass flats. Most pleasure beaches in the Keys are man-made, with sand imported from the U.S. mainland or the Bahamas. There are public beaches in **John Pennekamp Coral Reef State Park** (MM 102.5), **Long Key State Recreation Area** (MM 67.5), **Sombrero Beach** in Marathon (MM 50), **Bahia Honda State Park** (MM 37), and at many roadside turnouts along the Overseas Highway. Many hotels and motels also have their own small, shallow-water beach areas. One of these open to the public, with a delightful tiki bar just behind the crescent beach, is at **Plantation Yacht Harbor Resort & Marina** (MM 87, BS, Plantation Key, ☎ 305/852–2381).

When you swim in the Keys, wear an old pair of tennis shoes to protect your feet from rocks, sea-urchin spines, and other potential hazards.

Key West

Public beaches in Key West are open daily 7 AM–11 PM, and admission is free.

Atlantic Shores Motel (510 South St.) has a beach where women can go topless.

Dog Beach, at Vernon and Waddell streets, is the only beach in Key West where dogs are allowed.

Ft. Zachary Taylor State Historic Site has several hundred yards of beach near the western end of Key West, and an adjoining picnic area has barbecue grills in a stand of Australian pines. Snorkeling is good except when winds blow from the south–southwest. This beach is relatively uncrowded and attracts more locals than tourists; nude bathing is not allowed.

Higgs Memorial Beach, a Monroe County park near the end of White Street, is a popular sunbathing spot. A nearby grove of Australian pines provides shade, and the West Martello Tower provides shelter should a storm suddenly sweep in.

Simonton Street Beach, at the north end of Simonton Street, faces the Gulf of Mexico and is a great place to watch boat traffic in the harbor. Parking, however, is difficult.

Smathers Beach features almost 2 miles of sand beside South Roosevelt Boulevard. Trucks along the road will rent you rafts, Windsurfers, and other beach "toys."

Southernmost Beach, on the Atlantic Ocean at the foot of Duval Street, is popular with tourists at nearby motels. It has limited parking and a nearby buffet-type restaurant.

DINING AND LODGING

Dining

Denizens of the Florida Keys may be relaxed and wear tropical-casual clothes, but these folks take food seriously. A number of young, talented chefs have settled here in the last few years to enjoy the climate and contribute to the Keys' growing image as a fine-dining center. Best known among them are Susan Ferry and Doug Shook, who have made their reputations at Louie's Backyard, along with Norman Van Aken (formerly of Louie's), whose book, *Feast of the Sunlight* (Random House, 1988), describes the delights of Key West's "fusion cuisine," a blend of Florida citrus, seafood, and tropical fruits with Southwestern chilis, herbs, and spices.

The restaurant menus, the rum-based fruit beverages, and even the music reflect the Keys' tropical climate and their proximity to Cuba and other Caribbean islands. The better American and Cuban restaurants serve imaginative and tantalizing dishes that incorporate tropical fruits and vegetables, including avocado, carambola (star fruit), mango, and papaya.

Freshly caught local fish have been on every Keys menu in the past, but that is starting to change. Because many venerable commercial fish houses have abandoned the business in the past decade, there's a good chance the fish you order in a Keys restaurant may have been caught somewhere else. Since 1985, the U.S. government has protected the queen conch as an endangered species, so any conch you order in the Keys has come fresh-frozen from the Bahamas, Belize, or the Caribbean. Florida lobster and stone crab should be local and fresh from August through March.

Purists will find few examples of authentic Key lime pie: a yellow lime custard in a graham-cracker crust with a meringue top. Many restaurants now serve a version made with white-pastry crust and whipped cream, which is easy to prepare and hold for sale. For the real thing, try **7 Mile Grill** (MM 47, BS, Marathon) or **Mangrove Mama's** (MM 20, BS, Sugarloaf Key).

Note that small restaurants down here don't hold too strictly to their stated hours of business; sometimes they close for a day or a week, or cancel lunch for a month or two, just by posting a note on the door.

Lodging

Some hotels in the Keys are historic structures with a charming patina of age; others are just plain old. Salty winds and soil play havoc with anything man-made. Constant maintenance is a must, and some hotels and motels don't get it. Inspect your accommodations before checking in. The best rooms in the Keys have a clear bay or ocean view and a deep setback from the Overseas Highway. The city of Key West offers the greatest variety of lodgings, from large resorts to guest houses in wonderful old ship-carpentered houses.

In Key West, three services can help arrange for accommodations. **Key West Reservation Service** (628 Fleming St., Drawer 1689, 33040, ☎ 305/294–8850 or 800/327–4831, ℻ 305/296–6291) makes hotel reservations and helps locate rental properties (hotels, motels, bed-and-breakfasts, oceanfront condominiums, and luxury vacation homes). **Key West Vacation Rentals** (525 Simonton St., 33040, ☎ 305/292–7997 or 800/621–9405, ℻ 305/294–7501) lists historic cottages and condominiums for rent. **Property Management of Key West, Inc.** (1213 Truman Ave., 33040, ☎ 305/296–7744) offers lease and rental service for condominiums, town houses, and private homes, including renovated Conch homes.

Accommodations in the Keys are more expensive than elsewhere in south Florida. In part this is due to the Keys' popularity and ability to command top dollar, but primarily it's because everything used to build and operate a hotel costs more in the Keys.

Big Pine Key
DINING

$ **Island Reef Restaurant.** This Keys-perfect cottage-style foodery was built in the Flagler era and has six counter seats, 15 tables covered with bright beneath-the-sea-blue prints, and outdoor tables—outdoor rest rooms, too. Nightly dinner specials, which start at $9 and don't run much higher, all come with soup or salad; potato; vegetable; rolls and scones; homemade pie, pudding, or ice cream; and tea or coffee. Entrées include seafood, steaks, veal, frogs' legs, and vegetarian stir-fry. ✗ *MM 31.25, BS,* ☎ *305/872–2170. MC, V. Closed Dec. 25. No breakfast or lunch Sun.*

LODGING

$$–$$$ **The Barnacle.** Three bed-and-breakfasts, all Keys-y, all up on stilts, all
★ serving full breakfast, and all within a mile of each other, make Big Pine Key the B&B hub of the Keys shy of Key West. The Barnacle is run by Wood and Joan Cornell, who for years operated the well-known Reluctant Panther in Manchester, Vermont. There are two rooms in the main house, both on the second floor, and two in the Cottage, one upstairs and one down but each with its own kitchen. Guest rooms are large, and those in the main house open to an atrium, where a hot tub sits in a beautiful garden screened to the sea and sky. Throughout both houses, furnishings are colorful and whimsical, and many were collected from around the world. Wood Cornell's stained-glass windows are very impressive, and floors are mostly paver tiles. ⊞ *Long Beach Dr., east off Overseas Hwy. just south of MM 33, Rte. 1, Box 780 A, 33043,* ☎ *305/872–3298. 4 rooms. Hot tub, beach, dock, boating, bicycles. No credit cards.*

$$–$$$ **Casa Grande.** This B&B, right next to the Barnacle, is run by Jon and
★ Kathleen Threlkeld, longtime friends and former business associates of the Cornells in upstate New York. Though operated separately, the inns share many facilities, such as rafts, rubber boats, and kayaks, and are connected on the land side by a pond and drive and on the sea side by the beach. (It's important to note, however, that although all three B&Bs are on the beach, the sea deepens very gradually and the shore is often covered with seaweed. The B&Bs provide saltwater sneakers, or you may take a boat to deeper water for swimming.) Casa Grande is markedly Mediterranean, with a massive Spanish door and mucho Mexican furnishings. The spacious guest rooms have carpeting, high open-beam ceilings, and a small fridge. Here, too, there is a screened, second-story atrium facing the sea. ⊞ *Long Beach Dr., east off Overseas Hwy. just south of MM 33, Box 378, 33043,* ☎ *305/872–2878. 3 rooms. Beach, hot tub, dock, boating, bicycles. No credit cards.*

$$–$$$ **Deer Run.** Just down the road is the most casual of the three B&Bs, populated by lots of animals: cats, caged birds, and a herd of deer, which forages along the beach and lush seafront gardens. The inn is run by burned-out real-estate operator and 35-year Big Pine resident Sue Abbott, who, like her fellow innkeepers, is caring and informed, well settled and generously hospitable. Two downstairs units occupy part of a onetime garage area. Though a wall blocks any sea view from one of them, the other two units, including one upstairs, have wonderful sea views, variously through the trees and mulched pathways. Guests have use of a living room and screened porch. Like its neighbors, this offers some of the best value for the money in the Keys. ⊞ *Long Beach Dr., east off Overseas Hwy. just south of MM 33, Box 431, 33043,* ☎ *305/ 872–2015. 3 rooms. Beach. No credit cards.*

Florida City/North Key Largo
DINING

$ **Alabama Jack's.** In 1953 Alabama Jack Stratham opened his restaurant on two barges at the end of Card Sound Road, 13 miles southeast of Homestead in an old fishing community between Card and Barnes sounds. The spot, something of a no-man's-land, belongs to the Keys in spirit thanks to the Card Sound toll bridge, which joined the mainland to upper Key Largo in 1969. Regular customers include Keys fixtures such as balladeer Jimmy Buffett, Sunday cyclists, local retirees, boaters who tie up at the restaurant's dock, and anyone else fond of dancing to country-western music and clapping for cloggers. There's a live band on weekends. You can also admire the tropical birds cavorting in the nearby mangroves and the occasional crocodile swimming up the canal. Though Jack has been gone since the early 1980s, owner Phyllis Sague has kept the favorites, including peppery homemade crab cakes, crispy-chewy conch fritters, crunchy breaded shrimp, homemade tartar sauce, and a tangy cocktail sauce with horseradish. The completely open-air place closes early because that's when the skeeters come out. ✕ *58000 Card Sound Rd., ☎ 305/248–8741. No credit cards. Closes weekdays at 7, weekends at 7:30 (unless it's busy).*

Islamorada

DINING

$$ **Green Turtle Inn.** Once upon a time, around 1947, this was Sid & Roxie's Green Turtle Inn, and women in Betty Grable hairdos and guys in crew cuts would drive from miles around to socialize over dinner and dancing. Third owner Henry Rosenthal is still devoted to the era. Photographs of locals and famous visitors line the walls, and stuffed turtle dolls dangle from the ceiling over the bar. The background music is "Speak Low" and "In the Mood" in wood-paneled rooms kept on the dark side. Specialties remain from the old days, including a turtle chowder; conch fritters, nicely browned outside, light and fluffy inside; conch salad; alligator steak (tail meat) sautéed in an egg batter; and Key lime pie. Whole pies are available for carryout. ✕ *MM 81.5, OS, ☎ 305/664–9031. AE, D, DC, MC, V. Closed Mon. and Thanksgiving.*

$$ **Marker 88.** The best seats in chef-owner Andre Mueller's main dining
★ room catch the last glimmers of sunset. Hostesses recite a lengthy list of daily specials and offer you a wine list with more than 200 entries. You can get a good steak or veal chop here, but 75% of the food served is seafood. Specialties include a robust conch chowder, banana blueberry bisque, salad Trevisana (radicchio, leaf lettuce, Belgian endive, watercress, and sweet-and-sour dill dressing—former president Bush's favorite), sautéed conch or alligator steak meunière, grouper Rangoon (with papaya, banana, and pineapple in a cinnamon and currant jelly sauce), and Key lime pie. ✕ *MM 88, BS, Plantation Key, ☎ 305/852–9315. AE, D, DC, MC, V. Closed Mon., Thanksgiving, Dec. 25. No lunch.*

$$ **Papa Joe's Landmark Restaurant.** Never mind the heavily chlorinated water and the pasty white bread when you can savor succulent dolphin and fresh green beans and carrots al dente. Here, they will still clean and cook your own catch: $8.95 up to 1 pound per person fried, broiled, or sautéed; $10.95 any other style, which includes meunière, blackened, coconut-dipped, Cajun, amandine, or Oscar (sautéed, topped with béarnaise sauce, crabmeat, and asparagus). Joe's—which dates from 1937—includes an upper-level, over-the-water tiki bar with 25 seats. "Early American dump" is how owner Frank Curtis describes the look: captain's chairs, mounted fish, hanging baskets, fish buoys, and driftwood strung year-round with Christmas lights. The decor never gets ahead of the food, which is first-rate. An early-bird menu from 4 to 6 is priced at $7.95–$9.95. For dessert dive into the Key lime cake, peanut-butter pie, Grand Marnier cheesecake, mud pie, or rum chocolate cake. ✕ *MM 79.7, BS, 78786 Overseas Hwy., ☎ 305/664–8756. AE, MC, V. Closed Tues., Thanksgiving, Dec. 25.*

$$ **Squid Row.** It may look like just another cutely named, affordable food
★ stop on the way to Key West, but this attitude-free roadside eatery is

devoted to serving the freshest fish you haven't caught yourself. Seafood wholesalers own it, and they supply the kitchen with fresh daily specials. Grouper grilled in a little vegetable oil, sprinkled with paprika, and drenched in fresh lemon comes divinely flaky. Alternately, enjoy it rolled in bread crumbs and sautéed, served with black pepper and citrus butter. Whatever's fresh and seasonal is best here: yellowtail, various snapper and shrimp dishes, and, of course, squid. Service is friendly and prompt, and the wait staff can talk about the specials without theatrics. They'll brew a fresh pot of coffee and volunteer to wrap what's left of the flavorful, airy banana bread that comes at the start of the meal but is best as dessert. There's also a bar with happy hour 5–7. ✕ *MM 81.9, OS,* ☎ *305/664–9865. AE, D, DC, MC, V. Closed Wed.*

$$ **Whale Harbor Inn.** This coral-rock building has oyster shells cemented onto the walls, an old Keys bottle collection, and a watermark at 7 feet, a reminder of Hurricane Donna's fury in 1960. Several employees rode out the storm in the lighthouse tower. The main attraction is the 50-foot-long, all-you-can-eat buffet, which includes a stir-fry area and a plentiful supply of shrimp, mussels, crayfish, and snow crab legs. The adjoining Dockside Restaurant and Lounge are open for breakfast, while the upstairs wood-trimmed raw bar and grill and the open-air bar, at eye level with the flying bridges of the marina charter fleet, are open to midnight. ✕ *MM 83.5, OS, Upper Matecumbe Key,* ☎ *305/664–4959. AE, D, DC, MC, V.*

LODGING

$$$$ **Cheeca Lodge.** Winner of many awards for its environmental responsi-
★ bility, this 27-acre, low-rise resort on Upper Matecumbe Key is the long-standing leader in green activism in the Keys' hospitality industry. One Cheeca policy, for example, imaginatively combats natural-resource degradation by letting guests decide if they wish to reuse sheets and towels. Camp Cheeca employs marine-science counselors to make learning about the fragile Keys environment fun for children ages 6–12. Biodegradable products are used, almost everything is recycled, and the resort has banned motorized water sports. The beachfront pioneer burial ground of the Matecumbe United Methodist Church is preserved on the grounds, and tranquil fish-filled lagoons and gardens surround. Guest rooms feature periwinkle blue/strawberry and green/hot orange color schemes; all have British colonial–style furniture of tightly woven wicker, cane, and bamboo. Touches include intriguing hand-painted mirror frames, faintly surreal art prints and romantic waterscapes, and natural shell soap dishes. Suites have full kitchens and private screened balconies; fourth-floor rooms in the main lodge open onto terraces with ocean or bay views. Rooms are available for nonsmokers and people with disabilities, and the Atlantic's Edge restaurant serves gourmet food. ☒ *MM 82, OS, Upper Matecumbe Key, Box 527, 33036,* ☎ *305/664–4651 or 800/327–2888,* FAX *305/664–2893. 139 rooms, 64 suites. 2 restaurants, lounge, 2 pools, saltwater tidal pool, 9-hole golf course, 6 lighted tennis courts, boating, parasailing, fishing. AE, D, DC, MC, V.*

$$$$ **The Moorings.** If your first glimpse doesn't convince you this is the finest
★ place to stay in the Keys, the facts will. This one-time coconut plantation has one-, two-, and three-bedroom cottages on 17 acres that even today remain luxuriously free of cluttering "profit centers." The beach has 1,000 feet of sea frontage, a scattering of Adirondack chairs, here and there a hammock, a dock you can swim from (no Jet Skis allowed), a pool, and a tennis court. Cottages are tucked in the tropical forest and furnished with quality wicker and artistic African fabrics against backdrops of pristine white kitchens. Peaked roofs rise behind French doors, lighting is soft, bathrooms romanesque, and touches exquisite

from towels thick as conspiracy to extra-deep cushiony bedcovers. The word "paradise" forms easily in your mouth. ⚒ *MM 81.5, OS, 123 Beach Rd., 33036,* ☎ *305/664–4708,* ℻ *305/664–4242. 18 cottages. Pool, tennis court, beach, dock. MC, V.*

$$–$$$ **Ragged Edge Resort.** Most downstairs units now have screened porches at this unusually spacious, grassy little oceanside resort, ¼ mile off the Overseas Highway. The two-story buildings are covered with rustic planks outside; inside, rooms are decorated with pine paneling, tile, carpet, chintz-covered furniture, and matching drapes. Each unit has a large tiled bath suite. The one motel room has a refrigerator, while all others have full kitchens with island counters, chopping blocks, lots of cabinets, and irons and boards. Upper units have more windows and light and open-beam ceilings. The resort feels expensive, though it's surprisingly affordable because there's no staff to speak of and there aren't a lot of extras (like in-room phones). Amenities take the form of a two-story thatch-roof observation tower, picnic areas with barbecue pits, and free coaster-brake bikes. Though there's not much of a beach, you can swim off the large dock—a virtual rookery when boating activity isn't disturbing the pelicans, herons, anhingas, and terns. Look north and south, and only mangroves cluster the near distance. ⚒ *MM 86.5, OS, 243 Treasure Harbor Rd., 33036,* ☎ *305/852–5389. 10 units. Pool, shuffleboard, bicycles. MC, V.*

Key Largo

DINING

$$ **Fish House.** Behind the screened, diner-style facade are a gorgeous and
★ amusing mural of the Keys and display cases filled with the freshest catches, which are then baked, blackened, broiled, fried, sautéed, steamed, or stewed as if every night were the finals in some Keys seafood competition. (In fact, there are many such competitions, and the Fish House often comes up the winner.) The dining room is as redolent of the Keys as a Bogart movie—festooned with nets and every imaginable fishy Christmas ornament. You can sit in captain's chairs or banquettes. Servers wear shorts, and the place is relaxed about everything except the food. The fish is whatever's freshest, and there are always lots of crustaceans. Fried entrées are lightly breaded with cracker meal and fried in canola oil. All come in generous portions with corn, new potatoes, and coleslaw, so adding an appetizer or dessert should satisfy most guests. Key lime pie is homemade, and there are a few wines and beers. You can't beat the fast service and great eats. ✕ *MM 102.4, OS,* ☎ *305/451–4665. AE, D, MC, V. Closed Thanksgiving.*

$–$$ **Crack'd Conch.** The new floor and ceiling make no difference. Behind the white clapboard and lattice exterior and the green and violet trim, foreign money and patrons' business cards still festoon the main dining room, where vertical bamboo stakes support the bar. There's also a screened porch and an outdoor garden. This was originally a fish camp from the 1930s. Specialties include conch (cracked and in chowder, fritters, and salad), an award-winning lobster taco, fried alligator, smoked chicken, and 115 kinds of beer. Portions are big; they use lots of take-out containers. ✕ *MM 105, OS, 105045 Overseas Hwy.,* ☎ *305/451–0732. AE, D, MC, V. Closed Wed. and holidays.*

$ **Harriette's Restaurant.** Typical of roadside places where the Coke signs outrank the restaurants', this eatery is thick with down-home personality. Owner Harriette Mattson makes it her business to know many of her guests by name and even takes the trouble to remember what they eat. Wisecracking waitresses, perfectly styled for this joint, will tell you that the three-egg omelet is usually a six-egg omelet because Harriette has a heavy hand. Harriette's is famous for its breakfasts: steak and eggs with hash browns or grits and toast and jelly for $5.95, or old-fashioned hotcakes with whipped butter and syrup and sausage or bacon for $3.25. A new Keys mural, a little paneling, some carpet, and acoustic ceiling tiles touch things up, but you can still count on a homey style punctuated with local crafts and photos on consignment. ✕ MM 95.7, BS, 95710 Overseas Hwy., ☎ 305/852–8689. *No credit cards. Closed Thanksgiving, Dec. 25. No dinner.*

$ **Mrs. Mac's Kitchen.** Hundreds of beer cans, beer bottles, and expired auto license plates from all over the world decorate the walls of this wood-paneled, open-air restaurant. At breakfast and lunch, the counter and booths fill up early with locals. Regular nightly specials are worth the stop: meat loaf on Monday, chef's choice on Tuesday, Italian on Wednesday, and seafood Thursday through Saturday. The chili is always good, and the beer of the month is $1.50 a bottle or can. ✕ MM 99.4, BS, ☎ 305/451–3722. *No credit cards. Closed Sun., holidays.*

LODGING

$$$$ **Jules' Undersea Lodge.** This, the world's first underwater hotel, consists of 600 square feet of space anchored at 30 feet. It has two bedrooms, two baths, and a dining and radio/TV corner that can accommodate a cramped six. The lodge takes reservations from divers throughout the year and offers a resort course for new divers (PADI and NAUI affiliations). Rates are steep ($195 per person, $695 for four to six) but include breakfast, a light dinner, and unlimited diving in a lagoon of limited visibility. Novelty is what this is all about. ☎ MM 103.2, OS, 51 Shoreland Dr., 33037, ☎ 305/451–2353, FAX 305/451–4789. *2 rooms. Dining room. D, MC, V.*

$$$$ **Marriott's Key Largo Bay Beach Resort.** At this 17-acre bayside resort, Marriott reimagines Key Largo as if it hadn't become one more sense-dulling suburb of Miami. Proximity to the mainland does, however, make this the easiest to reach by car of the Keys' glamour resorts. Its five lemon-yellow, grill-balconied, and spire-topped stories are sliced between highway and bay and give off an air of warm indolent days. The facilities are as good as the guest rooms, which are joyfully styled and fully furnished for resort comfort with chintz, rattan, and straw; paddle fans; and sliding glass doors to balconies from which, at least in the better rooms, you can watch the sunset sweep across the bay. The resort creates its own virtual reality. You might even end up believing it's real. ☎ MM 103.8, BS, 103800 Overseas Hwy., ☎ 305/453–0000 or 800/932–9332, FAX 305/453–0093. *122 rooms, 14 2-bedroom suites, 6 3-bedroom suites, 1 penthouse suite. 3 restaurants, bar, pool, saltwater pool, beach, fishing, game room. AE, D, DC, MC, V.*

$$$$ **Sheraton Key Largo Resort.** Of all the large, amenity-filled, enclave resorts on the way south, this is the original, and it's imaginatively done for a chain. A big bushy buffer between hotel and highway makes you feel you're a million miles from tumult. The building is long and lean; a three-story atrium fit into the trees has windowpane and coral-rock walls. Service is good and sometimes outstanding. All units are mini-suites or larger, and all are spacious and comfortable, even if the decor's not exciting. The least desirable rooms are the 230, 330, and 430 series, which overlook the parking lot. Mulched nature trails and boardwalks lead through hammocks to mangrove overlooks by the shore. (Bring bug spray for your walk.) Both Cafe Key Largo, for three meals a day, and Treetops, the gourmet dinner-only room, guarantee grand views three stories above the bay. ☎ MM 96.9, BS, 97000 Overseas Hwy., 33037, ☎ 305/852–5553, 800/826–1006, or 800/325–3535, FAX 305/852–8669. *190 rooms, 10 suites. 2 restaurants, 3 lounges, 2 pools, 2 lighted tennis courts, dock, windsurfing, boating, fishing. AE, D, DC, MC, V.*

$$$ **Holiday Inn Key Largo Resort & Marina.** New owners have spent $3 million refurbishing guest rooms and restyling public areas, so that even though this *is* a Holiday Inn, it's outfitted with Keys pride. New chintz and Keys-themed bedroom art have added to the aesthetics, while good sense has brought a new kids' playroom with an imaginative mural and convenient buffet meal service off the lobby to accommodate family vacationers. Former owner James W. Hendricks still docks the *African Queen* at the adjacent Key Largo Harbor Marina. This is the closest resort to Pennekamp Reef. ⊞ *MM 100, OS, 99701 Overseas Hwy., 33037,* ☎ *305/451–2121, 800/465–4329, or 800/843–5397,* FAX *451–5592. 32 rooms. Restaurants, 2 pools, hot tub, boating. AE, D, DC, MC, V.*

$$$ **Marina Del Mar Resort and Marina.** This personally run, two-, three-, and four-story resort beside the Key Largo Harbor Canal caters to sailors and divers. Heavy use doesn't show, as owner Scott Marr renovates rooms throughout the year. Units have original watercolors by Keys artist Mary Boggs, as well as refrigerators. Suites 502, 503, and 504 have full kitchens and plenty of room for large families or dive groups. There's live nightly entertainment in the restaurant and bar, a free Continental breakfast in the lobby, and spectacular sunrise and sunset views from the fourth-floor observation deck. Advance reservations are suggested for boat slips. Across the road is the Marina Bayside Resort with another 56 motel rooms. ⊞ *MM 100, OS, Box 1050, 33037,* ☎ *305/451–4107 or 800/451–3483,* FAX *305/451–1891. 52 rooms, 8 suites, 16 studios with kitchen. Restaurant, bar, pool, 2 tennis courts, exercise room, boating, fishing. AE, D, DC, MC, V.*

$$–$$$ **Largo Lodge.** No two rooms are the same in this vintage 1950s resort,
★ but all are cozy, with rattan furniture and screened porches with Cuban tile floors. The prettiest palm alley you've ever seen sets the mood. Tropical gardens with more palms, sea grapes, and orchids surround the guest cottages. There's 200 feet of bay frontage, and late in the day, wild ducks, pelicans, herons, and other birds come looking for a handout from longtime owner Harriet "Hat" Stokes. If you want a top-value tropical hideaway without going far into the Keys, this is it. ⊞ *MM 101.5, BS, 101740 Overseas Hwy., 33037,* ☎ *305/451–0424 or 800/ 468–4378. 6 apartments with kitchen, 1 efficiency. MC, V.*

$–$$ **Bay Harbor Lodge.** Owner Laszlo Simoga speaks German, Hungarian, and Russian and caters to an international clientele. Situated on two heavily landscaped acres, his little resort offers a rustic wood lodge, tiki huts, and concrete block cottages; every room has either a small fridge or full kitchen. Unit 14, a large efficiency apartment with a deck, has a wood ceiling, original oil paintings, and a dining table made from the hatch cover of a World War II Liberty Ship. Laszlo and his wife Sandra are the kind of caring hosts who make mom-and-pop lodges such as this worth your patronage. The rates and the waterfront setting make this place especially good. A pool is to be added by 1996. ⊞ *MM 97.7, BS, 97702 Overseas Hwy., 33037,* ☎ *305/852–5695. 16 rooms. Hot tub, exercise room, boating, 2 docks. D, MC, V.*

Key West

DINING

$$$ **Cafe des Artistes.** The classic Key West dining here is so good that guests
★ clad in T-shirts and shorts don't even blanch at a $100 dinner check for two. This intimate, 75-seat restaurant was once part of a hotel building constructed in 1935 by C. E. Alfeld, Al Capone's bookkeeper. The look is studiously unhip: rough stucco walls, old-fashioned lights, and a knotty-pine ceiling. Haitian paintings and Keys scenes by local artists dress the walls. Guests dine in two indoor rooms or on a rooftop deck

beneath a sapodilla tree. Chef Andrew Berman presents a French interpretation of tropical cuisine, using fresh local seafood and produce and light, flour-free sauces. Specialties include the restaurant's award-winning Lobster Tango Mango (lobster with cognac, served with shrimp in a mango-saffron beurre blanc), a half roast duckling with raspberry sauce, and the yellowtail Atocha (sautéed with shrimps and scallops in lemon butter with basil). Special orders can be accommodated, and the wine list is strong on both French and California labels. ✕ *1007 Simonton St., ☎ 305/294–7100. AE, MC, V. No lunch.*

$$$ **Cafe Marquesa.** This intimate restaurant with attentive service and su-
★ perb food is a felicitous counterpart of the excellent small hotel (*see* Lodging, *below*) of which it's a part. Accommodating maybe 20 tables, the café has a mellow atmosphere with bluesy ballads played in the background and an open kitchen viewed through a trompe l'oeil pantry mural. Ten or so entrées are featured nightly and typically make good use of regional foods—mango relish with the grilled boneless quail and veal and pork *boudin* sausage, coconut milk in the Caribbean shrimp chowder with sweet potatoes, and citrus marinade for the grilled chicken with roasted garlic light sauce. Many low-fat choices are featured, such as a grilled black grouper served in a tomato-ginger broth with white-bean succotash and baby bok choy. Desserts are quite the contrary: a Marquesa brûlée with almond chocolate macaroon, coconut cake with chocolate lattice and crème Anglaise, and a Key lime cheesecake with raspberry *coulis*. There's also a fine choice of microbrewery beers and fresh coffee. ✕ *600 Fleming St., ☎ 305/292–1244. AE, DC, MC, V. Closed Tues. in summer. No lunch.*

$$$ **Louie's Backyard.** Key West paintings and pastels adorn the interior of this oceanfront institution, while outside you dine under the mahoe tree and feel the cool breeze coming off the sea. The ambience shares pride of place with chef Susan Ferry's culinary expertise. The loosely Spanish-Caribbean menu changes twice yearly (December and June) but might include loin of venison with port, wild mushrooms, and goat-cheese strudel; pan-cooked grouper with Thai peanut sauce; and stir-fried Asian vegetables. Top off the meal with Louie's lime tart or an irresistible chocolate brownie brûlée. Lunch service, alas, can be out to lunch. ✕ *700 Waddell Ave., ☎ 305/294–1061. AE, DC, MC, V.*

$$$ **Pier House Restaurant.** The brick in this elegant dining room hints at the North, but guests in T-shirts and shorts are emphatically tropics. Steamships from Havana once docked at the pier jutting into the Gulf of Mexico. Now guests watch pleasure boats glide by in the harbor, while at night the restaurant shines lights into the water, attracting schools of brightly colored parrot fish. The menu highlights American and Caribbean cuisine, featuring such dishes as the Caesar Pier House salad with smoked shrimp; yellowtail snapper with avocado, papaya, and a Key lime butter sauce; orange duckling with a tawny port sauce and wild mushrooms; and chocolate decadence with raspberry coulis. Ordered specially, a poached yellowtail is served with broccoli florets and red peppers triangulated on alternate rounds of yellow and green squash. Even simple food becomes art. ✕ *1 Duval St., ☎ 305/296–4600, ext. 555. AE, D, DC, MC, V. No lunch Mon.–Sat. Easter–mid-Dec.*

$$ **Antonia's.** Northern Italian cooking reaches new heights in a smart set-
★ ting that was once site of the hippie coffeehouse Crazy Ophelia's. A woody bar opens to a darkly paneled and candlelit dining room with at most 30 tables. Chefs Antonia Berto and Phillip Smith turn out fluent renditions of Keys seafood and pasta, including a nightly grilled fish, a fresh catch prepared with a variety of sauces, and *capellini alla puttanesca* (angel-hair pasta with fresh tuna, tomato sauce, capers, anchovies,

olives, red pepper, and garlic). There's also veal, of course, and tenderloin fillets, rack of lamb, chicken, and various salads. All pastas and focaccia are made in-house. Guests can order half portions of pastas, and many Italian wines are offered by the glass. ✕ *615 Duval St., ☎ 305/ 294–6565. AE, DC, MC, V. Closed Thanksgiving. No lunch.*

$$ **Dim Sum.** In a sophisticated little Oriental kiosk set in a garden square off Duval Street, Burmese chef Michael Min Khin turns out Far Eastern cookery notable for its variety if not always its subtlety. Ask for dishes light on the sauces, and you'll enjoy the food as well as the captivating atmosphere. The intimate 15-table restaurant has a high-peaked bamboo roof, bamboo dividers, batik covers under glass, and Oriental art in lacquer frames. The culinary mix includes vegetarian dishes (spicy eggplant and tofu or a three-curry nan platter served with leavened nan and crackly papadum breads, and chutney), noodles (Singapore style with wok-fried chicken and Chinese sausage or the Coral Ruby Medley of fresh shrimp, fish, and scallops), and the so-called Delights Exotica (sweet and sour grouper, cashew chicken, and moo shu pork stir-fried with lily flowers, black mushrooms, and "blossoms" of scrambled egg). There's a good selection of beer and wine. ✕ *613½ Duval St., ☎ 305/294–6230. AE, DC, MC, V. Closed Labor Day–mid-Oct., Thanksgiving, Dec. 25, Jan. 1.*

$$ **Pepe's Cafe and Steak House.** Judges, police officers, carpenters, and fisherpeople rub elbows every morning in their habitual breakfast seats, at tables or high-back, dark pine booths under a huge paddle fan. Face the street or dine outdoors under a huge rubber tree if you're put off by the naked-lady art on the back wall. Pepe's was established downtown in 1909 (which makes it the oldest eating house in the Keys) and moved to the current site in 1962. The specials change nightly: barbecued chicken, pork tenderloin, ribs, steak, at least one fresh fish item, potato salad, red or black beans, and corn bread on Sunday; meat loaf on Monday; seafood Tuesday and Wednesday; a full traditional Thanksgiving dinner every Thursday; filet mignon on Friday; and prime rib on Saturday. ✕ *806 Caroline St., ☎ 305/294–7192. D, MC, V.*

$–$$ **Mangia Mangia.** Fresh homemade pasta comes served alfredo, mari-
★   nara, meaty, or pesto-style, either in the twinkly brick garden with its specimen palms or in the classic old-house dining room with the splashy Save the Rain Forests mural, where another 12 much-needed seats and an equally needed coffee bar were added. One of the best—and best-value—restaurants in Key West, Mangia Mangia is run by Elliot and Naomi Baron, ex–Chicago restaurateurs who found Key West's warmth and laid-back style irresistible. Everything served from the open kitchen is outstanding, especially the pasta, made with 100% semolina and fresh eggs. Made-on-the-premises Key lime pie or Mississippi mud pie are winners for dessert, after which you can now get a decaf as well as espresso and cappuccino. The wine list, the largest in Monroe County, contains excellently priced "reserve" wines (a good selection always under $20), or try talking Elliot into letting you sample his flower-light home-brewed lager. ✕ *900 Southard St., ☎ 305/ 294–2469. MC, V. Closed Thanksgiving, Dec. 24–25. No lunch.*

$ **Blue Heaven.** The inspired remake of an old blue-on-blue clapboard, peach-
★   and-yellow-trim Greek revival Bahamian house was, not too long ago, a bordello where Ernest Hemingway refereed boxing matches and customers watched cockfights. There's still a rooster graveyard out back, as well as a water tower hauled here from Little Torch Key in the 1920s. Upstairs is an art gallery of whimsical Key West work (check out the zebra-stripe bikes), and downstairs are affordable fresh eats, either in the old house or the big leafy yard. There are five nightly specials, and a good

mix of offerings covers natural foods (carrot and curry soup, grilled vegetable roulade, Caribbean tofu stir-fry) and more typical West Indian favorites (pork tenderloin pan-seared with sweet potato, veggies, plantains, chutney, and curry butter; Jamaican jerk chicken; Caribbean barbecued shrimp). Top it off with Banana Heaven (banana bread, flamed bananas with spiced rum, and homemade vanilla-bean ice cream). Three meals are served six days a week; on Sunday, there's a to-die-for Sunday brunch that includes humongous pancake or waffle platters, granola and fruit bowls, and the freshest coffee, all accompanied by an electric hammered dulcimer while kids swing on ropes and chase roosters through the richly decaying humus of the yard. Expect a line. Everybody knows how good this is. ✕ *729 Thomas St.,* ☎ *305/296–8666. D, MC, V. Schedule may change in summer.*

$ **El Siboney.** This sprawling, three-room, family-style restaurant serves traditional Cuban food, including a well-seasoned black-bean soup that's a blessing for vegetarians. Specials include beef stew Monday, pepper steak Tuesday, chicken fricassee Wednesday, a weekly surprise Thursday, chicken and rice Friday, and oxtail stew with rice and beans on Saturday. Always available are roast pork with *morros* (black beans and white rice) and cassava, paella, and *palomilla* steak. ✕ *900 Catherine St.,* ☎ *305/296–4184. No credit cards. Closed 2 wks in June, Thanksgiving, Dec. 25, Jan. 1.*

$ **Half Shell Raw Bar.** "Eat It Raw" is the motto, and even off-season the oyster bar keeps shucking. You eat at shellacked picnic tables and benches in a shed, with ship models, life buoys, a mounted dolphin, and old license plates hanging overhead. Classic signs offer homage to Keys' passions. Reads one: "Fishing is not a matter of life and death. It's more important than that." Once a fish market, the Half Shell looks out onto the deep-sea fishing fleet. Specials, chalked on the blackboard, may include broiled dolphin sandwich or linguine seafood marinara. Whatever it is, it's fresh. ✕ *Land's End Marina,* ☎ *305/294–7496. D, MC, V.*

$ **Sunset Pier Bar.** When the crowds get too thick on the Mallory Dock at sunset, you can thin your way out 200 feet offshore behind the Ocean Key House. A limited menu offers crispy conch fritters, potato salad, shrimp, and jumbo Hebrew National hot dogs. Live island music is featured nightly. ✕ *0 Duval St.,* ☎ *305/296–7701. AE, D, DC, MC, V.*

GUEST HOUSES

$$$$ **Curry Mansion Inn.** Careful dedication to detail by Key West architect
★ Thomas Pope and care for modern travelers by owners Al and Edith Amsterdam have made the annex rooms exceptionally comfortable, even if not as detailed as the now rarely used rooms in the main house, the first of the island's millionaire mansions (from 1899). Each room has a different color scheme using tropical pastels; all have carpeting, wicker furnishings, and quilts from the Cotton Gin Store in Tavernier. Rooms 1 and 8, honeymoon suites, feature canopy beds and balconies. In 1993 the Amsterdams added eight full-size suites at the restored James House across the street; 306 and 308 face south and have beautiful morning light. Guests are welcome to a complimentary expanded Continental breakfast and happy hour with an open bar and live piano music; they also receive privileges at Pier House Beach Club, Casa Marina, and The Reach. A wheelchair lift and rooms accessible to people with disabilities are available. ▨ *511, 512 Caroline St., 33040,* ☎ *305/294–5349 or 800/253–3466,* ℻ *305/294–4093. 15 rooms, 8 suites. Pool. AE, D, DC, MC, V.*

$$$$ **Island City House.** This guest house is actually three buildings: the vintage-1880s Island City House, Arch House (a former carriage house), and a 1970s reconstruction of an old cigar factory that once stood on

the site. Arch House features a dramatic high carriage entry from the street to the lush courtyard beneath its second story, and though all its suites (most old Key West in character) front on busy Eaton Street, only numbers 5 and 6 actually have bedrooms facing the street. Units in Cigar House are largest; those in the original Island City House best decorated. The chintz and Victorian patterns fit well in the house's somewhat darker (read romantic) spaces. Floors are pine, and suites (with parlor and kitchen) contain antiques. Guests share a private tropical garden and are given free Continental breakfasts. ⛶ *411 William St., 33040,* ☎ *305/294–5702 or 800/634–8230,* ℻ *305/294–1289. 24 suites. Pool, hot tub, bicycles. D, DC, MC, V.*

$$$–$$$$ **Artist House.** Dressed in French Empire and Victorian style, with lavender shutters on white clapboard, latticework, wrought-iron spear fencing, and a grand tin-shingled turret, this guest home is a real showstopper. All rooms are antique filled and have Dade County pine floors. Among the rooms you'll find a mix of brocade sofas, Japanese screens, pull-latch doors, claw-foot tubs, four-poster beds, and elaborate moldings. A small upstairs room configured into the upstairs rear of the house has a hot plate and full fridge, but it lacks the elegance of the others. The little garden out back has a Jacuzzi with a stone lion's head, surrounded by a brick deck, and there's a pond. A Continental buffet breakfast is included. ⛶ *534 Eaton St., 33040,* ☎ *305/296–3977 or 800/582–7882,* ℻ *305/296–3210. 7 units. Hot tub. AE, D, DC, MC, V.*

$$$–$$$$ **Heron House.** With four separate buildings centered on a pool, all slightly different but all Key West–style, Heron House feels like an old town within Old Town. A high fence surrounds the compound (just a block off Duval Street but quieter by a mile). Unlike other lodging owners, Fred Geibelt doesn't keep his place up just to stay in business; he simply can't resist showing how good he can make it. Neither antiques nor frills (even room phones) are Fred's thing. Superb detailing is. Most units feature a complete wall of exquisitely laid wood (parquet, chevron pattern, herringbone), entries with French doors, and bathrooms of rarely seen polished granite. Some have floor-to-ceiling panels of mirrored glass. Avoid rooms 3, 4, 43, and 44; though not bad, they're not yet redone and so only ordinary. Ask to make sure no construction will be going on when you plan to visit; Fred can hardly resist improving something. Instead, pick a time when he's just enjoying the place and enjoy it with him. An expanded Continental breakfast is included. ⛶ *512 Simonton St., 33040,* ☎ *305/294–9227,* ℻ *305/294–5692. 22 rooms. Pool. AE, MC, V.*

$$$–$$$$ **Watson House.** Small in number of rooms but big in amenities, this
★ guest house provides utmost privacy with Duval Street convenience: It's a block from the bustle but light years from the hassle. Ed Czaplicki, with partner Joe Beres, has restored the house to its 1860s Bahamian look, which guests find caressingly soothing. French doors and gingerbread trim dress up the pristine yellow-and-white exterior. Full kitchens are found in the deco Cabana Suite, by the two-tier pool gardens, and the second-floor William Suite, with new wainscoting and wallpapers. The connecting or private Susan Room also has new wallpapers. ⛶ *525 Simonton St., 33040,* ☎ *305/294–6712 or 800/ 621–9405,* ℻ *305/294–7501. 1 room, 2 suites. Pool. AE, MC, V.*

$$–$$$$ **Popular House/Key West Bed & Breakfast.** Unlike so many prissy ho-
★ tels that wall the world out, Jody Carlson brings Key West in. Doors stay open all day. Local art—large splashy canvases, a wall mural in the style of Gauguin—hangs on the walls, and tropical gardens and music punctuate the mood. Jody converted this onetime fat farm into a B&B in the late 1980s, offering low-cost shared-bath rooms and lux-

ury rooms in the same house, reasoning that budget travelers deserve the same good local style as the rich. Low-end rooms burst by day with the bright yellows and reds of their furnishings. At night they glow by candlelight. Hand-painted dressers will make you laugh out loud. Spacious third-floor rooms, though, are best (and most expensive), decorated with a paler palette and brilliantly original furniture: a bench made of newel posts from the old Key West City Hall, another piece crafted of attic I-beams. Terra-cotta tiles, rockers with cane insets, and arched windows overlooking Key West rooftops provide added pleasures. The Continental breakfast is lavish. ⌨ *415 William St., 33040,* ☎ *305/294–3630 or 305/296–7274. 10 rooms (5 with shared baths). Hot tub. AE, D, DC, MC, V*

$$–$$$ **Frances Street Bottle Inn.** With established guest houses going more and more for the luxury trade, this wonderful house, opened in 1994, offers a refreshing change. Owners Bob and Katy Elkins look after guests as if they were all favorite cousins coming down to get married. The two-story Conch house dates from the 1890s, and the clean and tidy rooms are all pale, with carpet and plain furniture, paddle fans, and ductless air-conditioning that's virtually silent. Dedicated to conservation, the Elkins have installed low-flow toilets and shower heads, and they compost and recycle. Two bedrooms are downstairs and open to a porch-patio (where a Jacuzzi may be coming), two upstairs open to a porch, and the two least-expensive rooms nonetheless have two exposures and four windows. The house's name comes from the antique bottles that Bob, a commercial spearfisherman, collects. Continental breakfast is included. ⌨ *535 Frances St., 33040,* ☎ *305/294–8530 or 800/294–8530. 6 rooms. MC, V.*

HOTELS

$$$$ **Banyan Resort.** Guests sitting on their porches reading the morning paper over coffee exude a wonderful feeling of proprietorship at this time-share resort across the street from the Truman Annex. The five houses that make up this jungle-landscaped compound include a former cigar factory and bottling works, both listed on the National Register of Historic Places, and three modern buildings in the Victorian style. The award-winning, colorful, and palmy gardens are a cornucopia of avocado, banyans, Barbados cherry, bromeliads, caladiums, crotons, cycads, eggfruit, elephant ears, ferns, papaya, Persian lime, sapodilla, and who knows what else. Living spaces vary widely—some two stories with circular stairs and stunning high ceilings fronted by walls of windows, others with palms growing up through holes cut in porch decks—but all are full of amenities even if the furniture in some is standard. Pools, an outdoor bar, lovely walkways, and fountains all surround the tropical Victorian architecture. ⌨ *323 Whitehead St., 33040,* ☎ *305/296–7786 or 800/225–0639,* ⅨⅩ *305/294–1107. 38 suites. Bar, 2 pools, hot tub. AE, D, DC, MC, V.*

$$$$ **Gardens Hotel.** In Old Town, small, unusual properties make by far the
★ best accommodations. Bill and Corinna Hettinger's grand place occupies almost a quarter of a city block—nearly an acre. In the '30s, the celebrated gardener Peggy Mills planted the site with orchids, bromeliads, palms, and other tropical exotica in full yet sensitive arrangements, making the gardens a work of art. In 1992 the Hettingers rescued the property from decline and have enabled hotel guests not only to visit the gardens but also to luxuriate there. The lodgings have the character of an English country home in the tropics. Furniture is distinctively yew and mahogany, overstuffed chintz strews indoor gardens across wicker, and baths are marble (most with Jacuzzi tubs). Original Key West art by Peter Williams deserves your attention. A Continental breakfast

and bottle of champagne on arrival are included. ☎ *526 Angela St., 33040,* ☎ *305/294–2661 or 800/526–2664,* FAX *305/292–1007. 14 rooms, 2 suites, 1 cottage. Bar, pool, spa. AE, MC, V.*

$$$$ **Hyatt Key West.** A first for Hyatt, this "baby grand" resort consists of three four-story buildings shoehorned into a tight waterfront site, but then everything built in Key West is a tight fit. Given the imaginative adaptation of traditional Old Town architecture carried out here, this compound comes off a winner. Rooms have Hyatt flair, many with irregular shapes, high tongue-in-groove wainscoting, three-way wall mirrors in the bathroom, one or more three-way lamps, and generally a good blend of muted and bold colors. In a city where water pressure is notoriously low, the showers at the Hyatt flow with knock-down force. ☎ *601 Front St., 33040,* ☎ *305/296–9900 or 800/233–1234,* FAX *305/292–1038. 116 rooms, 4 full suites, 4 minisuites. 2 restaurants, 2 bars, pool, hot tub, massage, fitness room, beach, boating, fishing, bicycles. AE, D, DC, MC, V.*

$$$$ **La Concha Holiday Inn.** This seven-story Art Deco hotel in the heart of downtown is the city's tallest building and dates from 1926. The lobby's polished floor of pink, mauve, and green marble and a conversation pit with comfortable chairs are among the details beloved by La Concha's guests. Large rooms are furnished with 1920s-era antiques, lace curtains, and big closets. The restorers kept the old building's original louvered room doors, light globes, and floral trim on the archways. You can enjoy the sunset from The Top, a lounge that overlooks the entire island. No-smoking rooms and rooms accessible to people with disabilities are available. ☎ *430 Duval St., 33040,* ☎ *305/296–2991, 800/745–2191, or 800/465–4329,* FAX *305/294–3283. 158 rooms, 2 suites. 2 restaurants, 3 bars, pool, bicycles. AE, D, DC, MC, V.*

$$$$ **Marquesa Hotel.** A near doubling of size at this coolly elegant, restored
★ 1884 home has traded an inspired intimacy for something more staged. Guests have become more visible. Where before they were largely confined to their rooms when not at the pool, now they come out to enjoy balconies, typically shoeless in Marquesa robes, seated beneath umbrellas at leisurely breakfasts. They appear as if models in a setting of pools and gardens against a backdrop of brick steps rising to a far perimeter of villalike suites. Space, if no longer intimate, is hardly less private, and former guests needn't worry that the change will be jarring. Elegant rooms are detailed with eclectic antique and reproduction furnishings, dotted Swiss curtains, and botanical print fabrics. The newer guest units are larger but equally well thought out—rubber silencers on the bottoms of chair legs, closets as fully detailed as the rooms, fans and air-conditioning as silent as machines can be, and lighting as bright as a hospitable operating room in the bathrooms and soft and golden in bedchambers. As ever, the lobby resembles a Victorian parlor, with antique furniture, Audubon prints, fresh flowers, and wonderful photos of early Key West, including one of Harry Truman driving by in a convertible. ☎ *600 Fleming St., 33040,* ☎ *305/292–1919 or 800/869–4631,* FAX *305/294–2121. 27 rooms. Restaurant, pool. AE, DC, MC, V.*

$$$$ **Marriott's Casa Marina Resort.** Flagler's heirs built La Casa Marina in 1921 at the end of the Florida East Coast Railway line. The entire 13-acre resort revolves around an outdoor patio and lawn facing the ocean. The lobby has a beam ceiling, polished Dade County pine floor, and wicker furniture; guest rooms are decorated in mauve and green pastels and Key West scenes. Among the best rooms are the two-bedroom loft suites with balconies facing the ocean and the lanai rooms

on the ground floor of the main building, which have French doors opening onto the lawn. Rooms for nonsmokers and people with disabilities are available. Flagler's, the showplace dining room, serves a light cuisine that emphasizes pasta and seafood. ☎ *1500 Reynolds St., 33040,* ☎ *305/296–3535 or 800/228-9290; in FL, 800/235–4837;* FAX *305/296–4633. 249 rooms, 63 suites. Restaurant, bar, 2 pools, massage, sauna, 3 tennis courts, exercise room, health club, boating, jet skiing, fishing, bicycles, children's programs. AE, D, DC, MC, V.*

$$$$ **Pier House.** This is Key West's catbird seat—just off the intersection
★ of Duval and Front streets and an easy walk from Mallory Square and downtown. It's the action here that makes the Pier House so desirable. Since the 1930s, when David Wolkowsky restored and began expanding this once-modest lodging, the Pier House has defined Key West for the middle-class mainstream on an unbuttoned spree. Weathered-gray buildings flank a courtyard of tall coconut palms and hibiscus blossoms, and the eclectic architecture includes an original Conch house. Most rooms are smaller than in newer hotels, but not in the Caribbean Spa's 22 rooms and suites, opened in 1990. Here you find hardwood floors and two-poster plantation beds. Baths in 11 of these units convert to steam rooms, while the others have whirlpool tubs. One-bedroom suites come supplied with VCRs with movies and CD players with compact discs. Gather with the locals around the thatch-roof tiki bar at the Beach Club or avail yourself of a loofah rub, massage, aromatherapy, or facial in the fitness center. ☎ *1 Duval St., 33040,* ☎ *305/296–4600 or 800/327–8340,* FAX *305/296–7568. 129 rooms, 13 suites. 5 restaurants, 5 bars, pool. AE, D, DC, MC, V.*

$$$–$$$$ **Best Western Key Ambassador Inn.** If you want to stay near the air-
★ port, this is the place to visit. Even though the rooms are typical motel style—functional and nonluxurious—and the Ambassador was built in 1952, the surroundings are well cared for and the property offers lots of resort features. Each room has a balcony and most offer ocean and pool views. The mood at the pool bar is upbeat and often swings to a reggae sound. A mangrove-lined stream runs through some of the 7 acres and connects the salt ponds in the back with the ocean in front across the road. A complimentary Continental breakfast is included. ☎ *3755 S. Roosevelt Blvd., 33040,* ☎ *305/296–3500 or 800/432–4315,* FAX *305/296–9961. 100 rooms. Bar, snack bar, pool, fitness course, shuffleboard, laundry. AE, D, DC, MC, V.*

MOTELS

$$$ **Harborside Motel & Marina.** The appeal of this ordinary motel is its affordability in a safe, pleasant section tucked between a quiet street and Garrison Bight (the charter boat harbor), between Old Town and New Town. Units (all efficiencies) are boxy, clean, basic, and carpeted and have little patios, phones, and basic color cable TV. ☎ *903 Eisenhower Dr., 33040,* ☎ *305/294–2780,* FAX *305/292–1473. 12 efficiencies. Pool, laundry. AE, D, DC, MC, V.*

$$$ **Southwinds.** A short walk from Old Town, this pastel, 1940s-style motel has mature tropical plantings and a pool in a raised deck, all nicely set back from the street a block from the beach. Rooms have basic furnishings. It's as good as you'll find at the price, and though rates have gone up, they drop if demand gets slack. ☎ *1321 Simonton St., 33040,* ☎ *305/296–2215. 13 rooms, 5 efficiencies. Pool, laundry. AE, D, DC, MC, V.*

Little Torch Key

LODGING

$$$$ **Little Palm Island.** The lobby sits blandly beside the Overseas Highway
★ on Little Torch Key, but the resort itself—sybaritic and secluded—daz-
zles 3 miles off by launch on a palm-fringed island at the western edge
of the Newfound Harbor Keys. There guests lodge in 14 thatch-roof villas, each close by the water, each up on stilts, and each with two suites.
Even guests to the manner born find the spaces well detailed—Mexican-
tile bath and dressing areas, Jacuzzis, beds draped with mosquito netting, Mexican and Guatemalan wicker and rattan furniture, air
conditioners, wet bars, stocked refrigerators, and safes. The only possible improvement might be to replace the commercial carpet with something more island in character. The only phone sits in a dolled-up former
outhouse, and there is no TV—a blessing. Instead, a fountain-fed pool
beguiles, and the crescent of beach beckons you to some of the best snorkeling, diving, and fishing waters in the continental United States. The island is in the middle of Coupon Bight State Aquatic Preserve and is the
closest land to the Looe Key National Marine Sanctuary. The food rates
as many stars as your personal rating system awards. Yachtfolk from
up and down the Keys know their way into the Little Palm Marina and
sooner or later at dinner time tie up. 🖼 *MM 28.5, OS, 28500 Overseas
Hwy., 33042,* ☎ *305/872–2524 or 800/343–8567,* 📠 *305/872–4843.
29 suites. Restaurant, bar, pool, sauna, exercise room. AE, D, DC, MC,
V.*

Long Key

LODGING

$$–$$$ **Lime Tree Bay Resort Motel.** Consider this the little resort that could—
and did. New owners of this long-popular 2½-acre hideaway in the Middle Keys have spent two years at work on a makeover. Gone are the
vestiges of a fish camp, replaced by attractive wicker- and rattan-fur-
nished guest rooms, tropical art, and new kitchens in cottages. New,
too, are a boat-rental hut, little sandy beach, landscaping, beautiful pool
deck, hammocks, a gazebo, and covered walkway. The best units are
the cottages out back (no bay views, unfortunately) and the four deluxe
rooms upstairs, which have high cathedral ceilings and skylights. The
upstairs Tree House is the best bet for two couples traveling together;
it has a palm tree growing through its private deck and a divine canvas
sling chair with a separately strung footrest. You can swim and snorkel
in the shallow grass flats just offshore. 🖼 *MM 68.5, BS, Box 839, Layton 33001,* ☎ *305/664–4740,* 📠 *305/664–0750. 29 rooms. Restaurant,
picnic area, pool, hot tub, tennis court, horseshoes, shuffleboard, beach,
boating. AE, D, DC, MC, V.*

Lower Sugarloaf Key

LODGING

$$$ **Sugar Loaf Lodge & Marina.** This well-landscaped older motel overlooking
mangrove islands and Upper Sugarloaf Sound has one building canal-
side, with soft beds and an eclectic assortment of furniture, and another
bayside, with high ceilings, wall murals, and balconies on the second
floor. A friendly dolphin named Sugar inhabits a lagoon just outside
the restaurant; diners can watch her perform through a picture window.
Several additional dolphins were at least temporarily cared for here in
1995 as part of a train-for-release program. 🖼 *MM 17, BS, Box 148,
33044,* ☎ *305/745–3211,* 📠 *305/745–3389. 44 rooms, 11 efficiencies.
Restaurant, deli, lounge, pool, miniature golf, tennis, laundry. AE, D,
DC, MC, V.*

Marathon Area

DINING

$$ Kelsey's. The walls in this restaurant at the Faro Blanco Marine Resort are hung with boat paddles inscribed by the regulars and such celebrities as Joe Namath and Ted Turner. All entrées here are served with fresh-made yeast rolls brushed with drawn butter and Florida orange honey. You can bring your own cleaned and filleted catch for the chef to prepare. Dessert offerings change nightly and may include Mrs. Kelsey's original macadamia pie (even though she's sold out and gone to the old Riverview Hotel in New Smyrna Beach) and Key lime cheesecake. ✕ *MM 48, BS, 1996 Overseas Hwy.,* ☎ *305/743–9018. Reservations required. AE, MC, V. Closed Mon. No lunch.*

$$ WatersEdge. The name of this popular restaurant at the Hawk's Cay Resort (*see* Lodging, *below*) has changed, but you can still dine indoors or under the dockside canopy. A collection of historic photos on the walls depicts the railroad era, the development of Duck Key (which later became Hawk's Cay), and many of the notables who have visited here. Dinners include soup and a 40-item salad bar. Specialties range from homemade garlic bread, Swiss onion soup, Florida stone crab claws (in season), and steaks to mud pie and coffee ice-cream pie. ✕ *MM 61, OS,* ☎ *305/743–7000, ext. 3627. AE, D, DC, MC, V. No lunch Easter–mid-Dec.*

$ Grassy Key Dairy Bar. Tables, counters, and even white shirts in the kitchen are now found at this ever-improving little landmark that dates from 1959 and is marked by the Dairy Queen–style concrete ice-cream cones near the road. Locals and construction workers stop here for quick lunches. Owners-chefs George and Johnny Eigner are proud of their fresh-daily homemade bread, soups and chowders, and—a surprise to those who expect a vegetarian place—fresh seafood and fresh-cut beef. ✕ *MM 58.5, OS,* ☎ *305/743–3816. No credit cards. Closed Sun., Mon. No lunch Sat.*

$ Herbie's. A local favorite for lunch and dinner since the 1940s and winner of many local awards, Herbie's has three small rooms with two counters. Indoor diners sit at wood picnic tables or the bar; those in the screened outdoor room use vinyl-covered concrete tables. Specialties include spicy conch chowder with chunks of tomato and crisp conch fritters with homemade horseradish sauce. ✕ *MM 50.5, BS, 6350 Overseas Hwy.,* ☎ *305/743–6373. No credit cards. Closed Sun. and 1 month in fall (usually Oct.).*

$ 7 Mile Grill. This open-air diner built in 1954 at the Marathon end of
★ Seven Mile Bridge has walls liberally lined with beer cans, mounted fish, sponges, and signs describing individual menu items. It's open breakfast, lunch, and dinner, and favorites include fresh-squeezed orange juice, a cauliflower and broccoli omelet, conch chowder, the fresh fish sandwich of the day, and a foot-long chili dog on a toasted sesame roll. The daily special could be a Caesar salad with marinated chicken, popcorn shrimp, chicken almondine, grouper, or snapper. Even if you're not a dessert eater, don't pass up the authentic Key lime pie or, for a change, the peanut-butter pie, served near frozen, in a chocolate-flavor shell. Made with cream cheese, it's a cross between pudding and ice cream. ✕ *MM 47, BS, 1240 Overseas Hwy.,* ☎ *305/743–4481. No credit cards. Closed Wed., Thurs., Dec. 25–1st Fri. after New Year's, and at owner's discretion Aug.–Sept.*

LODGING

$$$$ Hawk's Cay Resort. Morris Lapidus, architect of the Fontainebleau
★ Hilton hotel in Miami Beach, designed this rambling West Indies–style resort, which opened in 1959 as the Indies Inn and Marina. Over the

years it has entertained a steady stream of film stars and politicians (including Harry Truman, Dwight Eisenhower, and Lyndon Johnson), who come to relax and be pampered by a friendly, low-key staff. Decor features wickerwork rattan, a sea-green-and-salmon color scheme, and original contemporary artwork in guest rooms and public areas. Most rooms face the water. Twenty-two two-bedroom marina villas and rooms for people with disabilities are available, and hotel guests can enjoy use of the Sombrero Golf Course in nearby Marathon. Dive trips, including some for people with disabilities, are available. Also on site is a Chicago Zoological Society dolphin research facility, ⌨ *MM 61, OS, 33050,* ☎ *305/743–7000 or 800/432–2242,* ℻ *305/743–5215. 160 rooms, 16 suites. 4 restaurants, 2 lounges, pool, 8 tennis courts (2 lighted), fitness center, boating, fishing, video games, summer children's program. AE, D, DC, MC, V.*

$$$–$$$$ **Conch Key Cottages.** It's getting kind of trendy, this happy hideout on its own little island slightly larger than a tot's sandbox and bridged by a pebbly causeway. The look is castaway, hidden; the mood live-and-let-live. Allamanda, bougainvillea, and hibiscus jiggle colorfully, and the beach curves around a little mangrove-edged cove. Lattice-trimmed cottages (with equipped kitchens) rise up on pilings, old-fashioned in Dade County pine; try to get one of the three that directly face the beach. Owners Wayne Byrnes and Ron Wilson have lately replaced pine floors with cool tile, and pine doors with glass, mucking up the authentic look somewhat. Furnishings are reed, rattan, and wicker, with hammocks out front. New additions include a pool, dock carts for moving gear around beyond the parking lot, Bahamian-color paint, and two two-bedroom cottages. People are meant to live comfortably here, without a lot of fuss and without a lot of clothes. ⌨ *MM 62.3, OS, R.R. 1, Box 424, 33050,* ☎ *305/289–1377 or 800/330–1577,* ℻ *305/743–8207. 12 cottages. Pool, beach. D, MC, V.*

$–$$ **Bonefish Resort.** A caring, competent pair of nurses, Jackie and Paula,
★ know how to make guests at their little oceanfront motel resort comfortable, to the point of driving them around if need be. They provide the hospitality of a B&B yet leave you a little more on your own. All the rooms and efficiencies are different—some have futons, some tub-showers, some tropical covers on director's chairs, some daybeds, some fishnets strung on walls, and others original art sent by former guests—but all are clean and well maintained, and all have newly painted palms on the doors. If you sleep lightly, ask for one of the rooms set back from the highway. The small waterfront has freely available canoes, a Windsurfer, pedal boat with ocean bucket for viewing beneath the surface, rowboat, shore pavilion, loaner fishing poles, and a Jacuzzi under a thatch hut. It's a wonderfully tropical atmosphere, utterly informal and perfect for slowing down. ⌨ *MM 58, OS, Grassy Key 33050,* ☎ *305/743–7107. 12 units. Hot tub, boating. MC, V.*

$–$$ **Valhalla Beach Resort Motel.** Guests come back year after year to this unpretentious motel with the waterfront location of a posh resort. There are no less than three little beaches here, whereas many Keys resorts have none. Bruce Schofield is the second-generation proprietor of this 1950s-era plain-Jane place. Clean and straightforward, with rattan and laminate furniture and refrigerators in the rooms, it's excellent for families because of the safe, shallow beaches. It's also far off the highway, so don't miss the sign. ⌨ *MM 56.5, OS, Crawl Key, Rte. 2, Box 115, 33050,* ☎ *305/289–0616. 4 rooms, 8 efficiencies. Beaches, dock. No credit cards.*

$ **Sea Cove Motel.** "So un-Sea Cove," is how one of the owners of this cheapest-of-the-cheap, yet not uncharming, motel described the considerable improvements lately made here. Next to the motel rooms and efficiencies, which poke down a gravel lane, are three houseboats at a plain but private dockside. One has multiple rooms on upper and lower decks, the other two are self-contained units. Rooms on the larger houseboat now have bathrooms with makeup lights, tile, and pretty floral papers. Low lighting over the beds gives the tiny rooms an intimate feel. Air-conditioning is now in all but one unit. Otherwise the motel has zero amenities. Don't expect housekeeping. Expect savings. Pets are allowed for an extra $5 a day. ☎ *MM 54, OS, 12685 Overseas Hwy., 33050,* ☎ *305/289–0800. 22 rooms (13 with shared baths), 4 efficiencies. Picnic area, fishing. AE, D, MC, V.*

THE ARTS AND NIGHTLIFE

The Arts

The Keys are more than warm weather and luminous scenery—a vigorous and sophisticated artistic community flourishes here. Key West alone currently claims among its residents 55 full-time writers and 500 painters and craftspeople. Arts organizations in the Keys sponsor many special events—some lasting only a weekend, others spanning an entire season.

The best of the Keys publications is *Solares Hill,* published by Key West Publications, Inc. (330-B Julia St., Key West 33040, ☎ 305/294–3602, FAX 305/294–1699). The monthly is witty, controversial, and tough on environmental issues and therefore gets the advertising of the best of the Key West arts and entertainment scene. The best monthly for the rest of the Keys is the equally controversial libertarian organ *Island Navigator* (81549 Overseas Hwy., Islamorada 33036, ☎ 305/664–2266 or 800/926–8412, FAX 305/664–8411). It's free at banks, campgrounds, and stores, and its monthly community calendar lists cultural and sports events. A sister publication, the *Free Press,* fills in by the week. The best weekday sources of information are the *Keynoter* (3015 Overseas Hwy., Marathon 33050, ☎ 305/743–5551), for the Keys north of Key West, and the *Key West Citizen* (3420 Northside Dr., Key West 33040, ☎ 305/294–6641), which also publishes a Sunday edition. The *Miami Herald* (218 Whitehead St., Key West 33040, ☎ 305/294–4683 or 800/437–2537) publishes a Keys edition with good daily listings of local events. Free publications covering Key West arts, music, and literature are available at hotels and other high-traffic areas.

Key West
Red Barn Theater (319 Duval St. [rear], ☎ 305/296–9911), a professional, 94-seat theater in its 15th year, performs dramas, comedies, and musicals, including plays by new playwrights.

Tennessee Williams Fine Arts Center (Florida Keys Community College, 5901 W. Junior College Rd., ☎ 305/296–1520) presents chamber music, dance, jazz concerts, and plays (dramatic and musical) with national and international stars, as well as other performing-arts events, November–April.

Waterfront Playhouse (Mallory Sq., ☎ 305/294–5015) is a mid-1850s wrecker's warehouse that was converted into a 185-seat, non-Equity community theater presenting comedy and drama November–May.

Nightlife

Islamorada

Back behind the big plaster mermaid on the highway sits the Keys-easy, over-the-water cabana bar **The Lorelei** (MM 82, BS, ☎ 305/664–4656). Live nightly sounds are mostly reggae and light rock.

Key Largo

Breezers Tiki Bar (MM 103.8, BS, ☎ 305/453–0000), in Marriott's Key Largo Bay Beach Resort, is popular with the smartly coiffed, brochure-look crowd. **Caribbean Club** (MM 104, BS, ☎ 305/451–9970) draws a hairy-faced, down-home crowd (and those drawn to them) to shoot the breeze while shooting pool. It's friendlier than you might imagine. **Coconuts** (MM 100, OS, ☎ 305/451–4107), in the Marina Del Mar Resort, features year-round nightly entertainment. **Groucho's** (MM 100, OS, ☎ 305/465–4329), in the Holiday Inn Key Largo, hosts comics Friday and Saturday nights. **Holiday Casino Cruises** (MM 100, OS, ☎ 305/451–0000 or 800/971–1777) operates four-hour night (and day) sails aboard the 92-foot custom yacht *Pair-A-Dice* out beyond the 3-mile limit.

Key West

Capt. Tony's Saloon (428 Greene St., ☎ 305/294–1838) is a landmark bar, owned until 1988 by a legend in his own right, Capt. Tony Tarracino—a former bootlegger, smuggler, mercenary, gunrunner, gambler, raconteur—and lately Key West mayor. The building dates from 1851, when it was first used as a morgue and ice house; later it was Key West's first telegraph station. The bar was the original Sloppy Joe's from 1933 to 1937. Hemingway was a regular, and Jimmy Buffet got his start here. Live country and rhythm and blues make the scene nowadays, and the house drink, the Pirates' Punch, contains a secret rum-based formula. **Havana Docks Lounge** (1 Duval St., ☎ 305/296–4600, ext. 571, 572) is a high-energy disco popular with young locals and visitors. The deck is a good place to watch the sun set when Mallory Square gets too crowded. **Margaritaville Cafe** (500 Duval St., ☎ 305/292–1435) is owned by Key West resident and recording star Jimmy Buffett, who has been known to perform here but more often just has lunch. The house special drink is, of course, a margarita. There's live music nightly. (The Margaritaville Store is at the same address.) **Sloppy Joe's** (201 Duval St., ☎ 305/294–5717) is the successor to a famous speakeasy named for its founder, Capt. Joe Russell. Ernest Hemingway liked to gamble in a partitioned club room in back. Decorated with Hemingway memorabilia and marine flags, the bar is popular with tourists and is full and noisy all the time. Live entertainment plays daily, noon to 2 AM. The **Top Lounge** (430 Duval St., ☎ 305/296–2991) is on the seventh floor of the La Concha Holiday Inn, Key West's tallest building, and is one of the best places to view the sunset. (Celebrities, on the ground floor, presents weekend entertainment and serves food.)

Marathon

Nightly, four-hour, offshore casino gambling cruises operate on the **Mr. Lucky** (Marathon Marina, MM 47.5, ☎ 305/289–9700), with day cruises on weekends. There's also gourmet dinner service.

FLORIDA KEYS ESSENTIALS

Arriving and Departing

By Plane

Continuous improvements in service now link airports in Miami, Fort Lauderdale/Hollywood, Naples, Orlando, and Tampa directly with **Key West International Airport** (S. Roosevelt Blvd., ☎ 305/296–5439 for information, 305/296–7223 for administration). Service is provided by **Airways International Airlines** (☎ 305/292–7777), **American Eagle** (☎ 800/443–7300), **Cape Air** (☎ 800/352–0714), **Comair** (☎ 800/354–9822), **Gulfstream International Airlines** (☎ 800/992–8532), and **USAir/USAir Express** (☎ 800/428–4322).

Direct service between Miami and newly expanded **Marathon Airport** (MM 52, BS, 9000 Overseas Hwy., ☎ 305/743–2155) is provided by American Eagle and Gulfstream International. USAir Express connects Marathon with Tampa.

Another option is to fly into Miami International Airport (MIA) and take a van or taxi. **Airporter** (☎ 305/852–3413 or 800/830–3413) operates scheduled van and bus service from MIA's baggage areas to wherever you want to go in Key Largo and Islamorada. Drivers post Airporter signs with the names of clients they are to meet. The cost is $30 per person to Key Largo and $33 per person to Islamorada; children under 12 ride for half fare. Reservations are required. **Island Taxi** (☎ 305/664–8181 or 305/743–0077) meets arriving flights at MIA. Reservations are required 24 hours in advance for arrivals, one hour for departures. Fares for one or two persons are $80 to Key Largo, $100 to Islamorada, $175 to Marathon, and $200 to Key West; each additional person is $5, $10 to Key West. Accompanied children under 12 ride free. **Keys Super Shuttle** (☎ 305/871–2000) charges $77 to Key Largo for the first person, $15 each additional person; the prices to Islamorada are $88 and $22. To go farther into the Keys, you must book an entire van (up to 11 passengers), which costs $250 to Marathon, $300 to Key West. Super Shuttle requests 24-hour advance notice.

By Car

If you want to avoid Miami traffic on the mainland en route to the Keys, take the Homestead Extension of Florida's Turnpike; although it's a toll road that carries a lot of commuter traffic, it's still the fastest way to go. If you prefer traffic to tolls, take U.S. 1.

Just south of Florida City, the turnpike joins U.S. 1, and the Overseas Highway begins. Eighteen miles farther on, you cross the Jewfish Creek bridge at the north end of Key Largo, and you're officially in the Keys.

Work on improving U.S. 1 from Card Sound to Key Largo, which includes widening a large section of road to four lanes and replacing the Jewfish Creek bridge, is underway and will continue through the decade. In all likelihood, delays will continue to increase. Drivers can save time by taking Card Sound Road (Route 905A) from Florida City 13 miles southeast to the Card Sound Bridge (toll: $1.25), which will take you across to North Key Largo. Continue ahead until you reach the only stop sign, and turn right onto Route 905, which cuts through some of the Keys' last remaining jungle and rejoins U.S. 1, 31 miles from Florida City.

By Bus

Greyhound Lines (☎ 305/374–7222 or 800/231–2222) has increased service to the Keys. Buses run from downtown Miami, MIA, and Homestead to Key Largo (Wings, MM 99.5, BS, ☎ 305/296–9072 for all Keys stops), Islamorada (Burger King, MM 83.5, BS), Marathon (Kingsail Resort, MM 50, BS), Looe Key (Ramrod Resort, MM 27.5, OS), and Key West (615½ Duval St.). You can also try to flag down a bus anywhere along the route.

By Boat

Boaters can travel to Key West either along the Intracoastal Waterway through Florida Bay or along the Atlantic Coast. The Keys are full of marinas that welcome transient visitors, but they don't have enough slips for everyone who wants to visit the area. Make reservations in advance, and ask about channel and dockage depth—many marinas are quite shallow.

Coast Guard Group Key West (Key West 33040, ☎ 305/292–8727) provides 24-hour monitoring of VHF-FM Channel 16. Safety and weather information is broadcast at 7 AM and 5 PM Eastern Standard Time on VHF-FM Channel 16 and 22A. There are three stations in the Keys: Islamorada (☎ 305/664–4404), Marathon (☎ 305/743–6778), and Key West (☎ 305/292–8856).

Getting Around

The best road map for the Florida Keys is published by the Homestead/Florida City Chamber of Commerce. You can obtain a copy for $2 from the **Tropical Everglades Visitor Center** (160 U.S. 1, Florida City 33034, ☎ 305/245–9180 or 800/388–9669).

Throughout the Keys, local chambers of commerce, marinas, and dive shops will offer you the local **Teall's Guide**—a land and nautical map—free or for $1, which goes to build mooring buoys to protect living coral reefs from boat anchors. The whole set includes the entire Keys, John Pennekamp Coral Reef State Park, Everglades National Park, and Miami to Key Largo; you can buy the set for $7.95, postage included, from **Teall's Florida Guides** (111 Saguaro La., Marathon 33050, ☎ 305/743–3942).

By Car

If you don't have your own car, you can rent one at several places in the Keys. **Avis** (☎ 305/743–5428 or 800/331–1212) and **Budget** (☎ 305/743–3998 or 800/527–0700) serve Marathon Airport. Key West International Airport has booths for **Avis** (☎ 305/296–8744 or 800/831–2847), **Budget** (☎ 305/294–8868), **Dollar** (☎ 305/296–9921 or 800/800–4000), **Hertz** (☎ 305/294–1039 or 800/654–3131), and **Value** (☎ 305/296–7733 or 800/468–2583). Companies in other Key West locations include **Thrifty** (3841 N. Roosevelt Blvd., ☎ 305/296–6514 or 800/367–2277) and **Tropical Rent-A-Car** (1300 Duval St., ☎ 305/294–8136). **Enterprise Rent-A-Car** (3031 N. Roosevelt Blvd., ☎ 305/292–0220 or 800/325–8007) has several Keys locations, including participating hotels. Don't fly into Key West and drive out; there are substantial drop-off charges for leaving a Key West car in Miami.

Except for four-lane sections through Key Largo, Marathon, Boca Chica Key and Stock Island (just north of Key West), and, recently, Tavernier and Bahia Honda State Park, the Overseas Highway is narrow and crowded (especially on weekends). Expect delays behind large tractor-trailer trucks, cars towing boats, and rubbernecking tourists. Luckily, recent highway improvements, including replacement of almost all bridges and new four-lane sections, have reduced the driving time between Florida City and Key West to between 3½ and 4 hours on a good day, where five hours used to be advisable. After midnight, you can make the trip in three hours—but then you may miss the scenery.

In Key West's Old Town, parking is scarce and costly ($1.50 per hour at Mallory Square). Use a taxi, bicycle, moped, or your feet to get around. Elsewhere in the Keys, however, having a car is crucial. Gas prices are higher here than on the mainland, so it's wise to fill your tank in Miami and top it off in Florida City.

By Bus
The **City of Key West Port and Transit Authority** (☎ 305/292–8165) operates two bus routes: Mallory Square (counterclockwise around the island) and Old Town (clockwise around the island). The fare is 75¢ (exact change) adults, 35¢ senior citizens, students, children under 5, and riders with disabilities.

By Taxi
Island Taxi (☎ 305/664–8181 in Upper Keys, 305/743–0077 in Middle Keys) offers 24-hour service anywhere from Key Largo to Key West. Fares are calculated at $4 for the first 2 miles and $1.50 for each additional mile for up to two adults and any accompanying children; extra adults pay $1 per mile.

Four cab companies in Key West originate from the same dispatch area (1816 Flagler Ave.): **Island Transportation Services** (☎ 305/296–1800), **Maxi-Taxi Sun Cab System** (☎ 305/294–2222 or 305/296–7777), **Pink Cabs** (☎ 305/296–6666), and **Yellow Cabs of Key West** (☎ 305/294–2227). All operate around the clock. The fare from the airport for two or more to New Town is $5 per person with a cap of $15; to Old Town it's $6 and $20. Otherwise meters register $1.40 to start, 35¢ for each ⅓ mile, and 35¢ for every 50 seconds of waiting time.

By Limousine
Two services operate in Key West: **Paradise Transportation Service, Inc.** (3134 Northside Dr., ☎ 305/293–3010) and **Southern Comfort** (631 Greene St., ☎ 305/294–5279).

Guided Tours

Orientation Tours
The **Conch Tour Train** (☎ 305/294–5161) is a 90-minute, narrated tour of Key West, traveling 14 miles through Old Town and around the island, daily 9–4:30. Board at Mallory Square Depot every half hour, or at Roosevelt Boulevard Depot (just north of the Quality Inn) every hour on the half hour. The cost is $14 adults, $6 children 4–12.

Old Town Trolley (1910 N. Roosevelt Blvd., Key West, ☎ 305/296–6688) operates 12 trackless trolley-style buses, departing every 30 minutes daily 9–4:30, for 90-minute, narrated tours of Key West. The trolleys are smaller than the Conch Tour Train and go places the train won't fit. You may disembark at any of 14 stops and reboard a later trolley. The cost is $14 adults, $6 children 4–12.

Special-Interest Tours
AIR TOURS
Island Aeroplane Tours (3469 S. Roosevelt Blvd., Key West airport, 33040, ☎ 305/294–8687) fly up to two passengers in an open cockpit biplane. Tours range from a quick six- to eight-minute overview of Key West ($50 for two) to a 50-minute look at the offshore reefs ($200 for two).

Key West Seaplane Service (5603 Junior College Rd., Key West 33040, ☎ 305/294–6978) operates half-day and full-day tours of the Dry Tortugas in single-engine seaplanes, departing from Stock Island (last island before Key West). The capacity is five passengers per plane, and the cost is $139 per person for a half day, $239 for a full day (including refreshments and snorkeling gear). Round-trip transportation for those wishing to camp for up to two weeks costs $259.

BIKE TOURS

The **Key West Nature Bike Tour** (Truman Ave. and Simonton St., ☎ 305/294–2882) departs from Moped Hospital on Sunday at 10:30 and Tuesday–Saturday at 9 and 3. The cost is $12 per person with your own bike, or you can rent a clunker for $3.

BOAT TOURS

Throughout the Keys, many motor yacht and sailboat captains take paying passengers on day, sunset, or night cruises, and glass-bottom boats, which depart daily (weather permitting) from docks throughout the Keys, are popular with visitors who want to admire the reefs without getting wet. (If you're prone to seasickness, don't try to look through the glass bottom in rough seas.) For information on additional operators, contact local chambers of commerce and hotels or *see* Sports and the Outdoors, *above.*

Adventure Charters (6810 Front St., Key West 33040, ☎ 305/296–0362) operates tours on the 42-foot catamaran *Island Fantasea* for a maximum of six passengers. Trips range from a half day into the backcountry to daylong and overnight sojourns.

Back Country Eco-tours (Rte. 2, Box 669-F, Summerland Key 33042, ☎ 305/745–2868) runs tours into the Great White Heron National Wildlife Refuge aboard *The Gale Force,* a 24-foot skiff with a viewing tower. Departing from T.J.'s Sugarshack Marina (MM 17, BS, next to the Sugar Loaf Lodge), four-hour trips cost $45 per person for two to six people; seven-hour tours for two people cost $175, $50 each additional person. All tours include free snorkel gear, instruction, snacks, and beverages, and some trips add walking tours and beach time.

Everglades Safari Tours (Box 3343, Key Largo 33037, ☎ 305/451–4540 or 800/959–0742), departing from the Quay Restaurant docks (MM 102, BS, Key Largo), operates year-round, daily, 90-minute champagne sunset tours on a six-passenger pontoon boat ($15 per person); 105-minute mangrove tunnel, skiff tours ($25 per person); and a variety of custom tours.

M/V *Discovery* (Land's End Marina, 251 Margaret St., Key West 33040, ☎ 305/293–0099) and the 65-foot **M/V *Fireball*** (Ocean Key House, 2 Duval St., Key West 33040, ☎ 305/296–6293 or 305/294–8704) are two glass-bottom boats.

M/V *Miss Key West* (Ocean Key House, 2 Duval St., Key West 33040, ☎ 305/296–8865) offers a one-hour, narrated cruise that explores Key West's harbor up to ½ mile from shore. The sundown cruise includes live music.

Vicki Impallomeni (23 Key Haven Terr., Key West 33040, ☎ 305/294–9731), an authority on the ecology of Florida Bay, features half-day and full-day charters in her 22-foot Aquasport open fisherman, *The Imp II.* Families especially like exploring with Captain Vicki because of her ability to teach youngsters. Tours depart from Murray's Marina (MM 5, Stock Island), and reservations are recommended, at least a month ahead in winter.

Wolf (Schooner Wharf, Key West Seaport [end of Greene St.], Key West 33040, ☎ 305/296–9653) is Key West's tall ship and the flagship of the Conch Republic. The 74-foot, 44-passenger topsail schooner operates day cruises as well as sunset and starlight cruises with live music.

KAYAK TOURS

Florida Bay Outfitters (MM 104, BS, Key Largo 33037, ☎ 305/451–3018) operates a year-round schedule of sea kayak tours from half-day to weeklong tours in the backcountry, into Everglades National Park, and along the edge of the Crocodile Lakes National Wildlife Refuge. Camping trips are fully outfitted. Prices range from $45 to $650 per person, and you must book the longer tours well in advance.

Mosquito Coast Island Outfitters & Kayak Guides (1107 Duval St., Key West 33040, ☎ 305/294–7178) runs full-day, guided sea kayak tours around the lush backcountry marsh just east of Key West. Reservations are required. The $45-a-day charge covers transportation and supplies, including snorkeling gear, water, and granola.

Reflections Kayak Nature Tours (MM 30, OS/BS, Box 430861, Big Pine Key 33043, ☎ 305/872–2896) operates daily trips into the Great White Heron National Wildlife Refuge and Everglades National Park from the Upper and Lower keys. The Lower Keys are considered home, however, and "away" trips depend on the number who sign up. Tours last about three hours, and $45 per person covers granola bars, fresh fruit, raisins, spring water, a bird-identification sheet, and the use of waterproof binoculars; snorkeling gear (if you want it) is extra.

WALKING TOURS

The **Cuban Heritage Trail,** which comprises 36 sites embodying Key West's close connection to the historical affairs of Cuba, is detailed in a free pamphlet and map available from the Historic Florida Keys Preservation Board (*see* Tour 4 *in* Exploring, *above*).

"Pelican Path" is a free walking guide to Key West published by the Old Island Restoration Foundation. The tour discusses the history and architecture of 43 structures along 25 blocks of 12 Old Town streets. Pick up a copy at the Greater Key West Chamber of Commerce (*see* Important Addresses and Numbers, *below*).

"Solares Hill's Walking and Biking Guide to Old Key West," by historian Sharon Wells, contains eight walking tours, covering the city as well as the Key West cemetery. Free copies are available from the Greater Key West Chamber of Commerce and many hotels and stores.

Writers' Walk is a one-hour guided tour past the residences of prominent authors who have lived in Key West (Elizabeth Bishop, Robert Frost, Ernest Hemingway, Wallace Stevens, Tennessee Williams, among others). Guides share richly from the anecdotal trove. Tours depart at 10:30, on Saturday from the Heritage House Museum (410 Caroline St.) and on Sunday from in front of Hemingway House (907 Whitehead St.). Tickets, which are $10, can be purchased from Key West Island Bookstore (513 Fleming St.), Blue Heron Books (538 Truman Ave.), or Caroline Street Books (800 Caroline St.) or at time of departure if the tour isn't full.

Important Addresses and Numbers

Emergencies

Dial 911 for **police** or **ambulance. Florida Marine Patrol** (MM 48, BS, 2796 Overseas Hwy., Suite 100, State Regional Service Center, Marathon 33050, ☎ 305/289–2320), a division of the Florida Department of Natural Resources, maintains a 24-hour telephone service for reporting boating emergencies and natural resource violations. **Coast Guard Group Key West** (*see* Arriving and Departing by Boat, *above*) responds to local marine emergencies and reports of navigation hazards.

HOSPITALS

The following hospitals have 24-hour emergency rooms: **Fishermen's Hospital** (MM 48.7, OS, 3301 Overseas Hwy., Marathon, ☎ 305/743–5533), **Lower Florida Keys Health System** (MM 5, BS, 5900 Junior College Rd., Stock Island, ☎ 305/294–5531), and **Mariners Hospital** (MM 88.5, BS, 50 High Point Rd., Tavernier, Plantation Key, ☎ 305/852–4418).

LATE-NIGHT PHARMACIES

The Keys have no 24-hour pharmacies. Hospital pharmacists will help with emergencies after regular retail business hours.

Tourist Information

Florida Keys & Key West Visitors Bureau (Box 1147, Key West 33041, ☎ 800/352–5397). **Greater Key West Chamber of Commerce** (402 Wall St., Key West 33040, ☎ 305/294–2587 or 800/527–8539, FAX 305/294–7806). **Islamorada Chamber of Commerce** (MM 82.5, BS, Box 915, Islamorada 33036, ☎ 305/664–4503 or 800/322–5397). **Key Largo Chamber of Commerce** (MM 106, BS, 105950 Overseas Hwy., Key Largo 33037, ☎ 305/451–4747 or 800/822–1088). **Lower Keys Chamber of Commerce** (MM 31, OS, Box 430511, Big Pine Key 33043, ☎ 305/872–2411 or 800/872–3722). **Marathon Chamber of Commerce & Visitor Center** (MM 53.5, BS, 12222 Overseas Hwy., Marathon 33050, ☎ 305/743–5417 or 800/842–9580).

INDEX

Escape to ancient cities and

journey to  *exotic islands with*

CNN *Travel Guide, a wealth of valuable advice. Host*

Valerie Voss will take you to

all of your favorite destinations,

including those off the beaten

path. Tune-in to your passport to the world.

CNN TRAVEL GUIDE
SATURDAY 12:30 PMet   SUNDAY 4:30 PMet

CNN.

Fodor's Travel Publications

Available at bookstores everywhere, or call 1–800–533–6478, 24 hours a day.

Gold Guides
U.S.

Alaska

Arizona

Boston

California

Cape Cod, Martha's
Vineyard, Nantucket

The Carolinas & the
Georgia Coast

Chicago

Colorado

Florida

Hawaii

Las Vegas, Reno,
Tahoe

Los Angeles

Maine, Vermont,
New Hampshire

Maui

Miami & the Keys

New England

New Orleans

New York City

Pacific North Coast

Philadelphia & the
Pennsylvania Dutch
Country

The Rockies

San Diego

San Francisco

Santa Fe, Taos,
Albuquerque

Seattle & Vancouver

The South

U.S. & British Virgin
Islands

USA

Virginia & Maryland

Waikiki

Washington, D.C.

Foreign

Australia &
New Zealand

Austria

The Bahamas

Bermuda

Budapest

Canada

Cancún, Cozumel,
Yucatán Peninsula

Caribbean

China

Costa Rica, Belize,
Guatemala

The Czech Republic
& Slovakia

Eastern Europe

Egypt

Europe

Florence, Tuscany
& Umbria

France

Germany

Great Britain

Greece

Hong Kong

India

Ireland

Israel

Italy

Japan

Kenya & Tanzania

Korea

London

Madrid & Barcelona

Mexico

Montréal &
Québec City

Moscow, St.
Petersburg, Kiev

The Netherlands,
Belgium &
Luxembourg

New Zealand

Norway

Nova Scotia, New
Brunswick, Prince
Edward Island

Paris

Portugal

Provence &
the Riviera

Scandinavia

Scotland

Singapore

South America

Southeast Asia

Spain

Sweden

Switzerland

Thailand

Tokyo

Toronto

Turkey

Vienna & the Danube

Fodor's Special-Interest Guides

Branson

Caribbean Ports
of Call

The Complete Guide
to America's
National Parks

Condé Nast Traveler
Caribbean Resort and
Cruise Ship Finder

Cruises and Ports
of Call

Fodor's London
Companion

France by Train

Halliday's New
England Food
Explorer

Healthy Escapes

Italy by Train

Kodak Guide to
Shooting Great
Travel Pictures

Shadow Traffic's
New York Shortcuts
and Traffic Tips

Sunday in New York

Sunday in
San Francisco

Walt Disney World,
Universal Studios
and Orlando

Walt Disney World
for Adults

Where Should We
Take the Kids?
California

Where Should We
Take the Kids?
Northeast

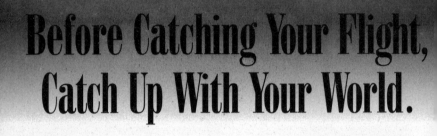

Before Catching Your Flight, Catch Up With Your World.

Fueled by the global resources of CNN and available in major airports across America, CNN Airport Network provides a live source of current domestic and international news,  sports, business, weather and lifestyle programming. Plus two daily Fodor's features for the facts you need: "Travel Fact," a useful and creative mix of travel trivia; and "What's Happening," a comprehensive round-up of upcoming events in major cities around the world.

Fodor's
TRAVEL FACT
In 1985, 10.7 million Canadians traveled to the United States; by 1994 that number had risen to 17 million.

Source: Fodor's Worldview Travel Update

With CNN Airport Network, you'll never be out of the loop.

CNN✈
Airport Network
A CNN NETWORK

HERE'S YOUR OWN PERSONAL VIEW OF THE WORLD.

Here's the easiest way to get up-to-the-minute, objective, personalized information about what's going on in the city you'll be visiting—before you leave on your trip! Unique information you could get only if you knew someone personally in each of 160 destinations around the world. Everything from special places to dine to local events only a local would know about.

It's all yours—in your Travel Update from Worldview, the leading provider of time-sensitive destination information.

Review the following order form and fill it out by indicating your destination(s)

and travel dates and by checking off up to eight interest categories. Then mail or fax your order form to us, or call your order in. (We're here to help you 24 hours a day.)

Within 48 hours of receiving your order, we'll mail your convenient, pocket-sized custom guide to you, packed with information to make your travel more fun and interesting. And if you're in a hurry, we can even fax it.

Have a great trip with your Fodor's Worldview Travel Update!

Fodor's WORLDVIEW
TRAVEL UPDATE

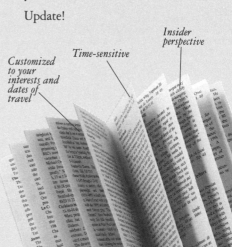

Insider perspective

Time-sensitive

Customized to your interests and dates of travel

DESTINATIONS

Worldview covers more than 160 destinations worldwide. Choose the destination(s) that match your itinerary from the list below:

Europe
Amsterdam
Athens
Barcelona
Berlin
Brussels
Budapest
Copenhagen
Dublin
Edinburgh
Florence
Frankfurt
French Riviera
Geneva
Glasgow
Lausanne
Lisbon
London
Madrid
Milan
Moscow
Munich
Oslo
Paris
Prague
Provence
Rome
Salzburg
Seville
St. Petersburg
Stockholm
Venice
Vienna
Zurich

**United States
(Mainland)**
Albuquerque
Atlanta
Atlantic City
Baltimore
Boston
Branson, MO
Charleston, SC
Chicago
Cincinnati
Cleveland
Dallas/Ft. Worth
Denver
Detroit
Houston
Indianapolis
Kansas City
Las Vegas
Los Angeles
Memphis
Miami
Milwaukee
Minneapolis/St. Paul
Nashville
New Orleans
New York City
Orlando
Palm Springs
Philadelphia
Phoenix
Pittsburgh

Portland
Reno/Lake Tahoe
St. Louis
Salt Lake City
San Antonio
San Diego
San Francisco
Santa Fe
Seattle
Tampa
Washington, DC

Alaska
Alaskan Destinations

Hawaii
Honolulu
Island of Hawaii
Kauai
Maui

Canada
Quebec City
Montreal
Ottawa
Toronto
Vancouver

Bahamas
Abaco
Eleuthera/
  Harbour Island
Exuma
Freeport
Nassau &
  Paradise Island

Bermuda
Bermuda Countryside
Hamilton

**British Leeward
Islands**
Anguilla
Antigua & Barbuda
St. Kitts & Nevis

British Virgin Islands
Tortola & Virgin
Gorda

**British Windward
Islands**
Barbados
Dominica
Grenada
St. Lucia
St. Vincent
Trinidad & Tobago

Cayman Islands
The Caymans

Dominican Republic
Santo Domingo

Dutch Leeward Islands
Aruba
Bonaire
Curacao

**Dutch Windward
Island**
St. Maarten/St. Martin

French West Indies
Guadeloupe
Martinique
St. Barthelemy

Jamaica
Kingston
Montego Bay
Negril
Ocho Rios

Puerto Rico
Ponce
San Juan

Turks & Caicos
Grand Turk/
  Providenciales

U.S. Virgin Islands
St. Croix
St. John
St. Thomas

Mexico
Acapulco
Cancun & Isla Mujeres
Cozumel
Guadalajara
Ixtapa & Zihuatanejo
Los Cabos
Mazatlan
Mexico City
Monterrey
Oaxaca
Puerto Vallarta

South/Central America
Buenos Aires
Caracas
Rio de Janeiro
San Jose, Costa Rica
Sao Paulo

Middle East
Istanbul
Jerusalem

**Australia & New
Zealand**
Auckland
Melbourne
South Island
Sydney

China
Beijing
Guangzhou
Shanghai

Japan
Kyoto
Nagoya
Osaka
Tokyo
Yokohama

Pacific Rim/Other
Bali
Bangkok
Hong Kong & Macau
Manila
Seoul
Singapore
Taipei

INTERESTS

For your personalized Travel Update, choose the eight (8) categories you're most interested in from the following list:

1.	**Business Services**	Fax & Overnight Mail, Computer Rentals, Protocol, Secretarial, Messenger, Translation Services

Dining

2.	**All-Day Dining**	Breakfast & Brunch, Cafes & Tea Rooms, Late-Night Dining
3.	**Local Cuisine**	Every Price Range — from Budget Restaurants to the Special Splurge
4.	**European Cuisine**	Continental, French, Italian
5.	**Asian Cuisine**	Chinese, Far Eastern, Japanese, Other
6.	**Americas Cuisine**	American, Mexican & Latin
7.	**Nightlife**	Bars, Dance Clubs, Casinos, Comedy Clubs, Ethnic, Pubs & Beer Halls
8.	**Entertainment**	Theater — Comedy, Drama, Musicals, Dance, Ticket Agencies
9.	**Music**	Classical, Opera, Traditional & Ethnic, Jazz & Blues, Pop, Rock
10.	**Children's Activites**	Events, Attractions
11.	**Tours**	Local Tours, Day Trips, Overnight Excursions
12.	**Exhibitions, Festivals & Shows**	Antiques & Flower, History & Cultural, Art Exhibitions, Fairs & Craft Shows, Music & Art Festivals
13.	**Shopping**	Districts & Malls, Markets, Regional Specialties
14.	**Fitness**	Bicycling, Health Clubs, Hiking, Jogging
15.	**Recreational Sports**	Boating/Sailing, Fishing, Golf, Skiing, Snorkeling/Scuba, Tennis/Racket
16.	**Spectator Sports**	Auto Racing, Baseball, Basketball, Golf, Football, Horse Racing, Ice Hockey, Soccer
17.	**Event Highlights**	The best of what's happening during the dates of your trip.
18.	**Sightseeing**	Sights, Buildings, Monuments
19.	**Museums**	Art, Cultural
20.	**Transportation**	Taxis, Car Rentals, Airports, Public Transportation
21.	**General Info**	Overview, Holidays, Currency, Tourist Info

Please note that content will vary by season, destination, and length of stay.

Name

Address

City   State   Country   ZIP

Tel #   (   )   -   **Fax #**   (   )   -

Title of this Fodor's guide:

Store and location where guide was purchased:

INDICATE YOUR DESTINATIONS/DATES: You can order up to three (3) destinations from the previous page. Fill in your arrival and departure dates for each destination. **<u>Your Travel Update itinerary (all destinations selected) cannot exceed 30 days from beginning to end.</u>**

		Month	Day		Month	Day
(Sample) **LONDON**	From:	6 /	21	To:	6 /	30
1	From:	/		To:	/	
2	From:	/		To:	/	
3	From:	/		To:	/	

CHOOSE YOUR INTERESTS: Select up to eight (8) categories from the list of interest categories shown on the previous page and circle the numbers below:

1 2 3 4 5 6 7 8 9 10 11 12 13 14 15 16 17 18 19 20 21

CHOOSE WHEN YOU WANT YOUR TRAVEL UPDATE DELIVERED (Check one):
❏ Please send my Travel Update immediately.
❏ Please hold my order until a few weeks before my trip to include the most up-to-date information.
Completed orders will be sent within 48 hours. Allow 7–10 days for U.S. mail delivery.

ADD UP YOUR ORDER HERE. SPECIAL OFFER FOR FODOR'S PURCHASERS ONLY!

	Suggested Retail Price	Your Price	This Order
First destination ordered	$ 9.95	$ 7.95	$ 7.95
Second destination (if applicable)	$ 6.95	$ 4.95	+
Third destination (if applicable)	$ 6.95	$ 4.95	+

DELIVERY CHARGE (Check one and enter amount below)

	Within U.S. & Canada	Outside U.S. & Canada
First Class Mail	❏ $2.50	❏ $5.00
FAX	❏ $5.00	❏ $10.00
Priority Delivery	❏ $15.00	❏ $27.00

ENTER DELIVERY CHARGE FROM ABOVE: +

TOTAL: $

METHOD OF PAYMENT IN U.S. FUNDS ONLY (Check one):
❏ AmEx ❏ MC ❏ Visa ❏ Discover ❏ Personal Check (U. S. & Canada only)
❏ Money Order/International Money Order

Make check or money order payable to: Fodor's Worldview Travel Update

Credit Card _/_/_/_/_/_/_/_/_/_/_/_/_/_/_/_/_/ **Expiration Date:**_/_

Authorized Signature

SEND THIS COMPLETED FORM WITH PAYMENT TO:
Fodor's Worldview Travel Update, 114 Sansome Street, Suite 700, San Francisco, CA 94104

OR CALL OR FAX US 24-HOURS A DAY
Telephone **1-800-799-9609** • Fax **1-800-799-9619** (From within the U.S. & Canada)
(Outside the U.S. & Canada: Telephone 415-616-9988 • Fax 415-616-9989)

(Please have this guide in front of you when you call so we can verify purchase.)
Code: FTG   Offer valid until 12/31/97